# A Store of Memories

*Portrait of G. Allan Burton in oil by Cleeve Horne, RCA.*

*G. Allan Burton*

# A Store
# of Memories

McClelland and Stewart

McClelland and Stewart Limited
*The Canadian Publishers*
481 University Avenue
Toronto, Ontario
M5G 2E9

**Canadian Cataloguing in Publication Data**
Burton, G. Allan, 1915-
  A store of memories

Includes index.
ISBN 0-7710-1792-8

1. Burton, G. Allan, 1915-  .  2. Businessmen – Canada – Biography.
3. Directors of corporations – Canada – Biography.   4. Simpsons
Limited – Biography.   I. Title.

HF5465.C34S52 1986      381′.45′000924      C86-094173-6

Printed and bound in Canada by T. H. Best Printing Co. Ltd.

*To Betty*

# CONTENTS

# PREFACE

"Why don't you write a book of memoirs?" asked my wife Betty.

"Because I am a watercolour painter, not a writer. You are the author in the family," I replied.

Betty is also a lovely and persistent promoter of a cause, especially if it concerns her loved ones. So to appease her, I tried to imagine how one would start a book of memoirs. "I was born on a snowy day, January 20, 1915, at home . . ." hardly seemed adequate. I had no memory of such an occasion.

Resisting, ever more weakly, my wife's constant reminders, I decided there was one way in which my story could be brought to life and that was through telling stories and anecdotes about the people, institutions, churches, schools, travels, and events that influenced my life the most. For the majority of people, the amusing, hilarious, or just plain ridiculous incidents in life are more often remembered than the tragic, although the trauma of tragedy may leave indelible marks on the soul. So I sat down one night and listed, decade by decade, as I remembered them, the important characters and events in my life. As I added a name or a place to the list, a floodtide of memories – mostly good, some amusing, all true – swamped my mind. I started to write about horses first because, as I explain, "They have always fascinated me," and only then about people and events.

Writing these memoirs has been an absorbing, interesting, and exhausting experience. But mostly it has been enjoyable. Over the past three years the task has made me think harder than I have for years. How do you tell it as it was without hurting anyone, when giving pain was never the purpose of these memoirs? How do you express your love, account for your hopes and fears, and explain the lessons learned? These are some of the questions I had to consider – and answer. The reader will have to judge how well I handled them.

My working title was "Half-Remembered Lies." It amused half of my friends and horrified the other half. It comes from a quotation attributed to Napoleon which runs: "History is mainly composed of half-remembered lies." But according to my editor, an authority on such things, the authentic quote is "History is made up of lies agreed upon." Anyway, whichever version of Napoleon's quotation is correct, my life story, or memoirs, contains no lies that I know of and only the tiniest bit of history.

I would like to acknowledge the encouragement and loving patience of my wife Betty, who, before the ink was dry, listened to each episode as I read it; the research and support of Mark Kennedy, my stepson; the devoted toil over many months of my secretary, Mrs. Ruth Carlisle, assisted sometimes by Daryl McDonnell and Denis Cheevers; and the enthusiasm and interest of our children.

I thank also Jack McClelland, publisher and staunch Canadian, whose generous praise and encouragement was like the Balm of Gilead to a fledgling author, and to John Robert Colombo, my editor, a sensitive and understanding man.

# HORSES
# AND HOMELIFE

Horses have fascinated me for as long as I can remember. At age five or six, on a summer vacation on Gertie Hines's father's farm near Bath, Ontario, I was allowed to ride Bess, an old and very gentle mare, bareback, of course, to get the cows and bring them in to milk. My moment of terror came when I hugged her huge foreleg and she put her ponderous hoof squarely on my small foot, squashing it into the muck. Not only was I pinned and in pain, but I was terrified that no one would help me. My little fists beating her foreleg seemed to Bess to be a sign of affection, so she turned and nudged me lovingly with her soft nose. She calmly surveyed my terror and frustration with tender brown eyes, snuffled, and then shifted her weight, thus releasing me.

At about the same age, I followed our local garbageman around Rosedale on his appointed rounds, dreaming that someday I could be a garbageman and have a beautiful "circus horse" like the one he drove. I had never seen such a huge and gentle animal, especially never a horse with a waxed mustache wearing a straw hat! The Toronto refuse collectors of the day drove large, two-wheeled Belgian carts, each hauled by a Clydesdale complete with shining brass and gleaming harness. Each man looked after his own horse and equipment. With great pride and dignity, he collected the trash, especially when passers-by remarked how fine his animal looked in its gleaming harness. My friend assured me that his mustachioed partner, with the hairy white socks covering his hooves, did this menial work only in the summer; all winter he worked with a circus down South. This only made me more keen to be a garbageman.

I hated winter. At the first sign of frost, as I was considered to be undersized and delicate, my mother forced me into long woollen underwear and pinned a pad of impregnated wool across my chest next to the skin. It was terribly itchy and uncomfortable. By opening my pores, it laid me low with the croup seven years in a row. Spring release from the trappings of winter was a joyous time.

I started school at the old Rosedale Public School, which necessitated walking, ambling, playing, and running a mile or so each way. It was located in south Rosedale, which was separated from north Rosedale by "our" ravine. It was always ours and never seemed to belong to the people in south Rosedale. The ravine was spanned by a long, narrow iron bridge. Each day a mounted policeman used to meet our group of north Rosedale children, and in turn would hoist one child up on his horse while he walked solemnly, leading the parade like the Pied Piper of Hamelin across the creaking and rattling old structure.

When my turn came and I was hoisted onto his tall bay horse, with its large trooper's saddle, I was surrounded by a rolled rain cape on the cantle, an impressive pistol case on the pommel, and a four-foot-long dog whip swaying by my short legs. With the wonderful aroma of horse and leather in my nostrils, my imagination ran to the great deeds to be done on a shiny police horse as one of Toronto's finest. I changed my mind about professions. A garbage collector was out; a mounted policeman I was to be.

In the 1920s, the mounted policeman on his horse who patrolled our ravines, and the officer on his Planet bicycle, whose beat was Binscarth Road and the rest of north Rosedale, were our friends and confidants as well as protectors. We would have been deeply shocked and dismayed had anyone called them "fuzz" or "pigs" as a later, ruder generation did. They wore high-domed pith helmets, like English bobbies, and we called them "coppers." In our books they were always the "good guys."

At about age ten I started at the University of Toronto Schools on Bloor Street. To be accepted, I had to write competitive examinations, because U.T.S. was an experiment in providing a cross-section of Toronto students with a private-school atmosphere at public-school prices. It took me two years to gain admission and seemingly a long time to graduate. Although I never failed a final exam, I kept my family and supporters on tenterhooks year in and year out.

At U.T.S., after an intense morning of work, we were dismissed at 2:30 p.m. I would dash to Whitewood's Stables where I was learning to ride. Whitewood's Stables were down a lane behind Yonge

Street, where the Rosedale Subway Station is now. Prince, my horse, would be waiting, tacked up and ready, with Jose Welsh, my instructor, on his horse, a cow pony. Jose, who had been with his father's rodeo, which had gone broke, was groom and man Friday to Bob Whitewood, a dapper little horseman with a very short fuse.

I was glad Jose was my teacher because he had great patience, good horse sense, and never abused an animal or a pupil. Our daily hour's ride in the ravine was filled with his stories of the excitement of rodeo life and bucking broncos. I was so fascinated by his tall stories that I was riding without fear and with good balance before I knew it. From now on, the circus was out. Toronto's finest mounted division would have to get someone else; life as a cowboy on the open range was for me! I have owned several horses since those days, some truly memorable, others best forgotten, but no one ever forgets his first horse or his first true love. Yet, nearly sixty years later, I cannot remember when or how Prince and I parted company.

I never knew my grandfathers. Both were dead and gone before I was born. Grandfather George Burton was the original merchant, operating a general store in Green River, Ontario, where my father, Charles, was born. Grandfather loved to race his standard-bred trotter, so Grandma Burton was left to run the general store whenever he slipped away.

Grandfather Leary built houses and was apparently wise and far-seeing. In the 1890s he built three houses on Manning Avenue in the western outskirts of Toronto. Manning was not the most fashionable street in that section of the city. Palmerston Boulevard, the next street east, with its special globe street lamps on iron posts, easily won that title. But owning three houses on the second-best street was doing well. One house was occupied by Grandmother Leary (née Rutherford) and my mother's two sisters, Aunt Annie York, who was a widow, and one of the early head nurses of Western Hospital, and my unmarried Aunt Ada, a dedicated teacher at Clinton Street School for forty or more years. Her brother, my Uncle Joe Leary, was the principal for almost as many years at Givins Street School. The other houses were occupied by Grandmother Burton (née Barclay) and by our family before our move to Rosedale. I always found Grandma Burton stiff and formal, whereas I was always delighted to be in the company of Grandma Leary. I grew up surrounded by females, at least for my first decade. I still enjoy their company a half-century later!

Close to the top of my list of unforgettable characters was Grandma Leary. She was petite and quick, ancient but spry. It seemed to me that she wore the same costume every day of her life. When I knew her, from her eighty-sixth to her ninety-seventh years, she wore a very stiff, full-length black grosgrain silk dress, a Brussels lace choker around her neck, with two sturdy wire supports on each side, which gave her a very erect, military bearing. She loved to fish and, in her ninety-second year, went out in a boat alone on Lake Rosseau to fish, still in her black dress. Rumour had it that she had come over from Scotland with her parents on a sailing vessel in 1833 when she was three months old. She had been born in Dunfermline, a Rutherford, her mother a Gordon. With Gordons, Rutherfords, and Barclays in my background, and with no disrespect to the Burtons, I often describe myself as eighty-five per cent Scotch and the rest soda!

Grandmother Leary was a school-teacher before she married Grandfather Leary. They had four children, all delivered by Dr. Jack McCullagh, a good doctor who served our family for forty-five years. All my aunts and uncles were delivered under a bed sheet, as modesty then dictated! At ninety-six, when she was in a coma and dying of "old people's pneumonia," Dr. Jack, as he was called, slipped his stethoscope under her flannel nightgown next to her bare back to take a sounding. Modesty used to dictate that such soundings were taken over the night garment, but Dr. Jack figured she was too far gone to notice this time. Feeling the stethoscope against her bare back, she woke up, looked directly at my mother, who was in the room on constant watch, and said, "Ella, is there any possible excuse for this indecent exposure?" Then she died. Dr. Jack said the shock killed her. Mentally she was as bright as a dollar to the end. I was just under ten when she died at the ripe age of ninety-six.

The person who had the greatest influence on my life was my father. Charles Luther Burton, C.B.E., D.Sc., was born in Green River, Ontario, in 1878, over the general store owned by my grandfather, George Burton, merchant. In 1890, after selling the Green River store, the family moved to Toronto where Charles attended the Toronto Collegiate Institute, now Jarvis Collegiate Institute. He started work at age fourteen for H.H. Fudger, owner of the Fancy Goods Company, wholesalers. Mr. Fudger, along with Joseph Flavelle and A.E. Ames, also had a one-third interest in The Robert Simpson Company, the department store and mail-order house. During his fifteen years at the Fancy Goods Company, father rose from office boy, to head book-keeper, to buyer, to owner of a considerable portion of the business. In 1911, expressing a wish to sell out and start a retail business, Mr. Fudger offered him a position in Simpsons as assistant general manager. He quickly became general manager and at one time managed both Simpsons in Toronto and Murphy's in Montreal, a new business acquired by Simpsons in 1914. Profit-sharing was introduced in 1919.

In 1929, after Mr. Fudger died and A.E. Ames had sold his interest, Sir Joseph Flavelle made a deal to sell the Simpsons' stores and mail-order service to a prominent American retailer. Part of the deal was the condition that C.L. Burton stay on as general manager. Sir Joseph Flavelle had not consulted father, who refused to work for the new American owner. Instead, with the help of J.H. Gundy of Wood Gundy & Company, a very generous personal loan for several million dollars from the Canadian Bank of Commerce, and a large sum raised by Simpsons managers, $8.5 million was paid to Sir Joseph Flavelle for his share of Simpsons. Father became president of the new company. Simpsons Limited was profitable. Even during the Great Depression, it lost money in only one year, 1931.

Father, who had made a dozen or more European buying trips for the Fancy Goods Company, soon established an elaborate overseas buying organization, headquartered in St. Pauls Churchyard, London, England, to service Simpsons' buyers. The London Office, as it was called, controlled all the European agents in Paris, Brussels, Berlin, Florence, and Scandinavia. Until 1937, the London Office acted as agents for the Hudson Bay Company's buyers, who often accompanied Simpsons' buyers in the various markets. My brother Edgar was appointed general manager in 1937, succeeding my father as president in 1948, and as chairman in 1956. My father continued to go to his office daily until his eightieth year, insisting he had not retired. He came in every day to give useful advice!

Father was always active in civic affairs. He served as president of the Toronto Board of Trade, as founder of the Industrial Commission, as fund-raiser for Big Brothers, and as a friend of the YMCA and many other worthwhile projects. He spoke German and French and sponsored the Alliance Française in Toronto. When his book *A Sense of Urgency* was published by Clarke, Irwin in 1952, he gave half of his royalties to the University of Toronto to teach better French and the other half to the Université Laval to teach better English. Laval rewarded him with an honorary degree, a Doctor of Commercial Science degree (D.Sc.). During World War II, he co-ordinated all wartime charitable organizations, for which he was made a Commander of the British Empire (C.B.E.).

My father and my mother enjoyed a long and happy marriage. In 1950 they celebrated their golden wedding anniversary. Some two thousand guests attended the celebration at Thornlea, their country place near Thornhill, north of Toronto. Following my mother's death seven years later, my father in 1958 married Joyce Richardson, R.N., who had nursed members of our family for several years, and a son, Charles Robert, was born of that union.


Just as my father had a great influence on my life, so in his own way did my older brother Edgar. Edgar Gordon Burton, C.B.E., was born in 1904, attended the University of Toronto Schools, and studied one year of political science at the University of Toronto before leaving to work for Carson, Pirie, and Scott, the department store in Chicago, in a junior position in the Women's Fashion group. At age nine he started violin lessons and by fourteen was proficient enough to give a solo concert. His ambition to be a concert violinist was shattered when his left hand was crushed and crippled for life in an automobile accident. He was then seventeen, and after three months in hospital he spent a year convalescing in England and France. While *en pension* in Paris, living with a French family and learning French, he often visited Simpsons' Paris office and accompanied the buyers in the market, acting as an unofficial interpreter. As a result of these visits, most of his exposure to retailing was in the fashion end of the business.

At age twenty-four, having been promoted several times at Carson's, and after having spent a couple of years in Simpsons' Coat Department, he married a lovely southern girl, Clayton Calloway, who was attending the University of Toronto. My father was delighted and arranged a year-long honeymoon for the young couple. During the honeymoon, Edgar visited most of the industrial zones of England and France, and this added to his knowledge of merchandising. Edgar and Clayton had four children – Ted, Mary Alice, Anne, and Merrill. Edgar became general manager of Simpsons Limited in 1937 and finally president in 1948. Edgar was largely responsible, along with General E.R. Wood, chairman of Sears, Roebuck, Chicago, for the concept that led to the formation of Simpsons-Sears in 1952. This fifty-fifty combination of Simpsons Ltd. and Sears, Roebuck grew over the next twenty-five years from $100 million to nearly $2 billion in annual volume of business.

I was eleven years younger than Edgar. He was away in Europe or Chicago as I was growing up, so I really did not know him well until I returned from overseas in 1945, when I was thirty and he was forty-one. During the war years, Edgar served under Donald Gordon as retail administrator of the Wartime Prices and Trade Board for a dollar a year. He was awarded the C.B.E. for this service, and the National Retail Merchants Association, in their first International Award in the 1950s, designated him International Retailer of the Year. It was a great honour from his peers.

Edgar was somewhat shy – a much-respected businessman, conscientious, knowledgeable, public-spirited, with a serious air about him. No doubt he developed the latter to look older as a youthful president. His great problem was that he worried constantly. If all was going better than expected, he would start worrying about the fact that there was nothing to worry about! In this regard we were different. I admitted to concern, but not worry. This may be semantics, but I do not think so.

In the early fifties, when I was general manager, Toronto had a transportation strike. Business was affected severely, of course, as there was no public transportation to bring in customers. The store transported two thousand employees a day in our furniture trucks hastily equipped with benches. One day Edgar called me into his office and asked, "Aren't you worried?"

I said, "What about?"

"Why, the TTC strike and business!" he exploded.

"We are transporting two thousand employees a day. We are open for business. We have done everything we know, short of kidnapping customers, to handle the situation," I replied. "If you know anything more we can do, tell me. We'll be happy to do it."

"I don't think you are serious about the business," Edgar replied.

"Then that is the greatest mistake you could make, Edgar," I said quietly.

When Edgar's son, Ted, came into the business, after studying at Upper Canada College and working a spell at J.L. Hudson's in Detroit,

where he apprenticed in the Fashion Division as his father had at
Carson's, he had the further advantage of seeing how they proposed
to handle the merchandise needs of their suburban stores, then in
the planning stage. Ted is gregarious, good-looking, bulky, and ener-
getic. He has a burning desire to at least match everything his grandfather, father, and uncle have accomplished both in retail trade and
in public service. He has achieved some of his ambitions, becoming
the fourth Burton to be appointed president of the Toronto Board of
Trade, fourth president of Simpsons Limited, a bank director, and a
trustee of the Toronto General Hospital.

As was the custom of the day, I was born at home, not in a hospital.
Our home was on Manning Avenue, and my birth, on January 20,
1915, was celebrated by a record snowfall. It coincided with further
promotion for my father in The Robert Simpson Company and much
better remuneration, so when I was one year old we moved to north
Rosedale to 52 Binscarth Road, a large house with a beautiful view
of the ravine.

There were very few houses in Rosedale at this time. But at the
end of our street, there was a huge one of baronial size. It was owned
by a Mr. Osler, and it was well set back from the road in a park-like
setting. It was dark and forbidding and quite obviously haunted, at
least to our young minds. The Osler children were hurried along the
street by their nannies as if everyone else on the street had the plague.
The Oslers owned all the property across the street from us, except
for a section owned by the Merediths. With an eye to future profit,
Mr. Osler allowed the city to create a refuse dump to fill in some of
his land for future development. My father was horrified and disgusted to find a six-foot plank fence erected across from our proud
new house. It completely blocked his view of the ravine, and, to make
matters worse, there was a daily convoy of horse-drawn, two-wheel
garbage carts. The garbagemen dumped their interesting but odorif-
erous loads within hearing and smelling range of us. This went on
for some four or five years with no recourse and little love between
Mr. Osler and Mr. Burton.

For a youngster, it was exciting to live opposite a dump. There
were frequent outbreaks of fire in the refuse, which had to be quelled
by fire reels. We scavenged and found many interesting things, and
we became skilled with slingshots, practising on the huge rats that

infested the site. There was a rumour that Ambrose Small, the theatre-owner who had disappeared without a trace, was "done in" and hidden in our dump. Our house on Binscarth Road is still occupied by members of the family, but the old Osler house has had several owners in the intervening years. I am pleased to record that the Osler-Burton children got along well, once the haunted house and the dump no longer spoiled the atmosphere.

My father bought a piece of property on Glen Road, around the corner from Binscarth, which had a small park opposite it, to guarantee our view. It framed the imposing Rosedale United Church on the east side of Glen Road. Just along from the church was the Lieutenant-Governor of Ontario's huge official residence in Chorley Park, which was surrounded by thirty or forty acres of parkland.

One of the things that has made Toronto the financial capital of Canada and the great city it has become is that it has never had a leisure class. Torontonians, when they were not working for themselves, worked for the betterment of their city and the many institutions in it to improve the lot of its citizens. Others looked down their noses and called it "Hogtown," but we called it "The Queen City."

In the 1920s Lake Simcoe developed as the main summer colony of those Torontonians who could afford cottages. The area was readily accessible by train and automobile. For the adventurous, there were the Muskoka lakes, with their crystal-clear water, rugged rocks, pines, and little in the way of such city amenities as electricity and telephones. My father bought Pinerocks on Florence Island, Lake Rosseau, Muskoka, in 1925, and it has remained in the family for over six decades. The nearest village was Windermere, now a mere two-and-a-half-hour drive from Toronto. Then it was a full seven-hour drive and the last twenty miles was over a bone-jarring, log corduroy roadbed. There was no dashing back and forth between the city and the cottage on weekends. Mother and the smaller children spent the entire summer on the island. The lake steamer dropped off essential supplies once a week.

As much as I enjoyed Muskoka, what I found particularly exciting was the farm owned and operated by Gertie Hines's father. He farmed one hundred acres near Bath. The farm was not overly prosperous, but he had a large and airy clapboard house and the Hines family certainly was not poor. We had vacations there.

Gertie left the farm at age sixteen and came directly to work for us in Rosedale. For the next forty-five years she was part of the family. While she did not own anything, everything, lock, stock, and barrel, was hers, in a manner of speaking: "Don't dirty my floor . . . my curtains need washing . . . my vegetables won't be cooked for another half hour!" Gertie had little formal education but was gentle and wise as country people often are, and everybody loved her. In all the time I knew her, I never heard a cross word between Gertie and my mother, who was also gentle and wise. Both were reasonable enough to co-operate when they got "bees in their bonnets." They were forever having "sewing bees" and "spring-cleaning bees," or meetings of the Bethany class of the church ladies or the Missionary group which raised much clatter and little money to support "our missionary in China." Mother was especially wise to co-operate with Gertie because raising five children, with a considerable disparity in age, ensured that there was always a crisis of health or happiness. There were the comings and goings of babies, young men, and maidens, all sizes, and a large house in Rosedale to keep up. Without Gertie, mother would have been lost. Gertie was a real centre of calm and domestic efficiency.

She was deeply religious and devoutly superstitious. As we all did, she attended Hillcrest Church of Christ Disciples, on Bathurst Street, three times on Sundays. I am sure she prayed more for us than she ever did for herself. We were her whole life. On at least two occasions Gertie took her whole city family – father, mother, and all of us – for a summer vacation on her family's farm. That is when I first met Bess, the old mare who pulled the hay wagon and anything else that needed pulling on the farm, except teeth and tits. I was quite startled when I saw my father throwing bales of hay, because I had never seen him do such physical labour before!

Gertie was about forty when her father, a widower for years, married again. She never visited the farm after that. It was not hers any more. At age sixty, Gertie married for the first and only time. The groom was an old retired farmer who had a comfortable house in Bath. After ten years of married comfort, she outlived him, then sold out and moved near Maple to live in one of my sister Dorothy's houses until she died, well over eighty years of age. From Gertie I learned by example the love and devotion that develops when people are simple, honest, and caring. We all missed her very much.

During these very early years, my father spent four months of the year overseas buying merchandise for Simpsons. Our main contact with him was through the mail. He sent long and wonderful letters written in his fine, copperplate script. His letters had something for everyone: poems for the youngest, me; advice to the lovelorn, a condition which seemed to affect my sisters, then in their teens; admonishment for my brothers in anticipation of some startling act, or praise for one of their better accomplishments; a hearty, keep-up-the-good-work for Gertie; and a private love page for my mother.

I was nearly ten before I got to know my father really well. He was forty-nine then. Overworked and fatigued, he consulted his doctor, who ordered him to relax. He also suggested he stop smoking and drinking and give up golf. Being perverse, my father, who did not smoke or drink, bought himself a horse and taught himself to ride. Then he took his first cigarette and drink of hard liquor. A year later he was examined again by the same doctor, who was amazed to find him in first-class condition. He never really did like smoking and labelled it the difference between doing something and doing nothing – and quit! He did become very fond of horses, riding, and Scotch whisky, but not necessarily in that order. My early recollections of father, when he was home, were of family picnics to which my mother was addicted; summers in Muskoka, when Dad and I would go fishing together for hours without saying much, but mutually absorbing the constant yet ever-changing beauty of water, rocks, and sky.

My earliest vivid memory is of when I was six or seven. I had inadvertently, while playing ball in our garden, hit a pitched ball, knocking it cleanly through a pane of the garage window. Mother descended like an avenging angel, claiming that this was too much. This crime could only be handled by Daddy himself. My father almost never laid a hand on any member of the family. Mother disciplined the children if they needed it, sometimes with the back of a hair brush (cruel and unusual punishment). I was frightened enough at the enormity of my crime, but having to endure the hours of waiting for my father to return home from work stretched my over-wrought nerves to the breaking point.

When father got home and had the situation explained to him, he took me out to the garden to survey the slight damage. I was so abject that he burst out laughing at my terror, which suddenly infuriated me, and enraged I ran up to him and kicked him in the shins, shouting, "Nobody laughs at me!" Then I got the spanking I had anticipated. My outburst amused him all the more but in a curious way earned me the beginning of his respect. I think for the very first time he realized I was not just another baby, and I began to realize that he was more human than I had suspected. As I discovered, he was the most human of human beings, with frailties as well as great strengths. At ten, for a full and happy year, father rode with me one hour a day five days a week from Whitewood's Livery. He and I became very close friends through our mutual love of horses and riding, and the many hours we spent together were an important time in both our lives. We established a rapport and loving respect for each other that survived as long as he lived, and beyond.

# EARLY LESSONS

## 2

George Mougenel was our "driver" for most of my early years. Along with Gertie Hines, he organized and ran everything mechanical and otherwise at 52 Binscarth Road and later at 136 Glen Road in Rosedale. "Mouge," as everyone called him, was a Simpsons' driver of the old school, trained under Mr. McCaig, the head of the drivers in the horse days.

Simpsons had all-matched, dappled-grey delivery horses, and each driver looked after his assigned horse and rig. The large brass plate on the side of the rig which read "The Robert Simpson Company Ltd." had to be polished to a mirror-shine or Mr. McCaig would literally pull the hapless driver off his seat, saying, as he thrust his face toward the plate, "Can you see your ugly face in that, Mr. Smith? No, you can't? Now, be a good lad and go back and polish it properly, so not to disgrace the company." Mr. McCaig always called his drivers "Mr." One of the grandest sights in Toronto was to see, first thing in the morning, twenty or more dappled-grey horses pulling Simpsons' rigs and trotting smartly up Jarvis Street in line. What one could not see was that a high proportion of the smart drivers on the seats were glowing with gin, supplied by a house on Mutual Street. A few tots of gin kept the cold wind out. Amazingly, the horses knew exactly their allotted routes and turned off without too much direction.

Mouge graduated to chauffeur and drove us for many years and many miles. He learned to pack mother's clothes for a trip neater than a French maid could. Unfortunately he drank, more as time went on. He was the first in a succession of fine men who have driven us over the past seventy years.

Our delivery-route man was Norman Jones, and he allowed me to help him cover his route. I discovered the Simpsons' man was a very special man to his customers, who would think nothing of leaving him notes reminding him to do small, friendly chores: "Please turn off the hose," "Let the cat out," and so on. It was a friendly world in those days.

When my mother was a young girl, young ladies painted china as a pastime and as an artistic accomplishment. But, when I was young, to play a musical instrument was much admired. Even better was to sing and join the Mendelssohn Choir or be a soloist in the church choir.

My brother Edgar, as mentioned earlier, took the violin very seriously, until the accident ended his playing.

My sister Blanche sang and had several instructors or voice coaches, but she never made the Mendelssohn Choir. She sang at church socials or after lunch on Sundays. The effort was as hard on her as it was on everyone else, except mother, who adored seeing any spark of accomplishment in any of her children.

My sister Dorothy, nine years older, and my brother Carl, three years older than I, dutifully took piano lessons from Madame Penley, who was famous mainly for her teaching room at the Hambourg Conservatory on Wellesley Street at Sherbourne. Carl and Dorothy advanced as far as a mechanical rendition of "In a Country Garden," a song with no good memories for me.

At age eight I was shipped off to Madame Penley for my first piano lesson, and my last. I owe Madame Penley a very great deal because it was she who inadvertently got me started drawing and painting. Doing watercolours has been a life-long hobby of mine. It happened this way. I was small, timid, and undersized, but sitting next to the florid expanse and offensive fragrance of Madame Penley and trying not to be sick, I made a firm resolve not to take any more piano lessons. Lessons stank! There was no way I could tell my mother why I was not going to study piano, at least no delicate way, so I was very evasive when asked, "How did you like Madame Penley? She's coming to tea today." Along with Madame Penley came an elderly gentleman, her father, A. Freeman Smith, an artist and architect who was to have a great effect on my life and with whom I studied for the next seven years.

Mr. Smith was an average-sized, English gentleman, with white hair and a neat, pointed Vandyke beard, rather like the man who played Santa Claus in the movie *Miracle on 34th Street*. I saw in him at once my saviour! Marching over to him and facing him squarely, while he balanced his teacup and himself on a small drawing-room chair, I said, "Can you draw a maple leaf, sir?"

Having been a teacher at the prestigious Birmingham School of Art in England for forty years, and a specialist in Gothic church architecture as well as a published author on the subject, Mr. Smith said the English gentleman's equivalent of "sure," probably, "I believe I can." Smiling and at ease for the first time at the party, he put aside his teacup, drew out a pencil and paper, and with great speed and economy of line drew the most perfect maple leaf I had seen.

"Could you teach me to do that, sir?" I asked.

"I would be delighted," responded Mr. Smith.

I marched over to my mother and Madame Penley and with firmness declared that henceforth I would take painting and drawing from Mr. Smith and no more piano from Madame Penley. From then on I went to Mr. Smith's twice a week for nearly seven years. Mr. Smith gave me one lesson a week in geometry, to learn perspective, and one in drawing and watercolour technique. As a result I completed Junior Matriculation level geometry by the time I was ten years old.

My mentor was of the old school – no white or black paint or fancy effects you could not wipe out or scratch; much better to leave the whites the pure white of paper. He did allow the use of ox gall to break the surface tension of some paper so the colour flowed more smoothly, and, to this day, I can still taste the extreme bitterness of the gall. But his influence extended beyond the mechanics of art. Mr. Smith was a deeply religious man and a devout admirer of John Ruskin, the great Victorian critic and social thinker. I remember him telling me, quoting Ruskin, "Watercolour painting is a series of happy 'accidents' due to the different drying effects of the atmosphere. The true watercolourist is an artist who can capitalize on these 'accidents' and incorporate them into his design as if he had planned it that way, thus achieving a beautiful effect even beyond his normal ability." What impressed me deeply was the belief of Ruskin and Smith that beauty and good will endure in a society, even when sullied by temporary periods of ugly, fashionable excesses, fashions which they equated with "decadence." I was confident that the artist could bring forth this unsuspected beauty to the view and understanding of many people and help mould a better world.

After my abrupt refusal to take piano lessons, deserting music in favour of art, I seldom saw Madame Penley again. However, as I left the Ernscliffe Apartments on Wellesley and Sherbourne Streets, where she shared an apartment with her father, and where I had my lessons, I passed the Hambourg Conservatory of Music on the north side of Wellesley. I could hear the distant echo of sweet and sour notes, a scraping and tinkling of students, some studying strings with Boris Hambourg, some absorbing the essence of piano technique from the formidable Madame Penley. I never regretted my choice.

In 1929, at age fourteen, I went to study for a year at Lycée Jaccard in Lausanne, Switzerland. It was a sad parting for Mr. Smith who, in view of his advanced age, did not expect to see me again in this world. He wrote a farewell letter to me, one of several I still cherish. It goes as follows:

> *August 16, 1929*
> *48 Ernescliffe*
> *Wellesley Street,*
> *Toronto 5*

*My dear Allan:*
*In a few days you will be hoping to cross the ocean towards Europe. I hope you progress in your studies, your recreations in your new environment will all be good, and that your hopes will be realized.*

*Keep your face to the sunshine and the shadows will fall behind you.*

*There is but one source of all good – look to Him daily and in all difficulty and He will help you. Read a portion of the Scripture daily, especially the New Testament, and learn at least some of Matt. V, VI, VII, our dear Saviour's own words.*

*And now I say goodbye to you and God bless you.*

*With kindest regards to your parents, your affectionate friend and former art teacher.*

(signed) *A. Freeman Smith*

I wrote him later from school, telling him I was studying under a Swiss called Claude Jeanneret, an artist of international reputation, adept in many mediums, who was trying to change my technique, "to loosen me up." Mr. Smith replied on March 29, 1930: "Your art masters are likely to be different because I suppose they will be under French influence, where the best continental art schools exist. I hope, while you have opportunities so near, you will visit the picture galleries in France (Paris) before you come away, and if you visit London, don't miss the Victoria and Albert Museum. I think there is none better in Europe." But by this time, I was deep into sports – sculling, soccer, riding, skiing, skating. Art and architecture were for a future life!

I did see Mr. Smith on my return, but he was getting very old. As I had turned fifteen, I was full of the present and the future. I visited him a few times, but mostly for conversation. He had taught me as much as he could, and now he lived only with his memories and Ruskin's quotations. He was as dear to me as the grandfathers I never knew.

Clare Conner was a couple of years older than I. We first met at Rosedale Public School when I was about six and he was eight. He was slightly built with flaming red hair and freckles, a dreamer with a Huckleberry Finn look of mischievousness, contemplated or just accomplished! I played Tom Sawyer to his Huck Finn and admired his strength and lack of fear. I never got the strap at school. Clare always did, often for things he had not done, but he never complained. I could protest "till the cows came home" that I was responsible for all that had brought down the teacher's wrath, but the teacher would never believe me. "It's noble of you, Allan, to try and protect your friend, Clare, but I know he did it." Poor Clare would wink, shrug his shoulders, and stoically take another strapping on my behalf.

During your lifetime, if you are lucky, you will make many good friends. Some may be very special, but only a few can ever be counted "best friends," people you never forget and who never forget you. Clare was one of my "best friends."

Clare lived on Highland Avenue in Rosedale, so we walked to school together each day. After school, we roamed the heavily forested ravine half a block away from his home, playing out the Indian stories we had read, such as *The Last of the Mohicans*. Together we read *The Boy Allies in the Trenches, Tom Swift and His Flying Machine, Boys' Own Annual, Chums Annual,* and, best of all, the wonderful G.A. Henty stories for boys. Clare took art lessons with me from Mr. Smith for one year, but I think the Conner budget did not need the extra expense, and Clare was becoming interested in other things. I lost track of him when I was in Switzerland. On my return we saw less of each other but remained "best friends."

At the outbreak of war, Clare became a pilot with the Royal Air Force and took part in the early bomber raids on Wilhelmshaven. On one of his first raids he brought his plane home on fire, with most of the tail burned away. He had instructed his crew to "bail out." All did except his sergeant, who remained and battled the blaze. For this action the sergeant received the Victoria Cross; Clare, the Distinguished Flying Cross. I was terribly proud of my old friend. Clare was given one week's leave, during which he married an English girl. Then he tried the same manoeuvre of bringing another crippled plane home. Tragically, he was lost in the Channel.

There is a sequel to this story. One day after the war, I was picking up my small son, Jamie, at school, and before he ran over to get in the car, he called out and waved to a little girl with flaming red hair, "Goodbye, Claire." There, before me, was a small female version of Clare Connor. I asked, "Who was that?"

Jamie said, "She's my special friend, Claire Connor. She's from England. Her daddy was killed in the war."

I drove off with a huge lump in my throat.


In the twenties, adolescence was referred to as "reaching puberty." Every mother with a son at U.T.S. wanted him to be in Tommy Porter's class before he reached too far and too often. Tommy was ahead of his time because he conducted what must have been among the first official sex-education classes in the Ontario school system. U.T.S. had many outstanding masters. Some, like the headmaster, Dr. Althouse, went on to more senior posts in the system, but none was more honoured than Tommy, because he dared to explain things to his boys that most of the mothers did not know or would not admit to knowing. Such "things" as semen, eggs, embryos, wombs, and masturbation were never even whispered in polite society. How things have changed!

I never knew why the tall, slim, grey, rather distinguished Mr. Porter was always referred to as "Tommy." Perhaps it was because, as he had discussed the ultimate intimacy of sex with their sons, the parents looked on him as a family friend. Tommy told us a lot we already knew or had heard about in varying forms from older boys, but he also had some bizarre, frightening information that worried us a great deal. Too many "wet dreams" could sap your strength! One ounce of semen was equivalent to forty ounces of blood! If we felt a strange phenomenon coming on, we were advised to jump immediately into a cold shower or go for a long walk, preferably alone. We also learned some strange things about our sisters and their friends. These things did not apply to our mothers because to our minds they must be quite different. We presumed that as one got older one got over "that sort of thing."

One of my problems at U.T.S. was that every class I went into the master used to say, "Oh, you are Carl Burton's brother. We expect great things from you." My brother did very well academically, usually getting straight A's. My sights were set on the safe harbour of a "passing mark." I worked hard enough to ensure that happy result, and thus avoided the storm that would surely ensue if I failed. I never did fail a final exam, but I sure worried everyone – masters, family, and me most of all, when I thought about it.

Because I had been underweight and was considered to be delicate for the first ten years of my life and because I had suffered seven severe bouts of the croup in seven years, great efforts were made to fatten me up. A fat child was, in those days, considered to be a healthy child. By the age of eleven, I was twenty-five pounds overweight, too heavy and soft to do field sports or games like rugby, as football was called. So, instead, I became an excellent swimmer, a fair wrestler, and runner-up to the junior champion in fencing with foils. Individual sports at U.T.S. were encouraged. Varsity Stadium was our playing field.

One of the school highlights each year was "the play," which I always enjoyed. Everyone took part in it because there was something for everyone to do, even if only to appear as one of the rabble in *Julius Caesar*. Our production of that play was a hilarious sellout. Members of the Junior School were the rabble. They wore short togas and stood with their backs to the audience, facing Caesar downstage on his throne. In high-pitched voices they shouted, "Hail, Caesar!" while bending and bowing. With each "Hail, Caesar!" and each bow, forty little pink bare bottoms, with male ornaments dangling in the full glare of the footlights, were "flashed" to the audience. The first "Hail, Caesar!" drew a snicker, a titter, and a ripple of embarrassed giggles from the audience. The second "Hail, Caesar!" brought forth guffaws and gales of laughter, as the little "flashers" went through their act, basking in the applause. The next performance everyone had to wear his shorts, and clean ones, too!

One of life's biggest adventures must be going to one's first summer camp, not the tailor-made camps with all the conveniences that kids go to now, but the rustic style of camp, like Cochrane's Camp on Bear Island, Temagami, a half-century ago. For me, it was a wilderness adventure never to be forgotten. There was a long journey by train to Temagami, then by steamer some hours up Lake Temagami until I arrived at Cochrane's Camp, elated but exhausted.

I was rather timid as a child, and this was the first time I had been away from home for more than overnight. Strangely, I was not homesick, as I was to be several years later in boarding school in Switzerland; rather, I was determined to become physically strong and not let anyone know how terrified I was of the dark. If I had a goal at this moment of my life, it was to become strong enough to lick my brother Carl who, being three years older and many times stronger than I, used to tease me by holding me down on the floor, enraged but powerless, until I cried in frustration. When I was eleven he was fourteen, so there was a vast difference in animal strength. So determined was I to toughen up that at Cochrane's Camp I volunteered for work beyond my years, and talked my way on to the exclusive Moose Island where the bigger boys, called "Moosus," lived in tents rather than in the cabins the younger boys shared on the large island.

I was a good swimmer and earned my Royal Life-saving Badge, which enabled me to go on one of the really memorable canoe trips of that camp year. We started off three to a canoe. Our counsellors, eighteen- and nineteen-year-old students, knew more than we did, but not really enough more when it came to map-reading and wilderness lore. The fact that we survived is a credit to them, but we lost our way and were gone three or four more days than planned. Our food ran out and we lived on gruel, hardtack, and plum jam for three days. It was a miserable time for me because I had heavy bands on my upper and lower teeth and could not chew hardtack, our main food. I pulverized it between two stones, mixed it with plum jam, and ate the gooey mess. I could not face plum jam for the next twenty years!

Our course took us well on our way to James Bay. Each day was exciting, shooting rapids and portaging, sometimes three or four long portages a day. I carried upwards of ninety pounds on a tumpline, Indian-style, with a broad band across my forehead which led back to the pack. My hands clutched the straps on either side of my head to steady the load. I could not lift my load so I had to have it placed on a rock high enough for me to get under it.

Half way through the voyage we ran across some Americans beside a river, miles from nowhere. There was a huge hole in their canvas-covered cedar canoe. They were near desperation when we found them, as they had no means of repairing their canoe, had run out of food, and had no wireless or radio. We had canvas and pitch and repaired their canoe and told them to follow us. They also shared our meagre hardtack. Little did they know that we were not too sure where we were going! But all of us made it back safely.

When I think of the elaborate equipment of sleeping bags, insect repellants, and other "necessary" items that present-day children take to camp, I am struck with the ultra-simplicity of the gear we had, *viz.*, two grey army blankets, pinned together with blanket pins for a sleeping roll, a rubber ground sheet, a towel and a bar of soap, sneakers and shirts and shorts.

On our memorable trip we encountered a most violent storm while on the lake and sought refuge on a small uninhabited island. Our blankets were soaked, and so we lit a huge bonfire around which everyone sat, gamely trying to imagine that this was really roughing it and that it was fun. It was miserable! All the more so when, for some ill-conceived prank, I was banished from the light and warmth of the bonfire and friends to my bedroll, damp as it was. My overactive imagination and natural fear of the dark transformed the flickering light of the bonfire into weird shapes and the blackness of the forest behind me full of lurking beasts of prey. The chatter of my companions in the distance around the fire served to emphasize the creeping silence of the woodland creatures surrounding me. Exhausted, I fell asleep but a short while later awoke, horrified to discover that a four-foot-long snake had crept under my blankets to share my body heat. My cries brought the whole camp to my side. The snake was killed and, to everyone's misery, we found the place was overrun by these large reptiles – king snakes, I believe they were. In the morning their home, or den, was found under a huge boulder. An orgy of slaughter ensued. We did not realize that these creatures were completely harmless.

Our wilderness was then unspoiled, and most of the animals seemed to sense we meant no harm. We carried no firearms, and I suppose the most alarming thing about us was our noisy chatter and natural body fragrance. Chipmunks, always cheeky, chattered and teased us. Rabbits and deer bounded a short distance before stopping to stare. Whiskey-jacks, chickadees, crows, and red-winged blackbirds followed us on portages, relaying us from one flock to another until we cleared their area. By mutual consent we detoured porcupine and skunk.

I saw real suffering on this trip for the first time in my life. One poor lad, in the sweat and prickly heat caused by being city-soft and the chafing caused by the unusual prolonged exertion of paddling and portaging, developed a huge boil for every button on his pants around his waist, six in number. He was in agony and could not carry his loads. His pain was terrible to witness when one of the counsellors applied iodine to these festering sores. This young counsellor, so inept in first aid, later became a well-known medical doctor, but he nearly killed his first patient!

The summer came to an end. We survived, strong, tanned, and much less timid, with a whole new appreciation of the beauty and joyful solitude one experiences on a wilderness lake in Canada's northland. Mother was astounded when I walked into our house on my return and, without even saying hello to Carl, tackled him down on the floor and walloped him. He quickly negotiated a permanent truce. Thus another of my life's goals was achieved.

# LYCÉE JACCARD

## 3

On his annual buying trips to Europe, my father had learned to speak German quite fluently and later learned to speak French. He spoke French with a heavy, guttural Germanic accent, so much so that in Paris sometimes he had a hard time, having the accusation flung at him, "Vous-êtes Allemand!" He was a devotee of Goethe and all his works, so he really thought more in German than in French. Anyway, he was a firm believer in the broadening experience of a year or so in Europe. Just as learning to play a musical instrument was *de rigueur*, one after another of my brothers and sisters had their "overseas experience," the main purpose of which was to learn another language, preferably French.

My sister Blanche, the oldest, was sent to a finishing school in Paris. She was a handsome eighteen-year-old, well-rounded and naïvely romantic. She learned how the nuances of a language can get one into trouble before one understands the colloquialisms. At a party in Paris, Blanche met a dashing young Parisian, Maurice Duclos. They stepped out onto one of those beautiful curving balconies, with turn-of-the-century ironwork, to see the full moon. Blanche, pulling a simple phrase from her limited French vocabulary, said, "Regardez la lune." *La lune* being slang for *derrière*, the gallant Frenchman stepped back, regarded her shapely bottom carefully, and, with that typically Gallic gesture of admiration, kissed his fingertips, threw a kiss to the breeze, and said, "C'est magnifique." Blanche later told us that when she refused to marry him he said he would join the Foreign Legion. The family dismissed this as the romantic roamings of a young girl's mind. As it turned out, he did join the Legion, or so he said. He also served with the underground in World War II, but he did not say on which side. Following the war, he spent the next few years in South

America. Appearing in Toronto forty years after meeting Blanche in Paris, he said "hello" and disappeared again!

When I reached age fourteen, arrangements were made to send me to the Lycée Jaccard in Lausanne for a year to learn French. I was to go to Switzerland with a boy whose father, Colonel Snell, was general manager of the Simpsons' store in Montreal. Young Herb Snell and I lived together for a whole year, but had little in common except our loneliness and our desire to return home. Mother, my brother Carl, and I sailed on the *Duchess of Athol*, a Cunarder, later lost as a troop ship in World War II. We thrilled to the horns, hoots, and streamers of departure and watched the brave pushing and pulling of the tugboats with admiration. Then, suddenly the ship began to move. We watched in sadness as the shore receded and we left Canada and friends behind. We were in first class, but in a modest section of it. My mother's Scottish background – "There is no use wasting money" – dictated economy. Our accommodation was quite adequate, and the stewards and stewardesses were very well trained and eager to offer a level of service unknown today. True first-class travel is a thing of the past.

My father was not with us on this 1929 trip. I believe he was deep in the negotiations with J.H. Gundy of Wood Gundy and the Simpsons' managers to buy out the Sir Joseph Flavelle interest in The Robert Simpson Company Limited, thus creating Simpsons Limited, and becoming the major shareholder block in the new company. If my father had been with us, we would not have had our first – that is, Carl's and my first – experience with getting "tiddly," as it was quaintly described. In the beautiful main dining room, wine flowed freely and was served at nearly every table but ours, Mother being very much against "drink" – wine and alcohol in all its forms. Carl at seventeen and I at fourteen had had no experience with the substance. However, about the third day out, when we all felt better, which was called "getting your sea legs," Mother gave way to the urging of the wine steward and ordered a bottle of sparkling burgundy for the three of us. Mother had very curious ideas about alcohol and liquor. If it was colourless, like gin, it had no alcohol; if it bubbled, like champagne or that fearsome drink, sparkling burgundy, it was sinful but harmless. When offered a drink by my father, Mother used to say in perfect innocence, "You know very well, Daddy, I don't drink, but I wouldn't mind one of those refreshing gin and tonics!" In her opinion the tonic water, which contained quinine, transformed the gin into a medicine to ward off malaria, and other fearsome diseases. Simpsons once sold thousands of bottles of Beef Iron and Wine Tonic to ladies who would have been horrified had they known the glow it gave them came not from the beef extract or the iron, but from the twenty-five per cent sherry!

Our bottle of sparkling burgundy was duly poured, and after one sip Mother had no more. But she insisted that Carl and I must not waste the bottle at these prices. So I got "tiddly" and Carl got drunk, so drunk that he locked himself in the ship's elevator for about two hours and ran it up and down without letting anyone else inside. Our helpful steward talked him into the open and to bed. The next day Mother felt miserable at the disgrace. Carl felt deservedly poorly, and I felt that sparkling burgundy was a waste of time. I still feel the same way.

We arrived in London via the boat train from Southampton and took up residence in the huge new Grosvenor House Hotel on Hyde Park. The doorman – a magnificently top-hatted, gold-braided, six-foot, ex-Household Cavalry Corporal of Horse – was a visible declaration of what to expect inside London's newest and most luxurious hotel. This huge and haughty man opened taxi doors, holding the handle between thumb and forefinger at arm's length, as if to avoid contamination, while he caressed the handles of the stately Rolls-Royces as they arrived, as if welcoming old friends. Only later did I realize that doormen did not get paid but made large incomes from tips, a few coins at a time.

I wanted to go riding in Rotten Row, that historic and lovely strip in Hyde Park where Guards' officers exercise their chargers and others ride sedately, with or without their grooms, to be seen more than to be exercised. Mother was game, so we went to Selfridge's department store and she bought me britches, boots, and jacket, then back to the hall porter's desk to order me a mount. I suggested a ride of two hours. I was to meet the groom with my horse at Hyde Park Corner, he to return in two hours to take it away. I mounted and rode off with not a care in the world. About fifteen minutes later it started to pour rain, not the gentle rain that is supposed to give English girls their fine complexions but a pouring, drenching, miserable rain that drove everyone off Rotten Row but me. I did not know which stable my horse came from, and I still had an hour and a half to go before the groom came for the horse. I rode up and down in the deluge for another half hour before deciding the only thing to do was to ride the horse back to Grosvenor House, up the road in among the hundreds of taxis. My teeth were chattering from the chill, from being wet to the skin, and from not knowing what to do when I arrived at the magnificent doorman's post. I could see, as I approached, he was now in a raincape holding a huge umbrella over the heads of the patrons as they descended from their vehicles. I rode up to him, dismounted, pulled the reins over my horse's head, handed them to the astonished doorman, and said, "Please hold my horse while I phone!" My last view of him was him holding the horse's reins in one hand, an umbrella in the other, still trying to open car doors as they arrived. I never did phone but went upstairs to a hot bath and a sound sleep – and never used that entrance of the hotel again for the remainder of our stay in London.

Our next exciting adventure was our first air trip. We flew from Croydon to Le Bourget in an Imperial Airways "Cyclops Class" biplane that had two enormous wheels almost six feet in diameter. Its top speed was ninety miles an hour. The interior looked like a gentleman's clubroom, with large mahogany armchairs placed along each side facing each other in pairs, with a solid mahogany table in a fixed state between them. There were no seat belts. A smartly uniformed attendant in a starched white linen military jacket, complete with brass buttons, served each of the twelve passengers hot roast beef carved at his table from a traditional trolley with a domed silver cover. There was no hurry because Croydon to Le Bourget was a two and a half hour flight! We arrived feeling very much like world travellers. Flying in those days was for the sophisticated few.

We were met by our Paris representative, M. Castenet, a distinguished-looking, middle-aged man who was beautifully and extravagantly dressed, complete with light, pearl-grey Homburg with a shining white, silk hatband and trim – a sight to behold! He soon had us settled in the luxurious Plaza-Athenée hotel and instructed us as to when our train left for Geneva and Lausanne. We went to the Louvre and made a quick sightseeing tour of the Ile de la Cité and Notre-Dame Cathedral. Mother was always a little nervous, even suspicious of the motives of Frenchmen. Not able to speak the language, she felt threatened by the babble and chatter of unfamiliar sounds around her. She was uneasy in Paris.

We were walking down the Champs Elysées to meet M. Castenet at our office when, some distance away, we saw the unmistakable pearl-grey Homburg with white silk hatband visible above the iron shield of a corner *pissotière*. The shield covered the person relieving himself from the shoulders to the knees. The round *pissotière* contained many Homburgs, some blue, some black, but only one pearl-grey with a white silk band! As we approached, it was clear that the man under the hat was the gallant M. Castenet, our representative. Catching the pair of us out of the corner of his eye, he used his free hand to doff his Homburg and greet us with "Bonjour, Madame Burton et Monsieur." Mother tossed her head in the air in startled embarrassment, quickened her pace, and passed the *pissotière* without returning the salutation. Some distance past, her cheeks flaming, she hissed at me, "Nasty Frenchman, the *least* he could have done was *ignore* us." Only later did she realize that poor M. Castenet meant only to be courteous.

The Gare de l'Est, the railway station, a monochrome of soot, was a bedlam of noise and confusion. The sounds of travellers were punctuated now and then with the urgent cries of lost ones or of happy recognitions. There was the hissing and grumbling of the panting steam locomotives, which shrieked occasionally in a ridiculously high-pitched sound of frustration. The cavernous station was full of passengers and baggage, of sad-looking porters in blue sloppy work-clothes, each wearing a black beret and a leather apron, a heavy strap across one shoulder. Our haven of refuge was the tall, gold-braided representative of Thomas Cook & Sons who, recognizing us as one of his own, quickly got us and our large number of bags directed to our train. "Thomas Cook" and our porters found our staterooms in one of the spotlessly clean *wagon-lits*. Carl and I shared one room and Mother had one to herself. M. Castenet did not think Mother was quite up to sharing sleeping accommodation with a stranger, so he wisely rented both the upper and lower berth for her exclusive use. It was not unusual for a female passenger travelling alone to find a male stranger in the upper berth, or vice versa, if only one berth had been booked. The arrangement must have led to some interesting trips.

Lac Léman, the Lake of Geneva, and Geneva itself seemed clean and tranquil after the hurly-burly of France. When we finally arrived at Lausanne, we were driven to the Hôtel Beau-Rivage, a grand hotel in the old fashion, with lace curtains and tea on the terrace. Our first night was disturbed by bone-chilling screams which, we found out the next morning, came from an Italian woman in labour across the street. Lausanne, a pretty town, boasted 127 private schools, the main industry.

Lycée Jaccard was situated at Pouilly, about one-and-a-half miles from Ouchy, as the lakefront district was called. The Lycée was the largest boys' school in the district and one of the most prestigious. It stressed physical fitness and sports of all kinds. Academic subjects were not taken as seriously, except for languages, Latin, and mathematics. The school was owned and operated by the Jaccard family – Papa Jaccard, Momma Jaccard, and their four sons, whose names all started with "M," Maurice and Marius being the two I remember. All the schoolboys called the senior Jaccards "Momma" and "Papa" behind their backs. Papa Jaccard was a towering figure, all in black, square-set, with a full, iron-grey "spade" beard. In dress and deportment, he was a picturesque character from a previous century. Momma Jaccard was also dressed in black, but with white lace collar and cuffs. She was a kind, motherly woman with strong peasant features. Her sons taught different sections or disciplines. All were tall men, physically strong, good-looking, and dedicated, mainly to keeping Lycée Jaccard solvent at all costs.

On arrival, Mother and I had tea with the senior Jaccards in their quarters, an ordeal each student endured on his birthday. My room was on the third floor, a pleasant airy room with a balcony and a wonderful view across the lake to the French Alps. Herb Snell, my roommate, had not yet arrived, so I settled in alone. Finally the time came to part and, having said goodbye to Mother and Carl, I ran to the highest window under the eaves to watch their car recede to a speck in the distance and disappear. The growing lump in my throat burst into sobs and tears. I had never felt so completely cut off and alone. I was surrounded by foreigners and unable to converse in their language.

As boys will do, it was not long before I found my way around and made some friends. Fourteen different nationalities were represented at the school. Students were English, French, German, Swiss, Italian, American, and Canadian. There was a Prince of Siam as well as boys from several South American countries, not to mention Hong Kong and Singapore – a veritable League of Nations. We quickly grouped into cliques and alliances – roughly Latin and non-Latin. It was the English, German, North American, and, curiously, the two French students (both colonials) against the Italians, Spaniards, and South Americans. The Siamese Prince sided with "us." This division was not too apparent during the daylight hours; we played on the same teams and got along fine. But after the lights went out, silent raids or noisy donnybrooks took place in the corridors, "us" against "them" over imagined insults or just for the fun of it. The Jaccards did not interfere unless something was broken. No boy dared complain.

We rose at 0600 and were out in the yard by 0615 for physical exercises, summer or winter, in cotton singlet and cotton shorts, no sweaters allowed. Breakfast was at 0700, classes were from 0800 to 1200, with a break at 1030, when we were each issued a block of the bitterest chocolate and a fist-sized piece of bread. Lunch followed from 1230 to 1300, then enforced rest until 1400 hours. Compulsory sports went from 1400 to 1600 hours. Dinner was from 1800 to 1900. Classes were held once more from 1930 to 2130 hours. Lights out at 2200 hours. The regimen was good for me. I got healthier and healthier, as we all did. Our fare, simple but ample, included, to my disgust, horsemeat and jugged hare. My chest expanded six inches during the year, principally from rowing or sculling.

There were two other masters, in addition to the Jaccards, a German Swiss, whose name I have forgotten, and a deflated little Englishman called Mr. Cove. I soon got into trouble with the German Swiss, who attempted to teach me German in French before I knew any French! I called him *sale cochon* under my breath, partly because I was outraged at some penalty he had imposed on the class, partly to see what would happen. I did not realize calling a person "dirty pig" could be at all serious. I soon found out! I was marched to be reprimanded by Papa himself. I quickly apologized, but the German Swiss and I were never friends after that.

Mr. Cove, the quiet little Englishman, won our hearts and shared our loneliness. He had been an English teacher in Germany at the outbreak of World War I and had been interned as a prisoner of war for several years. He told us he had worked in a salt mine. He had eventually escaped penniless to Switzerland and had taught English at Lycée Jaccard ever since, virtually as an indentured slave. He never made enough money to return to England, which was his professed goal, because whenever he got a bit ahead he would be fined by Papa for getting drunk or for some other infraction and so returned once more to drudgery and bondage, forever dreaming of England.

To my surprise and delight I took a leading part in most of the team sports. I had trimmed down and muscled up. I was goalkeeper on the Junior soccer team. We won the Junior Championship of Switzerland in 1929. I was stroke on the four-man sculls, played tennis, hockey, and rode. Every Sunday we were allowed to row our four-man scull down to Ouchy and back, unsupervised. We had been watching the paddle-wheelers that crossed the nine-mile stretch of open water between Swiss Lausanne and French Evian-les-Bains. We thought it looked easy so we decided to row there and home. We did beat the paddle-wheeler across the lake, but not having passports could not land in France. We had no money and could only rest on our oars. The nine-mile return journey was a nightmare of fatigue. Fortunately the lake was as smooth as glass. Marius Jaccard, the athletic coach, was beside himself with worry. We saw him on the dock, and with our final strength came in the last mile as if we were in a race and collapsed at his feet. We could not lift our shell out of the water, and we were banished to bed. Fifteen minutes after our return, one of those extremely violent and noisy storms broke over the mountains. Lac Léman was churned to waves with whitecaps. We would surely have capsized and likely drowned had we been caught out on the open lake. Marius came to our room to tell us privately how proud he was of our strength and ability. I think the good Lord must have overlooked our foolishness, while approving our spirit, just as Marius had.

I commenced painting once more in watercolours under the noted Swiss artist, Claude Jeanneret. Whereas my first teacher, Mr. Smith, had a white beard and was very neat, Claude Jeanneret had a black, rather greasy beard, which completely hid a kindly spirit. The white dandruff on his beard was like snowflakes, but, appearance notwithstanding, he was a most accomplished artist in a variety of mediums. My weekly lesson was a happy time.

I also got permission to ride once a week at the army barracks. The Swiss officers had substantial Irish hunters for their chargers. The Cavalrymen rode lighter Hungarian horses. Our mounts were the officers' Irish-breds, mine a powerful chestnut called Sidi, which I was told meant "Lord" in Arabic. Our riding class was taught the basic Swiss cavalry instruction. I was allowed to lead the ride on Sidi because I was the most experienced. A couple of weeks' allowance went to purchase a cheap pair of spurs, which I proudly wore to and from my classes but never on Sidi. He was well-behaved but exuded power and thrust in response to a light heel. If I had worn my prized spurs, he would have taken me to the next canton!

I gradually became moderately competent in the French language and tried hard to make up for the weeks of schooling during which, not knowing French, I might as well have been somewhere else. For

three days at the start of the year I took algebra, not knowing that
"Y" in French was called *y grecque*! Lycée Jaccard was hopeless for
me academically, but marvellous for the whole of me, and I grew in
strength and confidence.

The first school break came at Christmas, and the manager of
the London office, H.G. Colebrook, and his wife, a reluctant partner, agreed to have Herb Snell and me visit them for the Christmas
holidays. Mr. Colebrook was a fine merchant and a meticulous gentleman. He took great pride in the fact that his brother was the best
"whip" in England, famous for his coach-and-four. We arrived at
their beautiful home at Henley-on-Thames outside London but there
was no one about. Mr. Colebrook had gone off to our offices in St.
Paul's Churchyard, and Mrs. Colebrook was in her chambers. Herb
and I, being hungry, found our way to the diningroom for breakfast.
A real-live butler – a "Jeeves" – bade us good morning and announced
he had a special treat for us – shad's roe! Not only did we not know
what a shad was, but when a brown pyramid of the roe was put before
each of us, one taste convinced us it tasted like sawdust from a very
bland tree. We asked the lordly butler, who apparently adored shad's
roe, if we could have plain bacon and fried eggs. I suspect he knew
we would reject this English delicacy and had offered it so he and
the kitchen help would be the recipients of the prized roe.

One unforgettable memory of this holiday was of a glorious afternoon at the Bertram Mills Circus, famous all over Europe for its marvellous act of twelve or fourteen pure-white Arab stallions in the ring,
doing a flawless routine in unison. The trainer, who merely stood in
the middle of the ring, issued quiet verbal commands, never crack-
ing his long whip, yet getting complete synchronized obedience. These
beautiful horses ended their act by lining up and bowing on one knee,
heads and flowing manes touching the ground. After London, we
were almost glad to get back to the exhausting routine of Lycée
Jaccard, because we had neither the money nor the freedom to do
justice to London, my favourite city – after Toronto!

Easter was the next break from school, and Mother reappeared
with my maiden Aunt Ada and Mrs. Maggie Hambly, mother of my
father's secretary, Grace Hambly. The ubiquitous Thomas Cook &
Sons arranged a two-week trip to Italy for all of us. I suppose these
ladies were only in their early fifties, but to me they were elderly,
presumably fragile, and obviously unsophisticated. The Victorian
myth of the fragility of women, which lasted another thirty years,

was deeply entrenched. I achieved new importance in their eyes because now I could converse in my limited French. They did not know I knew how to swear in fourteen different languages, one of the first things every student learned at the Lycée. I took charge because I was male, young, and had a new-found confidence and assurance in dealing with porters, cabbies, station-masters, and desk clerks. Secretly I was still in awe of *maître d's* in posh restaurants.

In Milan we had been put up in a quaint *hôtellerie*, noted for its cuisine but not for its comfort. No one except a religious fanatic who believed in self-mortification would stay there. The pillows were completely round bolsters filled with sand, the rooms as dark and plain as monks' cells. We visited Milan Cathedral, a triumph in perpendicular Gothic and one of the most exciting buildings of its style in the world. Inside the huge entrance doors is a life-size, seated statue of a saint who was skinned alive. Here he sits in solid white marble, his skin draped over his arm as casually as if it were cashmere. The sheer artistry of turning a huge block of Carrara marble into a beautiful figure and of etching out the very veins of the skin and the muscle layers underneath is a remarkable achievement. We also enjoyed Florence and visited the antique palaces of the Uffizi and the Pitti, now famous galleries of art treasures. We explored the Ponte Vecchio, the bridge over the river Arno, with its accumulation of goldsmiths and jewelry shops clustered along its span like barnacles on a ship. We marvelled at the beautiful Della Robbia enamelled *terra-cotta* plaques of the infant Jesus surrounded by flowers, a reproduction of which was purchased by my mother.

The nineteen-year-old son of the representative at Simpsons' Florence office was detailed to take me out for an evening's entertainment. We walked through the Piazza feeling dwarfed by its huge statues, still in those days lit by flambeaux on the corners of the ancient buildings. The flames from these torches cast grotesque and ever-changing shadows of Michelangelo's statues on the vermiculated stonework and deepened the shadows under the arches and in the alleys. The square was deserted except for us, and our footsteps sounded loud in the darkness, alerting, I was sure, the lurking cut-throats in the shadows. My nerves were taut, and I was so carried away by my overactive imagination that, by the time we got to the Arno River and its dimly lit cafés, I was ready to go home! I did not drink and in lieu accepted my first espresso, which I did not like, the taste for which I eventually acquired some twenty years later. The café's featured act was an illusionist of great skill, and the magician's illusions heightened my feelings of insecurity – so much so that, chastened, I was dumped back at my hotel by my despondent and disgusted companion.

The countryside and hills above Florence have a beauty of their own. When I first saw them, they were serene and bathed in sunshine. Fourteen years later, when we were fighting to take Florence from the Germans, they seemed not so benign and sleepy. At each railway station in Italy we had a routine argument with the conductor of the train. Seeing a young boy and three middle-aged, Anglo-Saxon women, he would claim our reserved seats were already taken, a racket that apparently worked well with most Americans who produced a tip to get things straightened out. These poor conductors did not count on my Scottish-Canadian mother, who simply refused to pay. Once the train moved and no one else appeared, we would occupy our rightful space with the smug satisfaction of not having been "bamboozled" by a crooked Italian conductor. In the high days of 1929, before the bite of the Depression, it was worth your while to make it clear that you were Canadian, not American. In most cases, the asking price would be promptly cut in half!

Our next stop was Rome. Again we stayed at a small hotel, clean but austere. Rome was a constant delight and source of wonderment: the Catacombs, the Christians and the lions, the Coliseum, the Forum, and hundreds of antiquities, historical remnants of ancient Rome. What a wonderful place for a student of architecture! Our visit to the Vatican was prearranged. His Worship, Sam McBride, mayor of Toronto and an Orangeman (no other could be elected mayor of Toronto at the time), had secured for us an introduction to the Pope. We duly went to the Vatican, toured the Basilica of St. Peter, and lined up with several other people who had a prearranged audience. A splendidly uniformed officer of the Swiss Guard was in charge, and I was intrigued to be advised that the Guards really were Swiss, the honour often passing from father to son. As our time to be ushered into the audience chamber drew near, Mother got increasingly nervous and uncomfortable. The whole show was against her upbringing of no "graven images" and simplicity of worship, so in an outburst of guilt she said to the resplendent Swiss Officer of the Guard, "I have changed my mind, I would rather see the gardens!" The officer displayed no alarm or emotion and instructed another guard to give us a tour of the lovely gardens, not usually shown to tourists.

So we never did see the Pope or receive his blessing. However, on the way out of St. Peter's, as we passed a shrine with hundreds of votive candles flickering, the monk or priest in charge offered to keep a candle burning to protect me for the next twenty-five years for the equivalent of only six dollars. Mother, notwithstanding her faith or lack of it in Roman Catholicism, thought that was too good a bargain to miss and had one lit for me. Perhaps that act together with a sense of good luck was why I came unscathed through years of active service in the war to come! She also bought St. Christopher medals, the patron saint of travellers, to see us safely to the end of our journey. Innocents abroad need all the help they can get. The Church eventually repudiated poor St. Christopher, but we kept them close to us until we got home and then gave them to George Mougenel, our Catholic driver, who valued them highly.

Next we went to Naples where we saw Vesuvius and toured the ruins of Pompeii. Mother was upset to see the erotica on the walls. I was allowed into one series of rooms that had sexually explicit murals, but Mother was excluded because she was a woman. Venice we visited on our way back to Lausanne, and we did St. Mark's and saw the beautiful Roman horses and the thousands of pigeons. The canals seemed less than romantic when a load of garbage narrowly missed our gondola.

Back at school there were goodbyes once more. Before Mother left, Mr. Cove, the English master, pleaded with her to take me home with her! He could not escape himself, and he felt anything he could do to help someone else escape was worthwhile. By this time I wanted to stay in Lausanne to compete in the sculling championships at Geneva in June, but this was not to be.

My father had business in London, so once more Mother came to Switzerland, this time to see me out of school and return to the bosom of the family. We had steamer trunks in those days, large impregnable upright pieces of luggage that could only be handled by strong men with suitable dollies. They were different from today's air luggage, which is made of two wisps of space-age plastic and a prayer that it will hold together for more than one flight. I had arranged for my heavier baggage, including my steamer trunk, to be prepaid and forwarded to London. I had carefully considered the difference between the Swiss and French franc and made sure we had sufficient French francs for a meal, as we transferred from the Gare de l'Est to the Gare du Nord for the Channel train. On arrival in Paris, this time without Thomas Cook & Sons, because we did not need them, the station-master asked to see me because he claimed I owed an excess baggage charge. I was understandably upset because, if his claim was correct, we would not have enough French francs left with which to eat. Confident of my spoken French and the rectitude of my position, I argued with the station-master, but got nowhere. Mother, not understanding one word, but feeling that I was not winning the battle, finally said, "What does he want?"

I said, "He is falsely claiming we owe one hundred and forty francs for excess baggage, which I have already prepaid."

Mother, with determination, said, "I will handle this!" Grasping her umbrella halfway up its length, she advanced belligerently toward the station-master and shook it in his face, saying, with controlled ferocity, "You nasty Frenchman, you will not get away with this."

The station-master blanched and backed away, saying to our porter, "Ça fait rien. It doesn't matter, get them out of here quickly!"

When we resumed our seats in our coach, Mother said, "Remember, Allan, that sometimes it doesn't do to know too much!" So much for my beautiful French.

My new-found confidence had been badly shaken by the experience with the station-master, and I was anxious to see my father again. To me he represented a great sea of calm, a world traveller with knowledge and sophistication. Now I was going to see him in London. The rough Channel crossing of the steamer was in contrast to the calm dignity of the boat train, the friendly grey hum of London traffic, and the warmth of Dad's greeting.

During our few days in London, I decided I would take Mother out to dinner. I had the huge sum of four pounds. The two of us walked down to Piccadilly toward the Ritz Hotel, and seeing the sign "Ritz Grill" I had the wild and totally erroneous notion that a grill was somehow more affordable than a restaurant. So we descended and were seated by a startled maître d' as we were the only ones in the grill not in evening dress, black tie for the men. The menu was à la carte, and I quickly discovered we could afford only consommé and coffee before becoming bankrupt. I was upset because I had wanted to give Mother such a splendid meal, but when I explained the problem, she declared the consommé was superb and was all she wanted before the theatre. I expect the maître d' was glad to get rid of us as we were to leave, although it was all very courteous and dignified.

The next day we were to get packed and on our way to the boat train for Southampton, and Mother and I were in the throes of stuffing and repacking to accommodate presents and purchases. Father did nothing, declaring that the valet would pack him as valets had always done on his fourteen trips to the Continent.

Time was running out. The valet had packed Dad's valises. Dad was in the process of getting dressed when he could not find his braces anywhere. The valet, accused of packing them, unpacked the trunk looking for them. Dad finally discovered them under his shirt, much to his chagrin, because Mother was making unseemly remarks about "the great international traveller." We made the boat train with minutes to spare.

# BACK HOME

4

When I returned home from the Continent, I re-enrolled at the University of Toronto Schools, very conscious of the fact that, despite my lessons in how to survive amid fourteen different nationalities, academically I had learned very little except French grammar. I pleaded with the headmaster to return me to the class that I had been in before I left for Switzerland because I did not deserve promotion. Dr. Althouse did not agree and insisted I advance with my age group or an older one. So, my junior-matriculation year was not very happy, as I was struggling to catch up. However, I succeeded and passed all subjects. No one was more surprised or impressed than I. Actually, I did very little work during the year but drove myself to exhaustion swatting for the final exams, hardly sleeping the last month.

Three momentous things happened to me in the year 1931. First, I joined the Eglinton Hunt Club Mounted Cadets, the officers' training unit for the old Governor General's Body Guard, Canada's senior regiment. Second, I passed the test for my chauffeur's licence and acquired a car, a Model A Ford roadster with a rumble seat and four-wheel brakes. It had a red metal triangle fixed to the left rear fender to warn other drivers to beware that I could stop quicker than they could. Third, I discovered girls.

I rode at the Eglinton Hunt almost every day in the cadet drills or at indoor polo on rented ponies. Captain Dick Paton, M.C., was the stable manager of the old Eglinton Hunt Club on Avenue Road and a remarkable man in many respects. He had been overseas with the cavalry in World War I and won himself a Military Cross for personal valour. Mr. Beardmore, M.F.H., of the Beardmore Leather Company (later taken over by Canada Packers), was Master of Foxhounds in the early twenties when the Toronto Hunt was split in two, one half becoming the Toronto and North York at Aurora and the other half the Eglinton Hunt. Just before the 1929 crash, Beardmore had sunk a personal fortune into the magnificent club, arena, and stabling on Avenue Road above Eglinton. He had a groom, Sam Calhoun, who was as Irish as Paddy's pig, and two great hunters, Kilkenny and Countess. My father bought both these horses and Sam Calhoun into the bargain. Sam had raised Countess from a filly, and never could a man love a horse more. It was understood that if Beardmore ever sold Countess, Sam would go, too. I learned to hunt on Countess, as generations to come did, for she hunted till age twenty-six and lived to the amazing age of thirty-six, about the equivalent of one hundred and fifty in a human. She was never lame or sick a day in her life. Kilkenny, a large horse, toed in, and was less reliable due to his slight conformation defect, but still a good horse for disposition and hacking.

The May show at the old Eglinton Hunt was a week-long gala social affair, held in the arena which seated about six hundred people. In the early days it was as popular as the Royal Winter Fair. I teamed up with Jack Rawlinson Jr. for the pair class in the May show of 1932, a momentous occasion in my life. Jack's father was Lieut.-Col. Jack Rawlinson, Commanding Officer of the Governor General's Body Guard and the principal in the well-known Rawlinson Furniture cabinet-making firm. The pair class was hilarious. I got "outjumped" on the first of an in-and-out jump and somehow went over the second obstacle with an arm and one leg on Jack's horse alongside me as well as on my own. I have never seen anyone do this before or since and still clear the obstacle!

After the class we went to the Rawlinson box, and Jack introduced me to two of the loveliest-looking females I had ever laid eyes on, his cousins, Audrey and Constance Syer. Audrey was seventeen, dark-haired and stunning; Constance, sixteen, fair-haired and glowing. I was seventeen and smitten with both! Best of all, they lived only a couple of blocks away from the Hunt Club. In our house at 136 Glen Road we had a large basement recreation room, pine-panelled, with a small stage and its own kitchen facilities. I quickly organized a party of some of my U.T.S. friends and their girl-friends and invited Audrey Syer as my date. When I picked her up at her house on Avenue Road, I met her mother and father for the first time. Caro Syer was a very handsome woman, and Roy a good-looking man who had put on some middle-aged "rugged" quality weight.

He was far from flabby but looked as if he could hold his own in a brawl. He greeted me gruffly and, without putting it into words, seemed to say, "Bring my daughter home safely and untouched or I'll break you in two!" I was suitably intimidated. Later, I found Roy to be soft-hearted and sentimental, a man of fine voice and gentle disposition.

On that first date I must have seemed less than bright because, as I recall, I spent much of the time staring at Audrey, absorbing her beauty. We talked and talked. I was so sure that I did not ever want her to go away that I did not even try to kiss her, which seemed to suit her fine at that moment. My friends, meantime, were engaged in frivolous flirtations, dancing, mild necking, and games. Watching them gave me some pangs of jealousy at their easy approach to the opposite sex. Unlike them, I was not interested in playing the field, but found myself watching my companion's graceful moves, enjoying her exclusive attention, powerfully attracted by her delicate feminine fragrance, and visualizing spending the rest of our lives together. From that moment on, by mutual yet unspoken consent, Audrey Syer and I were one – until her death forty-three years later.

The next evening, having borrowed my father's Cadillac to pick Audrey up for a drive, I found I had very little gas in the tank and no money. So, after suitably impressing the neighbours with the magnificent vehicle, when Audrey got in I said, "I have no money and very little gas. Which corner do you want to park at?" I pointed to several corners within eyesight.

"That one will do fine," she said, pointing to the nearest corner, where we sat for hours clinging together, blissfully happy and unconscious of time. Nothing more happened than hugs and kisses delivered and received with considerable passion, because society had strict views on premarital sex. On everyone's lips was the version of the old saying that runs "Familiarity breeds contempt and babies." However, that did not stop me from asking her, before we drove the half-block home, "What shall we name our children?" And to my delight and surprise, she started naming them!

When I recounted the latter part of this story to my father, he quickly decided he must see this young woman and asked me to invite her for dinner. On her arrival he obviously appreciated her beauty as much as I had. After dinner he asked us to join him in the library, a beautiful room with walnut panelling and a fireplace on one wall, two complete walls of books from floor to ceiling, and a huge window. It was an amazing interview because he had quickly assessed that our attraction to each other was very strong. He gave us a small sermon on the theme that "young blood runs hot" with the admonishment that "at all times one of you has to be strong and keep your head." I suspected his "old blood" could get heated to boiling as well. Audrey and Dad became very close, but Mother became the pattern of motherhood and family love Audrey emulated – her simplicity, taste, quiet dignity, love of house and home, and patent honesty in all things.

Our Sunday dinners following church usually ran to fourteen or more people because Dad, in an excess of Christian zeal and natural *bonhomie*, would invite the minister and his wife, one or more distinguished visitors to the church, and assorted relatives. Conversation ranged from Russia to missionaries, to Charles Dickens – Dad was the president of the Dickensian Society, to the theory of relativity and physics (if Uncle Frank was there – he was head of the Department of Physics at the University of Toronto), to music and the new soloist in the church choir. None of the subjects concerned me, but I could not exclude myself. I often wished our diningroom table had been wired for sound so I could have plugged into whatever discussion I wished or cut them all off. Whenever I ventured a remark, it was so tentative and hesitant that the conversational surf rolled over me before I could catch my breath, quickly drowning any pretence I had at wishing to be heard. Dear Audrey changed all that! At her very first Sunday dinner, when one of my hesitant remarks drew laughter, she – all seventeen years and one hundred pounds of her – stood up from her chair in indignation and said, in effect, "You leave Allan alone. You will listen when he speaks before too long and you won't laugh!"

There was no question in my mind that I loved Audrey, but I was sick with apprehension waiting for the conversation to resume, thinking that we were ruined. Audrey calmly sat down. After dinner, Dad called Audrey into his library and said, "You were magnificent, Audrey dear, and you were right about Allan." He, too, fell in love with her.

When Audrey "ticked off" the family, Dad must have recalled an incident that had taken place at our church three years earlier, when I had spoken up. The Disciples of Christ believed that you should not be baptized until you were old enough to know what you were doing, which usually meant one was baptized at about fourteen years of age. The Disciples also believed in "total immersion," and the minister wore hipwaders under his robe, a modern version of "the Fisherman." On Baptismal Sunday, as my father and I were leaving the church, an eager member of the Woman's Christian Temperance Union stopped us and asked me to sign "the pledge," a form which said I would avoid alcohol in all its forms forevermore. I had been so indoctrinated in our basic belief that one did not act until one knew what it all meant that, spontaneously and seriously, I said, "I am sorry I can't sign the pledge because I am not old enough to drink. I don't drink, but I am not sure at this point whether I want to become a drunkard or not!"

Dad, with a twinkle in his eyes, said, "That's a good answer, I won't sign either!" He was a non-drinker at the time, too. That evening I attended my first and last meeting in the basement of the church. The purpose of the meeting was to decide whether the congregation would pay the young minister, The Rev. Andrew Lawson – later of Eaton Memorial Church – $1,200 a year or $1,500. The haggling was very annoying, so I stood up finally and said, "I have never seen so many un-Christian attitudes displayed in my life. I think Mr. Lawson should get at least the $1,500." Then I left the meeting, enough for one day!

The Eglinton Hunt Club Mounted Cadets, twenty all ranks, were composed entirely of boys from University of Toronto Schools and Upper Canada College. In 1930, when I joined, Lieut. Ted Crease, an officer of the Governor General's Body Guard, was in charge. As the Mounted Cadets were an officers' training unit for the Governor General's Body Guard, one had to become a sergeant of the troop through riding ability, hard work, and dedication before being asked to join the regiment and accept the King's Commission. One purchased his own cadet uniforms, navy blue, silver, and white, and provided his own horse for drill, owned, borrowed, or rented from the Eglinton Hunt Club.

After two years of great fun and hard work, I became Troop Sergeant. As the third year came to a close, no Royal Military College graduate yearned more for his commission and his chance to become an officer of Canada's senior regiment, the Governor General's Body Guard, than I. The fact that I was coping with my Senior Matriculation at U.T.S. was far less important than my commission. In the left corner the document was signed "Bessborough," and in the right it had my number, 49486.

GEORGE THE FIFTH by the Grace of God of Great Britain, Ireland, and the British Dominions beyond the Seas, King, Defender of the Faith, Emperor of India, etc. – To Our Trusty and well-beloved George Allan Burton, Greeting! We, reposing especial Trust and Confidence in your Loyalty, Courage, and good Conduct, do by these Presents Constitute and Appoint you to be an Officer in Our Active Militia of our Dominion of Canada from the Twentieth day of January 1933. You are therefore carefully and diligently to discharge your Duty as such in the Rank of 2nd Lieutenant or in such other Rank as We may from time to time hereafter be pleased to promote or appoint you to, of which notification will be made in the Canada Gazette or in such manner or on such occasions as may be prescribed by Us in Council, and you are in such manner and on such occasion as may be prescribed by Us to exercise and well discipline in Arms, both the inferior Officers and Men serving under you and use your best endeavours to keep them in good Order and Discipline.

AND WE DO HEREBY COMMAND them to Obey you as their superior Officer, and you to observe and follow such Orders and Directions as from time to time you shall receive from Us, or any your superior Officer according to the Rules and Discipline of War, in pursuance of the Trust hereby reposed in you.

IN WITNESS WHEREOF Our Governor General of Our Dominion of Canada hath hereonto set his hand Seal at Our Government House in the City of Ottawa this Fifth day of March in the Year of Our Lord One Thousand Nine Hundred and Thirty-Three and in the Twenty-Third Year of Our Reign.

BY COMMAND OF His Excellency The Governor General

> *L.M. La Flèche*
> Deputy Minister of National Defence

2nd Lieutenant George Allan Burton
Governor General's Body Guard

Thus read the King's Commission for which I had yearned so much. It was dated on my eighteenth birthday, as young as anyone could receive it!

Without doubt, next to family, the regiment has had the most profound influence over my life and has been the source of most of my best friends. My first major goal in life was achieved when I became a cavalryman and, best of all, a Body Guard. My father had agreed that I could accept my commission in the Body Guard on condition that I not have a drink in the mess for two years. I did not drink, so that was no particular hardship. The protocol and traditions of the mess were strictly adhered to, and as a junior subaltern I was the lowest of the low. My job was to see that the guests of the mess were well served and to keep an eye on the Honorary Lieutenant-Colonel, the Mess President, the Mess Secretary, and the Commanding Officer, in that order. Audrey, as girl-friend of the junior subaltern, found no lack of ogling company from senior officers who kept me busy running errands.

It was the beginning of a long apprenticeship for both of us. I was the junior subaltern for the next two years, as there was no intake of new officers and no promotion. My routine was parade Tuesday nights, squadron work Friday nights, officers' league baseball and dance Saturday nights, and every Sunday afternoon Audrey and I drove miles around town to visit the homes of "my men" to ensure their attendance the following Tuesday night. As I walked up to the door in my uniform, many a worried mother came to meet me asking, obviously expecting the worst, "What has Johnny done now?" The result of this active solicitation, however, was one hundred per cent attendance and a waiting list of some fifteen to join my troop. Anyone who missed two parades in a row had his uniform collected, and we dismissed him summarily. This was not as easy as it sounds because, in the depths of the Depression, many men signed up to get the "issue" boots and the streetcar tickets to attend parade. The men received no government pay for regular parades. They did receive $1.50 a day for attending summer camp at Niagara-on-the-Lake. I found that while I could get the uniform back from a discharged man, it was nearly impossible to get his boots, which were on squadron charge. These bloody boots caused much paperwork, a foretaste of the mountain of paperwork to come my way over the years.

I will never forget my first formal parade in my new khaki service dress, Sam Browne and cavalry sabre in leather-covered scabbard, riding breeches, and custom-made field boots and spurs, all painfully new and determined to shape my civilian softness into a more military mould. I had barely learned troop drill and some squadron drill, but my first parade was Regimental Drill, with spectators, including Audrey, and I felt very awkward and self-conscious. I lined up with the officers facing the regiment, while the Regimental Sergeant-Major, a most impressive character, had the squadrons dressed and coerced into a rigid body of men in regimental formation worth allowing the commanding officer and officers to inspect. I thought to myself, "God, I hope I don't faint."

I was Second Troop, "C" Squadron. First Troop was "Swatty" Wotherspoon, now Brigadier Gordon Deward de Salaberry Wotherspoon, D.S.O., K.St.J., E.D. "Swatty" was not only a Royal Military College graduate, but had been cadet sergeant-major – number-one cadet! However, I did not think he looked as smart as I did because he had on a pair of his grandfather's field boots. They were so comfortable on him that he could mark time in them without the boots moving at all, whereas mine were so smart they were slowly cutting off the circulation. My feet felt like lead. We moved off without too much trouble, but when I did not know a command, the help did not come from my sergeant, named White, but from a prompting voice from the ranks. Before we dismissed, I asked the men who had been so helpful. A mature trooper admitted he had spoken out. He wore a string of ribbons on his chest from World War I, including the Military Cross, only awarded to commissioned officers. Tpr. Reginald Wedge, M.C., I found out, had been commissioned. His Military Cross was authentic. He had rejoined the ranks because he could not afford the cost of officer rank. He loved the army. Reg and I became very close friends over the years. During World War II, he once more became Major Reg Wedge, M.C., with the Second Regiment, Governor General's Horse Guards.

My friend "Swatty" of First Troop, "C" Squadron, was soon promoted to captain and adjutant, his place being taken by Lieut. John W. Eaton. Jack Eaton was also a graduate of R.M.C., and son of the honorary lieutenant-colonel of the Regiment, Lieut.-Col. R.Y. Eaton, then president of Eaton's and brother of Lieut. Erskine Eaton, whom I had displaced as junior subaltern. Erskine and I had been to U.T.S. together, where he had earned the nickname of "Irksome" because he had a puckish sense of humour and little regard for authority.

At the end of our first year as newly commissioned officers, as was the regimental custom, a subaltern's court-martial was conducted, an unofficial but deadly serious affair conducted on trumped-up charges by the junior captain and two next most-senior lieutenants.

It was serious in that if you did not withstand the grilling and questioning with composure and humility, the court could recommend dismissal from the regiment. If this happened, the next morning the unhappy officer received a letter from the adjutant suggesting a letter of resignation be forthcoming.

My charges were: 1. Complete ignorance of the rudiments and fundamentals of cavalry training. 2. Undue familiarity with senior officers. 3. Improper salute. The charges were all fairly mild, but I was apprehensive because my court-martial followed Erskine's. The tribunal kept him at attention for three-quarters of an hour before they could discern a modicum of remorse or humility in him. Either the tribunal was exhausted or I somehow soothed their vindictive natures, but I was in and out in ten minutes. Erskine, as I remember, got only a probationary passing from them, and some time later, after further escapades, quietly left the unit, but not before he and I together with Major Hilton Wilkes won the Hamilton Merrit Trophy for the best cavalry team in Canada in 1933. The test included riding, jumping, carrying messages mounted across difficult terrain, and so on, and each of us was given a sterling silver plate and tie-pin in the shape of a horseshoe nail made of platinum. I still have mine and wear it on occasion. After leaving the regiment on the outbreak of World War II, Erskine joined up with Les Fusiliers de Montréal as the only English-speaking officer in that unit. Lieut. E.R. Eaton is on the Horse Guard Roll of Honour, having died of wounds received at Dieppe while serving with Les Fusiliers. Once a Horse Guard, always a Horse Guard!

As the years passed, most of Jack Eaton's troop was composed of Eaton's employees, and most of my 2nd Troop of Simpsons' employees. His troop was known as the Eatonia and mine as the Simco. When we marched out of the old University Avenue Armouries for route marches, Simpsons' and Eaton's delivery drivers were amused to be cheered by one troop and booed by the other. Company loyalties at times exceeded regimental discipline. But out of it all came a great *esprit de corps.*

Lieut. Jack Eaton, Lieut. Donald Hunter (later Chairman of Maclean-Hunter), and Lieut. Marshall Cleland had represented the regiment as a military jumping team at the Dublin Horse Show, under Lieut.-Col. Joe Streight's guidance, bringing much credit to Canada and the Governor General's Body Guard. Jack Eaton and I and our sergeants were chosen as the rough riding detail to go to Niagara-on-the-Lake in the advance party to accept two hundred horses which came from the Indians on the Caledonia Reserve after careful examination by veterinarians. Our task was to saddle and ride each horse, or attempt to ride it, to get it ready to issue to the incoming troopers. About fifty of the horses refused to be ridden and simply threw themselves down on the ground, quite unlike the bucking broncos of rodeos. Rather than go to the trouble of refusing them, we hid the worst rascals in a local wood called Paradise Grove and let them forage for themselves, while we drew extra feed for the more willing animals.

A trick the Indian horse-suppliers used to pull was to rub iron filings in the rear of the fetlock and pastern joints. The filings were almost impossible to detect in the long shaggy hair, but after three or four days a swelling and running sore would develop. Then the outraged owners claimed compensation from the government for three times what the horse was worth.

It is not hard to imagine the dust, confusion, hullabaloo, and pandemonium that existed the first day of mounted drill, trying to get unbroken horses ready to be saddled, bridled, and ridden by city boys, some of whom had never been on horses before. An apparently impossible task, yet a miracle was in the making! In under a week Regimental Drill was performed mounted on the new horses, complete with sabres and lances, as if we had been doing it for months. One officer, Alec Roberts, was over six feet tall and over 250 pounds. He was a marvellous piano-player and a most popular man who excelled on the baseball diamond as our pitcher. However, finding him a suitable horse was a serious problem. Jack and I found a huge black mare, so strong she could have carried a knight in full armour. So she became Alec's officer's mount. Her nickname was Stagnant Stella. She had two speeds, slow and stop, and once stopped she was not easily coerced into shuffling forward again in her parody of a trot.

At the end of each parade the colonel would call "Officers!" Each one of us would surround him smartly in a semi-circle, salute, and wait to be dismissed. Poor Alec would still be kicking, beating, pleading, and trying to convince Stagnant Stella to join the other officers' smarter chargers, when we would be off parade and in the Mess tent. One day the sergeant behind Alec's mare, thinking to help him respond to the call for Officers, jabbed the mare under the tail. Stagnant Stella screeched and sprang forward one leap, much to Alec's surprise. Unseated, Alec fell off one side with his foot still caught in the stirrup, hanging upside down in front of the whole regiment, while Stagnant Stella breeched herself and cascaded a torrent of urine on the parched ground near his head. It would have been a dangerous situation with any other horse, but once Stella relieved herself, she sighed and looked around in calm contentment at her rider's unusual antics.

I achieved two of my early life's goals in the year 1933. First, I became an officer in the Governor General's Body Guard. Second, I was accepted by the School of Architecture at the University of Toronto. Our class had only nine students. Nowadays there would be two hundred or more. The Depression was at its height, no one was hiring architects, and few could afford the tuition fees. The course was five years long with one year of practical experience in an architectural firm before one was given an iron ring and became a practising registered architect. From the first day, I was in heaven. Education, history, design, even mathematics took on a whole new meaning for me. I had tolerated U.T.S. and high school or, more properly, they had tolerated me. But in architecture, I was starting on my own career.

Our masters were Professor Harry Madill and Professor Eric Arthur. Eric Arthur became a life-long friend, and we had much to do with each other. In school he was the gentle critic, the exponent of good design and good taste. His critique of one's work was highly prized and helpful. The late John B. Parkin was in fourth year when I was in first. He later became the head of John B. Parkin Associates, one of the most important architectural firms in the postwar years. Many years later I awarded him and Parkin Associates their first major job, a multi-million dollar contract on Simpsons' Lawrence Avenue Service Building, for which they won the Governor General's Gold Medal.

I passed my first year at university with flying colours, working harder than I had ever done before. I was initiated into Psi Upsilon fraternity. Our second-year class was only six strong. I found the structural, descriptive geometry and the calculus much more difficult in the second year, but got honourable mentions for my design projects and, again, high marks for the year.

I went to New York to work for the summer of 1934. The National Reconstruction Administration of the Roosevelt administration was

in full force and any job I got would be illegal as I had no work per-
mit. However, I found out that F. Schumacher & Company at 60 West
40th Street was looking for stockboys. Schumacher's even then was
one of the foremost decorative fabric houses in North America. I
applied for the job because I was becoming more and more interested in interior design. I was interviewed by a Mr. Gadabusch, who
was no less a person than the president himself. Mr. Gadabusch tested
my colour perception using a book called *Pseudochromatic Colour
Charts* prepared by a Japanese scientist. There were varied colour
dots on each page. If you were acute, you saw a number (say 97)
standing out of the maze of dots. If you were colour-deficient or colour-
blind, you would see other numbers (say 65 or 43). You could not
fake this test! I passed. Mr. Gadabusch told me I had the job, adding
that my colour-sense was one hundred per cent, the highest rating
anyone had received in the last fifty tests.

I was delighted. When he found out that I was eighteen he swore,
"Damn the N.R.A.! I'll have to pay you fifteen dollars a week instead
of the fourteen dollars had you been only seventeen." I was a bit
deflated at this outburst, having expected about thirty dollars a week in
the Big City, but I was in no position to argue. I started work the next
day on a mezzanine floor with no ventilation during the worst heat-
wave New York had experienced in years. For eighteen days it did
not go below eighty degrees, even at night. I worked with another
chap, whose name I cannot now remember, stripped to the waist,
ticketing, sorting, and rehanging thousands of samples a day. We got
to know the wares of all the other New York houses like Stroheim &
Romann by the type of design and feel, a skill that stood me in good
stead for many years to come. I worked very hard. Mr. Gadabusch
called me his "crazy Canadian." When I left he assured me that if I
ever wanted a job with them permanently I had but to ask.

I learned several important and startling things in New York. As
I had no friends in the city, I visited art galleries and museums, walked
up and down night-time Broadway, listening and watching but never
getting involved. I did not dare because I was working illegally. The
New York Public Library was across 40th Street from Schumacher's, and I used to browse through their shows of prints and books
until one day I sensed I was being followed step by step by a man
who eventually came alongside me and placed his hand over mine.
Startled, I ran out of the place, never to return. I discovered the library
was a notorious pick-up place for homosexuals. I also found out that

Child's and the YMCA had that reputation. I wasn't even sure what a homosexual was but I did not want to find out.

My fifteen dollars a week did not go very far – a movie cost a dollar. So I walked and looked and painted scenes from my bedroom window and in Central Park and read. I took a girl to a movie one night after work. She worked at Schumacher's. I had been brought up to believe that if you took a girl out you saw that she got safely home. After the movie I took her to the subway and rode for two hours with her to Flatbush, Long Island, walked her home, turned around, and got the late train back to my hotel, getting in about 4:30 a.m. I took her to the movies once more, but this time fulfilled my escort duties by taking her to the Long Island train, putting a nickel in the slot for her and saying goodnight! She told me that is what every date did. Nowadays it would be as much as your life is worth to ride alone on that subway trip, or even sketch in Central Park as I used to.

When I returned to Toronto, I was ill with assorted colds and flus for weeks. I had seen a great deal of life in New York and much of what I saw I did not like. New York has never been as high on my list of favourite cities as London or Toronto.

# WITH SIMPSONS

## 5

My first work experience at Simpsons was over Christmas 1932 as an "extra" in the picture department under the late Percy Moyer, a diminutive man, neat, soft-spoken, and kind. We were open every night of the week until 10:00 p.m. Supper money was 35¢. No overtime was paid. I was instructed to sell $100 worth of goods a day. The very first day on the job we had a huge sale of 39¢ "oilettes," which were small prints with a simulated "oil painting" look. So I ploughed in and sold $125 worth of "oilettes" and other more expensive paintings, covering about two tally sheets, which we had to add up for our sales total for the day. Years later I developed a feel for figures, but at that time math was not one of my great subjects. After several tries, getting a different answer every time, the girl in the office took pity on me and added my tally on her machine.

The second day I began to slow down, but just made my $100 total. The third day I had not sold a thing all day when I noticed my father coming along the floor toward the picture gallery. There was a fine etching, a huge one, a Landseer-type drawing of King Edward VII's wire-haired terrier, conveniently priced at $100, which I sold to my father, making my day. For thirty years this picture hung in a very conspicuous place in the house on Glen Road. With a wry sense of humour, he left King Edward VII's dog to me in his will, ignoring my desires to have one of his better paintings! I can see him chuckling when he made that bequest!

In 1935, at the start of my third year in architecture, I made a momentous decision. As much as I loved university, architecture, and my professors, the fact was plain that students several classes ahead of me could not graduate with their iron rings because no architects would employ them, even without pay. Without practical experience you could not complete the course. The architects had no work. It was said that only two firms that year in Toronto made $10,000 or more. So I decided to quit architecture and get a job. Naturally I turned to Simpsons. I lined up with dozens of job applicants at the Employment Office and was able to put down on my application "Previous Experience – F. Schumacher & Co., New York City." The interviewer, with great foresight, hired me as a stockboy in the drapery department at $12.50 a week. This was $12.50 a week more than the architects were making. Audrey and I wanted to get married someday, and we had set $40 a week as the benchmark for marriage.

I worked at Simpsons for three weeks before my father found out. It happened in a strange way. One night after supper, both my professors, Harry Madill and Eric Arthur, came to our house to plead with my father to let me continue in architecture for my third year. "But he is doing his third year. I drop him off at the university at 8:00 a.m. every morning," exclaimed my father.

"Well, he hasn't been in a lecture for three weeks," said Eric Arthur, adding, "too bad, because he showed great promise as an architect."

I was called in and had to explain that I had been working for three weeks and had found no convenient way to tell my father of my decision. It had been my decision and mine alone.

The employment manager at Simpsons at that time was Ed David, a clean-cut, youthful person in his mid-thirties. The morning after my confession, he was summoned to the president's office to explain why I had been hired as a salesman. I had embellished my "stock job" with some selling duties. "My son, Allan, tells me he's working as a salesman in the Chintz Department, Mr. David." Poor Ed David did not even know I was in the store.

"Oh yes, sir," replied Ed.

"I ought to fire you, Mr. David," said Dad. "My son isn't fit to handle our customers. He should be behind a parcel desk. He will never even learn how to tie a parcel."

"I'll see that he is put in the parcellers right away, sir," said Ed.

With that my father burst out laughing and said, "No, don't disturb him. Let's see how he will work out in the Chintzes."

Poor Ed David, slightly shattered, left the president's office, no doubt to pass on some pearls of wisdom to one of his subordinates, in particular the one who had hired me.

In the meantime I was getting my lumps. Bill Hunter, the manager of the Chintz Department, put the section head, Mr. Hutchings, in charge of my education. "Hutch" was a tall, straight-backed, grey-haired man with clipped military mustache and the manner and authority of a sergeant-major. My first day's "work" was to move several dozen sale cushions from under one row of tables and neatly store them in a similar position under the row of tables across the aisle. I got the job done in relatively short order and happily reported to Mr. Hutchings for my next assignment. Hutch looked at my handiwork and said, "Quite good, now put them back where they were." I was hurt and disgusted to have such an infantile test put on me, but proceeded to move the cushions back to their original position. I moved the same cushions, except for the few that were sold, back and forth for the first three days while Hutch watched me for some sign of resistance or insubordination. I refused to give him the satisfaction of seeing me "blow my stack" and was rescued when Bill Hunter came by and asked me, "Mr. Burton, what are you doing to those poor cushions?"

"Don't ask me, sir, ask Mr. Hutchings," I replied.

Hutch got a quiet dressing down in Hunter's office. The office partitions did not reach the ceiling, so I was able to hear a bit of the reprimand without actually eavesdropping.

First thing in the morning before opening, our major chore was to chalk a long string and, with the help of Charlie Jevons, another junior salesman in the department, we stretched the string taut on the carpet and flicked it like a bow string. We lined the tables up on the chalk mark to satisfy the sergeant-major streak in Hutch.

Charlie Jevons had watched my three-day torment and sympathized with me. We laid a trap for Hutch, with the help of several other people in the office. Just as we were ready to flick the string, our accomplice called Hutch to the phone in the office. We caught him neatly with the string as he passed, bringing his six-foot frame crashing to the ground. He rolled in a most undignified way toward the office before rushing back, face red with fury, to accuse us of a deliberate act of sabotage. I calmly said, "I have, I hope, much more important things to do than tripping you up, sir, or, for that matter, wasting time endlessly rearranging the same cushions. In fact, you seem to have tripped yourself up quite well." Strangely, as the years went on, Hutch and I became good friends, and Bill Hunter an even better one.

I resolved to advance from the Chintz Department as quickly as possible and determined I would use my design ability in Interior Design. At home in the evenings I designed a series of three model apartments. Apartment living was the newest thing. These designs were based on the one-and-a-half-room concept of the living-dining space in one open area, the dining area part of, yet distinct from, the living area. In very short order I had put them on paper. The renderings showed one very contemporary, one classical, and one colonial design. I had some acquaintances at Eaton's, so I got an interview there before showing them to Simpsons. If Eaton's liked them well enough to build them, I felt I would have enough courage to propose them to Simpsons. Eaton's did like the idea and offered me a job and a salary close to my marriage-goal figure and several times what I was making at Simpsons. That was on a Thursday. I said I would let them know Monday morning and asked for a showing at Simpsons Friday morning.

My judges in the boardroom were H.G. Colebrook, vice-president, Merchandise, the same Mr. Colebrook whom I visited in London for Christmas; the advertising manager; and a Mr. Grimbly, who had little or no artistic sensibilities but was in charge of Engineers, Interior Design, our Contract Division and Buildings, and other non-merchandise services. This group liked the ideas and asked how much I thought they would cost. I estimated I could build the three apartments and furnish them, largely from stock, for $10,000, a tidy sum in those days. I was elated when they agreed to proceed, but stunned when they asked who would decorate them. I replied I would, of course, because they were my ideas and so I could do the job best. They balked at that suggestion and countered with a question. "What have you ever decorated?"

"Nothing, but I know what I want them to look like," I said.

"No, we can't allow that," they said.

Crestfallen, I rolled up my drawings and headed for the door. "Where are you going?"

"Up to Eaton's," I replied. "I have a job there starting Monday morning."

"Okay, you can decorate them, but with Guy Mitchell as consultant."

Delighted, I moved from Chintzes to the drafting room and became associated with two fine men, the aforementioned Guy Mitchell and the chief architect, Frank Corley, both of whom remained my close friends until their deaths.

Guy Mitchell was our number-one decorator in Simpsons, and there was none better for the most beautiful houses in Canada. Guy was an unusual man, sensitive, wise, with great taste. He analysed his customers' lifestyles, family needs, and recreations, and gently nudged them to his proposals. His work, like a Rolls-Royce, was elegant, understated, comfortable, and never went out of style. More, he was a wise teacher.

Frank Corley, my direct boss – I was technically a draftsman in the Design Studio while I completed my plans – was a quiet Englishman, a competent architect and engineer, with enormous integrity. He was greatly respected by everyone in Simpsons and by the contractors. The senior draftsman, later called designer, was a young Dutchman, Adrian J. Vandervlis, an artist of good quality as well as a competent designer. I was given a raise to $16 a week, a long way from the salary I had turned down at Eaton's. Even so, I was completely happy. Horace Grimbly was a hearty, gruff, strong Scot, a simple, genuine man, whose chuckle had in it the flavour of Santa Claus, while his generosity with his staff had the strong taste of Ebenezer Scrooge. These were the people with whom it was my lot to work and, years later, to have work for me. A better group of colleagues would be hard to find.

One pleasant interlude occurred shortly after I started in the drafting room. This was a trip to New York, my first as a legitimate visitor. Mr. Grimbly, Mr. Mitchell, and I took the night train, arriving in New York the next morning. We stayed in modest rooms in the Roosevelt Hotel, which gave Simpsons a substantial discount to have their buyers stay there. It was also connected by tunnel to Grand Central Station, saving cab fare and time. Mr. Grimbly did even better than that. He refused to take a cab because of the cost, so we walked everywhere until my feet ached.

One night we got tickets to *George White's Scandals,* an innocuous evening of showgirls which emulated the follies. The finale of the first act, before intermission, was a ring of showgirls, several rows deep on a dark stage. A single strong spotlight illuminated the centre, from which up popped the most divine naked female form I had ever seen up to that point in my life. She was stark naked, except for a fig leaf, which I mistook for a maple leaf. Suddenly a hand from my next-door neighbour, Mr. Grimbly, reached out and covered my eyes! I batted it down to get a better look, much to Guy's amusement. Mr. Grimbly got up and said, "Well, I am leaving. I won't stay

and see that kind of filth!" And he stalked out. I thought it was deli-
cious, as did Guy. We repaired to a cosy bar in the New Weston Hotel,
under the pretence that Guy wanted me to see the latest in decor. We
also had a drink – Mr. Grimbly would not have approved of that either –
and discussed women, girls, and life in general.


The Depression had left its mark on the world, and for the average
person the memory of hard times dictated extreme caution when
buying more than was needed for everyday use. For the majority of
people in Toronto, frugality was the way of life. After all, none had
more than a fleeting glimpse of the vast wealth and frivolous leisure
that had been exhibited in older capital cities in the world for centuries. Toronto had never had a leisure class. Toronto did not achieve
world-class status until well into the middle of the twentieth century
when it ousted Montreal as the financial capital of Canada and led
the way in civic planning and services.

In 1936, Toronto was very much a provincial capital, known with
some derision in the rest of the country as Hogtown. I never knew
exactly how it earned that nickname, whether because the rest of
the country was jealous of it "hogging" most of the manufacturing
and growth in prosperous times or because, as Jack McLaren suggested in his book *Let's All Hate Toronto,* a bylaw was passed in
1849 as follows: "It is agreed by a majority of the citizens that no
hogs of any description shall be allowed to run at large within the
limits of the city from and after the first day of May." The town had
at one time been overrun by a horde of hogs, a squealing squad of
half-wild pigs. The situation was cleaned up so well that soon the
city became known as "Toronto the Good." That was the town I grew
up in. It was church-going, clean, dull, hard-working, with Orange
Protestants in City Hall.

After nearly a year in the Design Studio, my project of three model
apartments, planned on the "open" basis, was ready to be built and
decorated by me. I had much help in completing this project, which
was much larger than I had imagined when I "sold" it in the boardroom. It is hard to recapture the heart-pounding excitement of creating and producing this rather expensive permanent exhibit, "The
Apartments of Today." I had only just turned twenty-one. The night
before the date set for the rooms to open to the public, I had a hor-
rendous, debilitating migraine headache, with more colours explod-

ing behind my eyes than the strobe lights at a modern rock concert. I finally fell asleep exhausted, only to waken later in terror and bathed in cold sweat because in my nightmare someone had come on the set and painted every last article red, white, and black! The hours the master painter Teddy Bowman and I had spent to achieve a "honey-beige" effect by overglazing were lost in a moment of horrifying dream. Awake, the full terror of what I had to face the next day thrust itself into my consciousness. For the first time I had self-doubts. I inwardly cringed at the thought that my apartments on the new room-and-a-half concept would be laughed at or, worse, few would come to see my work. Only one other time have I ever felt such utter loneliness and fear, and that was years later on the approach march to our first battle in the Liri Valley at Monte Cassino, Italy. I survived both experiences.

I was stunned and overjoyed when I saw the huge crowds lined up to go through my rooms. There were 4,400 visitors on the first day. This was many more than the famous "House of Years" at Sloane's in New York had in one day, I was told by a Sloane manager. I stood all day in the foyer of the first apartment, eagerly listening to and noting the comments as our customers filed through. The modern foyer had a niche containing a curved settee, behind which was an original mural in oil of a nude Diana the Huntress done by Rene Kulback, a brilliant artist who at the time worked in Simpsons Display Department. We had taken the precaution of doing it in a monochromatic shade of beige, but it still shocked many people who remarked that it was "beautiful but indecent . . . I must warn Aunt Mabel not to come to see this." I was delighted because word-of-mouth advertising is the best and cheapest you can get. Besides, I banked on the fact that Aunt Mabel would like it. I knew we had a winner.

The success and joy was that people loved the display and bought everything in sight. We immediately started planning the next showing six months away. I kept track of every sale and sent weekly reports of comments, trends, and sales to the managers of the various departments, although I had no official status other than Interior Designer. In those days such regular "trend" records were not kept, only reports on sale or volume items.

There were thefts from the rooms. In broad daylight the "portable" radios were stolen, and people actually used the toilets in the model bathrooms despite the fact they were not connected. An undercurrent of discontent resulted in individuals who came through our fine furniture departments, known as the Avon House Galleries, and with razors slashed thousands of dollars worth of upholstered furniture. They also ruined expensive evening gowns in The Room, our most exclusive fashion area. We were not singled out for this sabotage; other stores got it, too.

After the success of my exhibition, I did a lot of work for our Special Contract Department, then headed by Harry Haynes. It was a particularly interesting time for me. I designed everything from a funeral parlour in Scarborough to a whorehouse in Barrie. The funeral director and the madame in Barrie had more cash to spend than many wealthy customers. They both, especially the madame, ordered only the strongest and the best furniture. My most important design job was for Ferde Marani, the architect of the new Bank of Canada building in Ottawa. I designed for him all the boardroom furniture and senior executive office furniture, a very large job. Donald Gordon, secretary of the bank, was the man I had to please, and he scared the hell out of me. He was a large man, loud-voiced, bluff, more like an outcropping of the Precambrian Shield than the suave international banker one might envisage. The government specifications were so excessively stringent that Berry Bros., the wood importers in New York, were unable to find any mahogany of the specific gravity called for by the Bank of Canada. In the decades they had been importing the finest woods for the finest furniture in North America, they had never been asked for such a grade. A special team was sent to Cuba and a single huge tree was selected and cut for this job. Only one such tree grows per acre on high ground and the wood is white and pure as birch – the lower in the forest, the redder the mahogany, the more open the grain, and the less dense the wood. The cheapest quality is "swamp" mahogany, very red and coarse-grained, often from Honduras or the Philippines. It is not really mahogany at all but a distantly related wood. Most of the mahogany furniture of the last century was made from these lesser grades. Without fear of contradiction, I can say the Bank of Canada furniture was made of the highest quality materials ever used in this country to that time. Even the webbing was specially woven in Scotland.

I talked Donald Gordon into using only a traditional oil finish. It would be worth it, I argued, as he had gone to so much trouble to have furniture made that would last for centuries. I warned him that it would take years of proper housekeeping to achieve the patina of the brown English mahogany antiques he so admired. I refused to stain the wood, which we had oiled and rubbed dozens of times before delivery, more than was called for in our contract. Although beautiful in design and exceptional in manufacturing detail, there was no denying the pieces looked like yellow pups when delivered.

Fortunately about this time the Governor General's Horse Guards, as my regiment was then known, was put on active service in World War II. I left final instructions for Donald Gordon to make sure that he saw the furniture was properly oiled and said I would see him after the war. I imagined I could hear his cries of outrage at the look of his expensive furniture all the way to England, even over the roar of the tank motors when we became an armoured regiment. When I finally did come home, some five years later, I was invited to my brother Edgar's house to a cocktail party in honour of none other than Donald Gordon. Edgar had worked for him when he was head of the Wartime Prices and Trade Board. When Gordon saw me enter the room, he bellowed at me from across the room, "Young man, come here!" I thought, "Oh God, he is still mad about the bloody yellow furniture." Instead, he smiled broadly, welcomed me home, and said, "It worked out just as you said. The furniture is magnificent, but it took the whole five years of war to do it!" He never scared me again.


Audrey Syer and I were inseparable and planned to marry, but in 1937 I was sent to England to work for a year in London for Trollope & Sons, West Halkin Street, Decorators to Her Majesty Queen Mary. The shop, just off Belgrave Square, was well situated because most of the distinguished houses of Belgrave and Eaton Square and others in the West End, whose owners patronized Trollope's, were within walking distance.

It was a sad blow to our plans that I had to depart for England for a full year, but we were not making enough to get married on. Audrey was working in the Shopping Service at Simpsons and we were both twenty-two, too young to marry. I never knew whether my father planned to separate Audrey and me for a trial period or he merely seized the opportunity that arose when we hired a young Englishman, Henry Leo (Tom) Deacon, recently arrived from Trollope's to work for Simpsons. Tom, as I knew him, and I became close friends, and he was an usher when Audrey and I finally married in 1938.

The awful reality of a year's separation struck us with a great weight of sadness when Audrey accompanied me and my parents to New York to see me off on the *Queen Mary*. After dinner at the Waldorf-Astoria, where we were staying, Audrey and I went for a long walk, ending up much later in the famed Peacock Alley. We sat there, saying little in our profound misery at the thought of parting the next day. Audrey had been posted to a buyer's position in our New York office for the year, so she would remain in New York when I sailed away. Mother was quite relieved the next morning to find that we had not eloped, as she had half-expected us to do. The thought never entered our minds. That was not the way we wanted our life-long marriage to start.

# APPRENTICESHIP AND MARRIAGE

## 6

There was much for me to do when I arrived in London. My father had given me a £400 letter of credit to be used only in an emergency. Because I was cautious and frugal by nature, the £400 remained unspent until my homeward-bound trip.

I worked out a budget and looked for a place near enough to walk to work in Belgrave Square. I was told a good address was important to have, and I certainly had one in Fountain Court, Buckingham Palace Road. But by the time I had paid my rent, I had exactly £1/10, about $7.00, for my week's food, transportation, and entertainment. I did not even own a radio, but I opened my window to get the free programs from my downstairs neighbour! My bachelor apartment windows looked across the road to Pimlico, my apartment being on the traffic side. As this was the less desirable side of the building, the rent was reasonable.

The constantly changing scene across the road in Pimlico, with its pubs and prostitutes, fascinated me. I had a perfect vantage point from which to watch the tableau. I got to know by sight all the prostitutes who worked the pub opposite Fountain Court, for it is the width of a street in London that makes the difference between a "good" address and a "poor" one. I got to know when each girl came to work and the little boy runners they employed to solicit in the pubs. I was truly amazed to see these same girls on a Sunday morning pushing prams, as well dressed and quiet as any good mother should be!

I walked everywhere in London, from one end to the other, enjoying and absorbing the ever-changing patterns and people, from quiet, dignified squares, to bustling, slippery avenues, crowded with the noise and smell of people working and quarrelling, laughing and swearing, as only the Cockney can swear. I walked and ate mostly alone, and watched the classes walk or ride in their distinguishing "uniforms" because there was, in those days, a proper dress for every station or activity in life. The clerks wore bowlers, black short jackets, and striped grey morning pants, and carried briefcases, all trying to look as if they worked in "the City," because the City was the only decent place to work if indeed one had to work. The upper classes had always depended on their bankers, stockbrokers, and auctioneers, and often rewarded them with titles and pretended that what they did was not work.

Having come from a society that admired people who had what was called "get up and go" and who worked for their life's gains, I found it confusing and even disturbing to realize that the so-called upper crust felt it undignified to have to work, only the Army, the Church, and the Civil Service being exempt from scorn. On my side of the ocean, a career in the Army, the Church, or the Civil Service was all right, but there seemed to be a general feeling that those in them could not or would not be very successful in the real world of commerce and trade. Besides, to me a tradesman meant a grocer, a butcher, or a milkman, and so I never used the tradesman's entrance to the grand houses I visited as I did not consider myself a tradesman. The assistant who accompanied me used the rear entrance, but I used the front door where I was convinced I belonged, and no one ever questioned me. In fact, I was often asked back to tea, but the assistant, who knew his place, was not.

Every Friday night my chief amusement was to walk from Fountain Court, down Buckingham Palace Road, to the Victoria Railway Station. Just across the street from the station was a pub that many Chelsea pensioners from the military hospital frequented. After "Time, gentleman, please" was called, I would ride, for a couple of pence, the No. 11A bus all the way to Chelsea with them. These old warriors wore their distinctive uniforms that date back to the last century. They wore long black frock coats with brass buttons and pillbox caps with peaks and red bands. They had served in the Crimea, in the Boer War, and in World War I, so their uniforms were well decorated with campaign medals. They loaded on my bus, full of cider, beer, and good cheer, along with frowzy old women, many of whom were plain drunk. I wished I could have remembered the tales and jokes they told and made. I was amused and fascinated by my weekly show.

It was near midnight when, on arrival at Chelsea, I got off with the pensioners. I then walked back several miles through Pimlico to my "good" address. Pimlico in those days had a reputation for toughness and sin, second only to the East End docks. Nowadays, pretty and prim Pimlico, with its artists and fashionable vices, is a far cry from the pre-war slums. Then, on each and every block there would be a free show of fights, arguments, noises, smells, humour, and laughter. A sad show of derelicts sometimes listened to an Army band or sidewalk preacher. I stood aside as a spectator and watched and listened and laughed with the crowd, but never spoke to anyone, and I was never in a moment's danger. I suppose I was not worth "mugging" in those lonely days. It is curious how your loneliness increases in a crowd of strangers. I felt the same on New York's Broadway, when I first became a people-watcher. It is an inexpensive form of entertainment.

Trollope & Sons, my new firm, had such a fine reputation for design throughout Europe that having worked for them in their London interior design studio was an entrée and hallmark for a position in most countries. Because I had drafting experience and had studied architecture, I was allowed to work for them for nothing! As an apprentice, of which I was one of five, I would normally be expected to pay up to £320 a year. There were seventeen people all-told in the design studio, not including the director of design. This dignified gentleman had a small office off the studio, large enough for a desk and a tilt drafting table, but hardly large enough for his ego. He was always dressed in morning clothes with striped trousers and never did any work that I could discover. I soon found out that when you had done a particularly fine piece of work, he would say, "Nicely done, very good. When you have finished, would you put it on my table for my signature?" The best work went out of the place bearing his signature, which I thought rather unfair of him. But I am sure he thought he was paying the artist a compliment!

For my first two or three days, I was told to wander through their beautiful antique galleries and draw various pieces in my sketchbook. It was a sort of test to see how skilled I was in freehand drawing. I still have all these sketches, and I wish I could draw as well today. My next visit was to the managing director, a very charming man, Mr. Ebel. He was half-American and half-French, but wholly English in dress and manners. I felt that his welcome was genuine and warm, and he quickly put me at ease. Not so the concierge who guarded the front entrance. An ex-warrant officer of the Lifeguards, over six feet tall and ruddy complexioned, he looked down on us from his elevated position on the front steps, as we apprentices descended to the basement entrance, with the calm look of superiority that a Great Dane gives a terrier. We always slipped past him with a "Good morning, Mr. Tomkins," and he would nod in recognition.

Merely three years later, during World War II, when I was a field officer of the Governor General's Horse Guards and staying at the Guards' Club in Brook Street, I decided, on a whim, to visit Trollope's to see how they were weathering the war. In uniform and wearing my Guards' cap, blue with a scarlet band and a band of silver woven on the black patent peak, I turned into West Halkin Street from Belgrave Square and could see my huge old friend still by the door. When I turned in and mounted the steps toward him, he threw me his very best Guards' salute with a "Good morning, sir!"

"Good morning, Tomkins," I replied. "You don't remember me, do you?"

"Can't say I have had the pleasure, sir," he replied, uneasily.

"Why, Tomkins, I slipped past you every morning for the year of 1937. Burton is my name, Governor General's Horse Guards."

He beamed and was so obviously overjoyed to see me that tears came to his eyes. He was also quite mystified how an apprentice in 1937 could have become a major in a Guards Regiment by 1940. It could never have happened in England.

He preceded me through every inch of Trollope's, opening wide each pair of doors and announcing in a loud voice to the few people left in each room, "Major Burton of His Majesty's Canadian Horse Guards!" The war had taken its toll. The wonderful galleries were all stripped of their antiques, and in their place were long tables on which several women were cutting airplane fabric. Of the original seventeen in the design studio, only three were left, and there was no design director. The designers were working on camouflage patterns for various shapes.

But the war was still in the future when I met the head designer. He was a wonderful artist but I am sorry to say that I do not remember his name, so I will call him Smith. Mr. Smith and I became quite friendly, because I soon was doing quite important jobs. Poor Smith was paid, as senior designer, £7, the equivalent of $35 a week. I was appalled because in New York he could have made ten times that amount, and in Toronto at least $150. He lived in Southend and had to rise at 5:30 a.m. to catch his train and he never got home before

8:00 p.m. One day I half-jokingly told him I would guarantee him $150 a week if he would come back to Toronto with me. "What they are paying you for a man of your ability is a shame. Have you ever suggested you are worth a good deal more?"

"No," he replied.

"Well, damn it, I'd tell them you want £25 minimum or you'll get another job," I said boldly.

So poor Smith went in, made his pitch, and a few minutes later settled for a raise of £3 to make his salary £10 a week. I suspected he never asked for £25, and no one suspected I was the one who put him up to it.

One day I was sent along with a junior to a beautiful house on Eaton Square to measure the library for new panelling. I went to the front door, while the assistant went to the tradesmen's entrance. I knocked and asked the trim and prim maid who answered to see Lady so-and-so.

She smiled at me and said, "Whom shall I say is calling, sir?"

"Mr. Burton from Trollope's."

Her face froze in astonishment and she said, "Tradesmen use the rear entrance."

"I am not a tradesmen, so please tell your mistress I am here," I demanded.

Meanwhile, my poor assistant was still trying to be let in the tradesmen's door. I had stepped into the charming hallway when a fine-looking woman came down the stairs saying, "Who is raising this commotion in my front hall?"

"Your servant, madam," I replied, and introduced myself.

The maid was dismissed to let the other lad in the tradesmen's entrance, and in short order I had taken the measurements, sketched, and added some marginal notes of design details her Ladyship wanted. I was prepared to go back to start work on it when she asked me if I would stay and have tea with her. I readily agreed because, while I looked well dressed, my food intake was not great. The assistant was not invited and returned alone.

When I returned to work, there was a commanding message to report to the office of the managing director, Mr. Ebel. In some trepidation I went in, expecting a dressing down or worse. "You were a very long time at her Ladyship's in Eaton Square. Tell me what happened."

So I related the whole affair, ending up with "and she invited me to tea and I stayed; what should I have done?" Mr. Ebel beamed with laughter. He said, "You obviously did the right thing because her Ladyship just called me to say what a charming young man had come to call on her and how pleased she was with your quick sketches. Burton, it is remarkable because she is known to be one of our most meticulous and difficult customers. Furthermore, she asked if I could include you in Princess Schleswig-Holstein's party for the Catholic Charities Ball at the Dorchester next week. It seems that the daughter of an admiral is coming to town and needs an escort. I said of course you'd be delighted. You do have full evening dress, white tie, and tails, don't you?"

Curiously, I did have both white and black tie with me, never expecting to use either. I left his office with my head swimming at this unexpected reversal of events. Almost immediately I began to imagine my hostess-to-be, the Princess, as a beautiful, graceful, and charming eighteen-year-old. When the night of the Catholic Charities Ball came around, I had other worries because I was a long way from being a Roman Catholic, the Bishop of London was to hold court, and I did not even know what my hostess looked like. Mr. Ebel, who was invited to the ball but not included in the Princess's party, said he would try to keep an eye out for me.

I arrived, with some two thousand others, at the Dorchester Hotel, all in white tie and tails, and stood uncomfortably switching from one foot to the other, trying to plan what to do next. I soon became aware that a long line was forming leading up to the resplendent Prince of the Church, where men were bowing and women curtseying to kiss his ring. I also noticed a pleasant-looking, middle-aged lady who was next to me and who asked me whose party I was with. "I am a guest of the Princess of Schleswig-Holstein, but I have never met her and I don't know what she looks like. Do you know her?" I introduced myself and found out her name was Mrs. Ryan.

"Yes, I know the Princess well," she said. "But before you go to greet her, aren't you going to kiss the Bishop's ring?"

"But I can't do that," I gasped. "I am not a Catholic."

Mrs. Ryan laughed merrily and said, "I'll bet you ten shillings you are afraid to get in line and kiss his ring."

I had only ten shillings in my pocket, so with the thought of doubling my money and no harm done, I said, "You're on!"

As we worked our way toward the dais where the Bishop was seated, I asked Mrs. Ryan, "Just how well do you know the Princess?"

"Very well," she said. "She's my sister!"

I was breaking out in cold sweats and hot flushes as my moment of truth came, standing in front of a rotund, silver-haired, pleasant-looking old man, who was extending his hand so I could kiss his ring. "I can't kiss your ring, sir," I whispered. "I am Protestant."

"Welcome, my son, you're an honest man." He chuckled as he shook my hand warmly.

I dug in my pocket and fished out my one and only ten-shilling note and sadly gave it to Mrs. Ryan, saying, "I couldn't do it, you won."

She added her ten shillings to mine and handed me back the pound, saying, "That took more guts than kissing his ring and, what's more, His Grace enjoyed it."

Then Mrs. Ryan introduced me to her sister, the Princess. She was not, as I had imagined, eighteen, but nearly eighty; not slim and graceful, but heavy and matronly; not dressed in gossamer silk, but dripping in ancient lace and exuding good humour. When her sister told her about the episode with the Bishop, she laughed out loud. Emboldened, I said, "You are the first, real-live princess I have ever met. I am afraid I don't know how to address you properly, but this may amuse you. I asked my brother-in-law, who is widely travelled, and he said in his experience all princesses loved to be called 'Maisie.'"

She shrieked with laughter and said, "I would love to have you call me 'Maisie.' You will sit at my right hand. Who are you escorting?"

"I am afraid I have never met her, either. She's an admiral's daughter."

I was invited to join the Princess. Some of her guests were not pleased to have her table rearranged at the last moment, but I felt flattered, if apprehensive. "Maisie" turned out to be a better dancer, in spite of her age, than my timid date, whom I eventually met. I caught Mr. Ebel's eye as we whirled by and he winked and nodded in approval!

My shillings slowly disappeared as my date wanted to have her face sketched for two bobs' worth of charity, wanted to spin a wheel of chance for another bob, and so on, until, with five shillings left, I dug my toes in and said I would dispense no more charity that night.

About 2:30 a.m., I grandly got in a cab, as everyone else was doing, said to the cabbie, "I live at Fountain Court, Buckingham Palace Road. Head in that direction, and when the metre gets to two shillings, stop." Then I got out, paid him half a crown, and walked the rest of the way home, having had one of the most unusual evenings of my life. The next morning I was again called into Mr. Ebel's office. He said, "You got on extremely well last night. The Admiral has called up to ask if you could join his party at Epsom this weekend." I thanked him, but declined, saying I did not have the proper clothes for Epsom and, more importantly, I had no money to spend there.

Such interludes were few and far between, with long periods of acute loneliness and boredom. My daily round was a shredded-wheat breakfast and a walk to work, arriving at 8:00 a.m. One saving grace was that most days the staff enjoyed a joint of beef or lamb for one shilling, all you could eat. So I learned to live on essentially one meal a day. I wrote long and amateurish love poems to Audrey, who apparently was enjoying New York more than I thought appropriate. Working with her friend Jean Harris in our New York buying office, and living together, the two attractive young women were more often than not included in the buyers' dinners when they went out to relax on the town. I tried to tell myself I was not jealous.

Before long I met two English girls who were shop assistants, one of whom had a Riley car, the other of whom could cook. One was named Audrey. I chuckled at my astuteness in finding a girl called Audrey, in case I later talked in my sleep! Actually, I did not have much to talk about, but once a week the girls would come to my flat and cook dinner, and most weekends we toured the countryside far and wide in the Riley, a most platonic and happy threesome. The "Riley girl" was engaged to a chap in India who had sent her the money to buy the car. It had quite a few miles on it by the time he got home.

It was from these girls that I learned such colloquial English expressions as "hedge and ditch" (to relieve oneself by the roadside), "Fannie" (it didn't mean the same thing in Canada and was more than a girl's name), "half and half," "mild and bitter," and, of course, to be "knocked up" (a wake-up call).

One job that kept me busy for many weeks was redesigning and supervising the replacement of all the twisted Jacobean chimneys on a huge country mansion called Sussex House owned by a Mr. Burton of Burton's Fifty Shillings Tailors. Mr. Burton was a man of substance and taste. I drew sketches of the twisted chimneys for his architect, then did full-scale renderings for the eighteen or so chimneys. These were pasted on plywood forms and then hoisted into place. When approved, we then made full-sized replicas of each of the ornate groups and put these in place for final approval. The models were then carefully dissected, numbered, and given to the only family of stone masons who could take on this intricate job. The finished work, I was told, authentically restored the ancient house to its proper proportions and workmanship.

Once or twice a month my brother-in-law, Gordon Graham, then general manager of our London and European Buying Offices, would take me to dinner at the Royal Automobile Club in Pall Mall. The RAC was not an exclusive club, like White's, but a luxurious and very large spa for the great variety of people who proudly displayed RAC emblems on the hoods of their cars. Their headquarters had fine dining facilities. The dining-room was a heaven to a half-starved apprentice, and Gordon Graham was always amused to see me gorge myself at his expense.

Gordon was a wonderful man, never in robust health due to his having worked in the sulphide room of a Kapuskasing papermill, which caused him to have periodic bouts of pneumonia. In the spring of 1937, I accompanied Gordon on a three-day trip to Paris to see the Exposition, which included the latest in home-furnishing designs, and discovered Montmartre and other side of nightlife in Paris. It was an unforgettable trip, and Gordon and I remained life-long friends. He went on to be the first president of Simpson-Sears, when Simpsons and Sears Roebuck & Co. formed that company from Simpsons' Mail Order business in 1951. That he was able to direct this young company during its first years, while suffering nearly annual bouts of pneumonia, was remarkable, but to do so with diplomacy and efficiency, while engendering loyalty in our managers and staff and respect for Canada and Canadians in Sears men in Chicago, was an outstanding contribution. He was annoyed at me that I would not work for him in the Mail Order, but my greater loyalty was to Simpsons' retail stores.


As the year wore on I became more and more lonely for home and pined for Audrey. One day, I wandered down the Haymarket and from one tiny shop a gypsy fortune-teller beckoned me to have my fortune told, which she would do for half a crown, about fifty cents. On an impulse I undertook this unnecessary extravagance. The woman started on her humdrum routine of palm reading when, suddenly, a great change came over her and she gripped my hand more firmly and peered at it with new intensity and excitement. For the next fifteen minutes she told me a lot about the past, something of the present, and even things concerning the future. In conclusion, breathing heavily from mental exertion and emotion, she assured me that, in the many years she had been reading palms and telling fortunes, she was never so sure she had seen a person's life so clearly. Afterwards, out of amusement I noted down the salient points the soothsayer had predicted for me and sent them off to Audrey in New York.

To begin, she said, I was an artist, draughtsman, or designer, a fact that she could have told from my perpetually grubby hands. I had travelled far, my home being across the sea, which she could have told from my accent. I had a particular loved one who was not at my home but was also in a foreign place. It was at this point that she had changed her pace, her excitement had risen. Her first prediction was that I would leave London within the week to return home permanently. It would be sudden and unexpected and not in my current plans.

She continued that on my return home a new and more important job awaited me, that my love would return, that we would be married and have much happiness and children, but that we would be once more separated from each other for a very long period of time, separated by another assignment, and that I would be surrounded by great danger, possibly a war. I was not to worry because my life-line was long and strong, so once more I would be reunited with my wife and family and accomplish much, until I was head of a large corporation. Her actual words were even more specific, but as I could not see as far ahead as the gypsy, I was amused but unconvinced.

When I returned to my apartment, there was a cablegram waiting for me from my father, ordering me to return home at once. A director's passage had been booked for me on the S.S. *Normandie*, sailing from Southampton in exactly one week. I was astounded at this coincidence, and decided to write down the remaining predictions before I forgot them. In the sober light of next day, I realized that while a new job had been offered, no indication was included as to how much I was to be paid, so I wired Dad: "How much?"

He replied, "$45 a week."

"Not enough!" I wired back, with my last few shillings. "Want $75 a week."

The last cablegram in the series said tersely, "$60 final. Get on the boat!"

I hurried back to the Haymarket to tell the gypsy my good fortune, but she had gone and the shop was closed.

I packed hurriedly, said my "thank you's," gave some tearful goodbyes, and boarded the S.S. *Normandie* with the whole of the letter of credit for £400 intact, a princely sum.

I had no conception of what a director's passage meant and was awed when shown to my large panelled stateroom, with its twin beds and private bath, one of the most luxurious on that magnificent steamship. While I was in a hurry to get to New York to see my beloved Audrey, I quickly cashed in my £400 letter of credit, certain I could take this magnificent setting for longer than the four and a half days which the *Normandie* took to cross the Atlantic.

I had only forty-eight hours in New York with Audrey before I had to report back to Toronto to start my new job as assistant manager of the Furniture Department. We promised each other that we would soon be together permanently. But week after week went by. Audrey could not leave the market while pre-Christmas buying was to be done. Christmas came and went and I was feeling more and more despondent. Audrey's sister Conty was a constant companion and a sympathetic listener to my frustrations at not being able to get Audrey sent home. One day, in a desperate gamble, I wired Audrey in New York, "Come home this week or I'll marry Conty." She came home in the next forty-eight hours to her new job in the Shopping Service.

In the meantime, I was deep in my new duties in the Furniture Department. Alex Rollo, the manager, Harry Witherspoon, the buyer, and Frank Cameron, another buyer, were all past masters of their Masonic Lodge, and an extraordinary number of the members of the department were Masons. The most exciting trips of the business year were to the semi-annual markets at the Furniture Mart in Chicago and the Grand Rapids Market, the home of fine furniture. As a junior with some pretence to being a furniture designer, I was looked upon with a mixture of scepticism and tolerant amusement. After all, designers were lower on the social order than supersalesmen because most designers were lousy salesmen and even poorer merchants.

My avowed intention was to greatly improve the standard of design and the quality of furniture that one could buy on the Canadian market. Alex Rollo, a very wise man intent upon teaching me a lesson about the real world, took me to the display of the American Furniture Company in the Furniture Mart and introduced me to Abe Warshowsky, supersalesman.

The American Furniture Company at that time made and sold great quantities of what was known as "Borax" – gross pieces of indescribable taste, massive, ugly, but very cheap. Abe Warshowsky was their top salesman, and only because Alex Rollo was a friend did he waste his time on me. He usually dealt with Sears, Roebuck's volume-buyers by appointment. Abe himself was a large, bulky man who wore the latest white-on-white shirts and perpetually chewed on the three-inch stub of an unlit cigar, his face shining with energy, perspiration, and good humour.

I was appalled by what he so proudly showed me. One "soot" – his pronunciation of "suite" – was particularly repulsive, a huge four-poster bed whose posts reminded me of four misshapen limbs suffering from severe "dropsy" or phlebitis; an elephantine chest of drawers; and night tables complete with "Buick" ashtrays, an amazing feature of this dreadful design in soft southern pine. Six huge pieces for only $140. When he had completed the tour, Abe asked me what I thought of the collection. I thanked him politely and said, "Mr. Warshowsky, I just don't understand it."

A broad smile came over his shiny face, cigar stub twitching in his clenched teeth. He said, "Allan, I know you'll never buy this 'Borax' crap, you are a good boy. I know all that goes on in this market. Come and see me first and I will always have a good tip for you."

Abe was as good as his word. Each time I went to market, I would see Abe first and invariably I got a hot tip and the inside track on a good buy. We became fast friends. Abe Warshowsky, even during the Depression, never made less than $100,000 a year selling his "Borax" crap, as he called it. Five years later, after the war, I returned to Chicago, and my first visit was to search out the American Furniture Company and Abe Warshowsky. I was astounded at the transformation. It was now a large, glamorous showroom full of eighteenth-century mahogany reproductions and Swedish-modern designs and no "Borax." A very pretty receptionist said, "Yes, Mr. Warshowsky is our sales manager. No, he couldn't possibly see you today. He has Sears, Roebuck in today. Would you like to make an appointment for tomorrow?" I was about to leave a message that Allan Burton had called in to say hello, when the same old Abe, looking slightly out of place surrounded by these new "soots" of furniture of delicate and even elegant design, looked down the length of the gallery and saw me. He trotted down the showroom as fast as he could, beaming and waving, gave me a big bear hug, and shouted, "Thank God, my son has come home from the war!" He quickly dismissed the Sears buyers, his largest customers, telling them to come back tomorrow, same time, closed the showroom, and took me off to display me to his many friends in the Mart. He visited me in Toronto every year until his death, by which time we were also important customers of his.

Audrey Syer and I were married on May 12, 1938. Except for my year at Trollope's in London, we had been inseparable since we had met at age seventeen. By this time, our social lives and most of our friends were bound up with the regiment, now known as the Governor General's Horse Guards. Nearly every Friday night a large group of Horse Guard officers and their wives or girl-friends met at the Oak Room in the King Edward Hotel to dance to Luigi Romanelli's Orchestra. Saturday nights I played baseball in the Officers' League, and we partied in one of the many messes after the game.

The soldiers of the Non-Permanent Active Militia, as the militia was called, took their military duties very seriously. We received even less support than the pittance now expended on the present-day Reserves, but we were recognized as an important and worthwhile part of the armed services, particularly if called out by the Riot Act to quell civil disturbances or maintain public order, which had not happened since the Riel Rebellion. An officer in the Horse Guards could not marry without his C.O.'s permission, could not absent himself from the city for more than forty-eight hours without written leave, and was expected to attend all parades and exercises.

It was natural, then, to decide on a military wedding. This involved a full Guard of Honour of fellow officers in uniform who, with drawn sabres, created a steel archway as they lined each side of the exit from the church. Beneath the steel the happy couple would march to face the hail of rice and shrieks of excitement before entering the waiting limousines.

Audrey and I were married in Grace Church on-the-Hill on a hot and muggy day in May by an Anglican priest who was more interested in reminding me several times not to forget his "envelope" than he was in the huge assembly of friends, relatives, and onlookers who came to see this blissfully happy young couple joined in holy wedlock. Having received his cheque for one hundred dollars, the Canon presumably released his blessing heavenward for, as we marched back down the aisle triumphantly, the sun broke through the overcast sky and through the magnificent Gothic window in the chancel and suddenly outlined us with a celestial spotlight down the length of the nave of this beautiful church. We walked through the narthex and out to the brilliant glittering arch of sabres held aloft by my fellow regimental officers of the Guard of Honour, to face a pelting of rice and rose petals. We were twenty-three and very much in love.

My brother Carl was my best man and Alec Boothe and Alec Roberts, both over six feet tall and fellow officers, were ushers. These huge men had to march up the aisle echeloned, one slightly behind the other, thus completely obscuring my view of the approaching bridal party. My Guard of Honour included Gordon de Salaberry Wotherspoon, Donald Hunter, Marshall Cleland, Edgar Ogilvy, and Mark Auden, all of whom had roles to play in our subsequent lives.

The reception was held at the old Granite Club on St. Clair Avenue, and the wedding and reception were honoured by the attendance of the lieutenant-governor, Albert Matthews, and Mrs. Matthews. His Honour enjoyed the young and handsome bridesmaids so much that he forgot that protocol dictated that no one left until he did. Time dragged on and finally it was time to go, but where? We suddenly realized that our train to New York was not due to leave for about four hours, and yet everyone was waiting for the bridal couple to leave next! The late Donald Hunter, bless his memory, solved the problem by inviting an impromptu group of the Guard back to his house, and rather than getting rid of the bride and groom, we went along to the party!

Later, several whooping and hollering Horse Guards in a convoy of cars led us down to Union Station, Alec Boothe having preceded us. He greased palms so that before I could tell the porter our train and car number, he grabbed my bags saying, "I know, sir, follow me." Installed in our compartment at the end of the sleeping car, we shut out the gaze of the curious passengers by closing the door and sank back to relax. The window of the compartment was filled with the faces of laughing Horse Guards shouting, "No, no, not yet!" They had climbed onto two large baggage trucks in uniform and party dress and pushed them along to our car and our window! They shouted out advice, humorous, lewd, and loud to the newlyweds inside the compartment.

Finally the train pulled out, leaving the roisterers behind and a very limp couple in the compartment. The conductor came through and said, "I hope you will always be happy like this." The Immigration and Customs came through, winked knowingly and said, "No, I don't want to look in your bags. You never know what you'll find in newlyweds' bags. Have a great night, goodnight!" Finally we were alone.

The next interruption came from the porter, who asked if he could make up our beds. We had to move out into the aisle in full view of the curious passengers. The porter asked me, "Do you want the upper and lower made up, or just the lower, sir?"

I was thunder-struck, tongue-tied, spluttering, when dear Audrey said, "Just the lower, thank you!"

Gratefully alone at last, we quickly undressed and went to bed. It was one of the most uncomfortable nights I can ever remember. Finally, about 2:00 a.m., I realized that the streaming perspiration and breathtaking heat had nothing to do with sexual activity but with the heat valve which had been turned on full several hours before, presumably as a prank. The temperature in the compartment was nearly a hundred degrees!

All in all it was an exciting, memorable, and thoroughly exhausting day in May 1938.

# UP IN ARMS

## 7

The luxurious suite at the Waldorf-Astoria saw much of Audrey and me in the next three days, as we recovered from the ordeal of the wedding ceremony and luxuriated, totally absorbed in ourselves. We needed no one else.

We were flattered when a call came from the front desk, asking permission to allow a photographer from Associated News Services to come up to photograph us, presumably for the home papers, with permission for the *New York Times* to copy. Taken in by the phony name and believing that an alert press really wanted to get our pictures for a wedding story, we instantly and innocently agreed. I remember posing for a ridiculous picture, pipe in hand, although I did not smoke, while the horrible thought dawned on me that something did not ring true. I asked the photographer why he did not take our pictures on shipboard. It turned out that he had no association with the press at all, but "worked" the Waldorf, flattering innocents abroad like ourselves by alluding to the press and thus gaining entry, against hotel rules. I paid him the minimum and complained to the management about invasion of privacy. Remarkably, we later did receive a couple of heavily retouched salon photographs of ourselves.

On board the *Queen of Bermuda*, a shallow-draught, round-bottomed excuse for an ocean liner, we quickly experienced another upset in our plan for another three days of passionate embrace. Such things depend on the invigorating effect of the sea air to overcome the lassitude that must follow over-exertion. My Audrey got seasick. Very seasick! Pale green in colour and moaning, my lovely bride shivered under a rug while I, out of loyalty, ate dried-out chicken breast and sipped consommé and crunched celery with her, while dreaming of steaks and other things. I have always been a good sailor.

Bermuda never looked more charming or beautiful than it did in that May of 1938, when we disembarked at Hamilton. In those days no cars or motor vehicles were allowed on the island. The only mode of travel for tourists was by bicycle, horse-drawn carriage, or "shank's mare" – walking. The exception was a hotel bus which carried us and our luggage to our room in the Belmont Manor, the newest, smartest hotel on the island. Firmly on shore, my bride recovered quickly, and we hired bicycles on which to roam the length and breadth of this most beautiful island.

Awakening early the first morning, leaving Audrey in bed, I dressed and descended to the main desk and asked the price of the room we occupied. With a little quick arithmetic, I found out that we would run out of money in about two weeks instead of the planned three. I burst into our room and told Audrey to get up right away, we were moving!

Stunned, she asked incredulously, "Is the honeymoon over?"

We asked the hall porter where the nearest estate agent was located, and before noon we had leased a new cottage, fully furnished, overlooking Darrell's Shipyard and the bay and on the edge of the Belmont Manor property. We had it for a whole month for less than the two weeks in the hotel would have cost. We had two bedrooms, a large living-room, dining-room, full kitchen, and a daily maid for $180 in all. We could even open our windows on the Belmont Manor side and dance to the hotel orchestra's music in our living-room.

We explored the south shore, then wild and uninhabited, saw in the aquarium the horrible things we had been swimming with, rode our bikes twenty miles to explore Old St. George's, and came home exhausted on the narrow-gauge railway that then ran the length of the island. Then, once more, there was a minor disaster. Audrey fell off her bike and cut her kneecap badly on the coral. Not properly treated, it took a long time to heal. We did not know then that coral is poisonous and induces a severe inflammation in a wound.

Bermuda had completely won our hearts and we were sad to leave, yet excited at the thought of moving into our own home when we returned to Toronto. After looking at houses and areas from the Kingsway to North York, we finally settled on a two-bedroom apartment in a fourplex at 1665 Bathurst Street, complete with heated garage for $67.50 a month. This was the only building for gentiles in the predominantly Jewish district, but we never suffered from discrimination and the price was right. Holy Blossom Synagogue was across the street and Koffler's Drug Store was a short distance south on Bathurst. This was the original pharmacy of the Koffler family which later Murray Koffler, the son, expanded into Shopper's Drug Mart, a huge Canada-wide chain of drug stores, each from five to ten times the size of the original Koffler store.

Audrey quickly became pregnant. The "pill" was, of course, not yet invented, and we half-heartedly put our faith in foams. While not averse to starting our family, we were somewhat frightened at the prospect. John Mann, the obstetrician and inventor of the Mann forceps and baby ventilator, was our doctor and a great friend. To our sorrow, Audrey began to bleed and have other alarming symptoms that resting in bed with feet up would not cure. We lost our first even before it had a name, and I was saddened but thanked God that Audrey was none the worse for the ordeal. In defiance of fate, we then set out about stubbornly to have a baby, not sure whether it was our first or our second!

As 1939 progressed, our military exercises took a more serious turn. An Austrian ex-corporal named Hitler in a far-off country, Germany, kept strutting and "Heiling," and the headlines were full of *Anschluss* and book burnings and free peoples fallen under German rule. Most of the talk in the regimental messes was about when we would be called up and who would be first. The weekend of September 3, Audrey and I were guests of our life-long friend and fellow Horse Guard, Alec Boothe, at his summer log cabin on Riley Lake near Washago, Ontario. A pleasant, colourful weekend was shattered when we heard a radio bulletin: "Great Britain has declared war on Germany, and Canada is expected to declare war on Germany momentarily." We quickly and quietly packed and drove back to Toronto in grim silence, gripping hands, sure we would be needed and fully believing we would be called up tomorrow!

Alec Boothe and I, being overeager, dashed home, strapped on our .45 pistols over our civilian clothes, and drove down to the University Avenue Armouries at eleven o'clock that same night to report for duty. The streets surrounding the armouries were quiet and deserted, the armouries locked up and in total darkness. Alec and I stood forlornly in front of the huge, iron-reinforced oak doors, feeling exceedingly foolish and increasingly disillusioned. Silently we turned and went home, and no one cared.

The next few months we lived with a steel kit box, my campaign chest, fully packed in the small vestibule of our apartment on Bathurst Street. Some regiments had been mobilized and were concentrated in improvised barracks in the various Exhibition buildings, but not the Horse Guards.

Life went on. Audrey was to deliver our first-born in early December 1939, but the pregnancy dragged on, her poor distended form groaning with the delay. Finally, Dr. Mann put her in the General Hospital when the labour pains started, and they never stopped for three days. Audrey was exhausted from pain and lack of sleep. I was exhausted from maintaining anxious vigil in the spouses' room, seeing worried expectant fathers come in and happy proud fathers go out, while I became a permanent fixture. Finally, Dr. Mann induced delivery and our new-born daughter, Gail, was brought in for me to see. Audrey anxiously asked me, "What do you think of her?"

Poor Gail was small, red, and wrinkled. There was a worried look on her wizened face. It was quite a shock, for I had expected chubby pink cheeks and chuckles. "It's kind of funny-looking," I said, in a most undiplomatic outburst of frankness.

Poor lovely Audrey burst out in a flash of anger, "Well, a monkey would look good to me at this point!"

I still think new-born babies' looks are overrated by anxious parents and doting grandparents. It is amazing that they blossom into beautiful little people. Beauty is truly in the eye of the beholder. But I can quite understand how the mother, having nurtured this tiny new life, exhausted, bruised, and torn as she may be from giving birth, sees past the red and wrinkled face of the new-born to the miracle of life in the eyes and the beauty of spirit in the tiny body. I was even afraid to hold our daughter for fear I would crush her.

We had both "girl" and "boy" names on our list. "Gail" was high on the list because the beautiful movie star, Gail Patrick, reminded me of Audrey and her dark-haired beauty. Little Gail was as blonde as could be, and quickly became the chubby pink and chuckles I had expected from birth.

Several of my friends, like Clare Conner, had joined active units or gone directly to England to join the Royal Air Force so as "not to miss the fun." The Horse Guards, restless and somewhat envious of the soldiers on active duty, tired of pretending our civilian cars were armoured vehicles, were mollified somewhat when two squadrons were "called up," one complete with horses in our traditional cavalry role to guard the Welland Canal, the other to guard several vital areas in the Toronto area, including our own University Avenue Armouries.

The "call up" was high-school drama at its worst. Suddenly we were all ordered to report to the armouries under orders of silence. Poor Audrey came home to our apartment from shopping to find the steel kit box, which had resided in our vestibule for the best part of a year, gone. I was also gone, and there was not even a note or phone call to explain the sudden absence. We fully expected to be able to phone home from the armouries, once we knew our destiny. But we were incarcerated, held incommunicado, for the next forty-eight hours, while our wives and families feared the worst. Meanwhile, we were passing pseudo-medicals, while the quartermasters issued uniforms reeking of mothballs, stiff and itchy with the warmth and feel of steel wool, boots in two sizes too large or too small, Lee-Enfield rifles from World War I plastered with grease, mess kits, blankets, and so on, to a long line of bewildered and excited troopers. The air of excitement diminished as fatigue and frustration set in and reports and nominal roles were demanded by district staff officers who barked out orders right and left before they even knew what they were barking about.

Captain Magnus Spence of the Medical Corps, a great friend and a distinguished member of the Horse Guards and our long-time regimental medical officer, passed my flat feet without having me take off my riding boots, passed Col. Russell Locke, a diabetic for ten years, because he was the C.O., and Lieut. Dennis Fitzgerald, who had ulcers. Poor Magnus would have been lynched outright if any one of us had been turfed out as medically unfit on that first night!

The Welland squadron was soon relieved by the RCMP and our new duties were to provide security guards for the airport in Camp Borden, Ontario, where we relieved the Irish Regiment of Canada. Included in our task was the protection of new, Canadian-built Mosquitoes, sleek planes largely made of wood, and some old Anson medium bombers, also made of wood, used by the RCAF for navigational training.

Two ambulances were presented to the Horse Guards by the Detroit Canadian Veterans' Club. They were converted hearses of Cadillac origin, painted white with red crosses. Our "staff" car, for the use of Col. R.P. Locke, our commanding officer, was a second-hand Ford convertible purchased with regimental funds and painted khaki. A huge "GGHG" was painted in white on each side.

Col. "Rusty" Locke, as he was affectionately known by all ranks, was dignified to the point of pomposity. He was fiercely loyal to the regimental traditions, and if there was not a suitable tradition to cover a situation, he invented one. But Col. Locke was no athlete. A march to church on Sunday morning was about as physical as he got.

Our few weeks on Air Force guard was an experience few would forget, including the flyers who took us seriously after the first night. Flyers on night exercises were used to driving past the Irish Regiment guards with a wave of the hand, but when we took over, they halted for inspection or got a .303 bullet from a Lee-Enfield in the trunk of their car, on orders of Major Ian Cumberland, our guard commander. Ian Cumberland, an R.M.C. graduate, was probably the finest soldier I have ever had the pleasure to serve under. He was a martinet, a disciplinarian, a physically and mentally tough man, but a fair and loyal friend. Ian lasted only a few days as guard commander before coming off his motorcycle and hurting his leg badly. Captain Alec Boothe took over command to our delight and his dismay.

The Air Force guard contingent from the Governor General's Horse Guards was a truly frightening force, much more danger to the Officer and Sergeant of the Guard and to the Air Force than to any potential saboteur. Most of the men, from seventeen to nineteen years of age, had no training with live ammunition and were highly nervous in the shadowy dark and bone-chilling cold of the nights at Camp Borden. Now they all had live ammunition in their guns. One officer making his rounds saw a shadow silhouetted against a white hangar wall some distance away. "Halt!" he shouted, pulling out his .45 Smith & Wesson revolver.

The silhouette was cast by a guard named McCormack who had a terrible stutter when surprised or excited. "FFFFrien--" he stuttered.

"Halt or I fire!" the officer demanded.

"FFFFrien--" McCormack began, but before he could finish, the officer fired. The bullet fortunately missed poor McCormack who, feeling the wind of death pass by his face, shouted , "FRIEND, you goddamn fool!"

Poor Alec Boothe, acting commander, was in a dilemma, not knowing whether to court-martial the officer for careless discharge of a firearm or discipline the soldier for swearing at an officer. Boothe, being a realist, gave the officer hell in private and the trooper hell for not challenging in the first place. Such was our first action in World War II.

We did a good job for the Air Force and were soon on friendly terms with them, largely thanks to the good offices of Ft.-Lieut. Harston, a Protestant padre with the Air Force, a friend and mediator on all sides. Suddenly the regiment was mobilized as the 2nd Canadian Motorcycle Regiment (GGHG) with Col. R.P. Locke, E.D., commanding. There never was a 1st Canadian Motorcycle Regiment. We would never have permitted another to be first, and there never was a 3rd Canadian Motorcycle Regiment, because after a year of exhilarating training and sport on the "bikes," during which we became quite proficient, the Army Command in its wisdom thought better of the whole idea and killed the experimental organization. We became an Armoured Regiment (Tanks).

Two entire motorcycle clubs joined up with us, including the Canadian race champion, Thomas Neelands. These men were outstanding riders and fine men. In no way did they resemble the Hell's Angels or similar bikers' gangs. They immediately took over teaching us to ride. We had an assortment of bikes, Indians with sidecars, Nortons for dispatch riders, Harley-Davidsons for speed, and one beautiful, four-cylinder Ariel Foursquare, owned privately by Neelands.

Two quick methods were used to teach us to ride. One was the sandpits; the other, the convoy on sharp-gravel roads. Neelands, a tall, pleasant-looking man, physically powerful, with an expression of perpetual good humour on his healthy pink cheeks, was obviously a fellow you could trust with your life. I sat behind him on the rear seat of his heavy machine and drove out to a quarry of soft sand, the kind that covers the training area of Camp Borden like acne on a youth's face. He drove in a wide, slow figure eight until I began to sense the machine's reaction to the shifting surface and relaxed. Suddenly Neelands jumped clear as the heavy machine slid sideways, pinning my leg against the hot cylinders. He quickly lifted the machine off and laughingly said, "Lesson number one, always be prepared to disembark and get clear!" Nothing but my pride was hurt. I spent the next fifteen minutes getting the feel of the heavy machine in the sand until I could instinctively shift my balance to counteract any skid. Lesson number two was conducted on army machines, in single file on the sharp rolling gravel of a half-made road at twenty miles an hour. You did not dare fall off or you would be cut to pieces.

On the passing-out parade before hill-climbing competitions by the most advanced riders, Neelands would demonstrate how to disembark from a bike at fifty miles an hour and roll safely away from the machine, unless there was a tree or a post in the way! This remarkable man was a Class A fitter, which meant he could make any given part of a motor from a block of metal with tolerances of hundredths of an inch. He trained and led our best mechanics all through the war as a senior warrant officer of the Horse Guards. He kept us on the road.

The passing-out parade, to which wives and girl-friends were invited, featured hill-climbing races and joy rides for guests in sidecars. Col. "Rusty" Locke caused great merriment when, in all seriousness, he turned to Alec Boothe and said, "Alec, would you do something for my wife which I am unable to do?" Momentarily at a loss for words, Boothe slowly realized the colonel meant giving Mrs. Locke a spin in the sidecar. Conscious of the suppressed chuckles of his brother officers, he helped the lady into the machine and drove off. Thus another "Rusty" Locke story was born to be retold many times during the war.

A new mascot arrived in camp, a small black pony called Sea Biscuit. The pride of the regiment, he was at the head of every parade, a bright blanket with "GGHG" emblazoned on it over his back. Sometimes he took his own headstrong direction, to the embarrassment of his groom.

We moved to the Canadian National Exhibition grounds for the winter and trained in High Park and on surrounding highways. Best of all, we were allowed home most nights when not on official duty, until a trooper came down with spinal meningitis and we were confined to barracks for weeks. During the quarantine, our wives and families were permitted to come down to visit, but we could only wave from opposite sides of the street and shout love and encouragement to keep our spirits up. It was a medical miracle that no other case developed, but none did, so the quarantine was lifted.

I learned a severe lesson one night about 4:00 a.m. at four below zero while, as orderly officer, I was doing rounds of the Exhibition grounds with Sgt. Blackman, my troop sergeant. I felt that I was giving a first-class example to the younger, newer officers of how a troop should be run. After all, I was the senior subaltern in the regiment at this time, responsible for the dress and decorum of the other commissioned ranks junior to me. So to bolster my pride as we walked through the snow, I asked, "Sgt. Blackman, what do my men think of me?"

Fortunately Sgt. Blackman was a chunky, spunky individual, and he replied somewhat incredulously, "Do you really want me to tell you, sir?"

Huffily I said, "I wouldn't have asked you if I didn't want to know."

"Well, sir, they think you are a shit!"

I was stunned, almost as if I had been slapped across the face. "Why?" I asked wearily. "You know my troop means everything to me."

"Yes, sir."

"That there is nothing I wouldn't do for them."

"Yes, sir, I know that, and they know that," said Sgt. Blackman, "but they don't trust you."

"For God's sake, why?"

"Well," said the doughty sergeant, "you don't have much judgement. You believe the excuses and lies of smart alecks and let them off. The poor soldier who is honest and tongue-tied, you throw the book at him!"

"Okay, Sergeant, I asked for it. What do you recommend?"

"Read the rules to them, and warn them all to expect hell and damnation and the maximum punishment if they break them," Blackman replied.

"Okay, Sgt. Blackman, I'll speak to the troop in the morning and do as you advise. But let me warn you and your NCOs, I'll be even more strict with you and them. You'll get the book plus!"

"Great, sir," said Sgt. Blackman. "We'll get along just fine!"

Things were better after that conversation. Our first active-service Christmas dinner was held in the basement of the CNE's Government Building, with the full tradition of the officers of the regiment serving the men turkey and plum pudding and all the trimmings. The regiment was then paraded on the square and we were told that a new division was being formed to be called the First Canadian Armoured Division and that we were to be a part of its Second Canadian Armoured Brigade with the New Brunswick Hussars, the British Columbia Dragoons, and the Motor Battalion Perth Regiment.

We were disappointed to lose our traditional reconnaissance role, to which all our training had been directed, but our excitement grew anew when, in the spring, we were once more transferred to Camp Borden. Then our first tanks arrived on "lend lease" from the United States. They were six Renault tanks from World War I. These museum pieces had two-man crews and metal tracks with huge tailfins or skids protruding from the rear so they would not fall over backward while climbing a steep hill. The maximum speed, when you could get one working, was five miles an hour on the road. We found that the fin was in the way of cranking the engine. As well, they were impossible to start or steer; the mechanisms had not been used since they were mothballed in 1918. They inspired the best in our mechanics, who cannibalized all six for enough workable parts to make one run and steer. They also "souped up" the old Renault engine. These alterations were done with considerable secrecy until, one sleepy Sunday afternoon, this lone "mini-monster" roared and clanked with fearsome and appalling noise down the road, steam gushing from every pore, past the camp commander's headquarters at fifteen miles an hour, three times its best speed. The road was quickly lined with cheering men and a most irate brigadier camp commander and some of his headquarters staff. Our planned demonstration was that our tank would "hide" in the woods after the run, and the brave crew quickly disperse, but how do you hide a geyser of steam rising in puffs like Indian smoke signals? Needless to say, there was hell to pay. Tracked vehicles were expressly forbidden on the camp road. Five hulks of tanks grinned vacantly while one of their number gave the last clattering hurrah and retired a hero.

No serious punishment was handed out as the diversion of the arrival of our first real tank claimed everyone's attention. There was only one, but, after the ancient Renaults, it seemed an awesome thing. Our Ram tank had a two-pounder gun plus three machine guns encased in a moulded hull of three-inch steel, driven by a diesel engine and served by a crew of five men. Only the most experienced drivers were allowed to drive this wonder.

It took us about a week to turn our Ram on its side in the training area. Our punishment was to deal with reams of paperwork. We were pleased when a court of inquiry established that it was a pure accident and that the Ram tank, with its high profile and high centre of gravity, was far from an ideal armoured fighting vehicle.

Our divisional name was suddenly changed to the Fifth Armoured Division so that there would be no confusion with the First Infantry Division already overseas. Then we learned that our regiment and brigade headquarters would go overseas together very soon. We began packing in earnest. Those of us already married made last-minute arrangements about assignment of pay; others, like Capt. Alec Boothe, got married. As many of our brother officers as could got leave to attend the small wedding in St. Paul's Chapel. The bride was Bea

Bryan, a beautiful blonde nurse, Alec's fiancée of some months. Alec and Bea spent their short honeymoon with Audrey and me at our rented cottage on Big Bay Point, Lake Simcoe.

A few men in the ranks, when they learned we would be going overseas, overstayed and went AWOL. I was posted to a panel of officers that comprised a court-martial to try those men. The sessions seemed endless, and I began to worry that the regiment might leave without me if I did not get off this tiresome duty. Each case was much the same, mostly routine, and I heard the same excuses in a hundred versions. Only one or two were serious enough to be classed as ''desertion.'' These latter cases provided my release from the court-martial duty. In a court-martial, the lowest-ranking officer is required to give his verdict first, followed by the next senior officer, and so on. As time went on, I got more and more apprehensive that I might be left behind, and tired of the whole silly process. I chose to give the maximum punishment for each serious offence and recommended it up to and including death! It was obvious that I no longer took the court seriously, and I was quickly sent back to the Horse Guards without comment to resume my normal duties.


Padres play an important role in the army. The closer you are to the enemy, the greater the odds of meeting your Maker. As an American padre said in World War II, ''There are no atheists in the foxholes.'' But there are padres and padres. As a regiment, we had been badly spoiled during the thirties by a lovable, delightful regimental padre, an Anglican priest, the Rev. Clarke Wallace, and his wonderful wife. Clarke Wallace had been a young padre in World War I but was far from stuffy. He conducted an annual memorial, church-parade service once a year, and at the New Year's Eve party he would get what the Irish would describe as ''drink taken'' because, no matter how much he drank, he never fell down. Every New Year's Day, Clarke Wallace conducted a morning service in his church during which he invariably based his sermon on the evils of drink, while he gripped the edges of the pulpit to steady the church. He also played a gentle game of poker and was much beloved and respected by all.

Later in the war he ended up ill in Lady Astor's hospital in England. Lady Astor, M.P., was head of the Woman's Christian Temperance Union and a vinegary soul at best. During one of her daily inspections of the hospital she noticed some "Petty girl" pin-ups over some of the invalided soldiers' beds, laughingly inoffensive by today's liberal standards. Lady Astor shrieked, "This is intolerable, where are the padres?"

This was too much for Clarke Wallace. He meekly put up his head and said, "I am a padre, Lady Astor."

"You are a disgrace, sir. Why do you allow these terrible, lewd pictures to be displayed on the walls?"

Clarke looked at her with his most benign expression and said, "Lady Astor, my cardinal sin is not women, it's drink!" With that she reportedly stormed out of the room.

Lady Astor earned the dislike of the entire Canadian Fifth Armoured Division and the British Eighth Army in Italy when, after we had battled at Cassino and fought eight hundred miles up Italy for two weary years, she rose in the House of Commons and called the soldiers in Italy "D-Day Dodgers." We took the insult, delivered during the invasion of Europe, as a compliment, because of its source.

We had a succession of Anglican padres, high and low. Either they could not stand us or we could not stand them. We invariably parted company in short order. They, too, were all of Great War vintage, old men no longer fit for the job. For several months we were without a padre and, in fact, went overseas without one. Our last one in Canada was the reason why. He was High Anglican and, at first, seemed a nice enough fellow. Shortly after arriving, he pleaded with parade to come out to Holy Communion, stating that he could not celebrate it alone. Capt. Jack Eaton and I were not Anglicans, but we decided we would give the new padre a break, so we spoke to several of our men and got quite a decent turnout, in spite of the fact that the time of service was 7:30 a.m. and the place was a small, cold-as-a-tomb building. It was an extremely cold winter and the CNE buildings could barely be heated, some not at all. When we came to the prayers, both Jack and I sat down and bent over in that forehead-on-hand, embarrassed attitude that members of "other denominations" adopt when praying. The padre stopped the service, stormed down the aisle, and stopped in front of us, obviously agitated. He said, "When the Wise Men visited Our Lord at the scene of the Nativity, they knelt. What was good enough for the Wise Men is good enough for us!" To this my friend Eaton replied something that sounded like, "Yes, but the lucky bastards had straw to kneel on!"

We were forthwith cast out of the service, like the money-changers from the temple. I believe if the priest had had the courage, he would have hit us. Obviously he did not appreciate how hard we had worked to get the men to turn out at all. The men were on our side. The story got around the camp like wildfire, told and retold with humour tinged with anger at the action of the cleric. Within two days he was gone, to everyone's relief including his own.

# OVERSEAS AGAIN

## 8

After months of initial and basic training, we received news that we would be confined to barracks in Camp Borden after October 1, 1941. This signal of our imminent departure for overseas caused excitement amid the heavy work of packing for a regimental move. Audrey came up to visit with me in Barrie for a last weekend of leave. The only room we could get in town was in the ancient American Hotel, a joyless, drab, airless relic of a rural Ontario hotel of the turn of the century. We clung together for hours in our misery at the thought of once more being parted. Audrey was a couple of months pregnant with our second child, one I might never see. Sweating, hot and uncomfortable in our dingy room, I went over to open the window wide, only to discover it opened not to the outside fresh air but on the stairwell containing the musty, stale odours of generations long departed.

It was the start of worse to come. The cold grey morning goodbye at the Camp Borden barrier was gruff and almost impersonal. We had nothing more to say. As I watched the car disappear, bearing my wife and unborn child away, I felt once more the crushing loneliness that I had experienced twelve years before in Lausanne as I watched my mother drive away, leaving me alone at boarding school in a foreign land.

The day of our departure dawned mild and dull. In the evening we fell in and the regiment entrained amid pouring rain, the men wet and uncomfortable and grumbling at the inevitable delays. So we left Camp Borden behind on our way to the sea. But first we shunted to a halt in the North Toronto station where, to my surprise and delight, several hundred of our families were gathered, including Audrey and our little daughter Gail. The noise and excitement of the next ten minutes made it seem like a happy occasion. So much for security. We had thought our departure from Camp Borden was a secret!

By late afternoon the next day, we disembarked in Quebec City, formed up in regimental column, led by our Horse Guard band, and marched through the Lower Town of Old Quebec for a spell of exercise. One of our officers, Lieut. A.F. "Ding" Judd, was very young and had a particularly high-pitched voice of considerable clarity and carry. To this point "Ding" had never been known to indulge in coarse language, as did many soldiers from time to time. When extremely annoyed he would burst out with "Oh rats!" So his innocence was presumed to match his fresh, boyish appearance. As we marched through Lower Town, we passed a house, obviously a bordello, with dozens of girls leaning from the windows upstairs, yelling and shrieking. The band had ceased playing and amid the lull a high boyish voice exclaimed, "What a peculiar place for a girl's school." The voice could only be Lieut. Judd's, and the regiment exploded with merriment and laughter, all of which brought some of the girls alongside to help us complete the march back to the train.

We stopped also at Moncton and Debert, sober affairs, but when we stopped at Truro on the way to Halifax, the Ladies' Auxiliaries in town were waiting on the platform with trays of cigarettes and apples and words of good cheer. That night we embarked in Halifax on the *Capetown Castle*, a handsome cruise ship of the P&O line that usually sailed between Southampton and South Africa. As soon as the *Capetown Castle* was loaded, we moved out to the middle of Halifax harbour, where we sat for the next three days while our convoy assembled. It was the largest troop convoy to that date, six troopships with a naval escort of six destroyers and a depot ship. *Capetown Castle* was the Commodore's vessel, and we were stationed in the exact middle of the impressive array of ships.

On October 9, 1941, we sailed out of Halifax. Overhead was an escort of flying boats and only one cloud on the horizon. As we left Halifax, Lord Haw Haw, the traitorous Englishman who broadcast for the Germans, as Tokyo Rose later did for the Japanese, was heard on the shortwave wireless to say, in effect, "We know the Fifth Armoured Division has just sailed from Halifax and we have a large wolf pack of U-boats to welcome them."

There was a patch of about four hundred miles of ocean beyond the range of our aircraft from either shore. It was here that trouble was expected. The officer deck watches were doubled, and complete blackout was observed. Not even a cigarette was allowed on deck. We had just entered this most dangerous zone when an electrical box on the upper deck of our ship short-circuited and burst into flame. A stupid seaman, in panic, ran out a seahose and played water on it, with the result that our magnificent ship came alight from stem to stern! The horrified "whoop, whoop, whoop" of our attendant destroyers, as they began running emergency patterns in and around us, seemed amusing until we realized that they were also dropping depth charges on their runs. Suddenly the flames were extinguished, and the excitement was over.

We disembarked shortly after noon at Princess Landing, Liverpool. We had waited outside the harbour all night before steaming up the Mersey because Liverpool was undergoing another bombing. Our crossing had been twenty-four hours faster than any previous convoy's. A balloon barrage of silver blobs swayed at the ends of their cables over the port to discourage low-level bomb attacks. Sunken hulks of ships sat in the harbour. As we waited aboard our trains in the station tunnel, while another small enemy air raid was dispersed, we got our first real sense of war. Seeing some of the bombed-out buildings, as our trains pulled out of town, increased our sympathy for the hardships the English were enduring and whetted our appetite to get back at the Germans. The trains took us to Cheltenham, to Swindon (which we later called "Swindletown"), and then to Ogbourne St. George, in Wiltshire, where we finally detrained and marched two miles to the coldest, dampest camp one could imagine. We fell asleep exhausted. In each room there was a small iron stove and a minute supply of low-grade coal, the whole known as "stoves, non-combustible, officers, for the use of."

In the next three weeks of Wiltshire damp and cold, aided by the trauma of untrained cooks trying to cope with "Lord Woolton" sausage and unfamiliar rations, one in four of the hardy Canadians went to hospital with pneumonia, including my doughty friend, Alec Boothe. Lord Woolton was Britain's Minister of Food. His "national" sausage was ninety per cent sawdust and a little meat flavouring. It was colloquially known as "horse cock" and was a mainstay of our diet. I lost thirty-five pounds in the next five weeks but got healthier in the process.

•  •  •

Christmas 1941 was our first away from home. Christmas Eve was a sad and depressing time. Most of the officers not on duty had gone to various parties. Those of us left in camp on duty, about six in all, had planned a party in the mess. I went back to my room early in the evening to get an extra bottle I had put away for such an evening, because drinks in the mess were severely rationed. Passing by the junior officers' room, I saw a stranger sitting forlornly on an army cot, sunk in abject misery, and looking very chilled. I stepped in and learned that his name was Lieut. Jack Seale, that he had nearly frozen to death in the back of an army lorry for three hours coming from Southampton, and that he had been dumped unceremoniously in our nearly empty camp this Christmas Eve. I invited him to join our party. He perked up and produced a bottle to go with mine. We ended on a high note, covering the gnawing loneliness in our souls with Christmas tinsel and cheer that lasted for a few hours at least. Jack was with us the entire war and acquitted himself well. Thus are life-long friendships simply made, through shared loneliness in strange places, wrapped in the common bond of the regiment.

After a few weeks, during which alternate squadrons paraded to the local Church of England every Sunday, the authorities decided the Horse Guards needed a regimental padre of their own. The authorities finally found a young, athletic Roman Catholic priest and assigned him to our regiment, although less than two per cent of our men were Roman Catholics. His name was Father Percy Johnson.

Lieut.-Col. Hubert (Buff) Sharpe had become our commanding officer when Rusty Locke was refused permission to go overseas for medical reasons. Buff Sharpe, a graduate of R.M.C., was a mild-mannered man, quiet, reserved, and gentlemanly. Young Father Johnson, glowing with enthusiasm on his arrival in Ogbourne St. George, paraded himself to the C.O., and in the course of the first meeting he made the mistake of asking the colonel to instruct the men to call him "Father." He was abashed when the Anglican colonel said, coldly, "You will be known by your name and rank, which is Captain Johnson. You are entitled to be called 'sir' once a day by junior officers and 'sir' by all other junior ranks all the time. Anything else you are called you will bloody well earn!"

Father Johnson, with true humility and some missionary zeal, went into every nook and cranny of the camp to introduce himself to the officers, NCOs, and men, saying to each, "My name is Percy Johnson, what is yours?" Padres were distinguished from combatant officers by the purple felt base to their officers' "pips," or rank insignias on their shoulders, whereas tank officers had yellow or gold. So almost instantly Father Johnson earned his nickname Percy "Purple Pips," and is still referred to as such with warmth and respect by all those who served in the GGHG.

Father Johnson remained our regimental padre, coach of the baseball team, and friend of all who served in the regiment for the next two years until, to our dismay, he was promoted to 5th Brigade and had to leave us for the New Brunswick Hussars. His replacement was an Anglican, a Major Stone, a smaller man with a sense of humour who, to our delight, almost instantly won his "spurs" and the respect of all. We sensed he was too good to last and, sure enough, he quickly got a promotion, ending up some years later as the chief padre of the Canadian Army. Major R.J. Stone won our attention and respect in his first sermon in Maresfield Camp. He based it on some foul language the equipment repairer had been heard to use when he hit his thumb with a hammer just as the new padre passed by. His theme was that the constant repetition of the army's four-letter word, particularly when used ungrammatically, as the equipment repairer had used it, was pointless, degrading, and senseless. "My theme this morning," said the padre, "is f— the f—ing f—er. Now, let's examine this silly statement piece by piece." By this time everyone was sitting bolt-upright paying attention. The new padre was okay, he spoke our language! But, for the years since World War II, Percy "Purple Pips" Johnson has remained the padre of us all. The others came and went, but he was the one who never missed a regimental reunion.

As a squadron commander, twenty-seven years of age, I was one of the "older" men, and thus presumed to be wise, understanding, and experienced. Most of the troops, NCOs, and even some officers under my control were in the seventeen to twenty-three-year-old range and presumed to be less experienced in the affairs of the world, whereas the truth was that many were far more street-wise than I. One practice we perpetrated on junior officers new to the Horse Guards in England was to confine the new arrival to camp for the first three weeks while he was properly turned out and taught to hold his liquor, or at least to respect it. This latter process consisted of sitting the new officer at a plain wooden mess table on a hard wooden bench, a full bottle of Scotch whisky and a glass and water in front of him, a fellow officer behind him. The orders were to consume the bottle before leaving the table. It mattered not whether he took two hours or twenty to finish it off. If he slumped, the officer behind him picked him up and commanded, "Drink!" Some were sick, others plastered, but having passed the test and survived, they were presumed to be fit to be let loose on London Town on leave. This "training" appeared to work; we had little or no problem with public drunkenness. We did not realize until later that we could have killed one or two if they had absorbed too much alcohol too quickly.

Our new commanding officer, Ian Cumberland, R.M.C., graduate and martinet, was known by his message code-name "CUMI." CUMI was as fine a soldier as you will ever find anywhere, but his drive and unremitting strictness nearly caused a mutiny in the ranks and bloodshed among the officers. We were kept on exercises for six months, with only forty-eight hours once a month, to "pull" motors and do heavy maintenance on the vehicles. CUMI was completely unrelenting in his desire for perfection, rejecting a report if there was a single misplaced letter. "Goddammit," he would say, "this report is wrong. Redo it and remember we are reconnaissance and our reports must be one hundred per cent accurate. Our lives depend on it!" We were drilled, honed, and tested and became hard, fit, and efficient, developing a good deal of *esprit de corps* and professional pride in the process.

The GGHG were an unusual outfit. Fifty per cent of all ranks had high-school Grade XII or better; fifty per cent were hard-rock miners from Kirkland Lake or had similar backgrounds. This proved to be the perfect blend for armoured vehicle skills, which must range from high-tech to brute strength. Unlike other services who, having fought, were able to rest while maintenance crews replenished their fuel and ammunition, we had to do our own maintenance and refueling. Three hours of maintenance for every two hours' running time was the norm. Food and sleep became a major problem whenever an exercise or action extended over several days.

One afternoon my "C" Squadron was ordered to assist Divisional Headquarters on some experimental work with assault tanks that carried their own bridges suspended in front of them. Two cables ran from the front of the huge bridge structure over the turret, in which the crew commander stood, to the rear of the tank. The cables were to be released by a "quick release" consisting of two shotgun shells which exploded when a lanyard was pulled, blowing the connecting link apart, and dropping the bridge – ideally over the ditch to be crossed. It was a complete disaster, all done in front of senior officers from Army Headquarters. None of it was our fault. The gim-crack invention, a brilliant idea poorly thought through, nearly killed one crew commander when a supporting cable slipped over the tank turret and came close to slicing the poor man in two. The companion tank dropped its bridge over the ditch, backed off, and in attempting to cross on the unstable structure, completely turned upside down, bathing the badly scared crew in acid from the huge batteries under the tank floor. The exercise was called off for rethinking, and we, minus casualties, were sent home, wondering how we could possibly win the war when there was every chance of getting maimed by our own general staff before we ever saw enemy action.

Our next major experience nearly resulted in my being court-martialed. We were practising driving on the high cliffs above Brighton from where, on a clear day, you could see the coast of France. One of my Sherman tanks caught fire from an overheated clutch. The crew, aware of the two hundred gallons of one-hundred octane fuel situated over the seat of the fire, wisely abandoned "ship." The petrol was spewed in a fine stream upward against the red-hot "blanket box" on the turret and burst into a forty-foot-high blue flame like a gigantic Bunsen burner, and did so all through the night in plain view of the Germans on the French coast. The Navy was upset, the Army was upset, and the townsfolk of Brighton were terrified that this huge flame would bring yet another air raid, or even the long-range gun the Germans tried out on them from time to time. We were upset when a very high-level court of inquiry came down from London Army Headquarters to investigate the loss of a hundred thousand dollars worth of tank.

The court consisted of a brigadier, two colonels, and two majors, none of whom had ever been in a tank. The drill, as laid down in the manual, was to remain in the tank, don gas masks, and fight the fire with hand-held extinguishers after pulling the plugs on the $CO_2$ bottles. The gas masks were required because if you did not wear them you would die from the phosgene gas generated by the extinguishers, if you were not blown up or fried first! The question was: Had my crew followed the approved method? The answer was: No, of course, they had not. It was not practical; the rules were obviously ridiculous. In a desperate effort to prove my point, I challenged any two members of the court to climb in the turret and let me lock them in while we played blowtorches on the metal outside for a minimum of ten minutes without them screaming to get out! There were no takers, and they quickly agreed that the rules should be rewritten. I was asked to rewrite the script for a new pamphlet on the emergency procedures. We found out later, in action, that when a tank is hit, the crew has about eleven seconds to decide whether they will burn or not. We also found out the German crews felt exactly the same way. After setting off the fire-retardant bottles, you got out as fast as you could.

When we finally got a full complement of vehicles, the regiment moved up to West Tofts, near Brandon, in Norfolk, to the Wash district where a large, five-square-mile area had been evacuated and turned over to tank-training manoeuvres. "C" Squadron provided the enemy for the other two squadrons of the regiment. This was rather unfair because I knew the strengths and weaknesses of my two fellow squadron commanders and we led them a merry chase. We were so successful as enemy that "C" Squadron was left behind when the regiment departed to act as enemy to the other Canadian armoured regiments, as well as the British and the Poles. The Poles were the only ones we had real trouble with, so we resorted to craft and illusion to beat their superior numbers. In other words, while we stuck to the rules of the exercise, we did not play fair. Neither did the Poles! It was the best training of the war.

As the enemy, we could see clearly the wooden response to some of the standard classroom manoeuvres, and we devised all kinds of outrageous stratagems to confuse and destroy what was often a much larger force. What we did was not cricket. We played dirty, we were crafty, but our wireless discipline was superb and we usually won. One day we were up against the entire regiment of Lord Strathcona's Horse. The start time was 0500. One minute later, my tanks concealed in a "killing" area, alone in a scout car with my driver, I descended in the ground fog of early morning in among the enemy tanks, all busy "netting" their wireless sets (a difficult procedure with the old No. 19 sets). I inquired from the first troop I met where I could find their squadron commander. Then I drove over to his tank, climbed up on it, pulled out my pistol, and took him prisoner.

"Take me to your commanding officer," I said. Then I climbed up and took the C.O. prisoner. He was near apoplexy. I drove away with them in the low fog and ruined the regimental exercise, until an umpire caught up with me. The British umpire was most discourteous, saying that in real life I would never have gotten away with it. "But this is real life," I said, "and these officers are out of action!"

The umpire made me return the two officers so they could get on with the exercise. I am afraid Col. Pat Griffin, the C.O. and a permanent force officer, never forgave me or the Horse Guards for the indignity he had suffered.

Finally we were relieved and started the long drive back to the south of England and the regiment. At one place on the road we had to go over a hump-backed bridge and make a sharp left turn along a river, twenty-four tanks in column. The lead tank went over the bridge, misjudged the turn and ploughed right through the living-room of the house on the corner. The second storey of the house cantilevered over the gaping hole. The next five tanks followed the route through the living-room before we could slow the column down enough to negotiate the sharp turn. A sign hung drunkenly from the second storey of the house over the hole. It read "Norfolk Claims Commissioner." We continued on our way without let-up or further incident. We assumed the commissioner could settle his own claim satisfactorily and we returned "home" to the regiment, which was now stationed in Aldershot.

When I had left for overseas, my wife was pregnant with our second child. Now the baby should have been born, but I had received no word from Audrey. Days, weeks went by. Letters, when they arrived at all, were a month old. Priority telegrams were reserved to report deaths, not births. Each night as I paced nervously up and down the officers' mess, I was joined by more and more of my fellow officers. Finally, three weeks after the fact, I got a telegram. A son had been born; mother and baby, James Allan, were doing well. The next morning in Part II Regimental Orders, James Allan Burton, aged three weeks, was given a regimental number and taken on strength as a Horse Guard, the youngest recruit ever. The all-night party that ensued was called the "Relief Party."

We moved to Maresfield Camp near Tunbridge Wells. My sergeant-major, Cy Clarkson, M.M., nicknamed "Bottle Ass," was the epitome of what a sergeant-major should be. Always proper, he walked stiffly, buttocks hard-pressed, chest out, tummy in, and head held very high. He was loyal, fair, immaculate in turn-out, intelligent, tough, and hard on slackers, with a sense of humour hidden behind his healthy ruddy cheeks. We made a good team in our single-mindedness to achieve perfection in "C" Squadron. When I returned from one of the training courses we were sent on, Sergeant-Major Clarkson reported to me that we had been having a great deal of trouble with the tough, rugged individualists in the Transport Troop, an unruly bunch of men who acted less like a troop than they should. Now they were surly and sour and causing trouble in Tunbridge Wells.

Perplexed, I went to my C.O., Ian Cumberland, to discuss this unusual situation. I told him that I was going to force them to act together against me in a continuous exercise until one of us cried quits. I might be gone with the troop for several days. My plan was to have all the truck drivers drive for two hours while their co-drivers marched for two hours, then they would exchange places. I would march for two hours and be driven for two hours by Corporal Burgess in my station wagon. There would be four hours' sleep each night and one hour at noon each day. The exercise would go on until one of us quit. It went on for three days and two nights until I was exhausted. Corporal Burgess said finally, "What in the hell are you trying to prove, sir?"

"I don't really remember, Corporal," I replied drowsily.

"Well, sir, if you are trying to beat that troop, forget it. They'll see you in your grave before they will let you win!"

"Wonderful!" I exclaimed with a sigh of relief. "That's what I was trying to prove. They are acting as a troop at last. Now all we have to do is to get them on our side."

The Transport Troop became one of the best, and shortly after that test of wills and endurance, I recommended Corporal Burgess for officers' training. He got his commission as 2nd Lieut. Burgess in due course. My men had long ago given me the nickname of "Uncle Al" because of my earnest, heart-to-heart talks with them. I was usually trying to talk them out of doing something foolish, like going absent without leave. Now, the Transport Troop found a new nickname for me. In recognition of our new-found admiration for each other, they called me "Boss" and meant it.


The Governor General's Horse Guards is affiliated with the Royal Horse Guards, then known as the Blues (now the Blues and Royals). The Household Cavalry, the Blues, and the Life Guards have a unique place in the hearts of Londoners. They are highly visible as mounted escorts on royal occasions and are the senior military regiments. They had a well-run club, the Guards' Club, then located in Brook Street.

On leave in London, having just come off intensive training exercises, I was privileged to stay at the Guards' Club as an honorary member. I arrived with my valise packed as carefully as my loyal batman, Albert Presswood, could manage, but feeling very much in need of "sprucing up." On arrival I was assigned a room and a servant to look after me. As he unpacked my valise, he deposited my soiled clothes in a pile and then proceeded to place my clean clothes on the same pile, fingering their cloth as he did so. I remonstrated, "Those are my clean clothes!"

"Oh, sir," he said in an anguished voice, "we can't allow a gentleman from the Guards' Club to go about with clothes in that condition. May I suggest that I can have you properly turned out in two hours?" True to his word, in two hours I shone from head to toe as I had never done before. It was a miracle!

While I was awaiting this valet's miracle, I descended to the writing room to write a letter home. I became so engrossed in the scene around me that the club and the characters in it became the subject of the letter. As I started writing, a florid, aging, white-haired, and well-upholstered "full" colonel came into the writing room. He was in uniform, the red collar-tabs proclaiming his rank, which, along with his ruddy complexion, more whisky-flush than fresh-air induced, reminded me of wattles on an ancient rooster. The colonel ruffled the newspapers and magazines on the table and, obviously annoyed, pounced on a bell, clanging it several times. A very small boy in a blue uniform, a page, ran in and stood strictly at attention in front of the colonel and said inquiringly, "Sir?"

"Boy! Where is *The Times*, eh, eh?" the colonel demanded.

"I don't know, sir," the page boy replied.

"Don't know, boy? Well, go and speak to someone in authority and get me a copy of *The Times*!"

Away sped the boy and returned in short order with the missing newspaper. As he handed it over, the colonel, in a conciliatory tone, said, "Good boy! See, you spoke to someone and found *The Times*. Now where did you find it?"

"Please, sir, in the Ladies' Annex, sir," replied the frightened lad.

"What? Do you dare to lie to me, boy? Now I ask you, when did ladies ever start reading *The Times*?"

I took it all down as fast as I could write. The frightened boy ran off as the colonel, satisfied he had proved the absurdity of the lie, found a lounge chair as overstuffed as he was. He sank into it, and murmured to himself as he scanned the hard-won paper before dozing off.

After donning my beautifully pressed Guards' uniform, sparkling Sam Browne belt, and distinctive cap, I strutted down to the Haymarket Club, a wartime drinking spa catering to Canadian officers. There I found a friend, and we decided to see a local play. We joined the queue and awaited our turn to buy tickets when an usher came out directly to me saying, "You wished a loge, sir!" It was a statement, not a question. Before I could say anything further, he said, "Please follow me, sir." They did not want a resplendent Guards' officer like me standing in queue – it was not done!

Returning to the Guards' Club about 3:00 a.m., prepared to walk the two or three miles from Victoria Station to Brook Street because there would be no taxi at that hour, I heard the consumptive wheezing of a London taxi as it approached. On an impulse I shouted out, "Guards' Club!" The taxi immediately pulled over, took me to the club, and dismounting I gratefully pushed an enormous tip of one pound on the driver. The driver, grinning, gave me back ten shillings and said, "We only overcharge the gentlemen at the Guards' Club double, sir. Thank you!" and drove off.

It was typical of tailors, regalia manufacturers, and others who dealt with the "upper classes," including regimental officers, not to bill the customer more than once a year, if then. I have always hated owing money and, not understanding the system, I went to Miss Miller, who ran the regalia company, and suggested as I had not had a bill in over two years, it might be good business to send me one. It was becoming increasingly apparent that we were going to move to another theatre of war.

Miss Miller said, "Don't worry about it, Major Burton. It would just upset the counting house." I insisted, however, and received the bill by return mail, paid it instantly, and then received a series of dunning letters threatening lawsuits if the account was not paid promptly. Hurriedly I got a quick leave to go up to London to see Miss Miller to prove I had paid up immediately. She rocked with laughter, saying, "See, I told you that just asking for a bill would upset the counting house. Only bankrupts ask for bills, and so the usual dunning routine also goes into effect!"

The following months were hectic with reorganization exercises of every conceivable type. Major A.K. Jordan of "A" Squadron had become second in command of the regiment under Lieut.-Col. Ian Cumberland. Major "Kitch" Jordan was a tough, compact man of medium height and average intelligence. As an ex-cadet of R.M.C., he was disdainful of anyone who had not gone to "the college" and supremely confident of his own superior ability in all things military. In fact, he was a good soldier when sober, but he had a mean streak a mile wide when he had one too many. From the moment he became second in command, he began, in small ways, a campaign to force everyone to declare allegiance to him personally, rather than to the C.O.

At the time I was having problems with the Transport Troop, he called me into his room and asked why, when I had a squadron problem, did not I seek his advice. My answer was, "I suppose because you are not the commanding officer. When you become C.O., I'll certainly come to you for advice."

Jordan's answer was chilling and surprising. "When I become C.O., Burton, you will, every day you live, regret that at this time you chose Cumberland instead of me!"

We were never friends from then on. I later realized that many cadets formed deep animosities against fellow cadets and carried these feelings throughout their lives. Ian Cumberland and Gordon "Swatty" Wotherspoon had been Jordan's seniors at R.M.C. and apparently had earned his undying but well-concealed hate. It was a malevolence born of jealousy, no doubt. These cadet wars took their toll in many subtle ways. In my case, my devotion to Ian Cumberland and my trust in him as a soldier, leader, and friend increased as time went on. I saw him and Kitch Jordan in action, and Jordan's weaknesses in character stood out in contrast. Yet it was my lot to serve under Jordan as squadron commander and eventually his second in command for more than a year in Italy and Holland.

This came about when Ian Cumberland was promoted to command the 5th Armoured Brigade after our first battle in the Liri Valley at Cassino in May 1944. Major Jordan was promoted to lieutenant-colonel, commanding the GGHG. Ian had left a recommendation that I become second in command, but Kitch's first act was to call me in and tell me he would promote someone else, my friend Major Tim Hugman. I was relieved to retain my squadron and to avoid what Hugman would have to endure at Regiment Headquarters. A short time later, when I was awarded the Distinguished Service Order for our first action at Cassino, our noble colonel got drunk and announced in the Mess that no one else in the regiment was going to get a D.S.O. until he got his! Across the ocean, when my decoration was announced in the local papers with the citation, my mother said, "Oh, good work! Allan won the D.S.O.! What is next?"

When told the Victoria Cross could be next – but that the highest award was often given posthumously – she said, "Oh, well, tell him not to try for that one." Lieut.-Col. Jordan did get his D.S.O. later on, and he deserved it, but I could easily imagine how livid he must have been when mine was announced so early on.

Finally we got our orders to prepare to move. Rumour had it that we were destined to go to Northern Ireland, although the fact that we were issued with tropical kits caused considerable cynical comment as mosquito nets were not of much use in Antrim.

# WAR ZONE ITALY

## 9

On November 12, 1943, we embarked on His Majesty's troop ship *Scythia* in Bristol harbour. We proceeded to a port in the Clyde where the rest of the convoy joined us. Then we were off to Northern Ireland. For the next ten days we wandered in circles around the North Atlantic, and it was soon quite clear that wherever we were going, it was not Northern Ireland. The convoy had steamed far north before turning south to elude the wolf packs of U-boats that lay off the coasts of the British Isles. On the 19th, a message from Lieut.-Gen. H.D.G. Crerar was read out to all ranks, welcoming us to his formation. It was becoming clear that Italy was our destination. On the evening of the 24th we sailed through the Straits of Gibraltar and, after a two-day run down the coast, we docked at Algiers. Suddenly all Headquarters personnel, including medical doctors and padres, were disembarked and transferred to the *Ville d'Oran*, a French ship. The fighting troops were loaded into transport trucks and dumped twenty miles out of Algiers in the Forêt de Ferdinand, under my command as senior officer, along with several other headquarter-less units, some five thousand men in all.

No preparations for our arrival had been made. The camp left by the departing 8th Army Desert Veterans was filthy. No one was in charge. There were no medical facilities, no food or cooks, not even a pound of chloride of lime for disinfectant. The Horse Guards were the senior regiment, and I was the senior major, so I took charge and tried to organize things. Major Tim Hugman and I decided that we should go into Algiers in an attempt to see General Dwight D. Eisenhower, Supreme Allied Commander, Mediterranean and Italy. We were terrified that a plague would run through the ranks. Even as simple a thing as too much exposure to the tropical sun could ruin us. We were afraid also that men would go AWOL and slip away to explore the Casbah, an extremely dangerous quarter of narrow streets and unfriendly Algerians. So we hurried to Army Headquarters Mediterranean to go to the top, if necessary.

Tim and I got to the headquarters, and our red-banded Guards' caps fooled the American provost into thinking we were generals. We asked the way to General Eisenhower's office, signed in, and started to march to our goal. Before we got there, a full colonel of the British Army stepped out of his office and asked where we were going.

"We have an appointment to see General Eisenhower, sir," we lied.

"When?" he demanded.

"Any time now, sir. He doesn't know about it yet!"

"You had better step in and discuss this with me," he said.

It turned out the colonel was the British liaison officer whose main concern was to "commandeer" our *Scythia* to transport several units of the desert force home to England in time for Christmas. He was completely sympathetic when he heard our dilemma and signed an authorization to draw whatever we needed in transport and supplies. He "attached" a British Service Corps officer to us to draw rations. We got the camp settled and rationed. But what do you do with five thousand young "time bombs"? The men were anxious to bust out of camp and see the world. Route marches were the Army's traditional way to kill time and increase fitness. Swimming in the Mediterranean Sea was another exercise. But after two years of fog and dew in England, our lily-white skin could not stand much sun. I decreed there would be not more than five minutes total exposure in the morning and five minutes in the late afternoon. As it was, we had some severe cases of sunburn, and one of my NCOs died from an apparent heart attack while swimming in the surf, our first casualty. It was a sad day for all.

Our nearby neighbours were the Ghurkas. Their officers suggested that, to pass the time, we protect our flag, proudly flying from the camp flagstaff, against their attempt to capture it. We surrounded it, four or five deep, holding hands. Yet, in the dark of night, the Ghurkas did get through and stole the flag without us even knowing they had done so. We had a pool on the outcome and lost! From then on we had a great respect for the diminutive Ghurkas.

We finally got our orders to move to the ship waiting for us in the harbour at Algiers. The Horse Guards drove in style in our own vehicles. The other units crowded into the transport sent to the Forêt de

Ferdinand camp for the move. On our arrival at the pier, I dismounted the regiment and marched the Horse Guards on board, leaving the vehicles behind. We had not signed for them in the first place! After an uneventful trip to Naples, I disembarked with a small advance party. The troops stayed on board overnight while we were assigned new camp staging areas.

Naples was a filthy city with poverty on all sides. The poor people were dirty, ragged, and were begging even for garbage. They were as much in evidence in 1943 as they were in 1929 when they were pointed out to tourists as one of the "quaint things" about Naples. There is truth to the old saying, "See Naples and die." We were glad to get out of the city.

We moved by long convoys to the south of Italy, the Matera-Gravina districts. As we moved through Marigliano, Avellino, Grotta Minarda, Ariano, and Orta Nova, the countryside grew more attractive and the people cleaner. After Avellino, the landscape became very mountainous, a condition that would plague us for months to come.

Life in the Matera-Gravina districts, where the regiment had reassembled, can best be described by quoting the official regimental history. "Life in a pup tent in the midst of the Italian winter was an experience without parallel. Pup tents were built up, pup tents were dug down. Pup tents were fitted with tin-can stove pipes and tin-can fires. Pup tents were flooded. Pup tents were burned to the ground. There was nothing quite like a pup tent."

"C" Squadron dug into the hillside near Gravina, about ten miles from regimental headquarters in Matera, but we were soon reduced to a piteous state by the ravages of dysentery. Sanitation slit trenches were dug adjacent to each cluster of pup tents because that was as far as the sick, shivering men could crawl. Over one hundred and fifty men had "the groaning sickness" at one time and no medical help was at hand. For five days it rained and the mud became a morass like quicksand with the consistency of glue. For five days it snowed. We huddled around charcoal braziers for warmth at night, and in the morning we chopped the ice off the makeshift breakfast table. Boots were perpetually wet and the only replacements were nameless monstrosities manufactured in India. The other monstrosity was the lethal "V" (for victory) cigarettes the Indians sent us. Even the Italians, who were dying for smokes, would not accept them in trade. We celebrated Christmas 1943 over three days, a squadron at a time. Our first Christmas in Italy was forlorn.

We were in a war zone, and the sullenness of the civilians brought this fact home to us each day. After all, we were only one more occupation of foreign troops in the series of occupations they have endured for the past three hundred years. In January 1943, we were excited to find our new general commanding officer was Major-Gen. Guy Simmonds, formerly commander of the 1st Division in Sicily, a top soldier. We cleaned ourselves as best we could, carrying some men over swollen mountain streams to keep them clean for the new general's inspection. Col. Cumberland had us formed up hours before Gen. Simmonds appeared. On arrival, Simmonds did not bother to inspect even the first row, but jumped up on his jeep, aping his idol Montgomery, and made a short and amazing speech.

"I am General Simmonds, your new Division Commander. You are the Horse Guards" – which we thought we knew – "and as long as I command you, there will be no incidents or trouble. That's all!" This was his address to Canada's senior regiment! We were insulted and glad when, a couple of weeks later, he was promoted once more and left. We had never caused trouble and disliked his arrogance.

My men professed to be embarrassed because such a high proportion of them had earned good-conduct stripes. Some called it an award for undetected crime. I had to order them to put them on. I had trouble with one of the men in the squadron, a trooper who had a university education and used his intelligence to bait NCOs. They continually put him on charge and, as continually, I let him off for lack of evidence. He became a sort of squadron hero, and I finally had to take a hand myself. I had half a dozen different charges prepared in advance, had him paraded to my tent, and advised him that we were now isolated in a theatre of war and that I had the powers of a Field Court-Martial.

I had witnesses out of sight. I ordered him to stand at attention and not to speak under any circumstances until I gave him permission, at which he snarled, "Gee! I would love to slug you." In marched the witness, out came the charges – threatening, disobeying, and so on, and I awarded him one year in Field Punishment Camp, later reduced to six months by Divisional Headquarters. As he was marched away, he vowed to kill me when he got out, and I was quite convinced he meant it. He was slovenly, insolent, and fat. Three months later, he came back shining, smartly turned out, and polite. I was a bit nervous when the sergeant-major announced his return. I had him paraded and said, rather insincerely, "Glad to see you back, Trooper B."

"I doubt that, sir," he said, "but I would like to thank you for the best course I have had in the Army."

"Tell me about it," I said.

"Well, sir, the first twenty-one days I spent down a six-by-six-by-six-foot hole, covered with a straw mat, living on bread and water because I refused to 'double' around the parade square. I was brought up once every seven days. A big 'limey' sergeant, the same one each time, with a rifle and fixed bayonet behind me, ordered me to 'double.' I said, 'F— you, Sergeant,' each time, and he pricked my ass with his bayonet. He repeated the order with no other result, so he threw me down the hole again. I tried everything I could devise to escape, tearing at the hard clay walls till my fingers bled, but after twenty-one days I shuffled along at his order. He stopped me almost immediately, took me over to the shade of a tree, gave me a cigarette, and said, 'The C.O. wants to see you now.' I was put in charge of the library and got out in three months."

"Trooper B," I answered, "your punishment is not over yet. I am making you a corporal immediately in charge of a tank. If you think of what I could do to you as a trooper, let me tell you I can double it as an NCO." He was an excellent crew commander throughout Italy and Holland and never got in trouble again.

During the nervous exhaustion of the approach march to the Liri Valley and Cassino, we asked ourselves over and over, "Will we measure up? Will we be brave enough to stand the battle?" Yet this was what we had trained for all these long, tedious years. We acquired confidence in our abilities, if not in our equipment, which was no match for the German tanks and their 88 mm guns. As the regimental history put it, "On the eleventh of May 1944, after moving from camp to camp toward the Liri Valley, the huge offensive attack on the Gustav Line was commenced by the 4th British and 8th Indian Divisions preceded by a barrage laid down by two thousand guns, the largest concentration in one barrage up to that time. The famous battle for Cassino was under way with the bloody crossing of the Rapido and Garigliano River."

This was our first experience of action. The Liri Valley is a narrow passage that cuts northwest through the Appenines to the Romagna Plain. The slopes of the mountains on each side were occupied with well-dug-in German positions, and every inch of the valley was exposed to direct observation from the mountainsides. Every conceivable resting place on the valley floor had been preregistered by the German mortars whose accuracy was terrifying. "C" Squadron was given the extreme right flank of the divisional advance to protect Highway 6 immediately under the Monte Cassino and Monte Grande hills, the place of honour.

The C.O., Ian Cumberland, after giving me my orders, said, "Good luck and goodbye, Allan."

I said, "How about *au revoir* instead of goodbye?" Later he told me that he had a recce (reconnaissance) report of forty-eight German tanks in our "C" Squadron front but he only told me "a large force" was in our vicinity. We had twelve Shermans and eight armoured recce vehicles which, in fact, were American Honey tanks with their turrets removed. In place of the 37 mm cannon we mounted on each a .5-inch machinegun for which we carried a lethal and highly illegal aircraft load of armour-piercing, incendiary and explosive bullets.

The moment of truth had come. As my last vehicles descended into the small ravine and struggled up the steep slope on the far side to re-form around me, we were alone at last in enemy territory. We paused momentarily, half expecting all hell to break loose. Our light recce vehicles began to fan out in front of us, as planned, when suddenly my wireless "command" set refused to work. My troops were in sight but out of touch! I had no way to control them except by hand signals relayed ahead, as we had done when mounted on our horses as cavalry. Fortunately I was able to stop the advance for ten minutes while my wireless corporal, Walter Stitt, literally tore the controls apart and somehow rebuilt them!

The silence was broken only by the heavy throbs of our tanks and the sounds of distant battle. Our nerves were stretched to the breaking point, and the country ahead, with wires of highly strung grapevines, was just high enough to spoil a tank commander's vision or choke him. The prospect was as poor as one could imagine.

In control once more, thanks to Stitt, I ordered the advance to proceed slowly, keeping in visual contact and together as a unit. We saw the heavy tank-tracks of vehicles recently departed when we came to our first clearing, an inviting open space with a house about two hundred yards away. I kept our main body under cover while the light tanks under Sgt. Sewell slipped around on a flanking movement. When I thought he would be in position, even though there was no sign of life around the house, I ordered every tank available to open fire on it simultaneously with machineguns and high explosives.

Sewell's light tank was "Four Able" and an anguished, "Hello,

Four Able," "Hello, Four Able," came over my wireless. "For Christ sake, you are firing at me! Stop it or I'll come back and pistol-whip the lot of you!" A ripple of laughter could be heard as the firing stopped on my order. The tension was broken.

Lieut. Cyrus Gaskin ran his tank up to the house and jumped down. A small figure in black tank overalls and beret, he kicked in the door, threw in a grenade, and nearly fainted in amazement as over seventy Germans crawled out, tears streaming down their faces and thoroughly demoralized.

We found a 75 mm anti-tank gun on one side of the house and a huge tracked, anti-tank vehicle with an 88 mm gun called a Ferdinand on the other, both knocked out by our speculative barrage, along with the corpses of their crews. We also found the officer in charge of the Ferdinand shot through both legs and in great pain. The medical kit in his vehicle was full of pills of all descriptions but no regular supplies, so we eased his pain with our morphine kit. We had the foresight to make a note of the frequencies on their radio equipment and found a code book which appeared to be current. The Germans were unaware of its capture for the next three weeks.

What does one do with prisoners? We had no instructions except to send them back to our lines. We had no desire to have them attack our rear, but we could not spare any vehicles or men to escort them. So I had them pile all their arms and helmets and remove their boots, and I ran the tanks over the pile, destroying them. Then, barefoot, they began the march back to our lines carrying their wounded. I hope they made it. Our infantry was not in a charitable mood!

The squadron deployment continued, but I had to be careful that our elation and new-found confidence did not do us in. Finally, after many small encounters, we reached our allotted positions. We had been lucky. The fact that we steadily advanced and overcame the rearguard positions left by the Germans seemed to convince them we were supported by a large force coming up behind us. In fact, there was no one. We had been lucky and had very few casualties. With Capt. Douglas Crashley acting as my second in command, we found ourselves by late afternoon in an unenviable position for tanks, with individual troops a mile apart guarding vital spots to protect the right flank of the main divisional advance. The textbook said that the infantry would come up and protect us for the night. We were ordered to retire to the comparative safety of a strong point formed around the Lord Strathcona's Horse on the centre line. The LSH, still commanded by Col. Pat Griffin, whom I had taken prisoner on his exercise in Norfolk, sent our liaison officer back with the information that he had no room in his tank laager for the Horse Guards. So, in a moment of disgust and pique, I sent the officer back to Col. Griffin telling him it would be our privilege to protect them for the night!

Resigned to staying in our exposed positions, we took as much of a defensive position as we could, literally in full view of the Germans on Monte Cassino. We were not shelled as we dug our slit trenches, and we thought that at last there would be some quiet. Crashley and I, facing each other, settled deep into our slit trench beside our tank, and listened as our widely dispersed troops reported on the wireless – all quiet!

Our assault troop in "white" scout cars, which are clumsy, half-tracked armoured personnel carriers, had been lost all day. They had been unable to keep up with the tank advance over some of the rougher country. Now they were lumbering straight across the open fields toward us, raising a large column of dust. We could not raise them on the wireless to have them turn around. We watched with apprehension as they hurried to rejoin us. The Germans suddenly began firing their mortars as fast as they could. A rain of high explosive mortar shells hit us without warning. The blast from the first shell within yards of our slit trench plastered Crashley's shirt against his body as if hit by a hurricane. I thought we surely had been hit. Somewhat stunned, we saw the closely packed white cars receive shell after shell, as we scrambled in haste to the comparative safety of our command tank so we could communicate with the rest of the squadron. Seven of the assault troop were wounded, including Lieut. T.R. (Fuzz) Richards, the troop commander. One of his men, Trooper C.L. Axtell, died later as they tried to evacuate him. We dispersed, zig-zagging at speed to a more distant cover. The German mortars were accurate enough to put a shell in your turret if you stood still long enough! So we got out of range and reassembled as blessed darkness fell.

In true tank fashion, we then had to do our own maintenance, unlike the Air Force which had other crews to do its maintenance and refuelling. With two hours of maintenance for every three hours of running time, fatigue was a real enemy to us all. It was nearly thirty-six hours before we got a chance to rest. Only the young can take that kind of fatigue and come up for more.

A few days later, to my complete surprise and astonishment, I was informed by Divisional Headquarters that I had been awarded the Distinguished Service Order. What a recognition for "C" Squadron's first day in action! I could put the ribbon up immediately and did so with great pride. The actual medal would be pinned later at an investiture. I only found out what the citation said when a clipping from the *Toronto Star* was mailed to me by my mother. The clipping, dated May 24, 1944, read as follows:

> After breaking of the Hitler Line, the Squadron of a Canadian Armoured Reconnaissance Regt., commanded by Major Burton, was given the task of protecting the right flank of the Division behind the Hitler line. His Citation reads – "Although his headquarters was under intense mortar fire throughout the day, this Officer placed and controlled his troops with superb skill and cool-headedness, succeeding in locating them in every position ordered.
>
> "The Squadron destroyed at least three 75 mm guns and one 88 mm self-propelled gun, capturing approximately 100 of the enemy as well as killing many others.
>
> "This resulted in the right flank of the Division being kept entirely free from any interference by the Germans throughout the day in the Hitler line in the Acquino area.
>
> "Early next morning Major Burton led his Squadron in sweeping the area from the divisional centre line across the railway, back up the railway to Melfa and clearing the area of all enemy pockets.
>
> "During both these days the Squadron suffered no vehicle casualties, there were no personnel killed, and only four or five wounded by mortar fire.
>
> "The bold, skillful way in which he handled his Squadron without thought of personal danger was of material assistance to the general advance of the Division and the success of subsequent actions."

Several days later we relieved "B" Squadron in the dark and found that we were pinned in position behind a knoll by a German 88 mm from Monte Grande across the valley from our position. I ordered Lieut. C.C. ("Bud") Wass to try to pinpoint the enemy gun so we could destroy it with our artillery. This entailed sending my second in command, Captain Crashley, to liaise with the British from whose zone the gun was firing. The British Grenadier Guards had had a rough time on this hill the day before and retreated. Lieut. Wass very bravely showed himself in a top window of a house on the crest above us. Incredibly, the Germans took him on with the 88 mm large calibre instead of with a sniper's bullet. He was only some four or five hundred yards from the gun. The huge gun was inaccurate at such a close range, and a very pale and shaken Lieut. Wass was able to give me an eight-figure map reference. We "stonked" (bombarded with concentrated fire) the position with a battery of 25-pounders of the 8th Field Regiment, Royal Canadian Artillery, on which we had a priority call. Our heavy fire destroyed the enemy gun, with the result that the Grenadier Guards were able to walk up the hill on the next attack on May 27, with only minor opposition. Lieut. Wass was awarded a very well-deserved Military Cross for this act of personal bravery and important reconnaissance which saved many lives.

On June 10, there was regimental inspection by our divisional commander, Major-Gen. Bert Hoffmeister, who congratulated us on our work in the Liri Valley. Our general was a first-class commander and one who gave the men great confidence that we would win our battles under him. During six weeks of rest and sunshine near the Volturno River, a huge reunion and "bash" were arranged, attended by all the Horse Guard officers in Italy. We boasted we had at least one Horse Guard officer in every formation H.Q.! Brig. Ian Cumberland, accompanied by his Staff Officer Lieut.-Col. J.W. Eaton, my old friend of early Horse Guard days, and the Eatonia and Simco troops of "C" Squadron were there.

Drink flowed freely, as everyone pooled his rations. "Blue flame" made its first appearance at this party. Almost straight alcohol, this Italian schnapps gave me the worst hangover of my entire life! We were celebrating promotions and decorations but mainly just being alive and being Horse Guards together in this beautiful spot.

Then, on July 29, after hours of preparation, repainting all the vehicles and new equipment, where possible, the rumour that we were to be inspected by the King himself proved correct. His Majesty King George VI carefully examined every man. We were immaculate. Gen. Sir Oliver Leese, 8th Army Commander, of which our Division, the 5th Canadian Armoured, was proud to be a part, addressed us. Sir Oliver was a huge man, as bulky as a mountain, but his voice was as high-pitched as the scream of a French locomotive. "Jolly good show, Horse Guards," he piped shrilly, "and you stood well too!" His high-pitched voice, contrasted with his physical bulk, gave our regimental mimics a first-class line with which to perpetuate and recount the occasion for months to come.

For three weeks in August, the temperature in the tanks ran 115 degrees Fahrenheit each day. One day, between four in the morning and sunset, I drank four gallons of water or tea, all of which came streaming out of my pores. We could not get out to relieve ourselves in daylight. It was so hot it was nearly impossible to mark the changing situation on the map because the protective talc was slippery with sweat. Our final objective was to be the Valley of the Po, eight hundred miles north of where we had started in Gravina. No less than eight hundred bridges had been laid by the engineers up the length of Italy, one for each mile!

I saw through my binoculars a British destroyer off the Adriatic coast, on which officers in immaculate whites were being served tea on deck, while we were sweaty and covered with grime. I nearly turned my 76 mm tank gun on them, but figured they outgunned us! They turned their 4.5 inch ship's guns on targets we were engaging, so I felt better about them, though envious. A German coastal gun sent a couple of shells in the destroyer's direction, and they steamed hurriedly out of range, leaving the Germans and ourselves to our private war.

For three terrible weeks in the fall of 1944, our tanks were useless because of the rain and mud. We were dismounted to hold somewhat static positions as infantry. The Irish Regiment gave us a twenty-four-hour, street-clearing course, which I will never forget. This consisted of standing six abreast in front of a brick wall with our steel helmets on, while snipers, concealed from twenty to two-hundred yards away from us, fired live ammunition into the wall just over our heads! The object of this unpleasant experience was to be able to identify the source and position of the sniper fire without flinching. No one got hurt and, surprisingly enough, we caught on very quickly. But our nerves were a bit the worse for wear because no tank man likes to be out of his tank and exposed to fire any more than the infantryman, who is completely claustrophobic when confined in a tank, likes the thought of being a huge sitting duck!

To our considerable relief we regained our tanks. The devil you know is better than the one you don't! Unfortunately, due to Prime Minister Mackenzie King's conscription policies, we began to run out of volunteers to replace the comparatively small but steady drain

on our crews as casualties increased. At one point, one-fifth of my
tanks had only one driver in each of them, instead of the regular
crew of five men. Without crews, they were unable to fight. Small
wonder that in 1940 the troops voted solidly against the Liberals in
protest. This vote confirmed King's opinion that we were a bunch of
radicals to be feared on our return to Canada. After all, he had been
publicly booed while inspecting troops in England eariier in the war,
and now this.

I was proud of my men. All had acquitted themselves extremely
well, and having survived the first ordeal of fire together and having
been singled out for special recognition as a squadron, we knew,
as others had known before us, why the Regimental Horse Guard
slogan was *Nulli Secundus*, second to none. The training for battle
was suddenly worth it!

In the weeks that followed one acquired an awareness and a new
appreciation of life and death. The war deepened my knowledge
of myself and of how other human beings behave when stripped of
rank and social grace. When put to the ultimate test, immature persons often show great hidden strengths and courage and become confident leaders. Others, bully-like, glorying in their physical strength,
collapse when their puffed-up image of superiority has the air let
out, pricked by their own inner terrors. Each and every person is a
complex melding of strengths and weaknesses, nobility and selfishness. Each has his little superstition, the mores of his ancestors.
I had a ''lucky'' coin, a Canadian silver dollar. It was a constant
reminder of home, for it had been part of my pay as a part-time soldier in 1939 when King George VI and Queen Elizabeth visited Toronto
and I, as a Horse Guard, joined the crowds lining the streets to cheer.
It was fascinating to watch the private part of even the hardest person unfold, as stress, strain, and events peeled the protective layers
of social or anti-social behaviour from a vast cross-section of youths.
These ordinary Canadians, most between eighteen and twenty-five
years of age, some younger, a few older, were forced to ponder the
meaning of life as they learned to destroy it or be destroyed by it.

Once I watched a very personable, modest young officer get killed
through blind faith. After the painful experience I coined the phrase,
''God doesn't love a stupid person,'' that is, one who flaunts Him.
We were under heavy shellfire when Lieut. X suddenly got up from
his cover and walked around in a demonstration of his belief that his

own prayers and those of his wife and family would preserve him and keep him safe. I was furious with him when he paid no attention to my shouts, and came close to shooting him myself because he was disobeying orders, exposing our positions, and endangering the lives of fifty of his troops through his display of "faith." Then he went down, wounded. A small piece of shrapnel had nicked his neck, a minor wound but one that necessitated sending him out of action for medical treatment to avoid "gas gangrene" from the shell fragment. I warned him. The wound came close to being a "self-inflicted" wound, and I said I should court-martial him. He replied, "I knew my prayers would preserve me. Anyone else would have been killed." In a few days he came back to us and repeated the performance. In the flaunting of his faith and the trying of God's patience, he was killed by a shell. He was a nice young man and should have lived a good life, growing old gracefully in his church. But we did not miss him where the action was.

The long months from May 1944 to January 1945 dragged on, first in hundred-degree heat and then in bone-chilling damp fogs when autumn arrived. Endless moves, skirmishes, and some minor battles kept us busy during this time. I had upwards of two-hundred Italian partisans "under my command." Most came along only as a sure way of securing extra rations, but a few, less than ten per cent, were trustworthy, brave, loyal, and worthy of the highest praise. As soon as we arrived at a *paisan*'s house in his village, he stopped fighting, and when we reached the far side of the town, we had very few of the partisans left to face the enemy. This syndrome had little to do with bravery or lack of it, but rather with the peasant's view that, having regained his house, it would be foolish in the extreme to be killed in someone else's backyard.

I was never left out of battle and only missed one minor action of the regiment. Whether or not this was Kitch Jordan's attempt to make my life shorter and more miserable, I never could decide. As a matter of fact, I did not think about it much at the time, but the usual rule was that the C.O. was left out of battle every other engagement, while the squadron's second in command took over. As I was never left out of battle, my new second in command, who took over after Crashley, blamed me for taking each of the actions myself. It was certainly not my doing but Jordan's. My new second in command was Capt. Alexander H. Crosbie, of the Newfoundland Crosbies, a first-class soldier nicknamed, of course, "Bing."

Finally, in January 1945, having gone eight hundred miles "up" Italy, mostly the hard way, worn down to 132 pounds in my uniform and suffering from hemorrhoids, an affliction I had in common with Napoleon, and thinking the regiment would see no more action in Italy, as we were north of the Po River, I reported to the medical officer. I could hardly walk a hundred yards. After his examination, he announced I had dangerously infected hemorrhoids and must go to hospital immediately. Thus my "war wound" got me in the end!

# HOSPITAL AND HOME

## 10

I had over four years of overseas service, two in action, and had never been wounded or in hospital. I had to go out with such a mundane, albeit painful, complaint! In a moment of compassion, Col. Jordan allowed me to go to hospital with my own scout car and driver. Little did he realize that as we went from hospital to hospital, each chief surgeon in turn would examine me and say, '"There is only one man who can operate on that mess, Dr. Ernest Janes, the famous surgeon from Hamilton, Ontario." Dr. Janes was eight hundred miles away in Caserta, the town from which we had started our advance to the Liri Valley. My driver drove me down the entire way, in stages, during which I visited many old friends in hospitals along the way. As it turned out, my condition was far more serious than I had believed, and I was hospitalized in Caserta for three months. The first month was a constant round of sitz-baths and huge amounts of food and a brandy eggnog every time I woke up, interspersed with hour after hour of solid sleep. I put on twenty pounds my first twenty-one days in hospital before they could operate on me.

Major A.H. (Bing) Crosbie, now promoted to Command '"C" Squadron, took the squadron into a short engagement on the Po Estuary to clear out a pocket of Germans. He did so with such brilliance, taking a hundred prisoners, that he was awarded the Distinguished Service Order. I was delighted at the news and surprised when Bing, my rather reserved '"Newfie" friend, arrived in Caserta, having hitch-hiked eight hundred miles to visit me in hospital and bring me a bottle of rum! He told me, excitedly, that he had applied a stratagem that we had practised months ago and that it had worked perfectly. Months before we had read in an intelligence report that the Russian tanks had employed a certain manoeuvre when they had been held up by marshy country, racing the motors of their bogged tanks as if dozens were advancing, while dismounting the crews to attack on foot. I believe Bing forgave me for saving the last battle for him!

Early in 1945 the regiment left Italy for Northwest Europe, and I was left behind in hospital in Caserta. I had never been away from the regiment before for any length of time, and after three and a half months in hospital and convalescence, I was sent to a reinforcement depot. I became a self-appointed inspector general of the thousand-man unit with the enthusiastic concurrence of the commanding officer, who had never been in action and did not want to face that possibility. I was restless and, as I regained my strength, I drilled, inspected, and attempted to get some discipline and order into the men. We got orders to board ship for Marseilles, and I was appointed to command the troops for the move. We were loaded into freight cars marked *Huit Chevaux, Quarante Hommes* (Eight Horses, Forty Men), the same ones used in the First World War, which had straw on the floor but no sanitation or water. We started the long, slow journey up the Rhone Valley to Ghent in Belgium. This meant stopping the train every two hours for water, relief, and food. It took four days to do the trip that modern French trains now do in four hours.

Along the way, we passed through the Cote d'Or and the famous vineyards of Burgundy. On arrival, after turning the troops over to the depot staff, I got permission to try and locate my regiment, the Horse Guards. Security, of course, would not divulge their whereabouts, so I drove blindly in ever-widening concentric circles around Ghent until I came across some of the wine-coloured 5th Armoured Division shoulder patches. I bluffed a provost post sergeant into letting me examine his map and found GGHG headquarters and reported to Colonel Jordan at regimental headquarters in Iseghem. I was so glad to rejoin my unit, I would have gone back as a troop commander. When I appeared before Kitch, he, with typical heavy-handed humour, said, "Where have you been, you malingering son of a bitch?" Then he quickly said, "I want you up here tomorrow morning as my second in command. I'll see that you are released from depot today."

I was speechless and glad to be welcomed home. One real problem was that my mail never caught up with me, and for six months I did not receive a single letter or parcel from home. I could not imagine what was going on in Canada. I kept writing increasingly despondent letters to Audrey and whimsical ones to the children. Gail was nearing five, and Jamie, who was born six months after I went overseas, was four. It was hard to imagine them, as I had no pictures or reports because of the lost mail. Fortunately, I realized my incoming mail must be lost, because it seemed unlikely that my family and friends would all disown me at the same time!

One letter I wrote to little Gail one night, as I sat and watched the clear sky full of twinkling stars, became the basis of an advertisement for Victory Bonds. It was all about the "Twinkle Fairies." My brother-in-law, Gerry Maccabe, a brilliant and volatile advertising man, read it and changed the names and ran it as a successful magazine advertisement: "A real live letter from an overseas officer to his little daughter whom he hasn't seen for four years," and so on. I forgave Gerry for using my material when the ad won a top ad award! It went like this:

> *Hello Darling:*
> *I am on a big ship in the middle of the ocean, and thinking awfully hard about you and Mummy. Some day when Daddy is home again, we will get on a lovely big ship and sail away out where the winds come from – to an island Mummy and I know about that's all sunshine and flowers. Or maybe we'll just stay home for a while and play. We could go up to the farm and see the dogs and horses, or visit Grandma in the Big House and see the goldfish.*
>
> *I don't know when Daddy can come home, but if you say your prayers every night and wish very hard, it may not be much longer now.*
>
> *But darling, please try to be a good little girl. Remember the Twinkle Fairies that live in the stars and listen to the wishes of good little girls and boys. When you're good it makes the Twinkle Fairies happy – then they will pull the clouds away from the doors of their stars so that you can watch them twinkle and dance.*
>
> *Wish very hard and be good friends with the Twinkle Fairies – maybe they'll listen and help Daddy come back to you and Mummy soon.*
>
> > *Big hugs and kisses,*
> > *Daddy*

The Colonel seemed genuinely glad to see me once more. I was more than pleased, not only to be able to return to my old unit, but also to come back with a promotion to second in command of the regiment. The position is now called Deputy Commanding Officer.

I drove a regimental jeep back to Ghent and parked it in the guarded vehicle area overnight so I could leave at dawn the next morning. True to his word, Kitch Jordan cut through all the red tape and got my release from depot in a matter of hours. When I came to get my jeep in the morning, my high spirits were dashed. The trooper on guard duty overnight had stolen my jeep and gone AWOL. I was furious, but more worried what Jordan would say when I arrived late and reported my stolen jeep.

I hitched a ride back to Iseghem, where the Horse Guards were billeted, and as I drove up to regimental headquarters, low and behold, my missing jeep was parked outside the building at the front door, with a trooper from another unit at the wheel, asking directions to his unit, the New Brunswick Hussars. The poor fool had inadvertently brought my jeep home. I placed him under arrest, marched into the orderly room to report for duty, and then began to feel a pang of sympathy for a fellow soldier who went AWOL merely because he wanted to get back to his unit. I had my prisoner sent back to his regiment with a note describing the incident and recommending that the Hussars secure his release from depot and that the theft and AWOL charges be dropped.

Almost every house in the small town of Iseghem had one or more Horse Guards billeted in it, including two troopers at the local bordello. This was not discovered until the two troopers asked to be moved because, while they were more than happy at the life, they simply could not take it anymore. They were physically worn out. They could not make parades and accommodate the madam as well! I called the burgomaster in to explain how he came to allot two men to the whorehouse. He said he had been short two spaces so he had surveyed the ranks and had picked the two men most likely to enjoy it.

We soon got orders to move to Nijmegen, the area in Holland still littered with British glider wrecks from the abortive airborne assault on the bridges over the Rhine. Arnhem, Zwolle, Harderwijk, and Assen became familiar names as we mopped up pockets of Germans and Dutch left behind to protect their retreating forces. One of the greatest shocks we got was that not by any means were all Dutch people on our side, although we had always thought of the Dutch as our allies. At least 50 per cent of the people in every town we liberated were pro-German, and in each case half of the inhabitants upon their liberation put the other half under arrest as collaborators. We witnessed some shocking scenes of revenge. In one incident, the mayor of Arnhem was shorn of his hair completely, along with the women of the city who had collaborated with the Germans, in front of a large crowd. The mayor's shorn locks were put on a silver platter with mock ceremony, salted and peppered, then placed in the gutter where the mayor was forced to crawl on hands and knees and eat them, the crowd howling with laughter. The women, each bald as a billiard ball, were divided into labour gangs and marched to do menial jobs of cleaning up the town and spat upon as they passed.

On one occasion, some Dutch prisoners were taken and our Dutch liaison officer, a Count, lined them up for interrogation. They refused to talk, so he slapped the nearest man a stinging blow in the face and stubbed his glowing cigarette out on the next man's cheek saying, "Take them away and shoot them!"

I stepped in at this moment and said, "I am sorry, Captain, these are our prisoners and I can't allow that."

His rage subsided and he said, "Of course, forgive me, but these four men were my jailers in the concentration camp for four years and shooting is too good for them."


I was in action until four days before the end of the war in Europe. We all knew that victory was a matter of hours away, and we worried more about being killed needlessly now than we had in the heat of battle. So I was doubly relieved when a jeep arrived to the front with the message that I was due for a week's leave in London. I left immediately for our base and, passing a tent in our officers' lines, I saw my friend Tim Hugman sitting and drinking, all by himself. He waved to me to come in, obviously delighted to have a companion. "Have a drink," he said, offering a bottle of Scotch with very little left in it.

"Tim," I said, "you haven't got much there. I'll get mine. I have a full bottle in my kit."

Tim wagged his finger and said, "Allan, this is your bottle. You better have the rest."

I had saved that bottle for weeks and, enraged, I said, "You dirty son of a bitch, what a thing to do to a friend!"

"Allan, old boy, my only excuse is that I just got word I am going home and you weren't here to celebrate with me."

"Okay, Tim, good enough, but every time we meet in the future, as long as we live, you owe me a bottle of Scotch on demand." To this

he solemnly agreed. I have met Tim Hugman, honourable man that
he is, six or more times in the forty years since the war. He lives in
Vancouver, and at each meeting he has produced a full bottle of Scotch
in repayment of his solemn debt.

Accommodation in London was non-existent. By great good fortune, a group of us, all Canadian officers, ran into Countess Lloyd
George, whose daughter had married a wing commander in the RCAF.
We had all been to the wedding before going to Italy. The Countess
opened her flat to the six of us and could not have been kinder.

The great news came at last. The war in Europe was over, and
London became a madhouse. Along with thousands of others, we
tumbled along through Green Park to stand in front of Buckingham
Palace, choked with emotion and loaded to the brim with drink, while
the King and Queen came out on the balcony to acknowledge the joy
and cheerful roar of the multitudes below them. It was a once-in-a-
lifetime scene, the crushing good humour, a great city at a stand-still,
people everywhere, laughing, dancing, hugging, some crying and singing "There'll Always Be an England."

Every restaurant in London had been reserved by the civilian
population years before in anticipation of V-E Day celebrations. So
we resigned ourselves to sit around the Countess's flat and consume
a five-gallon cask of brandy we had acquired, when the Countess
came home with her lovely daughter and a couple of friends and
said, "Where do you boys want to go? Would the Savoy do?"

We hooted with laughter. "What a silly question! Would the Savoy
do?" we chortled, appreciating the joke. To our amazement, she had
a reserved table for twenty at the Savoy, and we ate, drank Dom
Perignon, and danced all night in a celebration that was like all New
Year's Eves rolled into one. We drank toast after toast to the generos-
ity and the beauty of Countess Lloyd George. Bless her, wherever
she is.

Back in Holland, a huge mound of letters, parcels, and other mail
was suddenly dumped in front of me. My mail, always weeks behind
me, had travelled all over Italy, through France, Belgium, and most
of Holland before catching up with me. I solemnly sorted the dozens
of letters from Audrey and Dad and Mother in piles according to
date and number. I quickly read the last letter first, hungry for news,
and then started reading them one by one. It was some time before
Audrey realized I was not getting any mail of any kind and that her
questions and loneliness were only answered by my miserable home-

sickness and self-pity. So we were each writing the other faithfully but without communication, as if addressing someone who could not answer.

In short order, the first experimental draft of veterans was assembled to be sent home to Canada. I was chosen to lead them because the authorities had discovered I had accumulated more "points," more hours in action, fewer leaves, and so on, than any other Canadian officer of field rank. Being put in charge of one thousand men of dozens of different units, all seasoned veterans, all anxious to get home, was a considerable challenge. My first problem was to assemble them on parade and check them off to make sure we loaded the correct number and names on the train that was to take us to the Channel port of Ostend. We could not afford any stowaways. My only speech to them, once assembled into their own units and under their own NCOs, was that we needed and expected complete obedience, and anyone who went absent, delayed, or otherwise gave us any trouble would be sent up to Germany for two years' occupation duty. Such a punishment was beyond me, and even if they suspected it was, not one man was willing to contest the issue. We had no trouble at all.

The Rev. Bob Snead, a Baptist minister, was assigned to us as padre, and we became close friends before our journey was over. We were marched down to the docks and watched young draftees from England disembark from the landing craft tanks that had brought them across the stormy Channel. They were on their way to occupy Germany and looked dejected. They had been seasick all the way. I was ordered to have my men board immediately. There was no chance to clean the filthy ships before we embarked. The poor fellows marched below decks on these crafts designed to transport tanks to beachheads rather than a thousand men across the English Channel. Sleeping hammocks were arranged in rows and tiers of four the length of the ship. Below deck, the stench of ancient vomit spoiled an already dank atmosphere. The poor men had to lie down one above the other, stacked like cordwood, and stay there for a trip which took eleven hours, while the cumbersome, ungainly ship was tossed and twisted by a severe storm and waves such as only the English Channel can produce. I was somewhat better off because I stood in the small wheelhouse on the bridge with the padre and Matthew Halton, the war correspondent for the CBC. Fortunately we were all good sailors, but for the next eleven hours we suffered, too. Halton did an interview with me, and his broadcast was heard by my wife and family, the first news they had that I was coming home!

When my sorry-looking contingent disembarked at Southend in the Thames Estuary, we assembled on the train platform, waiting for a fresh young contingent of Guards to vacate the waiting troop train so we could board it. My lot were tanned and bemedalled but sullen, unshaven, crumpled, tired, and in no mood to be shown up by the white, beardless conscripts who started to move past us. One of the conscripts said in a loud cockney voice, "Look at the filthy bloody Canadians! Gar, no wonder it took us so long to win the war!" There was a low growl from my men and, without any command, they encircled the contingent. The frightened young officer in the lead stopped his advance in bewilderment. I pushed my way in and advised him that he would, in a loud voice, humbly apologize on behalf of the British Army to the Canadian Army, and to veterans in particular, for the rudeness of his raw recruits. He jumped up on a nearby box and gave us a sincere apology. I ordered No. 1 Experimental Draft to fall back and reform ranks, while the young recruits quickly left the scene. Not another word was spoken on either side.

We were taken first to Aldershot. There we felt an atmosphere that was somewhat less than cordial and a bit bewildering to us. Aldershot had been an "Army town" since well before the Crimean War and was hardened to soldiers. Some weeks before, over a real or imagined grievance, some Canadian troops had rioted against the town. We were only too happy to get out of there in a few days.

We expected, on arrival at our new camp, well isolated in the countryside, that we would get leave to London in short order. But we were told no leave; in fact, no pay until just before embarkation and that would not be for at least two weeks. This was a great hardship because the men did not have enough money to buy cigarettes or beer. Even worse, there were no cigarettes in the canteens. The mood of the men became more difficult hourly, and they looked to me to correct the "snafu" – Situation Normal, All Fouled Up. No one could believe that the administration would deliberately be so stupid. We were certainly not being treated like returning heroes. As we soon found out, the politicians in Canada feared our return as a potential disruptive force to the docile democracy run by Mackenzie King's Liberals.

I did manage to get the men some pay and a small supply of cigarettes, but leave was withheld until each man had undergone a series of rehabilitation lectures on how to act once more as a civilian! These lectures were given by what in Russia would be called political commissars. Certainly none of the lecturers had seen action, unless it was in a back street in Hull or the Windmill Theatre in London. We were amused, bored, then insulted and infuriated in turn when the crassness of these civilians in uniform and their fears of us as returning veterans became daily more apparent. The lectures were suddenly stopped, leave rosters were produced, and a tentative date for embarkation was set.

When the men got back from leave, they were broke. That was their own fault, but once more there were no cigarettes. Yet we knew there were hundreds of thousands in cartons in the main postal depot in Slough. I found out the officer in charge at Slough was an ex-member of my regiment, and borrowing enough money from officers and NCOs to buy a carton for each of the thousand men on the draft, I set out to get them from the postmaster. He would not open his stores until another officer and I agreed to play poker with him while we consumed a bottle of Scotch we had brought him as a "softener." Several hours later, in the middle of the night, we had secured and paid for our thousand cartons of cigarettes and had earned enough money to pay back the majority of the "loan" from the officers and NCOs in addition.

On arrival back at camp, we found the truck convoys forming to be loaded, so as each man boarded his vehicle, he received a carton of cigarettes to take on board for the journey home. At quayside, Movement Control took over. All the officers were called out and boarded. All the NCOs were called out and boarded, and then the men were loaded alphabetically, without regard to unit. My well-organized unit was dispersed in an hour, and it took us six days at sea before we got them sorted out once more!

I was the officer in command of the troops, and the Rev. Robert Snead, as the padre, was my right-hand man. Bob was an extremely popular man. In action in Europe, he began collecting and cataloguing slivers and shards of stained glass broken from the windows of ancient cathedrals as the result of bombardment. He stopped the process when he discovered that some of his men were bringing him some pieces of stained-glass windows that had not been bombarded yet. When Bob returned to his church, Calvary Baptist in Toronto, he assembled all his glass, and an artist made him a large and most beautiful stained-glass window. There is a keyed drawing of the window at its base, which indicates where each historic piece of glass in the window came from. The Memorial Window was paid for in a unique way. K.O.R., or King's Orders and Regulations, have a habit of not changing very much. Bob found a passage in them dating back to World War I, which set down a daily allowance in cash to each officer travelling without a servant. He secured the proper forms, got each of us in the contingent to apply to Ottawa for the appropriate pay, and secured a promise from each of us to donate all the proceeds to him for his Memorial Window. God's work is done in mysterious ways!

When the ship docked at Halifax, all troops were confined on board except O.C. troops. I was allowed off to make a phone call home. I went to the nearest pay phone and asked for my home number, eager to speak to Audrey. There was no answer. Thinking she was possibly at my father's house with the children, I phoned there and was told no one was home and that my mother was in the Toronto General Hospital. I was troubled and worried. What a letdown after weeks of expecting to hear familiar voices. Depressed, I turned and spied a magazine stand which also sold light snacks. As I stepped up, tanned, fit, and with a full number of campaign ribbons on my chest, two young soldiers fell back. Their respect turned to a look of disbelief as I ordered a copy of *Canadian Homes and Gardens* and a large glass of milk. I was home! I had not had a glass of fresh milk in four and a half years, and no whisky in the world could have diverted me away from that first taste of home. The magazine had scenes of ordinary homes, with average people, and staring at them gave me the strange sensation of walking down Main Street.

Worried, I climbed the gangway and as I entered the ship, I heard a complete stranger in civilian clothes say to the purser, "Well, when Major Burton returns, tell him Charlie Jaggs was asking for him."

I went up to the stranger and introduced myself to him. He beamed and said, "Come on to my house, I have a surprise for you, and bring anyone you like with you."

"It's very kind of you, sir, but we are all confined to the ship."

"Not you, Major Burton. I have made all the arrangements." He showed me the necessary papers. Quickly deciding I would take Bob Snead with me, because I had no idea where we were going and he did not drink, I collected him and away we went in Charles Jaggs's car.

I still had no idea who Jaggs was. "Are you from the Citizens' Committee?" I asked.

"Yes, I am the chairman."

How nice of the Halifax Citizens' Committee to seek me out, I thought. No, that can't be the answer. "Are you Red Cross?"

"Yes, I am the chairman," Charlie Jaggs answered.

Mystified, I lapsed into silence until we entered his house. "Could I possibly phone Toronto? I tried earlier but couldn't raise anyone."

Charlie Jaggs said, "Let me get you a drink. I have held a line open to your father for the last two hours."

I dashed to the phone while Charlie Jaggs poured a drink. Almost before I asked any other question, I whispered, "Dad, who the hell is Charlie Jaggs?"

"Why, he is our Simpsons' general manager in Halifax. In fact, Charlie is Mr. Halifax."

Dad and Audrey were at the Caledon Club for the weekend. Mother was in hospital but it was nothing serious. The first words Audrey and I mumbled to each other after four and a half years were, "God, how I love you! How are the children?" Then there was a long silence, as we were too choked to speak but mumbled more unintelligible things. Then Dad filled me in on Mother and Charlie and Verna Jaggs, my host and hostess, who became good friends in the years to come.

We arrived in Union Station at Toronto at the ungodly hour of 2:30 a.m. The air was thick with the murmur of excited wives and parents while we detrained and formed up one last time, a relatively small contingent of some five hundred by now, because small parties had been detached for different destinations along the way. I wished them well and dismissed them.

Engulfed, I could not see Audrey in the milling crowd, and had a moment of panic that maybe she could not come. Then we were clinging wordlessly together until the spell was broken by Frank Heeney, Dad's faithful old driver, who welcomed me home and said, "I have the car outside. Your mother is waiting at the hospital. We had better go." We went to see Mother, then to 136 Glen Road to my father's, and then home at last at 4:00 a.m.

Home at last, alone with dear Audrey, the kids asleep upstairs. All's well that ends well, but this was the beginning of a new life. I was thirty and had much to be thankful for. Miraculously I had never been seriously hurt, even our families were intact, and my marriage was secure in our love for each other. I had experienced so many emotions – from joy to abject misery, from gnawing fear to flooding confidence – and had seen nobility, baseness, cruelty, warmth, terror, and sheer bravery in people of different races and all walks of life, stripped bare of the social veneer of manners and position. I had seen weakness in the physically strong and incredible strength in the frail and timid. I had observed blind faith and utter belief in God's protection through prayer that manifested itself in deliberate expo- sure to shellfire, a spiritual flaunting that ended predictably in the man's death, and great misery to those around him. This gave rise to my belief that God does not love a stupid person who will not help himself and leaves everything to God.

I had a new appreciation, not only of family and friends, but also of life itself.

When we returned home after the war, we were terribly anxious to get on with the rest of our lives. We were conscious that five years of what we presumed to be our "best" years had been spent cut off from family and business. We wondered what we had missed while we were away, and what we would have to do to "catch up" with those who had stayed home. Simpsons had promised all employee volunteers jobs when they returned, as had many companies. But in five years of learning how to fight, I had forgotten even simple busi- ness arithmetic and I was concerned about my business abilities. How- ever, my immediate concern was to get to know my children, Gail and Jamie, and outfit myself with clothes and the dozen things needed for my new life.

It was not just a life resumed; it was truly a new beginning. Much had changed, particularly within myself. I now had a hard-won con- fidence. I no longer stuttered. I had acquired a new position in the family. No longer was I the youngest member of the family, whose opinion was never valued, but one who was listened to, who had suddenly matured even beyond his years.

I must admit I liked the new-found respect and I was happy to be promoted to merchandise manager, Home Furnishings. I had learned how to plan, to do appreciations, and to organize my time. I had learned not to waste time in worry but to be concerned about detail and timing. The Army taught me that the best plan done too late was doomed to fail. Timing in life, being in the right place at the right time, is of the greatest importance. My father used to say that there is no such thing as pure luck. Luck is only the point in time where experience and opportunity meet.

I also had taught myself how to go to sleep within minutes, any- where, anytime. Without this I doubt whether I would have survived

Italy. At one period I averaged only one hour's sleep in twenty-four for three weeks running, and often this was broken into ten- and fifteen-minute snatches. Even more important, I could get real benefit from ten minutes, and awaken fully, instantly, without grogginess. I went away grown up, but unsure of myself, physically and mentally untried. I came home physically hard, confident, and with a new appreciation of the strengths and frailties of men under stress. I was mature and unafraid, ready to take on the world and make up for lost time. I was more alive than I had ever been.

Early the first morning home, Audrey and I went into the children's bedrooms to reintroduce myself to our children. Gail, who was barely eighteen months when I went overseas, had been well-schooled by my wife and had a picture of me on her wall. When I walked into her bedroom in my pyjamas and dressing gown, she threw her arms wide to hug me, squealing appropriately, "Daddy!" Next we tiptoed into Jamie's room. Jamie, whom I had never seen till now, when he had heard I was coming home, had immediately run to the livingroom window, looked out, and seeing a soldier, a kilted Highlander, walking down the street, had shouted, "Here comes Daddy now!" Jamie looked at this stranger in his bedroom with surly sleepiness and suspicion until Gail could stand it no longer and literally shook him, saying, "Stupid, don't you know Daddy?" Jamie suddenly came to life, squealed "Daddy," and in throwing his arms around my neck scratched the cornea of my left eye with his little fingernail! I was wounded on my first day home and it was a painful wound at that!

Audrey and I slipped away to Niagara Falls, leaving the children with their doting grandparents. I was still in uniform, beribboned, but now with a celluloid patch over one eye. As we checked out of the Inn, a dear little old lady came up to Audrey, voice quivering with sincere feeling. "How wonderful for you, my dear, to have your husband home again." Then she added in a whisper, "Isn't it too bad about his eye."

I had a month's leave before I had to report to my new position at Simpsons and I found that there were several adjustments that had to be made. For one thing, I still suffered from the "Italian complaint," dysentery. I went to the old Christie Street Veterans' Hospital to be re-examined by a panel of three doctors, the first of many such periodic tests over the next few months and years. They were very concerned about me because the emaciated little Roman Catholic priest who had occupied the next bed to me in hospital in Caserta in Italy had died of amoebic dysentery just a few weeks before in Toronto. Our house, which Audrey had bought while I was overseas, was right behind Chorley Park, the former official residence of Ontario's lieutenant-governor, now being used as a military hospital. I had gone to see the priest just before he died, so I took their concern seriously. Finally, Dr. Ian MacDonald, the senior medical testing officer, said, "Allan, let's face it. I have the same thing as you. Nearly everyone who was in Italy has. We just have to learn to live with it." It was a little hard on my pride, but I learned to live with it.

More difficult to overcome were some deeply ingrained instincts, some life-saving techniques learned in action. In our new house there was an open porch off our bedroom, with a door three or four feet away from the bed. One cardinal rule in the Army was to sleep with a solid wall at your back, facing any openings. I found I could not go to sleep, no matter how well-trained I was in that respect, until I had built up a small "booby trap" each night – a tin wastebasket with several things balanced on top – which would make it impossible for the porch door to open or for anyone to enter our bedroom from the porch without raising an alarm and giving me time to get my back to the wall. To do this, I had to wait each night until I thought Audrey was asleep, then wake early enough to take it all down again before she awoke. The slightest sound would waken me, a squeak, a voice on the street below. I would get up silently, check the windows, well back from them as trained, and go back to bed asleep in moments.

Unknown to me, Audrey had been watching these antics, wondering what kind of a "psycho" she had on her hands, when one night, about 3:00 a.m., I heard an unusual sound, got up, and saw two men coming up the side of our house toward the garage. I quietly sat on the edge of Audrey's bed and picked up the phone to call the police.

"What are you doing, Allan?"

"Calling the police," I replied.

"Now don't make a fool of yourself. I've been watching you night after night."

"Okay," I said, "but I just saw two men going toward the garage where we have some of our goods stored!"

"Call the police," cried Audrey as she covered up her head.

Gradually normalcy returned, but some of my survival skills became an integral part of my new awareness, and I never lost them.

# SIMPSONS
# AND FOX-HUNTING

## II

I had been appointed merchandise manager, Home Furnishings, at Simpsons downtown store in Toronto, and I was eager to start. When my brother Edgar wrote to me in Italy to hurry up and get the war over quickly because "we need you back in Simpsons," I wrote back to say that I had given the subject a lot of thought and I had decided that I would not return to Simpsons after the war, because I did not want to be his little brother all my life. I explained that, if I did come back, I wanted to be in charge of what was bought, how it was sold, who was hired and fired, how they were trained, and thus cut across all the normal lines of the organization. I also felt that if they were unhappy with their present Home Furnishings business, I would not want to serve under the existing merchandise manager. He wrote back and agreed.

When I reported to work, I reported directly to the general manager, Sydney Fletcher, a fine man but one of the old school, prim, stiff, a north of England bachelor. Syd was an excellent merchant and had been both the buyer of ladies' dress fabrics as well as the manager of our Overseas Buying offices in London. I was shown an office, assigned a part-time secretary, and for the first three weeks I did not receive a single phone call from anyone in the General Merchandise office or above. I was busy getting to know my departments and department managers and laying plans for major physical changes, basic things like new ceilings, lighting, and air conditioning. These simple amenities had not yet reached beyond the fashion floors.

I had inherited some of the best and toughest old-time merchants in my group. Most of them were rapidly approaching sixty-five, the retirement age, and they were not at all convinced that a thirty-year-old veteran, even with a fair war record, could lead them anywhere.

Such characters are no longer found in this modern age of computer analysis of customers and their needs by age, sex, and salary. These tools leave us nowhere as close to understanding a customer as these merchants' sensibilities did. I respected them, and I conceived my job to be one of letting them do what we had agreed on was the best course.

Cecil Budd, our rug buyer, was such a man. He was short, rotund, yet powerfully built, with ruddy cheeks and a sharply waxed, World War I mustache. His steely, small, alert eyes were not given to soft glances, and he had the strut of authority that any regimental sergeant-major would be proud to emulate. Cecil Budd was a proud man and had every right to be proud of his position in the rug business. He was the doyen of buyers at this time, finishing a career that had seen him as a young man buy oriental rugs in what used to be called Asia Minor, carrying a bag of gold with which to pay the tribesmen for his purchases. He hired a bodyguard to protect himself and his bag of gold, and another bodyguard to protect him from being robbed by the first guard. He told me that he would sit in a tent, cross-legged, with the rug vendor, their hands in a grip under a small prayer rug. As they haggled, they held each other's hand, the deal being struck when one or the other tightened his grip into a handshake. The heat in the tent was intense. Perspiring freely, Cecil Budd's hand tended to slip from the other's under the rug. He made several inadvertent purchases by trying to regain his hand grip. Then he found out that it was an old trick for the rug vendor to oil his hand to cause the slip. I learned much from Cecil Budd, but he was too old a dog to care about my new tricks.

Another famous merchant was Hugh Jolly in the linens, again a roly-poly man of sharp intelligence and Irish good humour, also near retirement age. Hugh had come over from Ireland as a young man, and he kept his Irish brogue till the day he died. Generally the Irish got jobs at Eaton's; the Scottish searched out the Scot, Robert Simpson. But Hugh, Irish as Paddy's pig, applied for a job at Simpsons, having worked as an apprentice for seven years in what the Irish call the "staples." When asked by the employment office if he had any previous experience, he said proudly in his slurring brogue, "Yes, sorr, seven years in the staples," upon which he was given an immediate job grooming and mucking out horses in our Mutual Street stables. The employment clerk thought he had said the "stables"! Hugh told me he worked there for three months before he could make anyone understand he meant the Linen Department, as we called it.

On an early trip of inspection and learning, I visited Hugh in his department where I was startled to see huge cardboard cartons full of sheets, and other linens, piled one on top of the other. I suggested that for less than one hundred dollars a strong shelf could be constructed to take the top carton so the stockman could get at any one without manhandling these huge, ungainly cartons everytime something was wanted from the bottom. Hugh exploded, "No, sir! I'll not waste the company's money that way. You'll not make a profit if you go around throwing good money away!"

I learned in the Army, and found it was borne out many times in business, that nearly all men emulate their trainer. If the teacher is strict but human and understanding, the pupil most likely will be the same. If the teacher is mean, hard, and unyielding, sooner or later, almost against his will, the pupil will copy. One such teacher was a certain Jackson, a hard and most difficult man in Hardware, who retired almost immediately after my return. Tom Dunne, his middle-aged assistant, said to me when I promoted him, "Allan, if I ever get as mean as Jackson you can fire me." Some years later, Tom, an otherwise first-rate chap now in the refrigerators and stoves, called Heavy Goods, had become very difficult. So I called him into my office – I was by this time general manager – and reminded him of our conversation years before. "You told me to retire you if you ever got like Jackson, Tom. Well, when do you want to go?"

"You can't be serious, Allan. Are you?"

"I sure as hell am serious, Tom, unless you want to change your ways," I replied.

"Well, I'll change then, Allan, because we have a lot to do together."

The interesting thing was he did change, and his relationship with his staff improved daily. We remained good friends.

The toughest man of all was Harry Ames, a slight, hook-nosed fellow in his sixties, with the cough of a chain smoker and a lined, grey face, whose humourless expression bore witness to the chronic pain of stomach ulcers. Harry had been "through the mill." To have a thirty-year-old thrust upon him at the end of his varied career was almost more than he could take. These men and many others like them formed the team that I had to work with in the early days after the war. They were not used to meeting together and felt strongly that their departmental results should not be discussed in public. After Jack Easton, the accountant and stock-control man, and I had done a lot of work on the departmental results, I called a meeting to discuss the net-profit results in detail. The irascible Harry Ames chose not to come to the meeting until it had been in progress for a good half-hour. He had been overheard saying that he was not going to attend any net-profit meeting as it was not any of my business what the net result was anyway as I was only the merchandise manager. As soon as Harry came into the room, I said, "Mr. Ames, you are late. This meeting is adjourned until ten tomorrow morning, here in this office. And, Mr. Ames, I don't mean one minute past ten, or come with your resignation in hand."

They filed out and shortly after Cecil Budd knocked at my door and came in. He was chuckling and said, "I am glad you handled Ames, he deserved it. We are on your side, Allan." I was relieved, to say the least.

Next morning Harry Ames was lounging around outside my door at 9:45 a.m. I said, "Did you want to see me before the meeting, Harry?"

"No," he said slyly. "I just didn't want to be late."

At which I said, "Don't waste the firm's time. Go away and come back at 10:00 a.m.!" He went.

The Interior Decorating Department, then called the Home Furnishing Department, was included in my group, and I discovered that the individual sales quotas of the decorators were very low and their salaries were disgraceful. We had lost one or two good people because of salary levels. So I set a reasonable cost-percentage to sales for the department and then broke it down to individual quotas and adjusted salaries accordingly. This meant an average increase per individual in the department of 100 per cent, some as much as 150 per cent, but the cost-percentage to sales, if they got the new sales budget, was 6 per cent instead of 15 per cent. By keeping down costs and increasing sales, everyone would benefit. I took this sheet of recommendations to the general manager, Sydney Fletcher, who looked at it in horror and tossed it back to me, saying, "I wouldn't touch that with a ten-foot pole. You are out of your mind, Allan."

I said, "I can't see how increasing sales and lowering costs is bad business. May I present this study to Mr. Clark, the general superintendent?"

Fletcher said, "I wouldn't advise it, but go ahead if you want to."

J.G. Clark was red-haired, bad-tempered, and a bully. He had every reason to be because he had been through the Depression as my father's right-hand man and chief expense controller. Some said he was a hatchet man, but he had done a great job. He and I had had a couple of run-ins before the war, and it was fairly obvious that he had little regard for me. I went up to the executive floor, then on the seventh, and I was courteously received by Mr. Clark, until I told him what I wanted to do and presented my study. He exploded in red-haired rage. "Ridiculous. You are just trying to make a Santa Claus of yourself!"

"Mr. Clark," I said calmly, as he no longer could bully me, "you have no reason to say that. Sign the increases and, if the sales fall short of my predictions in six months, fire me, if you have the guts."

He signed and said, "It'll give me great pleasure to fire you six months from today!"

"Brinkmanship" was not yet a word in vogue, but I quickly assembled the Home Furnishing Department staff, told them the name of the department was being changed to Interior Decorating, and explained the salary increases and new quotas to them. I said, "My job is on the line and I expect you to produce. For those who can't meet the quotas, a more suitable job will be found selling in one of the other departments."

We made all our quotas for the six months. In fairness, I must report that Clark, as tough as he was, called me up to congratulate me and added, "It'll be tough to fire you at Christmas."

Fletcher was delighted at the increased business. One of the interior decorators, a veteran at that, had come to me and confessed that he was a homosexual and had contracted venereal disease. This necessitated a period in Sunnybrook Hospital for treatment. I was somewhat taken aback and duly reported the incident to Fletcher. Prim, puritanical bachelor that he was, he recoiled in horror and said, "Allan, the place is full of them – in the Interior Decorating, the Display Department, even Advertising. I want you to search them out and fire the lot!"

I said, "Mr. Fletcher, I know very little about that sort of thing, and I suspect there is only one sure way to prove a person is a homo-sexual, and I am not prepared to go to those lengths for you or the Robert Simpson Company!"

He said, "Oh, I see, of course. Well, forget it, forget it, but keep your eye on them!"

• • •

I was rapidly getting on with my new job at Simpsons and, at the same time, began hunting once more with the North York Hunt Club on borrowed horses. In fact, Lady Eaton, who was Joint Master of North York with Frank Proctor, made me an Honorary Whip, assisting Bob Hollingsworth, her head groom, who doubled as First Whip. Hollingsworth was a typically small cockney and a gentleman whose whole life had been adapted to grooming, caring for, and riding horses. He was an excellent horseman and taught me my early lessons on fox-hunting and the way of the fox. What a golden opportunity for a young enthusiast!

Bob and I, on arriving at a cover, would slip quietly around to the opposite side of the woods before the huntsman sent the pack in to hunt, as he urged them on with the familiar cry of "Luu-in – luu-in – luu-in . . . hi wind 'im, hi wind 'im." Bob and I would sit motionless, watching the edge of the cover, listening to the cry of the huntsman and the solitary note of the horn. If the cover was dense, we heard only the yelps and cries of the various hounds tantalized by the remnants of scent of a fox long gone. Finally they would work it out, and a crashing babel of excited hounds converged on a hot scent, all "throwing their tongues," creating a symphony that reverberated throughout the woods as full and fine as any organ in a large cathedral. I defy anyone not to thrill to that glorious sound! Often before the hounds had found the true line, the hunted fox would slip out of our side of the wood. Once it came and sat alongside us as if to say, "Are they hunting you, too?"

More usually, "Charles," the fox, would come in view and give us a glance as he indulged in a variety of games to throw his pursuers off the track. I never saw one of these foxes at this stage show panic or even hurry about its business as it wove a pattern of scent along a fence rail, through water, or mingled with sheep or cattle. Their actions were convoluted and cunning. They even looked as if they enjoyed the game. They probably did because it was only an unlucky fox, indeed, that was killed. When they had had enough, there was always one of hundreds of groundhog holes to pop into for shelter. We did not, as they do in England, stop up the earths or dig them out. Seldom did we send the terriers in. Instead, we left the fox there and found another to give us a run for the money.

This was how I got hooked on fox-hunting for forty years! I started as Honorary Whip and ended as Master and Huntsman. As Mr.

Jorrocks, M.F.H., the principal character in R.S. Surtees's classic short story "Handley Cross," said while giving a lecture on hunting, "'Unting is the Sport of Kings – the image of war without its guilt and only five and twenty per cent of its danger." Jorrocks goes on, "In that word "unting' wot a ramification of knowledge is compressed! The choice of an 'oss, the treatment of him when got, the grooming at home, the riding abroad, the boots, the breeches, the saddle, the bridle, the 'ound, the 'untsman, the feeder – the Fox! The 'oss and the 'ound were made for each other and natur' threw in the Fox as a connectin' link between the two."

Lady Eaton, M.F.H., would appear at the meet mounted, but at this point in time she was not hunting actively. She entertained the hunt lavishly at Eaton Hall, her farm at King, for hunt breakfasts. Simpsons invariably provided the catering service because Eaton's did not have such a service and ours was the best in town. One day as we trotted back from the hunt up the long, tree-lined drive in from the road to Eaton Hall, I was horrified to see two large Simpsons catering trucks, red-and-black with yellow trim, parked behind dozens of cars that had arrived ahead of them. When I went into the Hall, my friends were quite snide in the remarks about "advertising" Simpsons at Lady Eaton's expense! The excuse that the drivers had taken a wrong turn and so were late did not impress Lady Eaton. So, after many years, we lost an important customer. We never catered for the Eaton family again, although she was personally very kind about the mistake.

Lady Eaton's Joint Masters were Frank Proctor, who, at ninety-two and still actively hunting, was by far the oldest Master in North America, and Bob Elder, father of the Canadian international riders of later years, Jim and Norman Elder. Frank Proctor was a jeweller by trade and a famous horseman, who rode his last steeplechase when he was over sixty years of age. Proctor always rode "hot" thoroughbred horses and, amazingly for his age, would vault into the saddle because he was too stiff to mount in the usual fashion! When the meet was at North York Kennels at Beverley Farm, he used to "warm up" his mount for the day by putting him around the steeplechase course at full gallop to wear him down a bit before the hunt started!

One day my brother Edgar and I were trotting home with Proctor after a long, hot hunt. I was tired and sweating freely. Proctor had not even perspired, being lean and "dried-out" looking. He turned to Edgar and me and said, "It's wonderful to see you young men out hunting. You know, those other fellows who sit in their offices down-town all day and never exercise, they lose their manhood by about thirty-seven!" Proctor was a wonderful sportsman and he wrote a large volume of hunting memoirs called *Fox Hunting in Canada*. It honours some of the men and women who made it a great sport. He was certainly one of those who did!

After the war I had wavered between golf and sailing and riding. My golf clubs had disappeared while I was overseas, and my beauti-ful thoroughbred chestnut hunter was no longer. As I got off the ferry at the Royal Canadian Yacht Club, I passed a sleek, wood-finished, Norwegian sailboat, a "tumlaren," with a large For Sale sign on it. As the "tumlaren" lay at its mooring each day, the lapping of the water against its beautiful hull had the near fatal allure of a siren's song for me because, next to horses, I loved sailing. I was saved when, as the summer drew to a close, my father bought a fine-looking hunter for me and offered to stable it at his farm in Thornhill. So I continued hunting and riding.

On a beautiful fall day in 1948, the North York hounds met near the Sharon Temple at Sharon, Ontario. I was riding my brother Edgar's horse and had been giving "leads" to Martha Eaton, Timothy Eaton's wife, over each fence. A great deal of the time I had been cut off and interfered with at several jumps by one very determined rider. In my opinion, he was making a deliberate nuisance of himself. We crossed a reedy marsh area which necessitated the field going in sin-gle file. Once more this rider thrust himself just ahead of me. Although his horse did not "carry a flag" – that is, have a small piece of red ribbon woven into the hairs of his tail to denote a "kicker" – his horse gave mine a powerful kick in the chest. I had visions of Edgar's horse crippled for life and shouted my displeasure at the beast ahead in strong language, suggesting that if the rider could not control him, he had better fall to the rear! Without a word, the pair moved off the track, let everyone through, and fell in at the rear!

We stopped for a sandwich lunch near the lovely old Sharon Temple. I was still fuming about that bloody Englishman and said to Martha Eaton, "Who is that chap?"

"Oh," she said, "don't you know Charles Kindersley? He's really a fine fellow and wants to apologize to you. He thought you were riding me off! When I told him you were getting me over the nastier chicken coops by giving my horse a lead, he was horribly embarrassed." Then Kindersley came over and we made a peace that has lasted forty years.

We were Joint Masters of Eglinton Hunt for over twenty-five of them. He taught me much about hounds, their keep and care and breeding, their training, and how to hunt them. Some of the best moments of my life have been spent fox-hunting with Charles.

My new horse, a halfbred bay with a fine white blaze, delighted me. I had to switch my allegiance from the North York to the Eglinton Hunt, my prewar club, because of its proximity to the city and our stable in Thornhill. It meant that once more my father and I could ride together, as we had done many years before. The new horse was a comfortable ride, but a dedicated coward when expected to leap over an obstacle more than one foot off the ground. It would gallop toward a jump and then, as you expected a couple of more strides before it sailed through the air, it sat down, front legs stiffly braced for maximum braking, and slid ingloriously into the jump! It was more humiliating than dangerous, so it was sent back to whatever cart it had pulled, and I was without a horse again.

My next horse, given to me by Gordon Perry, was an ancient "timber" steeplechaser, a fine-looking thoroughbred, but crippled by a badly festered pastern joint, which the non-horseman would call his ankle. If I wanted to doctor him, I could have him for nothing, Perry told me. The name of the horse was Vickers Lane. We went to work on the wound, and after hours of poulticing and probing discovered a large sliver of wood impaled in the swollen mass which, when removed, quickly restored the horse to soundness. Vickers Lane was a beautiful animal, comfortably constructed on the long springy fetlocks of the thoroughbred. He was a gentle ride until his blood was aroused on the hunt! Through long years of racing, the bars of his mouth had been severely damaged and quickly lost all feeling when you tried to restrain him. One could almost break his jaw in an effort to stop his wild gallop to get to the front because he felt no pain, and you careened like a kamikaze plane out of control, a danger to you and anything in your way. We had several severe falls, and it was obvious that one or both of us would be killed. Vickers Lane was a danger to the "field."

Once more my father came to the rescue and, through the good offices of Col. George Reade, an ex-cavalryman in the horse business, found me a three-quarterbred mare, a three-year-old chestnut of generous proportions and handsome. Sun-up was sixteen hands, two inches, with plenty of bone, huge girth, short-coupled, gentle, yet full of courage. She was never known to refuse a reasonable jump.

Sun-up carried me for eleven seasons and nearly four hundred hunts. She was always in front and never "on the ground" with me. The rougher the terrain, the smoother her gallop. She could leave most horses far behind across country at speed. She was my greatest horse and one of the best in the country. A good horse makes a brave rider!

When Audrey was pregnant with our third child, she was bedridden for nearly four months with a low-grade pneumonia. She seemed to get steadily worse. Finally, the trip from bed to bathroom became an exhausting, painful, gasping experience. Truly alarmed, I called on my brother Carl, who was a leading cardiologist, for help. Having interned at one point at the Muskoka Tubercular Sanitarium at Gravenhurst, he knew much about lungs. He examined her and took me aside and solemnly told me that Audrey's one lung was full and the other about three-quarters full of fluid and that she was in critical condition. "Can't you give her one of the wonder drugs?" I beseeched.

"No, there is nothing that we know of today that would do anything but maybe make her worse and endanger the baby. The body itself is the only thing that can fight this virus," Carl told me.

Audrey had not been able to eat anything for days, and Carl said she must have nourishment or the body could not do its work. "Give her a couple of good drinks of rye," he went on, "and have a meal ready for her. When she has drunk them, put it in front of her. If she eats it, she will probably live. If not, I don't know. Tonight is critical."

Thoroughly alarmed, I did as directed. She ate a good portion of the meal and slept while I watched all night. Early the next morning, Carl came and checked her lungs. One had cleared completely and the other showed some improvement – a miracle!

My admiration and respect for my brother, Dr. Carl Rutherford Burton, M.D., F.R.C.P. (Can)., F.R.C.P. (Lon.), knew no bounds. Here was a highly trained scientist who was wise enough to know when to let the body and the good Lord take charge. He told me afterwards that he probably could not or would not have advised that treatment to an outside patient. There was a fifty-fifty chance that Audrey would not live the night through. One can imagine the scandal if the doctor had advised getting the patient half drunk and she had not survived!

As Audrey slowly gained strength, I rediscovered my old love of watercolour painting. I painted in the bedroom, night after night, getting considerable facility back with drawing, brushwork, and washes. I did nearly eighty watercolours that year, some quite good. I was interested in technique at this time and tried everything. I sold my first picture of an old house in Thornhill that I had first sketched as an architectural student on condition that, if the buyer ever tired of it, I would buy it back at the same price. I did not know who wanted to buy it. It was purchased, as it turned out, by John D. Tory, the lawyer, who paid me two hundred dollars, enough to purchase a new forward-seat jumping saddle. My picture had a position of honour behind the chair and desk in his office for the next twenty years. When he died, he left it to me in his will.

As my work-load at Simpsons increased steadily, I did fewer watercolours, down to about four or five a year, but I did many sketches. People often asked me if I found painting or drawing relaxing. I found it absorbing and demanding but never relaxing. Painting has been an important part of my life, a wonderful hobby and a personal pleasure, but there was a long gap of several years during which I did not paint. Cleeve Horne, RCA, the eminent portrait painter and an old friend of mine, not realizing I might take his remarks seriously, kidded me about amateurs selling pictures and taking money away from professional artists. His remarks stung me so deeply I gave up painting for a long time. When Cleeve found out that he had caused me to quit painting, he was very contrite and offered to give me lessons to get me started again. I did not take up his offer but started once again on my own. Cleeve did a portrait of my father which hangs in our dining room at Limestone Hall, as does the one he did of me. Both are good likenesses.

The Eglinton Hunt Club had been kept alive during the war by Hal Crang and many of the old-timers who, except for Crang, gave it much advice but little financial support. The young members of the activity committee, of which I knew nothing, planned to elect at least one of their number to the board of directors. When the smoke cleared after the annual meeting, four of us had been elected and no one wanted the presidency. We argued until well after midnight when, in weariness, I said I would serve as president. Little did I know what was in store for me. Many of the old-timers were suspicious of the younger members. Two of the old guard, E.P. Taylor and Col. Eric Phillips, who were accumulating land in the vicinity of the club in the Don Mills and Bayview areas of the city, wanted a "watchdog." So they asked Richard Corbett to remain on the board to keep an eye on the new executive. I liked Dick and suggested that he be vice-president, to which he agreed instantly. In the course of the next few months he approved what we were doing and helped us to get the co-operation and support of Taylor and Phillips.

The Eglinton hounds were kennelled on a property nearby, and when Taylor added this estate to his growing real-estate hoard, he immediately sent me a letter ordering me to get the hounds off his property within two weeks. I was stunned and sensed that this was punishment for out-manoeuvring the old guard at the Club, petty as it seemed. In a moment of bravado, I sought an audience with E.P. Taylor and told him that he must give us six weeks to build new kennels on our own property at Leslie and Cummer, and said that no doubt he would contribute the first thousand dollars to the ten thousand we must raise in order to maintain his reputation as one of Canada's greatest sportsmen! He rippled with laughter and said, "Done," and wrote out a cheque for that amount. We raised the money, built the kennels in a nice colonial design, and moved the hounds, all in the six-week period. Syd Abbott, the kennel huntsman, was delighted, as was Charles Kindersley, the Master. As it turned out, it was the best thing that could have happened to the Club and started a whole new and very vigorous phase of the life of the Eglinton pack.

My father, meantime, was quite concerned that I might alienate such important businessmen as E.P. Taylor and Col. Eric Phillips. Without my knowledge, he took it upon himself to ask Eric not to be too hard on me. Eric told my father not to be concerned, that I could take care of myself very well, and that he was very pleased with the new vigour in the Club.

About this time, another prominent businessman built a huge Southern-style, plantation colonial house within sight of the Hunt. This was John Angus (Bud) McDougald, Eric Phillips's brother-in-law. Bud McDougald was always immaculately dressed in Huntsman's Saville Row suits and Lobb shoes. An eccentric and an antique-car collector, he was destined to become a potent force in business as a partner in Argus Corporation. Bud McDougald "ran" the exclusive Toronto Club and for years he was the sole arbiter of who could become a member. He set a high standard and carefully maintained what he conceived to be his "way of life." In the early days of Eglinton's postwar reorganization, he liked to have a lot to say about how things should be run and maintained at the club. But he put up very little cash to help us. One day I approached him for a much-increased subscription which, to my amazement, he gave me, saying that while he did not ride or hunt he would give it because he felt we were doing a good job of maintaining his "way of life"!

Bud and I became good friends. Although his political views made Genghis Khan look like a church warden, he insisted he was a Liberal. Years later I was a director of Standard Broadcasting, which was controlled by Argus, of which Bud was chairman. I attended a directors' meeting after a spell in the hospital. Bud took me aside and very seriously said, "Take care of yourself, Allan. There are few of us left." At that moment I felt I had arrived!

Bud had, as well as his "stable" of beautifully kept antique cars, a number of thoroughbred horses at his estate. Green Meadows was the real name of his estate, but because of the tall white classical columns which extended two storeys on the front facade, it was nicknamed "Southern Comfort" by some members of the Hunt. His horses had the reputation of looking much better than they ran. He won few races with them.

Bud gave me an extremely handsome chestnut thoroughbred gelding one day. It was six years old but had never raced or done anything else because it had constricted heels and "shelly" feet. This means that the horse had long hooves, narrow at the heel, with thin horn at the toes. It was difficult to nail a shoe to the hooves without splitting the hoof or laming the horse with a misplaced nail. I was taken with the animal. Some of the best horses I have owned have been rejected by others because they were unmanageable or needed some care to cure a deficiency. I sent a young man to bring him the short distance from Green Meadows to the Eglinton stables. I did not tell him the horse had not been ridden since he was a two-year-old and even then only partially broken. I thought he would lead the horse the half-mile, but instead he saddled up and mounted. The poor horse was so enraged at the unaccustomed weight on his back, and the rude dig in the ribs from the demon on his back, he shrieked and buckjumped in fury the whole way, trying to dislodge the boy. I arrived at the Hunt Club in time to see the tail end of this performance and wondered what I had taken on! I walked the trembling beast and cooled him out, speaking softly to him, bribing him with sugar lumps, rubbing his ears and muzzle, making friends before he started his journey to Milton and our farm, Limestone Hall Farms.

Bud had given this fine-looking animal the name Joe Schloss, the name of his farm manager. I renamed him Limestone Joe and set about teaching him manners. The first few rides I had on him in the paddock always started off with a minute or two of bucking, although with his long sloping fetlocks and springy step, his "bucks" were more graceful gestures of exuberance than the soul-shaking, bone-rattling experience that a fit pony could give.

One day I had had enough, and when he wanted to quit bucking, I kept after him until, after fifteen minutes, we were both near exhaustion. From that day on Joe never bucked again and became a very fine ride. Years later I gave him to the mounted troop leader of the Governor General's Horse Guards, my old regiment, and for twenty years he was the charger of the Officer of the Guard. He proudly stepped out at Woodbine when the Queen was escorted and when several governors general visited the Royal Agricultural Winter Fair. Limestone Joe had found his proper role in society, one that was quite in keeping with his former owner, Bud McDougald, and his "way of life."

# No Mean City

## 12

The late forties seemed to bear out the sentiment of a popular song of the period, "Everything is going our way." There was full employment; productive resources were strained to capacity; plants and equipment were being expanded, modernized, or rebuilt; the housing shortage was being alleviated; furniture and other household goods were in great demand; and the future looked bright. The Marshall Plan helped Europe make a dramatic economic recovery. And yet tensions between East and West increased to the breaking point, reaching a peak in April 1948 when the Russians blocked all road and rail communication from the Allied zones into Berlin, resulting in the Berlin Airlift. British and American fliers delivered such a quantity of food, fuel, and clothing that the daily rations of Berliners were actually increased.

At home in Toronto, we were busy and excited about the challenges of growth. Urban renewal and new housing had to cope with a population that was rapidly expanding because of immigration and a postwar baby boom. Large undertakings ranged from the huge Sunnybrook Veterans' Hospital and the new Hospital for Sick Children to the commencement of the country's first subway, originally known as the Yonge Street Rapid Transit Line. We welcomed hundreds of thousands of disillusioned and displaced persons, DPs, as they were called, to our vast country as eager new Canadians. About two-thirds of the immigrants came to Toronto, which put a great strain on our social facilities. These people brought with them cultural and social mores quite different from those of the society in which I had grown up. They were willing to do almost anything in the line of work to survive and prosper, as our forbears had done a hundred years earlier.

Toronto had never known a leisure class. "Handsome is as hand-some does" was still the credo in the work place. In 1949, with the construction of the subway, and over the next decade, came thousands of Italian labourers and their families. The city acquired the largest Italian community anywhere in the world outside Rome and possibly New York. One out of every five Torontonians is now of Italian descent. In effect, the Anglo-Saxon, Protestant, Orange-dominated Toronto the Good had ceased to exist. We became a multicultural metropolis, with a Roman Catholic majority.

The first wave of post-World War II immigrants came from the British Isles, as they had done in the past decades, seeking, as many of our ancestors had done, a life more prosperous and with more scope for themselves and their children than was possible in the social strait-jacket of the old countries. Others from Latvia, Estonia, and Germany came to escape political oppression, some hoping to make Canada a stage-stop on their way to the United States. Curiously, most of those in my acquaintance stayed as proud Canadians. It was a small number of ambitious Canadians who left for the United States for greater fields to conquer and greater wealth.

During one of my early inspection tours of our furniture ware-house, then housed in an old building on Front Street, I noticed a middle-aged man, neatly turned out in blue overalls and a small black beret. He was small of stature, grey-haired, and fine-featured. He was doing the most basic of labourers' jobs, cutting up and stacking the wooden shipping crates. Thinking him of French extraction because of the black beret, I asked him in French if he was from France.

"No," he replied in perfect English. "I am Dr. X of Latvia."

"You have the title of Doctor. What did you do in Latvia?"

I was stunned when he replied, "I was Chief Justice of the Supreme Court of Latvia at the time the Russians invaded our country."

I pressed on with my questions. "With your legal background, can't you study and resume your legal career in Canada?"

"No," he replied sadly, "I am too old. But please don't feel sorry for me, I am actually enjoying working with my hands and the daily contact with my fellow employees. I am more content now than I have been for years."

When the furniture warehouse was moved to the new Lawrence Avenue service building, designed by John B. Parkin Associates in

1948, the Chief Justice was made an inspector, someone who examines the shipment in detail to detect and correct any flaws in the furniture before delivery by truck to the customer's home. Each time I toured the building, he would be standing, as neat as ever, waiting to click his heels, bow, and wish me good morning. I always made a point to search him out before I left the building. He told me he had never been happier in his life than when working for Simpsons.

A short time after this I interviewed a tall, distinguished-looking man who was seeking employment. Colonel S's résumé listed three staff courses, Polish, French, and British; military decorations, including Poland's highest medal for valour, Britain's Distinguished Service Order, and other French and Allied medals. Colonel S had charged the invading German tanks on horseback with his cavalry regiment when Poland was overrun; had escaped through Portugal to England; had commanded an armoured regiment in the Polish Division in Europe; and had served as a staff officer. I had the greatest respect for the Polish Armoured Division, having first met its members in training in Norfolk and fought alongside them in the Liri Valley as part of the Eighth Army. Here was a young-looking, middle-aged man, who spoke English with a very heavy accent, with an illustrious military career, highly trained in several disciplines. But what could I offer such a man? As I hesitated, he said, "Please, don't hold my record against me!" I was embarrassed because he had obviously read my mind or had been told before that there were no openings worthy of his background. "Please, don't hold my record against me," he pleaded. "I will do anything. I am desperate. I must eat. I need a job!"

"Okay," I said, "the only thing I have at the moment is a job as a porter in the Rug Department. If you want it, it's yours."

He took the job eagerly, and soon thereafter changed his name to Col. Stevens, an anglicized version of his more difficult-to-pronounce Polish name, for business reasons. He soon revealed himself to be an expert in oriental rugs, rapidly becoming first section head and then manager of the the Rug Department, a position he held for many years.

Our immediate postwar problem was to obtain sufficient supplies of furniture to satisfy the growing demand. New houses were springing up in the new "towns of the future," the suburbs, like Don Mills. Here was a community where there were no very rich, no very poor, all working, all young parents with young children and a lifestyle that required the cars and gadgets of modern society. The young parents wanted to display their newly earned affluence for all to see and admire.

We had a real "boom-town" mentality in those days. We knew Toronto was the epicentre of industry in Canada, and we had been told that the twentieth century belonged to Canada. The evidence of this was the heavy foreign investment flowing our way. We were also growing faster, in almost every way, than Montreal, which still felt very secure in its position as the financial capital of Canada, where most of the head offices resided and everyone knew his place in the social scale.

In the furniture marts of Chicago and Grand Rapids, Michigan, we Canadians were not very important customers and were on quotas imposed to ration the demand equitably. The showrooms generally could sell their entire production allotment easily and quickly, leaving much time to socialize with their best customers or good "storytellers." A good fund of new stories became an important entrée to new accounts and suppliers. I was accepted as a good raconteur and became well known and received much help in the market as a result of these social contacts and friendships. We did not mind when American salesmen would call us "fresh-water immigrants," but when given extra quota our sales potential surprised them. With Canadian duties and freight imposed, we had to sell the same article at two and one-half times more than the price in the continental United States.

During these postwar years, I fox-hunted regularly with the Eglinton or North York hunts; found time to command the Governor General's Horse Guards; played baseball on second base with several successive GGHG-league winning teams in the Officers' League; joined the Toronto Board of Trade and several clubs; and took great delight in my growing family. We were young and healthy and every day was excitement and enjoyment.

I had built around me a young, talented team in the Simpsons' Home Furnishings group, each member having come my way either because of personality clashes with others or because each believed, as I did, in raising the design levels and real value, including the aesthetic value, of the everyday articles we used in our homes. My brother-in-law, Gerry Maccabe, a brilliant advertising man who had wide retailing experience in advertising in both Eaton's and Simpsons, was most helpful in the early days. We had a new promotion every Monday morning, ranging from amateur art shows to huge homemakers' shows. We co-ordinated house-and-garden colours, and were one of the very first firms to send our buyers to market with co-ordinated colour chips and instructions on which ranges of colours to buy this season and next.

Paul Johns, a graduate of the College of Art, was in charge of all display techniques. An artist, imaginative and finely tuned, he co-ordinated displays and headed our Home Furnishings Display group within the store's Display Department. One truly remarkable person was Frances Turner. Fran Turner worked for Harry Ames, an irascible and difficult man, who had a long career in retailing and was currently managing the basement store in Simpsons Queen Street Store. She used to come by my office from time to time in sheer frustration, and in blue language "sound off" about her latest fight with Ames, who was known to use shocking language to all and sundry when annoyed, which seemed to be a great deal of the time. Amused at these outbursts, I would calm Fran down by letting her "spout," and send her away once more to face her problems in the basement.

One morning I was surprised and delighted when the general manager, Sydney Fletcher, called me into his office to advise me that an assistant had been assigned to me. Fran Turner was waiting to report to me forthwith. I called her into my office and after welcoming her as my assistant, I said, "Rule number one – there will be no more unlady-like language, no more outbursts. You are a very talented, hard worker, and we have too much to do to waste any time, yours or mine, in outbursts of righteous indignation."

Fran said meekly, "I agree, Allan. Let's get to work!"

Fran's lifetime companion was, and is, Mark Napier, then the Canadian head of one of the largest advertising agencies in the world. When they married she changed her name to Peggy Napier. Why the change from Fran to Peggy I never knew. But whether as Fran or Peggy, she was a marvel of administrative genius and organization, and got along beautifully with our exciting young group promoting Home Furnishings in Simpsons' Queen Street store. No one could have had a better "staff officer" or assistant. Our Home Furnishing Division more than tripled and showed a good profit.

I laid out a five-year plan and budget for physical improvements and intensive training to achieve our sales goals. The plans included major items such as new ceilings, lighting, and air conditioning on each of the four 100,000-square-foot floors in turn. This alone constituted a $2 million expenditure in 1946 dollars. New fixtures and furnishings cost more than $200 thousand, and new warehouses and

*G. Allan Burton's grandfather, George Burton, seen here with his family circa 1887, was the first merchant of the Burton family, operating a general store in Green River, Ontario.*

*The author at age one in 1916.*

*The author (seated) at age ten with his brother, Carl, in 1925.*
[Dr. C.R. Burton and G.A. Burton.]

*G. Allan Burton became engaged to Audrey Caro Syer, daughter of Mr. and Mrs. John Roy Syer in 1938.* [Charles Aylett]

*In May 1938, G. Allan and Audrey were married at Grace Church on-the-Hill in Toronto. As they left the church, they were given a full Guard of Honour by his fellow officers in the Governor General's Horse Guards (GGHG).*

*Overseas, World War II, England in 1941, as a Captain in the 3rd Armoured Reconnaissance Regiment (GGHG).*
[Jarret & Jevons Portrait, London]

*Audrey Burton in 1948.*

TOP LEFT: *in the years 1949 and 1950, Lieut.-Col. G.A. Burton, D.S.O., served as aide-de-camp to Field Marshal Earl Alexander of Tunis, Governor General of Canada.*

LEFT: *In 1942, the author was promoted to the rank of Major in the Governor General's Horse Guards.*

TOP RIGHT: *The Governor General's Horse Guards in England, 1942. From left to right, standing: Lieut. A.H. (Bing) Crosbie, Capt. W.T. Aspell, Major G.A. Burton, Major W. Alex Boothe, Lieut. R.P. Weese, Lieut. Frank Essery. Sitting: Lieut. Ian (Bobo) Baxter, Capt. Frank Classey.*

CENTRE RIGHT: *While G. Allan Burton was overseas in England in April 1942, his son, Jamie, was born. Here he is shown at age seven months. Father and son did not meet until 1945.*

BOTTOM RIGHT: *In 1962, Jamie Burton followed his father into the GGHG. Here, Lieut. Jamie Burton (second from right) is on exercises in Petawawa.*

TOP LEFT: *The author on Sun-up, "the great mare," winner of the Eglinton Hunt's Master's Shield in 1955.*

CENTRE LEFT: *G. Allan Burton on Sun-up, riding in the Eglinton Hunt with Eddy Cooper (left), Whipper-In.*

BOTTOM LEFT: *Three Masters of the Fox Hounds in 1959 in England. The Duke of Northumberland, Master of the Percy Hunt, Alnwick Castle, Northumberland (centre), with G. Allan Burton (left) and Brigadier F.C. (Eric) Wallace, Joint Masters of the Eglinton and Caledon Hunt.*

RIGHT: *Joint Master of the Eglinton and Caledon Hunt, G. Allan Burton on Champ in 1971.*

*In 1950, G.A. Burton's parents, Charles L. and Ella Burton, celebrated their Golden Wedding Anniversary. [Norman Jones]*

TOP: *Under the portrait of their father, Charles L. Burton, Edgar Burton, chairman of Simpsons and president of Simpson-Sears, congratulates G. Allan Burton on becoming president of Simpsons in 1964.* [Everett Roseborough]

BOTTOM: *Edgar (centre), Audrey, and G. Allan carol singing at Simpsons' downtown Toronto store in December, 1953. Christmas carol singing was an annual event at Simpsons for fifty-four years (1925-79).*

TOP: *Murray Allen (left),
Eaton's general manager, and
a driver representing Eaton's
employees give donation
cheques to G. Allan in 1961
during his chairmanship of
Metro Toronto's United
Appeal. [J. Mitchell]*

BOTTOM: *Charles Stewart,
president of Simpsons, with
G. Allan and Audrey Burton
at the opening of the
Simpsons' store in Richmond
Hill, Ont.*

TOP: *"The Chairman." The award-winning photograph by Al Gilbert of G. Allan Burton, chairman and chief executive officer of Simpsons. The photograph was taken in 1971.* [By permission of Al Gilbert]

BOTTOM: *In 1978, G. Allan Burton, now chairman of Simpsons, and his nephew, Ted (left) President, present Joe Samalea of the Bakery Department with his 25-Year-Club Certificate at a Limestone Hall garden party.*

LEFT: *On October 15, 1976, G. Allan Burton married Betty Kennedy at Limestone Hall. The Rev. Douglas Stewart looks on as they sign the register.*

BOTTOM: *Limestone Hall, the author's residence for over a quarter of a century, was built in 1853.*

*The Burton and the Kennedy families joined together in celebration of the wedding.*

*Betty Kennedy Burton and the author at the wedding of his daughter, Lynn, to David Bennett in 1982.*

TOP: *Betty Kennedy and G. Allan Burton are shown here with A.J. Casson (centre) and his wife, Margaret, during an Arts and Letters Club sketching party at Limestone Hall in 1981.*

RIGHT: *A.J. Casson sketching the view from the author's studio window at Limestone Hall, 1981.*

*On April 9, 1986, G. Allan Burton was invested with the Medal of the Order of Canada by Governor General Jeanne Sauvé at Rideau Hall, Ottawa.*

handling techniques amounted to an additional $4 or $5 million. In today's dollars, this would run to $75 million or more over five years for one store. The usual store budgeting process, while done twice a year, was seldom, if ever, part of a long-term promotional plan to reassert Simpsons as the leader, the place to shop for design, service, and value when furnishing a home. Our slogan, "You'll Enjoy Shopping at Simpsons," we intended to make once more a pledge of complete satisfaction.

I was called into Syd Fletcher's office one day in 1950 and told confidentially that one year hence I was going to be made general manager of the entire store, which was then doing about $50 million business a year. I was flattered, stunned, and almost blurted out, "But I will only have finished four years of my five-year plan for Home Furnishings." Then an old Army saying came back to me, "Never refuse leave or promotion."

The entire next year can only be described as miserable. Fletcher had a daily session with me to expose me bit by bit to the wide range of things I would have to take care of as general manager. We spent a great deal of time on personnel changes. He seemed to be determined to place his personal choice of candidate in each job, which made life very difficult for me because he and I had widely divergent views of people. I worried that for years to come I would be forced to live with his selections.

Fletcher was an honest, good-hearted Christian and a loyal man to my father and Simpsons in all things. It became quickly apparent to me that he thought I was much too young, at thirty-five, for the "big job," and he was busily trying to save me from making as many mistakes as possible before I took office. At the same time, I felt old at thirty-five and, still concerned about the "lost years," I wondered if I could catch up enough to reach the top before I became too old! Fletcher would have been deeply hurt if he had realized what little confidence I had in his opinions on the character and reliability of people, particularly women, suitable to promote to managerial status. His outlook on life, in my opinion, was bent by bachelorhood and constricted by a puritanical if charming Victorianism.

One day that fall, a director and vice-president of Simpsons Limited, Norman Urquhart, C.B.E., asked me what was wrong. We were up at the Caledon Mountain Trout Club, fishing together alone on the pond. When I told him what I thought was my problem, he spoke sharply to me. "Are you the boss?"

"No, sir."

"Well, stop acting like the boss. Be confident that anything you don't like when you *are* the boss you can change. I'll support you all the way."

What a wonderfully simple solution! I relaxed and enjoyed myself for the first time in months. I think it is wrong to advise a person of his new job more than a few weeks in advance of the change – the fewer, the better – except where there is a chance the candidate, already selected for greater things but left unaware of the regard in which his superiors hold him, might jump ship to a competitor. Regular and good lines of communication should be maintained.

Later I maintained a "forty file," a danger file, because most men and women feel that if they are not within sight of their "goal jobs" in the company by the time they are forty, they wonder if they are appreciated. They receive and consider offers to join other companies, and you may have thousands of dollars invested in the person at this point of time. Interviews with those in my file were arranged. Their hopes and our expectations were discussed, so we both knew where we stood.

Norman Urquhart was a truly great friend. He was a wise, somewhat portly man, white-haired, sharp-eyed, astute, alert, with much "homespun" humour. Norman had been through the mill of the twenties and thirties and was connected with the mining business and a stockbroker. It was said that when he was in his mid-forties he walked into his office one day and announced that he had made all the money he wanted and that he was giving his business, then worth about two million dollars, to his faithful employees! He was a director of many companies besides Simpsons and was for many years chairman of the Trustees of the Toronto General Hospital, where an entire wing of this famous institution bears his name. Norman's guideline for investing in equities was simplicity itself. When you have doubled your money, sell half and re-invest; then you are riding the stock for free! He adhered to this rule, he informed me, with all stocks except Simpsons', which he never sold. Simpsons' stock was split at least fifteen to one during his time.

Facing the heavy demands of the general managership, I had to turn over command of the Governor General's Horse Guards to my successor, Col. Bud Baker. The Horse Guards have a saying, "Once a Horse Guard, always a Horse Guard," no matter where you go or what you do. I had served with the regiment from my eighteenth birthday in 1933, when I received my first commission, to 1950. Giving up the active role would have been more difficult except that there were many fine young men who had served overseas with the regiment who were anxious to take my place.

The honorary colonel of the Horse Guards is the Governor General of Canada, and the commanding officer is normally made one of his aides-de-camp, which entitled the C.O. to add A.D.C. to his name and decorations. I was privileged to serve His Excellency, Field Marshal Earl Alexander of Tunis, as one of his A.D.C.s, and Audrey served as Lady-in-Waiting to Lady Alexander whenever they were officially in town and I was on duty. Alexander was a remarkable and charming man. He and Margaret, Lady Alexander, made a handsome couple. Alexander was, like me, an amateur artist. He was fascinated by the Display Department at Simpsons, and we could hardly get him out of there to resume his tours.

Audrey and I were invited to spend a weekend at Rideau Hall as guests of Their Excellencies, and a more gracious host and hostess would be hard to imagine. Alexander sent his permanent aide, an Irish Guardsman, later destined to become prime minister of Northern Ireland, to meet us at the train station. As we drove up to Rideau Hall and got out of the car, who was waiting at the open front door for us but His Excellency, Field Marshal Alexander in person! It was about thirty degrees below zero and I was wearing a large coonskin coat, and Audrey mink, but the Governor General was standing in the cold, bare-headed and without a coat. Still abashed but being greeted warmly, I waited to follow him inside, when he "shooed" us into the house ahead of him, saying, "Get along, Allan, you're not on duty this weekend!"

He was wonderful to work for, if one knew his own business. Years later, after he had retired as minister of defence in Churchill's cabinet, he became a director of an important Canadian company and returned to Toronto to attend a board meeting. A reception was held in his honour at the Royal York Hotel. A line of guests quickly formed to shake his hand, from which I hung back. An official said, "Don't you want to meet Earl Alexander?" I said I knew him and thought I would wait until he was through so we could have a longer chat. With that, Alexander looked over and saw me for the first time. He left the line, came over to me, thrust his arm through mine, and turning to the crowd said, "Colonel Burton is an old friend of mine and we have much to talk about, so if you will excuse us!" With that, he marched me, arm and arm, with him out of the room, up to his suite for a drink and a chat. I thought it was a wonderful way to say "thank you."

Col. R.Y. Eaton, the long-time president of Eaton's, was also the long-time honorary lieutenant-colonel of the Governor General's Horse Guards. He had so served when I received my commission in 1933 and he was so serving in 1950. Col. Eaton was a huge hulk of a man, softly spoken, with an extremely sharp but dry sense of humour. He was "broad" Irish and very shy. He had kept the old Body Guard and then the Horse Guards in fine fettle with unfailing support for more than twenty years. When there is a change of command, the outgoing colonel advises the honorary lieutenant-colonel and introduces his successor. I arranged a date for Lieut.-Col. Bud Baker, my successor, and me to meet with Col. Eaton in his office at Eaton's downtown store. On arrival we were shown into his tiny office panelled in dark oak. The room was dark to the point of gloominess. The man loomed huge behind his desk in the shadows. Col. Eaton was never easy to converse with, partly because of his extreme shyness and partly because he did not believe in "small talk." I started the conversation by reminding him that I had been the youngest commanding officer of the regiment since 1812, and I went on to say that Col. Baker was three years younger than I had been and we had the youngest slate of field officers ever. Col. Eaton flashed a shy grin at me and pronounced in his Irish brogue, "Well, I guess time will cure that!" He thanked me for bringing Col. Baker to meet him and the interview was over!

My first important crises as the new merchandise manager of Home Furnishings occurred when Bill Hunter, the manager of the Drapery Department, suddenly became very ill with spinal meningitis and could not go to the New York markets to do his spring buying. Bill's second in command, a nice, competent floor manager, was not to be trusted with placing a couple of hundred thousand dollars' worth of orders in the New York drapery, chintz, or any other market because he was addicted to the bottle and might not remember where he had been. The junior assistant manager, Jim Agar, who had taste and moderate experience at that point in time, could not have handled the responsibility. Jim was mild-mannered and self-effacing, in contrast to his mother, Alice Agar, who was a strong, athletic woman and a top golfer well into her three score and ten. I decided that I must lead the foray into the market myself. After all, I had worked in Schumacher's and knew most of the principal fabric houses in New York better than the assistants did. Unfortunately, the day before we were to board the train to New York, Jim Agar had some sort of fracas and ended up with a severely fractured jaw, enpurpled and visibly tied together with black gut stitches on both sides of his chin. We boarded the train and mapped our final strategy to cover the vast market. Our goal was to buy the most attractive assortment of drapery chintzes Simpsons had ever seen. So we planned an early start in the morning.

The next morning, to my horror, I saw the senior assistant manager approaching with two black eyes and broken glasses. His story was that he had stumbled getting into the taxi, fallen, and done all this damage. With his track record, of course, no one believed him. Bravely we ventured into the marketplace, one senior assistant manager with two black eyes, one junior assistant manager with a broken chin, stitched, bruised, and purple, and one merchandise manager wet behind the ears but confident he could do the job.

In anticipation of my first buying trip in ten years, I had broken down our planned purchases into categories and quantities and price ranges so I would not get carried away and spend all my money in one place. The formidable House of Riverdale was our first visit because we were their largest customer in Canada. The salesman, who greeted us warmly, expecting large orders, on learning that I was the new merchandise manager, looked at my battered companions and said, "Gee! You Canadian merchandise managers are certainly tough on your buyers!"

He brought out his new line, almost every piece of which I rejected. I said, "I am sorry if that is your new line. I cannot find anything to be enthusiastic about, so I will not place any order with you. Have you nothing better?"

He was shocked to the core and hastened to bring out an entirely new, colourful, lively, saleable line of prints. As he showed the designs one by one and I enthusiastically bought more and more, I became somewhat annoyed that he had been trying to put one over on me. I demanded an explanation. The salesman said, "What I showed you first is known as our 'Mid-West Line,' and that is all Mr. Bill Hunter would buy. The line that you have purchased is known as our 'New York and California Design.' " Our new "New York and California Design" sold out at record speed and we never bought the dull "Mid-West Line" again.

· · ·

In the late forties and early fifties our growing family expanded. A daughter, Lynn, and a few years later another daughter, Janice, joined us. We succeeded in securing the services of a huge, robust, and cheerful woman, Madame Laura Racine, who was French Canadian and Roman Catholic. She was what Gertie Hines had been to our family when I was young. Her "babies" were then growing rapidly. Laura only left us when, not well herself, she moved back to the convent to once more take care of the nuns and be taken care of by them.

Our family was rapidly outgrowing the family house on Binscarth Road. After we moved in, we invited our neighbours, including Dick Fulford, the retired former owner of radio station CKEY, and his wife Muriel to our housewarming. The Fulfords were the last guests to leave and suggested that Audrey and I come across the street to his house at 47 Binscarth for a nightcap and listen to some of Dick's "studio" records. This small, exceptionally dapper little man was an enthusiastic amateur drummer, and his invitation was partly to acquire an audience for his virtuoso drum performance. About 3:30 a.m., after many drinks, I said, "Dick, this is a fine house, a gentleman's house. If you ever think of selling it, please give me first chance of refusal." Dick agreed that he would do so. We never got invited back to Dick and Muriel's house. They did little entertaining at home, and we were of a different generation. But seven years later, I was surprised to get a call from Dick saying that he wanted to sell his house. He had promised me first refusal, and he would give me one week to make an offer.

This was exciting news, but it came at an awkward time because Audrey had the day before taken the children to open our cottage at Pinerocks, Florence Island, Muskoka. I phoned her to come back immediately to view 47 Binscarth, which she did. When we examined the place together, Audrey was undecided, partly because the asking price was more than she thought we could afford. So I sent her back to Muskoka and bought the place.

My father always thought that he and mother would move out of their big house at 136 Glen Road and exchange it for his first house, 52 Binscarth, but mother, bless her, put her foot down saying, "Daddy, no, I will not, I am too old to be uprooted again." I could just see her "roots" going down through the polished oak floors into the good soil below! Most of my father's contemporaries, including himself, had built their "big" houses too late to enjoy their families growing up in them. They suddenly found themselves rattling around in too much space. So I was determined to acquire mine early. The deal completed, 47 Binscarth sat empty across the street from us for the next few months. We planned to redecorate completely before we moved in.

Thus began one of the loveliest periods of our lives. While the house at 47 was completely bare of furnishings of any kind, it never had that cold, ghost-empty feeling. Even in its nakedness it was a fine house, inside and outside. It sat on a beautiful property, four hundred feet deep, running down into a part of the Rosedale Ravine. In the basement there was a large recreation room, a replica of an English pub, half-timbered, with a fireplace and a full bar in dark oak, complete with brass rail. The only thing I had purchased from Dick Fulford, in addition to the house itself, was a collection of huge studio discs, dating from the thirties, and the player and turntable to play them. For nearly four months, three or four nights a week, Audrey and I would put the children to bed and then go over to 47, armed with folding chairs, the bar stocked with Scotch for me and Seagram's V.O. for Audrey, the fireplace lit, and night after night we danced to the wonderful old jazz records and made up for our years of separation, melting into each other's arms as we danced for hours on end. In the process that wonderful house wrapped its arms around us, and we knew exactly how we wanted our "big" house to look. It had already become "home" even in its empty state. I have never known another house, bereft of personal furnishings and art, to project this feeling.

Years later, when we had moved to the country and 47 was sold, although the new owners invited us several times, Audrey would not set foot in "her home" again and invariably found excuses to avoid going. I understood her feelings completely.

One of the most attractive features of the life of the department-store merchandiser used to be the buying trips, often to out-of-the-way places that he or she would most likely never see in a lifetime of other work. When my father did his travelling and buying, he would be away from home as much as eight months of the year. Travel then was luxurious and leisured, first-class all the way. Now the tendency is to rush around the world with the maximum amount of fatigue and the minimum amount of time spent socializing or searching out new lines.

In March 1949, I was privileged to fly to Europe on my first merchandise tour. The purpose of the tour was to visit our agents in several different countries to examine their markets and see if there were other new and interesting lines that we should add to our assortments. Audrey went with me, and we went overseas at the same time as Margery and William Finlayson, our neighbours. Bill was secretary-treasurer of the Argus Corporation. The plan was that, after travelling overseas together, we would go our separate ways but have the pleasure of each other's company on the return voyage on the S.S. *Excambrian*, sailing out of Genoa to New York.

Audrey had not flown before and was a "white-knuckler" all the way. We flew to London in a Trans-Canada Airlines North Star. These planes had four Rolls-Royce piston engines. The exhausts on the topside of the motors belched huge flames. This configuration may have derived from their use as bombers as the flames would not be visible from the ground. But it was frightening to non-flyers, especially as the motors varied in tone constantly, seldom being "in sync" with one another. After leaving Montreal a day late because of "equipment" difficulties, we stopped at Sydney, N.S., then Gander, Nfld., for refuelling caused by severe headwinds, then Prestwick, Scotland, and finally at Heathrow in a fog so dense we could not see our wing tips! We were airborne a total of nineteen hours. Quite apart from suffering what is now called "jet lag," we were exhausted. We stayed at the Grosvenor House, the scene of my boyhood horse episode with the doorman. Our rooms were icy cold because Bob Gibson, then our London office manager, had bouquets of flowers put in our rooms, and the housekeeping staff of the hotel had opened all the windows in the suite to keep them fresh! It was a shock to us to realize that England was still very strictly rationed.

Leaving Audrey in London, I visited Kidderminster to look for carpets – a poor, disheartening town. Then I went to Stoke-on-Trent, the home of many of the famous English pottery and china houses, where I met Leslie Irving of Paragon China, whose father before him, Hugh, had been a good friend of my father when Dad was in the china business. Maurice Pickles, our china buyer, and another supplier, Dick Plant, of R.H. & S.L. Plant, whose china production was sold mainly in Scandinavia, were also waiting to receive me. After our very cold drive, a lively party with many toasts took place before dinner at a hotel called Ash Hall, a converted large country house. It was very comfortable, so I phoned Audrey and suggested she join us the next day. We were going to tour the Paragon China plant and see their artisans make and decorate their famous china, which held the Royal Warrant. I also had a letter of introduction from my father to Hugh Irving, Leslie's father.

After we arrived at the plant, Leslie excused himself before he took me to see his father. He felt very poorly from the excesses of the previous night! He disappeared, leaving me alone, when along came a small man in a long white cloth coat, wearing a bowler hat. I thought that he was one of the foremen or an overseer of some sort, but he said, "Good morning. Can I help you?"

I replied, "Yes, do you know where I could find Mr. Hugh Irving?"

"I am Hugh Irving."

Taken aback, I said, "Then in that case, sir, I have a letter of introduction to you from my father, Mr. C.L. Burton!"

Leslie had not been wearing the traditional uniform that all pottery executives wore, the ankle-length white coat and black bowler hat, so I had no way of knowing the custom being observed by his father. I was told that Mr. Pickles, our buyer, was the best-liked buyer in the potteries and that Simpsons, Toronto, had the finest china department in Canada, which I firmly believed myself.

We visited Royal Doulton, famous for its figurines, and spent a day with Sir Ernest Johnson of Johnson Bros., another old friend of Dad's, and had tea and dinner with his family. Johnsons were large suppliers and even started a plant in Hamilton, Ontario. The next day, at Barlaston, we toured the world-famous Wedgwood Works, the newest and most remarkable china plant of one of the oldest and best-known firms in the world.

Back in London, I phoned Elias Svedberg, the internationally acclaimed furniture designer of Nordiska Kompaniet in Stockholm. It took me four hours to make the phone connection. I was told there were only thirty-nine telephone lines to the continent. I arranged to fly to Sweden. Audrey would stay in London and join me later in Brussels. I received word from Leslie Irving that if Simpsons would promise co-operative advertising with Paragon, they would eliminate Eaton's. I promised to work on it.

Next I went to the well-known makers of reproduction furniture, Wrestall, Brown & Cannel. I was advised it was no use seeing them because they were tied up to Eaton's. However, I spent most of an afternoon with Major Brown, sampling Red Hackle Scotch whisky at his insistence, and he decided to change his mind and sell both to

Eaton's and to Simpsons. I ordered a beautiful Queen Anne burl walnut desk, which I still use daily, to clinch the deal.

I met Sir Richard Burbidge, the chairman of Harrods' lovely store in London, and he arranged an unforgettable, behind-the-scenes visit to the rooms in Buckingham Palace, where all the state gold and silver plates and ornaments are kept. Two men polish silver all day long, every day, and at the end of the week they start all over again on the same pieces! It was a breath-taking display.

I flew Scandinavian Airlines four hours to Göteborg, then two and a half hours more to Stockholm. I had not realized it was so far! I was met by Elias Svedberg, the designer, and Harold Walther, the export manager, who drove me to the Grand Hotel, one of the few remaining *grand luxe* hotels in the world. There was a delay at the desk and I discovered that, thinking Audrey was coming with me, they had reserved the Royal Suite! I said that I did not mind as I was only going to stay overnight. But I was not prepared for a reception room the size of Union Station, with seven floor-to-ceiling French windows looking across the canal to the Royal Palace. My poor lone suitcase deposited in this huge apartment looked ridiculous. I went into the bathroom to wash up and, again, it was royally huge – two of everything, including two bidets, that most civilized of European sanitary inventions. All I could imagine was two lovers, on their own bidets, holding hands! Feeling somewhat giddy and a bit ridiculous, I filled both washbasins with water, put a hand in each, and shouted out to the Swedes, "Come, wash me!" They came in and, of course, burst out laughing. We were friends; formality had flown.

That night six Swedes took me to an eighteenth-century inn in the forest outside Stockholm, which was owned and operated by Nordiska Kompaniet, and I experienced my first formal Swedish dinner, an unforgettable experience. There was a small silk Swedish flag at one end of the table and a Canadian one at the other. The dinner consisted of fifteen courses, each with a different drink, and every time they ran out of ideas, they would have another schnapps! There were many speeches, including a long account of how they had discovered that I was in England and why they had persuaded me to come to Nordiska to see their factory and that they were most honoured that I had come. In reply, I recounted the flight over from London in detail, thanked them for their marvellous dinner and hospitality, and extended greetings from my associates in Canada who had had the pleasure of meeting Elias Svedberg on his Canadian trip.

I did not remind them he had come to Toronto at Eaton's invitation some years ago, and on that trip had decided to sell me his line instead! On that occasion I had taken him to the Royal Canadian Yacht Club for lunch. As the RCYC boat pulled away into the bay, Elias sighed and said, "Ah, this is the proper place from which to see a city – away from it!" Elias had been wined and dined for two days, and I took the low-key approach only because I had resigned myself to the fact that Eaton's had his line sewn up. All I said by way of business at the luncheon was, "Elias, if you want the largest possible volume of sales for your modern furniture, you were at the right place yesterday. But if you want someone who will vigorously promote your designs with sensitivity and understanding, you would be right to deal with me." On the way back to the city on the ferry, Elias suddenly looked at me and said, "Allan, I liked what you said. I also liked what you didn't say. I have decided to give Simpsons my line exclusively!" I was delighted and a bit thunderstruck. Bit by bit we were making great inroads.

So now back at the Grand Hotel, I reviewed our first meeting and made a note to appreciate much but promise little, and slept soundly. Awake at 5:00 a.m. the next morning, a crystal-clear day beckoned me outside to take snapshots until I was picked up at 7:30 a.m. by car to Nykoping, where the Nordiska furniture was made. I was very hungry although none the worse for wear, in spite of all the drink the night before, but at that hour no restaurant was open. We had been driving for about forty minutes, when I got the horrible feeling that possibly these Swedish gentlemen had had huge breakfasts at home. Inquiring if that was so, they said, "No, we are going to have breakfast at the King's Summer Palace," whereupon we turned into the royal driveway! We stopped at the Gatehouse – the King was away in Nice – and had a huge breakfast, milk, eggs, ham, all the things poor England was still without nearly five years after the war. Then we went on to the factory and straight to work. One curious thing I noticed was that all the woodworkers, including the labourers, stopped whatever they were doing and when we as a party stopped, they clicked their heels, bowed, and formally said the Swedish equivalent of "good morning." A vast difference in attitude was all too apparent in the metal-working shops. There was no "good morning." Instead, glowering looks and even the occasional spit on the floor near our feet greeted us. The contrast between the two groups in the same factory was astounding. I never did receive a satisfactory explanation, but it had something to do with the metalworkers being of a lower social order for centuries and the woodworkers being considered artisans and artists.

By this time lunchtime had arrived, and the Swedes said, "Ah, now we can go to the village and have some schnapps, ja?" They were crestfallen and put at a disadvantage the rest of the afternoon when I told them, "I will have milk, thank you. I never drink when I am working." They drank milk with me out of politeness. All afternoon I went piece by piece over their extensive line, making notes and telling them what I could pay for each item in krona, completely disregarding the price on the tag. After a couple of hours, I said, "Here's what I can do. Here's what I can pay. Just say yes or no." They said yes at once. I was then taken to Svedberg's house where once more we had an even more elaborate dinner, if possible, with the usual quantities of drink. I had been told by my host that it was the custom in Sweden if you really admired the meal to kiss the cook! So, going along with his suggestion, I asked Mrs. Svedberg if I might have the cook presented to me so I could thank her for the exceptionally fine dinner, with which she produced a plump, red-cheeked woman, plain-featured, short of ugly, with one huge front tooth visible in her gaping mouth when she grinned. I grabbed her to kiss her, as custom required, and she screamed and ran out of the room, thinking she was about to be raped rather than thanked, while my hosts hooted with laughter at my dismay!

During the flight back to Brussels we stopped at Frankfurt. Seeing the German police, whose military-type uniforms reminded me of the war, I did not disembark, as most did, to stretch their legs. To my delight Audrey was waiting for me in Brussels. After a couple of days' buying and being entertained by Simon Frères, our agents of long-standing, we headed for an Easter weekend in Paris. We travelled by train from Brussels to Paris and arrived at the Ritz at eight-thirty at night, dirty and tired.

This was our first experience at the Ritz. The doorman, to our annoyance, would not even take our luggage off the roof of the taxi until he had phoned in to make sure that we, indeed, did have reservations. We were hungry, but no supper was available from room service except for cold chicken salad. Demonstrating my beautiful but rusty French to my wife, I told the waiter to serve us breakfast "a huit heure et midi," meaning at half-past eight, not at eight o'clock and noon! The valet was just as astounded when I gave him my suits to be pressed and told him to press them and bring them back "at nine-thirty yesterday morning!" No one at the Ritz spoke English except the *concierge,* reputed to be the most powerful man in all Paris. And he was! If the *concierge* at the Ritz reserved you a table, or seats at a show, they were always the best in the house. There was no cab rank in Place Vendôme, so I arranged for an ancient Packard, complete with a chauffeur called Harvey, or as he said, "Aarrvay." Harvey's favourite sentence in his limited English was, "Ze traffique in Paree, she is something special." We had three glorious days in Paris and Versailles before we caught the Simplon Express for Milan.

The Ritz, in a complete reversal of their cool welcome, sent a courier with us to see that we were comfortably installed in our sleeping compartment. With six large valises, we were packed in like sardines. We were awakened three times, the first time at 5:30 a.m. at the Swiss border. We passed my old school, Lycée Jaccard, on the shores of Lac Léman, Lausanne. Finally, through the Simplon Tunnel, we arrived at Milan. The Excelsior Gallia was quite a comedown from the Ritz. We were met by Mario Ricci, our agent, who next day took me to buy carved Louis-style furniture chair-frames at a small village called Meda. The workmanship was exquisite and I was prepared to buy a quantity of frames. The owner of the small shop gave me a price on a fine Louis XVth Bergère. Thinking of negotiating a better price, I asked him his price on one hundred frames. Without hesitation, he quoted me a higher unit price than for just one! Thinking he had misunderstood, I asked Mario to explain to him that a large quantity deserved a discount. After a lot of voluble Italian, Mario explained that the shopowner said he would have to charge more per frame for one hundred of the same frame than for just one, the reason being that the carvers would be so bored doing the same one over and over, he would have to pay them a premium to complete such a large order!

However, Villa D'Este on Lake Como soothed my frustration before we went back to buy beautiful Como silks in Milan. The final morning, having carefully husbanded my money so that I would not end up with too many lira, I went down to pay my bill to find that Mario Ricci had checked out already, leaving me to pay his hotel bill as well as ours. We met the Finlaysons in Genoa on board the small S.S. *Excambrian* for a leisurely, ten-day sail back home across the south Atlantic, angling up to Boston. We never stopped elaborating on the experiences we had had on our separate travels. On arrival in

New York, Bill Finlayson found a letter from E.P. Taylor informing him he was fired as secretary-treasurer of the Argus Corporation, a result Bill anticipated, having converted all his stock to cash before our trip! E.P. had used Bill to the full, straightening out his newly acquired companies, and Bill had had enough.


When I became general manager of Simpsons and gave up command of the regiment I began to repeat the learning process I started in my previous division. Each general manager, it seemed, was encouraged to compete more vigorously against each other than against Eaton's, our main competition! This, to my mind, was most unfortunate. I was general manager of the downtown Toronto store, which was the largest and did more than half of the total business. The five stores in all did $100 million in sales each year. The Toronto store did more than twice as much as our largest store in Montreal. I felt we had much to offer the other stores, but even more importantly, our combined buying power in many fields would be very beneficial to our growth and strength and profits.

I made a practice of visiting the other stores and entertaining the out-of-town store officials as much as possible to sell my ideas of co-operation. Not all the resistance to this apparently radical idea came from the out-of-town stores. Several of my own store officials were concerned, saying that the general manager in Montreal would steal all our ideas but never give anything in return. A. Hartley (Bink) Lofft, our general manager in Montreal, was the oldest and most experienced of our general managers and a close associate and contemporary of my brother Edgar, our president.

I am sure Lofft was hurt when I got the "big job" in Toronto and he was moved from London to Montreal. Thus, when I suggested to Edgar that I wished to hold a regular general managers' conference, at which we could freely discuss our mutual problems, Edgar said, in effect, "You are mad!" My feeling was that no one of the rank of vice-president and above would be invited to or should attend the regular sessions, but would be invited to give papers on various subjects at stipulated times in the three-day seminar.

"Why am I mad?" I asked.

"Well," replied Edgar, "for one thing Bink Lofft will tear you to pieces."

I said I was prepared for his sarcasm or criticism. If he was right, I would deserve it; if he was wrong, the meeting would not stand for it. Edgar reluctantly agreed to let me proceed with the first general managers' conference. I acted as its chairman. The result was that we set up buying programs, joint promotional programs, study programs on future areas of improvement in the rapidly changing environment and the mechanization of "materials handling" and methods research. We also agreed that these conferences would be held a minimum of once a year, and that each general manager in turn would bear the overall responsibility of being chairman and running the seminar. It was surprisingly easy. Bink Lofft was generous enough to say that we had all benefited from the exchange of ideas. This was freely expressed in the absence of the senior officers, and I proposed that Bink be responsible for the next conference in the spring. Edgar was relieved and delighted at the results, but I did not tell him that one suggestion put forward anonymously as a means to expedite our work was to move the head office to North Bay!

During this time a tremendous amount of renovation – new escalators, lighting, ceilings, and air conditioning – was going on in the Toronto, Montreal, and London stores, and our Mail-Order Division, which in its own right was doing $100 million a year, needed many millions to expand and modernize. All the divisions and stores were profitable. Nevertheless, there was a constant, silent, but sometimes ferocious in-house battle to justify the demands on the available money. It must have been a terrible headache for my father, Edgar, and the Board to keep everyone, including our lenders, happy. However, they could feel the pulse of progress and the need to be the leader, as we did.

My predecessor as general manager, Sydney Fletcher, had sponsored a group of young men called "methods researchers," headed by an accountant named Elmer Rounding. The management needed greater expertise in the analysis of operations – how costs could be reduced, efficiency and productivity increased, and so on. Norman Agar, the comptroller of Simpsons, used to apportion common expenses between the Mail-Order Division and the various stores on an "assumed" basis rather than on any analysis. Thus Mr. Agar never lost – an adjustment was always in his favour. We, in operating, had a saying, "We have been Agarized again." So Elmer Rounding was sent to study the methods of time and motion study then popular in the United States.

Elmer Rounding was a tall, almost gangly individual, with a keen mind and a deceptive Gary Cooper-like ease of manner that hid his highly organized and competitive nature. He quickly added several other young men who were in their twenties and had different backgrounds but were similar in keenness and intelligence. My father used to refer to the members of the Methods Research group as "intelligently ignorant young men." There was no facet of the service or the administration of the business that they were afraid to tackle. In prewar days there was a sharp division, both in status and in remuneration, between the merchants and the service people, the highest and the lowest. The customer was the common bond between the two groups. There was little or no collaboration between them. It seems incredible that so much heavy work was "manhandled"–mechanized or automated systems, which we now consider the most basic of needs in warehousing and materials handling, were virtually non-existent.

Elmer Rounding was the right man at the right time. He was trained as an accountant but had much more imagination than most accountants. He was quick to see the benefits and opportunities of increasing production and profits while eliminating waste and unproductive drudgery. Soon we were studying everything from customer service to creating a workroom to service and repair the new television sets. Rounding and I became very close working partners, determined to keep Simpsons in the forefront of department stores.

Knowing that the ever-growing suburbs would lead to the development of shopping centres, or "plazas" as they were called, Elmer and I attended every possible seminar on the subject held in North America over a two-year period, learning about real estate, financing, development, and renting. In the meantime, others on Elmer's staff were sent to study workrooms and systems. Ronald Crichton, the young son of a long-time Simpsons floor manager, as part of the Methods Research group was assigned by me to examine and report on how we handled or mishandled customer complaints and service inquiries.

Ron Crichton was short and compact, quick in speech and action, and while not an accountant, he had come up through "service" and was not afraid to call a spade a spade. I had had several complaints from our customers that adjustments were difficult to achieve. This certainly did nothing to help them to "enjoy shopping at Simpsons," which our slogan encouraged them to do. Ron spent several weeks in the Adjusting Department, as it was then called, and soon found a logjam of unprocessed complaints that ran into the thousands. As a percentage of the total transactions in the millions, it was not alarming, but to the individual customer it was infuriating. He found no less than 1,900 unprocessed complaints in the manager's desk, under blotters, stuffed into drawers. Apparently the manager hoped that they would get lost. I removed the manager, who was in his early forties, young but lazy, and put Crichton, all of twenty-five-years old, in charge of the entire operation as acting manager to get the situation cleaned up in the shortest possible time and to select and train his successor – a feat he accomplished in about four months. The man he trained, and who was duly appointed manager of the Adjusting Department, was thirty-seven at the time and did an excellent job for some years.

Next Crichton was given the task of hiring electronics technicians and creating a radio and TV repair workroom. I wanted it to be the best in the business and to be in full operation six months later when television officially came to Toronto. We arranged for some of our technicians to work in various existing TV workrooms in the United States while we paid their full wages and expenses – Hudson's in Detroit, Abraham and Strauss in New Jersey, Rich's in Atlanta, Lord & Taylor in New York, among others. These firms received our men gladly, and although some tried to keep them, they all came back to Simpsons as foremen in the new TV workroom, becoming managers of the operation as further promotions were made.

Our next major project was a study of our delivery fleet. We designed and had made a special, reusable delivery-van body, incorporating both a skylight and a money safe to help prevent robberies. We avoided the forced obsolescence put on us by the motor companies, so we only ordered new chassis and motors, refitting the bodies to them as the mechanical features of the old trucks wore out. We sold these studies to competing firms for five thousand dollars apiece. Eaton's at one point adopted our basic van and we ordered for both firms, lowering the cost per unit, until some senior official in Eaton's, in a fit of pride, forbade their delivery people to co-operate with our purchasing. We saved literally hundreds of thousands of dollars annually over the next few years, and improved working conditions at the same time.

Once more, Ron Crichton, now barely twenty-seven, was promoted. This time I put him in charge of all our workrooms, which together employed some three hundred people.

Not afraid to tackle anything, we undertook to complete the upgradings of our main floor in downtown Toronto, reputed to have the longest continuous main aisle of any store in the British Empire, with new fixtures, new ceilings, air conditioning, new lighting, and escalators over the entire 100,000 square feet of selling space and yet maintain "the atmosphere" of Simpsons. One wag described the anxiety over doing the right thing to preserve our atmosphere as "giving mother a nose job – how do you want dear old mother to look?" We did this without shutting down any significant area, except where new escalators had to be boarded around for safety's sake. Max Miller, our store architect and successor to my old boss and friend Frank Corley, came up with a most ingenious solution to the problem of making repairs while remaining open for business. We made all the installations and increased our business while doing it. Max developed a mobile work platform that ran on steel rails sweated onto the store columns, which permitted us to continue to sell our goods underneath. As each section was completed, new rails were installed overnight and the huge work platform was rolled into the new work position, with the newly completed section open for business as well. The dust and debris from the work was carried in a long, galvanized sealed metal tube, or trough, to the outside under negative air pressure in a completely satisfactory manner. To this day its workings are a mystery to me. The hoardings around the escalators proved to be highly productive, becoming large selling backgrounds for specialty items.

Word had it that the discount stores, which offered minimum service but bare price, would soon put the traditional department stores out of business. We experimented with a small discount outlet in a small, 30,000-square-foot space in our Lawrence Avenue Service Building. It was very successful, but after a year we decided that it was not our business. We did $3.5 million worth of business in the space and made a $300,000 operating profit, but we lost ten times more inventory through shoplifting than normal. Most importantly, as I stood day by day listening to customers' comments, I heard, "Well, if we have to shop this way, we would rather have Simpsons or Eaton's do it, but why do we have to?" Then a major flaw became apparent. Customers had to line up, supermarket-style, at a few cash registers.

The average 100,000-foot discount store had a maximum of fourteen cash registers; our normal was forty-eight for the same area. We were able to do vastly more business than they at our busiest and most profitable periods.

Shortly thereafter, Leo Kolber, the new general manager of Cemp Investments, the Bronfman children's trusts, came to see me to offer us a store position in Cedarbrae in Scarborough. It was located half a mile east of the biggest discounter in town at that time, Towers. I went out to watch how Towers did business and to see how busy they were. They had it all to themselves. The store, by our standards, was dirty and untidy. Most, if not all, departments were franchised out to different merchants. The women customers were young, wore too-short shorts and hair curlers, and many were large with child. They did not look like our type of customer at all. Nonetheless, we found by survey that Scarborough families were made up of working people, neither rich nor poor, and we guessed they would respond to a beautiful clean store with services and better merchandise. So we took Cemp's offer and designed our new store as beautifully as we could. We were on tenterhooks as the opening day approached. The crowd we attracted looked the same as the one in Towers, pregnant and wearing curlers, but they bought everything in sight. I spotted an engineer pushing a disabled cash register on a wheeled work table through the main-floor crowd toward the service area. "What's wrong?" I asked him.

With a grin, he shot back, "Overheated!"

The miracle was that in a matter of weeks these same women started to make shopping an occasion. They arrived well turned out, hair groomed, the same people, but living up to the "atmosphere" for which Simpsons was justly famous. One year later the Towers store was in trouble. Their only defence to our competition was to slash prices till they bled to death. We were very profitable and much encouraged to take on all and sundry in the suburbs.

# THE NEW
# SIMPSONS-SEARS

## 13

In 1951, Simpsons' total business was $200 million in annual sales –
$100 million in the five retail stores and $100 million in the three
mail-order plants headed up by Gordon Graham. Gordon had wanted
me to come to work for him in the Mail Order, and while I greatly
admired him personally, I elected to take my chances in the Retail
Stores Division. The truth of the matter was I enjoyed the daily contact with customers and their changing needs, and the daily contest
with Eaton's for their trade. The Bay was not a competitor of ours in
those days. I preferred this close contact to the more distant and ana-
lytical approach needed to build a catalogue that required huge commitments many months before you could see any return on your
purchases. The retail merchant and the mail-order man will each
swear that he has the harder job. On a scale of one to ten, they both
rate about eight on the toughness scale.

There is no denying that the Simpsons-Sears arrangement for mail
order was a brilliant deal. My brother Edgar and General E.R. Wood
were the principal architects. The deal was simply to create a new
Canadian company called Simpsons-Sears, the voting stock of which
was owned equally by Simpsons Limited and Sears, Roebuck & Co.
of Chicago. Sears, Roebuck had never before concluded an arrangement with a partner on an equal basis. But no deal would have been
made on any basis that gave them control. Sears put up the cash.
Simpsons put up their mail-order plants and, importantly, the people who operated them, all Simpsons-trained. Simpsons sold its Mail-
Order Division to the new company for $20 million cash and access
to Sears lines and trademarks, such as Coldspot refrigerators, Craftsman tools, and the merchandising know-how that promoted them.
Sears did this better than anyone else in the world at that time.

Simpsons-Sears was given the right to develop retail stores, based on the Sears model, in all areas of Canada except within twenty-five miles of Simpsons' existing stores in Toronto, Montreal, Regina, London, and Halifax. While Simpsons was restricted from developing anywhere else in Canada, our retail business served the fastest-developing markets in Canada, and we knew we had our hands full for many years to come. In addition, we had a growing Contract Division, furnishing hospitals, hotels, and institutions all across Canada.

The contract that created Simpsons-Sears Ltd. was signed in 1952 amid many social events, much evidence of good will on both sides, and the immediate acceptance of the new arrangements by the press and other media. After the signing, my father invited General E.R. Wood of Sears, Roebuck to fish for trout at the Caledon Mountain Trout Club. The General had spent several seasons on the West Coast and Alaska fishing and hunting in the wilderness, from which sprang his love of Canada and affection for things Canadian – by which he meant the West. The old General, who, among other things, had gained his merchandise-control experience by serving as a supply officer when the U.S. Engineering Corps dug the Panama Canal, was forthright to say the least. He was notorious for his dislike of the East, meaning everything east of Chicago. In his view, the East was decadent.

The original officers of Simpsons-Sears in 1953 were the following:

| | |
|---|---|
| (Simpsons) | E.G. Burton, President |
| (Simpsons) | Robert C. Gibson, V.P. Merchandising |
| (Simpsons) | Gordon M. Graham, V.P. Mail Order |
| (Sears, Roebuck) | George F. Trotter, V.P. Retail |
| (Simpsons) | J.R. O'Kell, Secretary |
| (Simpsons) | J.D.H. Hutchinson, Treasurer |

My brother, Edgar, president of both Simpsons Limited and Simpsons-Sears Ltd., started off with offices and secretaries in both places, which proved too awkward and confusing at times. Simpsons-Sears adopted all, or nearly all, Simpsons' personnel perks and privileges, including their version of our profit-sharing plan and pension schemes. Simpsons, as far back as 1919, had one of the first half-dozen such schemes in North America. We never referred to our employees as anything but shareholders, and our stated aim was that our employees, through their Profit-Sharing Fund, would eventually own the largest single shareholding in the company. At this time the Profit-Sharing Fund held about 10 per cent of our Simpson shares.

Simpsons-Sears Ltd., which was a publicly traded company in its own right and thus able to raise its own capital and issue debt, had three classes of shares: "A" shares, voting, all held by Simpsons; "B" shares, voting, all held by Sears, Roebuck; and "C" shares, traded on the Exchange but non-voting. All shared equally in dividends, on a one-for-one basis. Interestingly, our profit-sharing plan, adopted by the Robert Simpson Company in 1919, was based on a plan in effect at the time in a Chicago company called Sears, Roebuck & Co.! My father, then general manager of Simpsons, had examined several plans in the United States – there were virtually none in Canada – and decided Sears' was the best. So, even in this area, there was little trauma.

Right from the start, we were most graciously received in all segments of Sears, Roebuck, but I am sure that there were some tense moments in the early days, on both sides, when Edgar and Gordon Graham were developing the plans for the new company. Gordon was immediately affected because, while we had patterned our profit-sharing on Sears, we, over the years, had patterned our mail-order book on Montgomery Ward's layout and presentations rather than on Sears' harder-hitting format. Very little of Simpsons' retail merchandise found its way into the Simpsons-Sears catalogue in Canada, whereas the Sears book advertised the same merchandise and more in their stores and even undersold the stores in some cases! Their success was hard to argue against. Both our Retail and Mail-Order divisions were successful and profitable, but we were geared to a much smaller market. The fifty-fifty deal proved its worth many times over. Never, to my knowledge, did we have to use our veto, nor they theirs.

Crowdus M. Baker, the Sears comptroller, a hard-bitten, burly man, and Arthur M. Wood, the secretary, tall, good-looking, and suave – no relation to the General – were both good friends of Simpsons-Sears during its twenty-five years of early development, and easy to work with as far as Simpsons was concerned. Joe O'Kell, originally from Simpsons, was the Simpsons-Sears secretary. A lawyer and our counterpart of Art Wood in Sears, Joe had the great facility of smoothly steering controversial decisions through the board at a time when dissenters had been programmed or outnumbered! Edgar would always delay a decision rather than fight, if there was any possibility of winning over the odd-man-out in a private session. In politics they call it reaching a consensus. The simple fact was, as time went on, we all thought that Edgar was being too pro-Simpsons-Sears in many of his decisions, none of which was easy. Our worst suspicions were confirmed when he was made a director of Sears, Roebuck in the United States. As great an honour as that was, many Simpsons people wondered how he could be dispassionate in his judgement. Being head of one partner company and on the board of directors of the other partner company was seen as a conflict of interest. Others argued that having direct representation in Chicago on the Sears board meant "our point of view" could be put across better. In Simpsons, however, we read "our point of view" as Simpsons-Sears' point of view rather than Simpsons Limited's. This was not entirely fair to Edgar, but that was how being one master and serving another was perceived by Simpsons' people.

The main reason Sears entertained the Simpsons-Sears deal was that it gave Sears immediate entrée in the Canadian mail-order field, associated with the best name in the business available, and with a complete staff of first-class managers. Except for George Trotter of Sears, who became V.P. Retail, and one or two early store managers from Sears, all the rest were Simpsons' men, a subtle drain on Simpsons Limited during the early years, for we at Simpsons were wholly enthusiastic about our new company and held nothing back to make it successful.

General E.R. Wood ruled Sears, Roebuck, and it was important that we got to know him better personally so, as mentioned earlier, my father invited the noted outdoorsman and fisherman to go trout fishing at Caledon Mountain Trout Club. When General Wood arrived at the club and saw the beautiful Caledon trout ponds, disdainfully he burst out, "Hell, them's 'stall-bred' fish!" We were amused when, try as he could, the "stall-bred fish" eluded the General, and my father and I quickly got our limit of eight each, the General finally getting two. The two men were remarkably similar. Both were in their seventies; both had been through the mill in many parts of the world; both were instinctive merchants because of their understanding of people. Both Dad and the General had strong opinions and genuinely admired each other. Both had "old-fashioned" values. The General and Dad, like two old male lions, never relaxed in each other's company, each keeping a watchful eye on the other for encroachments on his "pride." I liked General Wood and he seemed to like me. But then, I saw him mostly in his moments of relaxation, and he liked the fact I was "army."

Gradually as time went on, my father got more and more unhappy with certain Simpsons-Sears' board decisions, and he and Edgar would have a real donnybrook in private, each trying to make the other see his point of view. I would drop in to Dad's house each night after work – he was only one block away on Glen Road – and discuss with him our operating problems to benefit from his experience. More and more I had to listen to his latest disagreement with Edgar on Simpsons-Sears. Next morning, first thing, I would be called up to Edgar's office and he would unburden his soul to me about his problems with Dad. Finally I said, "Edgar, I will not and cannot judge between you and Dad. You are both right and both stupidly wrong. It is most important for all of us that you and he get along."

However, my father resigned from Simpsons-Sears' board in 1956 and I was put on it in his place.

I was elected to the main board of directors of Simpsons Limited in 1954. It was a very proud moment for me, a further sign that I was faced in the right direction! Being on the board was important to me in several different ways. Internally, it helped me to secure co-operation from our other Simpsons stores in merchandising and promotional matters. It had more clout than my then position as general manager of the downtown Toronto store. Externally, Elmer Rounding and I were getting ever deeply involved in negotiations with developers of shopping centres – real-estate entrepreneurs and, of course, Eaton's and Simpsons-Sears in some cases. So when Dave Kinnear of Eaton's came to me to propose that we take a position in the first truly regional shopping centre in Canada, to be named Yorkdale, in the Toronto borough of North York, Elmer and I were ready.

Eaton's had hired the Graham firm of Seattle as their architects, which was widely known for its regional centre in Seattle, Washington. We had no one in Canada to match their knowledge and expertise, so we placed a phone call to Victor Gruen in Los Angeles, whose reputation was at least equal to Graham's. Describing our dilemma to him, we asked if he could help us. His response was immediate. "Delighted. Our partner, Karl Van Leuven, is in Detroit working with Hudson's on their new suburban centres. I'll put him right on to you." Karl Van Leuven returned the call in short order, and I asked him how soon could he be in Toronto, thinking I would be lucky if I could get him in a couple of weeks. "Would this afternoon be too soon?" he replied.

"Wonderful. Come and stay with me," I answered. That was the start of a very close business partnership for the next twenty years, and Karl became a close and dear friend of my family.

We did not know what to expect. He arrived dressed in Ivy League black-and-white – black suit, white shirt, black tie – head shaven like Yul Brynner yet youthful and athletic-looking and soft-spoken. He looked very professional, but I may have been momentarily taken aback, expecting someone not so self-effacing. From our first session we knew we had hired a wonderful ally, one who could more than help us hold our own.

I well remember our first meeting at Eaton's. Dave Kinnear was flanked by Alan Eaton (R.Y.'s son) and Graham; with me were Elmer Rounding, Frank Corley, and Karl Van Leuven. As I recall, Eaton's had paid the princely sum of $1.4 million for the hundred acres of land between the proposed extension of the Spadina Expressway and Dufferin Street. They offered us any portion we wanted up to half the acreage, on the Dufferin Street side of the property, for $1.4 million, the full price they had paid. The Simpsons board had authorized me, solo, to make the best deal I could with Eaton's. This was on a Friday. I took Karl and Elmer up to Muskoka to my summer home, Pinerocks, for the weekend, so we could have our plan ready by Monday to discuss with Eaton's. We decided we needed a maximum of eighteen acres of land for present and future needs, which allowed a store expansion of forty per cent and the required parking to go with it. We also decided that we would pay the full asking price of $1.4 million with several important conditions attached.

Condition One. The land must be prepared, complete with sewers and electrical conduits, ready for blacktop surfacing. (The estimated cost for this work was $18 thousand per acre, so our real land cost was proportionately less.)

Condition Two. No one could build on or over our property without our permission, or west of an imaginary line bisecting the whole property from north to south.

Condition Three. Having paid Eaton's the whole price without discussion, we would not be required to pay anything more toward "off-site" improvements, such as a stretch of the convoluted ramp system that had to be built to connect Yorkdale to the Spadina Expressway, now known as the Allen Road.

Condition Four. Finally, anything the developer built on the Eaton's end of the property, which reduced the number of cars that could be parked below the standard set by North York bylaws, would force the developer to provide additional parking space above ground or below ground.

Eaton's were ecstatic that we had accepted the full $1.4 million asking price as our ticket of admission. They could not believe their ears that we expected only 18 per cent of their land for that price. They agreed instantly. We did not want to pay taxes or maintenance on one acre more than we needed. Dave Kinnear and I shook hands on the deal and turned it over to the lawyers to come up with a simple letter of intent and the subsequent agreement. It was only later that they wondered if they had outsmarted themselves. "Ready for blacktop surfacing" sounded innocent enough, but over the next year Eaton's spent the full $1.4 million and more on "off-site" improvements, without having recourse to us as partners to recover a portion, so our deal looked better and better. However, when I went to our board to report the agreement, the directors gasped at the "price" I had paid – $1.4 million for eighteen acres – mad, mad, I must be mad! But when I explained we had real control over the land and all we wanted for future expansion with no further liability, except for our fair share of common maintenance, their cries of dismay turned to paeans of congratulations.

Next I hired John B. Parkin Associates, the firm that had just completed our award-winning Lawrence Avenue Service Building, one-half mile south of Yorkdale, to start designing the most distinctive suburban store in North America, some 385,000 square feet, as originally designed and built. The formal agreement took months to be reviewed and signed. The lawyers on both sides were lint-picking. Access and egress to the site and agreement under circumstances that might arise seventy-five years hence, and the length of the agreement with several twenty-five-year extensions as options open to Simpsons, seemed to hold things up. I asked for a meeting with Dave Kinnear and his group and they came to the Simpsons boardroom. Our opposing team of lawyers, each about six in number, filled the room to capacity. I reminded Dave that we had had a quick and simple agreement when we had shaken hands on the deal and signed the letter of intent quickly. But now the lawyers were arguing interminably over the agreement, about minuscule details, and it was all costing us money. Could he speed things up? Kinnear, without hesitation, said, "You are so right, Allan," and turned to his lawyers and said he wanted the document for us to sign within forty-eight hours and no excuses. And we got it! This was typical of David Kinnear – tall, calm, urbanely handsome, a man of his word, truly a gentleman.

The successful conclusion of the Yorkdale deal only increased the mutual respect in which the age-old competitors, Eaton's and Simpsons, held each other. There was a time when Eaton's, being considerably larger than Simpsons for many of the early years, regarded us with amused tolerance. Now we could, and did, deal as equals. Both of us were faintly amused at the backwardness of the Hudson Bay Company generally and in particular their reluctance to go into shopping centres. Yet Eaton's tried to dictate a maximum size for our store in Yorkdale, but I refused, saying I would build the size we wanted and if Eaton's wanted to build more or less that was their prerogative!

About this same time, we were having more and more talks about shopping-centre locations in Toronto and Montreal with many developers, Leo Kolber of Cemp being the most active. We had learned lesson number one in Yorkdale, where Eaton's had purchased the land and could deal with developers as the owner, or share the development with them as partners with special privileges. With this in mind, we explored possible locations and situations in Toronto and all over the Island of Montreal, as well as Laval and locations on the South Shore. We were particularly excited about a piece of property of over one hundred acres in Pointe Claire, Quebec, on the west end of the island. When Elmer and I went out to examine the area, with a view to purchasing the location, it was a tranquil rural farm setting. There was not a house in sight and a large milk-cow mooed at us solemnly on the other side of the fence on the northern boundary. The largest segment of middle-class, middle-income English managers in any suburb of Montreal was found in Pointe Claire. This attracted us. The Trans-Canada Highway, which pushed through the middle of the island from east to west, would soon change the surrounding fields to new housing developments. We decided to go ahead and purchase the property so that rezoning applications could proceed. In the meantime, we concluded an "if-and-when" agreement with Cemp through Leo Kolber to share fifty-fifty in the project.

When these initial steps were completed, we invited Eaton's into our proposed centre to be the other major store at the other end of the mall from Simpsons. Each store was to be equal in size, which we suggested be 120,000 square feet. Eaton's wanted a smaller one, and we said they could be smaller if they wished! This was the time I learned that the Island of Montreal is rated a maximum risk for earth-quakes, as high as San Francisco! We were told that our buildings would have to be cross-braced to meet the building code, which added greatly to the initial cost. The fact that we had demonstrated our eagerness and ability to buy and become developer-owners of future shopping centres rather surprised Eaton's, I felt, so at the first opportunity I suggested to Eaton's that each of us, when we owned a property and started developing it, would give the other the *first* chance of refusal to join the development. They agreed quickly, because they knew we had an interest in Etobicoke, as they did, but in different areas. The importance of having the two major stores in the East – that is, Eaton's and Simpsons – as tenants could not be overstated, particularly when it came to long-term financing. Any centre with two leading department stores will dominate a wider shopping area than a centre with only one. Two well-known department stores ensures secure financing and attracts better tenants. The sum of the two is many times the drawing power of a one-store centre with second-class tenants.

Simpsons-Sears was very active during this period and under the planning and development guidance of Morgan Reid, vice-president, a former Simpsons' man, stores were built as large as the Sears main stores, 100,000 square feet, and locations were being purchased and stockpiled for future development. I had the pleasure of accompanying Morgan Reid on several of his exploratory trips, looking for new locations in the West, in Burnaby, B.C., and in Calgary. The latter location on the Trans-Canada Highway faced a particularly bleak section of prairie, which stretched uninhabited for miles on the other side of the road. The bleakness, even bareness, of the view put me off a bit, but the deal was good! Morgan was the counterpart of Elmer Rounding in Simpsons. He was as tall as Elmer but heavier set. He had a booming voice, a reverberating laugh, and an incurable optimism in the future of Simpsons-Sears and Simpsons and in the rightness of his views and opinions. Morgan, having assisted Edgar in Ottawa during the war years, was used to diplomatic manoeuvring and thus was admirably suited to deal with Sears in Chicago or with Ottawa bureaucrats or with a developer in Calgary. He was as good at his job as Elmer was at his.

For the first couple of decades there was little or no conflict between Simpsons and Sears. We operated in different areas of the country and complemented each other in many ways. Much more

Simpsons' effort in men and finances went into Simpsons-Sears' formative years than the general public perceived or that we got credit for. Inherent in the "grand scheme" were the growth restrictions on Simpsons, which became more apparent later on. But for the foreseeable future, we all had as much to do as we could afford or physically manage. However, those of us who looked ahead began to anticipate future problems in the possibilities and the options open to us.

The growth of the new company was phenomenal and more and more required Edgar's attention, which resulted in my being designated vice-president and managing director of Simpsons. The intent was to make me executive vice-president, but I objected to that much-abused title. Executive vice-presidents have some clout and seniority over ordinary vice-presidents, but are not in the position to make deals with outsiders or receive much public recognition. Edgar did not want to give up the presidency at this point in time, so I settled on vice-president and managing director as a title, which indicated that I was in charge. The very "Englishness" of the title carried more weight in the United States where, not being able to define the position as easily as executive vice-president (which is purely an American device), they allowed me extra latitude in negotiation. Today executive vice-presidents are necessary because of the proliferation of vice-presidents in modern companies of any size. But nothing has really changed except the upgrading of titles. When there was only one vice-president, the others were general managers or merchandise managers. Often the new upgrading of titles was in lieu of increases in pay, especially in the retail business, following a trend which started some years before in the chartered banks.

By the time I became vice-president and general manager, Simpsons had grown from five stores, doing $100 million worth of business a year when Simpsons-Sears was formed, to eight stores doing $400 million annually. Simpsons-Sears, in the meantime, had grown from the mail-order or catalogue business of $100 million a year to the catalogue and four stores doing about $600 million. Our combined turnover had risen from $200 million total to $1 billion in the seventh year of the new arrangement, and we were profitably expanding our customer base.

Simpsons always put great emphasis on the well-being of their employees. We did this through the proprietorship in profit-sharing and stock-option plans and by encouraging the family feeling engendered by individual recognition through the Twenty-Five Year Club, whose members had benefits in extra holidays and special discounts as rewards for their long service and devotion to the company. Simpsons-Sears at first shared our festivities. After all, they were all Simpsons men and women. As Simpsons-Sears grew and spread from coast to coast, the Twenty-Five Year Club festivities had to be held in several regional headquarters, as the logistics of moving so many people became a chore. Simpsons kept up the tradition of bringing each store contingent of Twenty-Five Year Club members to Toronto for a week-long round of festivities and sightseeing. The four hundred or more Simpsons people who came from Halifax, Montreal, Regina, and London arrived already in a high state of excitement. Some had never flown before; others, such as the Regina contingent, spent a couple of hilarious days on the Trans-Continental train living it up before the formal festivities commenced in Toronto. Friendships were made on these trips that lasted throughout the years, and the pride of being individually recognized and applauded for long service and devotion to the Simpsons family spread itself throughout their local stores when they returned home and enthusiastically regaled their fellow workers and customers with stories of what many called the finest week in their lives! It was truly a "family outing."

One of the first things I accomplished was to get recognition for the service people, both in pay and in the internal social hierarchy. The more we expanded to the suburbs and ·beyond, the more complex the service problems became, and the more important it was that service people were specifically trained for certain jobs. While apprenticeship is still the best grounding for a job, we could no longer tie a bright individual for a life-time career to one "dead-end" job. We needed the flexibility of the well-trained generalist to fill jobs as we expanded. Many of these job opportunities were filled by the graduates of the methods research group, the "intelligently ignorant" young men, as my father used to refer to them. Others came from university recruitment.

Before Edgar finally moved his Simpsons-Sears' operational office to Sears' Mutual Street building, the service and administration chores were split between T.L. Robinette and Ed Pickering. Tommy Robinette, Q.C., was a long-time career man with Simpsons Limited and my close associate for twenty years. Ed Pickering, who had served as principal secretary to Mackenzie King, was hired by

Edgar after the war to take over the Regina mail-order plant of Simpsons. Pickering was also in charge of the Regina retail store, which we had recently purchased from R.H. Williams & Co.

Ed Pickering, always a smooth operator, being well trained in Ottawa diplomacy and "stick-handling," and Tommy Robinette, soft spoken but direct, often came to disagreements about how a situation should be handled. After Ed came to Toronto to share the service responsibility, I found myself usually defending or being defended by Tommy Robinette, while Edgar and Ed Pickering nearly always shared the same point of view. Both Tommy and Ed were excellent men. Difficulties arose, I believe, because in the initial stages their respective responsibilities were not clearly enough set out by my brother.

My first experience with Ed Pickering in his new role came when we had a burst of union activity. Not being a labour lawyer and used to the effectiveness of army "shit meetings," where small problems could be solved on a direct basis, I suggested that I start a regular series of staff conferences during working hours. My reasoning was that if you could solve the little problems as they occurred, they almost never became big ones. When I suggested this, Ed strongly advised against the plan. "Why?" I asked innocently.

"They'll bring up all sorts of things that will embarrass you," Pickering replied.

I was stunned. "Like what?"

"Things like wages and working conditions," he replied.

"Well, by God, if they can embarrass me with questions about wages and working conditions, unless you know something that I don't know, I'll be on their side as quick as a wink. I am going into these discussions with a perfectly clear conscience that we, Simpsons, are good employers and fair, and that it has never been more important than now to talk directly to our employees. We must do so before some other persons get the right to act as go-betweens and interpret what you say in any way it suits them. When that happens the employees are prevented from talking directly to you, but must go through a grievance committee."

Ed reluctantly agreed that I should go ahead. I set up the first employees' conference in Toronto. The general rules were a maximum of ten employees at one time, each representing a different division or department of the store – a salesperson, an engineer, a driver – but no management. The conference was to be taken by the

most senior person available, general manager and above preferably. The final rule was that nothing was too small to be discussed. I
took the first conference, which was held in a private dining room of
our Arcadian Court restaurant. I saw only friendly faces down the
table, but one young man seemed bursting to speak. "You seem anxious to start, Mr. Jones. Let's hear from you first."

"What kind of company is this that kills men on the job?" he
shot at me.

I felt myself go cold, thinking, "Oh God, Pickering is right!"
Recovering, conscious that every face at the table was riveted on me,
I said, "If you could be more specific, possibly I could give you an
answer."

"Okay! Mr. Smith in the Stoves died pushing a stove last Tuesday," he said with obvious satisfaction.

"Now I know what you are talking about," I said. "Did you know
that Mr. Smith had had two heart attacks and was only working half-
time while receiving full pay? Did you know that Mr. Smith was under
orders never to push a stove? You are a young man. Where were you
when all this happened? Skulking behind a column, I bet, watching
a fine man kill himself, doing something you could do and probably
should have done." I gave it to him because I was familiar with Mr.
Smith and his medical problem.

"Yeah, where were you?" almost everyone else at the table asked
him, all eyes on the disconcerted young man.

The rest of the conference went well, and many small but important misunderstandings were corrected. These are the things that
rumours grow from, without much in the way of roots in fact, but
well fertilized by uninformed or malicious gossipers. I went upstairs
to discuss my experience with Ed, who was delighted at the outcome.
He informed me that Mr. Jones, the young man who had asked the
question, had abruptly resigned. As it turned out, he was a union
plant. He had lost his credibility with his fellow employees, who
made a point of seeing that he did his fair share of work, so he quit!

My point had been well made. Talk to people, know what you
are talking about, and above all *listen.* If you do not know the answer,
find out and take action so that little problems never can be distorted
into big rumours or grow into big problems. I do not much care for
the modern description "hands-on management," but that describes
the contact with people and knowledge necessary to run a successful and profitable store.

The "theorists" put the bottom line first and try school-book manipulations to achieve a respectable result. The object of their exercise is not well defined, and often established and loyal customers are driven away because of curtailed service and the lack of personal attention. The "theorist" worships "market share" and woos a "typical," statistically defined customer, one who is as faceless and as impersonal as a display dummy. My father always maintained that "the customer comes first." This may sound like a cliché but it was his philosophy of retailing – running stores to serve people – and it worked! When he said, "You'll enjoy shopping at Simpsons," he meant that he guaranteed satisfaction. "When you do everything right, profit will be the result," he said. If profit is your first and only goal, you will seldom make it, and your customers will quickly turn to the store that values their business more than you have demonstrated you do.

I got on well with Ed after this first experience and after the union effort fizzled out. The largest turnout the union organizers had on any one occasion was one hundred out of five thousand employees, and that was because someone issued a pamphlet which maligned my father. The "large" turnout was to tell the union organizers that they were all wet. The next "mass" meeting was attended by thirty-five employees. It was the last one before the union quit.

We made changes in benefits and improved working conditions, because it was the right thing to do, not because someone dictated the changes to us. We had the full support of our employee shareholders. We were confident and growing stronger, daily increasing the number of customers served. More and more of them carried our Simpsons' Charge-a-Plate credit card. Surveys showed that our charge cards were used more often than Eaton's and Bay cards by customers who identified themselves as Eaton's and Bay customers! We were growing faster than any other retail business in Canada, and we were always profitable.

Edgar was honoured by the National Retail Merchants Association as the International Retailer of the Year at their annual dinner in New York. Our stock rose accordingly.

# PUBLIC SERVICE

## 14

In the 1960s the Toronto Board of Trade had some ten thousand members and was the largest board of trade or chamber of commerce in the free world. I joined the Board of Trade in the early 1950s and worked my way through "the chairs" from treasurer to vice-president. Finally, in 1962-63, I served as its eighty-ninth president.

What was exceptional about my appointment was that, once again, a Burton was president. No other family at that time in the 118-year history of the Toronto Board could boast more than one president. I was following my father, C.L. Burton, who was president in 1928, and brother, Edgar Burton, who was president in 1949, as the third member of the Burton clan to become president of the Board, considered to be the most prestigious, business-oriented group in the city. I was, in due course, followed by Edgar's son, my nephew Ted Burton, who became the fourth Burton in the same family to serve as president.

I found it strange that, suddenly, as president, I was sought out by reporters and others for my opinions on hundreds of subjects, from world events to local gossip. The calls came at any time of day or night. This used to annoy me because, unlike the brash reporter who had just read a news item on the UP or CP wire service and then phoned me for my opinion or reaction, I most often had not a clue as to what he was talking about. If I expressed an opinion based on what I was told over the phone, I would be "near quoted" or "quoted out of context," which is sometimes worse than being "misquoted." So, I learned not to give telephone interviews without advance warning.

One of the most amusing incidents during my presidency took place at an official luncheon which was being tendered to a visiting trade delegation from Yugoslavia headed by Marshal Tito's number-three man. I was the official host. Our conversations took place through an interpreter, although it was obvious that the leader of the delegation understood English. When he was told that I was a keen hunter, he immediately invited me warmly to join him for a bear hunt on Tito's own preserves. Without a pause, I asked the interpreter, "Yugoslav or Russian bears?"

He looked horrified and said, "I don't think I'll interpret that!"

However, the Yugoslav leader burst into laughter and, smiling broadly, said in English, "*Yugoslav! Yugoslav!* Oh, that is good one!"

The worst period of my presidency came after I had a fairly serious fox-hunting accident. My horse fell at full gallop and I suffered a concussion. For many months I endured severe headaches and tired quickly, but nonetheless I spent only one night in the Toronto General Hospital and managed to fly to Vancouver to attend the Canadian Chamber of Commerce meetings held in that city. I existed on dozens of Aspirins a day. I had to make the key speech at the official dinner as president of the Toronto board, and having written it myself and worked very hard on the speech, I gave it. I was told later that it was excellent, but I could hardly remember delivering it! This was the only severe physical injury I suffered in forty years of cross-country riding and fox-hunting in Canada, the United States, and England.

As well as being president of the board, my duties as vice-president and managing director of Simpsons involved me in a considerable number of day-to-day civic matters. After my accident, my associates at Simpsons assumed extra loads and responsibilities without complaint. We were a well-knit team. But I was embarrassed to discover that my accident had something of the effect on my memory that medical electro-shock treatment has on patients. In the latter case it is designed to wipe the memory clean of worrisome things. In my case, a relatively small section of my memory had been erased by the blow to my head, but I never knew when or under what circumstances my memory would "deaden." I would be recounting some well-known fact when, suddenly, *blank* for an interval of time, and then full memory again, except for the missing section. It was nerve-wracking, to say the least. While I tried to conceal my memory lapses as best I could, my condition must have been apparent to my co-workers. It took me several months, reading files and "back" notes, to rebuild my memory. The good side of the story is that the concentrated study I was forced to do on our many and varied business deals and agreements not only rebuilt the "gap" but brought me up to date on their details and gave me an edge. So my damaged confidence was rebuilt as my physical condition was restored to normal.

In 1963 I joined the board of trustees of the famous Hospital for Sick Children, on which I served for the next fourteen years. It was a fascinating experience. The most dedicated chairman of Sick Kids, as it was known, was C.L. Gundy. Charlie Gundy, of Wood Gundy & Co., was on the Simpsons board until his death many years later. Charlie devoted much time, money, and energy to the hospital. He expected and got almost 100 per cent attendance at the regular meetings, and dished out enough committee work to keep the trustees busy the rest of the time. One drawback to being a trustee of the hospital was that, under John Ross Robertson's will, which bequeathed millions to Sick Kids, a trustee was not allowed to work for any other hospital or charity that supported another hospital, which ruled out the United Way and Red Cross, among other charitable organizations. There were some who considered the will's provisions to be a safeguard against having to work for other appeals or organizations, while I thought it was too confining. I have never worked with a more dedicated group of trustees or staff than at Sick Kids.

The next year, 1964, I was made president of Simpsons Limited. As president, I began working even closer with W.P. Scott. Pete Scott, chairman of Wood Gundy & Co., was vice-president of Simpsons and the senior outside director. Edgar was chairman and CEO, but he left the running of Simpsons more and more to me, as he became more involved with Simpsons-Sears and his American directorates, which included being a director of Sears, Roebuck in Chicago, of Procter and Gamble, of Johns-Manville, and of the Conference Board of America. We now had a jet plane, a De Havilland 125, and many and varied meetings hundreds of miles apart could be attended. You left home early and got home late, but at least now you could work a full day, on location, and sleep in your own bed at night. In the old DC-3 days, it would have been a two- or three-day trip to accomplish what we were now able to do in one day's flying.

There used to be a saying to the effect that the way to get rid of your chairman, "so you could get on with your work," was to keep him up in the air! Well, Edgar during this period did just that, with no help from me. He flew in ever-widening circles from meeting to meeting, and the constant flying took its toll. He began to suffer more and more from angina, a result, I am sure, of jet-lag fatigue and a natural disposition to worry about things – even when things were going so smoothly there was nothing to worry about! Edgar was highly respected wherever he went, and his council was sought by business and government. So, at Simpsons, we saw little of him on a daily basis. I depended more and more on Pete Scott, with whom I used to discuss most of my problems. His depth of experience and wide range of interests were a great source of strength to the organization. Through Wood Gundy, Pete had a connection with most of the major company mergers, buy-outs, and financings in Canada, and I never tired of listening to his early experiences.

Pete introduced me to the Ristigouche Salmon Club on the magnificent Restigouche River on the Quebec-New Brunswick border. The slight difference in spelling of "Ristigouche" and "Restigouche," as far as the club was concerned, merely highlighted its existence over more than a century on this magnificent river. "Ristigouche" was the original spelling of the Indian name. Pete, Gordon Bongard, and I fished together there for many seasons until Pete died and Gordon bowed to age. I began to trust and leaned increasingly on Pete's business judgement, and I became hooked on salmon fishing.

One of my concerns, which was highlighted in our five-year projections, was the need to continue our share of financing of our "child," Simpsons-Sears, so that the delicate, fifty-fifty balance of our agreement with Sears, Roebuck was not upset, and yet find enough money to fulfil our long-range commitments in Simpsons Limited. Financing was really Edgar and Pete's problem, but we were very dependent on Simpsons-Sears' payback to Simpsons in the form of dividends to cover debt payments that we had incurred, partially on behalf of Simpsons-Sears' insatiable appetite for expansion in the first place. Sears, Roebuck could not have cared less at this point if they ever took any dividends back to the United States. Our "child" was growing faster than at least one of its parents, Simpsons, and we began thinking about steps that should be taken to ensure our future.

We were in a fairly strong position, as about 30 per cent of Simpsons' voting stock was held by the employees' Profit Sharing Fund, the Burton family, and Wood Gundy executives. At the same time, we were limited in the long run to expansion only in the East, which in the first decade of the agreement seemed little or no problem at all. We had as much to do in the Toronto, Montreal, London, and

Halifax areas as we could handle. We had no plans to expand in the West and were content that part of our strength in men and money was used to "feed" Simpsons-Sears' exciting growth. However, our projections into the seventies showed that there were some problems in the offing. One solution was for Simpsons to become a truly national chain, coast to coast, possibly by making an accommodation with Woodward's, which matched our type of business and which was as dominant in British Columbia and Alberta as Simpsons was in Ontario and the East.

We could not complete such a deal without the concurrence of Sears, Roebuck, as spelled out in the agreement. Also, while "Chunky," as Charles Namby Wynn Woodward is known, and I were good friends, he had some problem with his family's interests in that company. Family members did not want to see any change in control, although they did talk from time to time about possibilities. My suggestion to Sears was that it would be beneficial to the long-term agreement for Simpsons to remain the strongest possible partner. Sears was non-committal. Another suggestion was for Simpsons to merge with Hudson Bay. Such an arrangement would see Sears, Roebuck's interest in Simpsons-Sears reduced from 50 per cent to 33 per cent, while the newly merged company would have control at 66 per cent. Again, we could not enter into any serious talks without Sears' approval. Much was to happen before either of these alternatives was explored further, although contacts were maintained in a loose way.

One factor that had not been explored in depth was what would happen to Simpsons itself when a small number of key players died and their holdings were taken over by their various beneficiaries, most of whom had interests other than Simpsons. First, in 1964, my father died. As he was eighty-six, this was to be expected, and his estate went largely to his grandchildren, with my brothers and sisters receiving incomes for life from tightly controlled trusts. My father had been most generous to us during his lifetime and had already distributed some of his Simpsons stock, starting during World War II and continuing at other intervals. So his residual estate, while modestly large, did not have a deleterious effect on the Simpsons position. Our business was so strong that Simpsons' stock was split several times in the next few years without any problem.

• • •

At the same time as I was pondering these issues, I was becoming increasingly involved in real-estate transactions, some of which had amusing results. On Jarvis Street in Toronto, Simpsons had been accumulating lot after lot opposite our Mail-Order building, which occupied the huge area between Church, Mutual, and Dalhousie streets immediately west of this new acquisition. Finally, we secured all the land to the east of the Mail-Order building fronting on Jarvis, and dreamed about a consolidation of Simpsons' service buildings on this land. This was also adjacent to our delivery, which served Simpsons-Sears as well as ourselves.

The first snag we ran into was on an old city map going back to the middle of the nineteenth century. This map showed a lane running through the middle of the block, serving the residential properties that faced onto the streets east and west. There was no problem, as we owned all the land. Or did we? To my amazement, the south end of the fictitious lane butted on the Warwick Hotel's property. The Warwick Hotel, with its striptease and bar, had an unsavoury reputation, exceeded only by the poor reputation of Jarvis Street itself at the time. It was said that if a retailer could turn his inventory over as many times a year as these establishments turned a bed a night, he would be among the retailing greats! We could not proceed with building on this property without clearance from the one common owner of the lane's south end, the Warwick Hotel. This most common of owners was represented by Senator Arthur Roebuck, Q.C., one of the few holdouts from the previous century, who still wore a starched wing collar every day and looked like an antique schoolmaster. There was nothing old-fashioned about his "horse-trading" sense. He demanded, as recompense for his client giving up his right of access to the non-existent lane, that we deed the Warwick Hotel owners a fifteen-foot strip of land along the south of our newly acquired property, from the east to the west, which they would add to their inadequate service area. We had to agree to this, but I never forgot Senator Roebuck.

The next time I ran into him was when we were completing the purchase of the Queen Street block adjoining the store on which the Simpson Tower now stands. We had acquired lots as they became available over thirty-five years, and now we owned all but the Bay Theatre and Bowles Lunch next to it on the corner of Queen and Bay streets. The Bay Theatre was a narrow movie house which was reduced to the continuous run of "B" movies. It was more an all-night hangout for winos to sleep off their excesses than it was a viable cinema. The tenant in the basement had a huge store of silver articles and was considered by some to be a "fence," although I cannot remember anyone ever seeing him thus engaged. The Bay Theatre was one of the very first reinforced concrete structures in Toronto, and was as strongly built as a wartime bunker. It turned out that Senator Roebuck represented the estate of the former owners.

I got into the act when I learned Roebuck was involved. The Bay Theatre had been owned in the early twenties by two sisters. In the real-estate boom of 1925, Simpsons had offered them $395,000 for this property, which they declined. Forty-three years later, the sisters having died, I sent Ken Kernaghan, our company secretary, to Roebuck with an offer of $385,000 but with a cheque in his pocket for $400,000. Roebuck, thinking to raise the ante several times in true "horse-trading" style, laughed and said, "Why don't you get serious. I wouldn't sell it for less than $400,000."

"Done," said Kernaghan, pulling the cheque from his pocket, and the deal was concluded.

When we came to demolish this bomb shelter, misnamed a "theatre," old Roebuck must have had the last laugh. It cost us an arm and a leg to raze it! The next property, Bowles Lunch, surrounded on all sides by Simpsons, was then owned by George Gardiner. We were able to come to a satisfactory arrangement with him, quickly and amicably. We began to think in terms of a several-floor office development on top of an expanded store on this important corner. I commissioned a new architectural firm, Bregman and Hamann, to do the original feasibility studies. It was one of the first jobs in the big time for Sidney Bregman and George Hamann, now one of Toronto's largest architectural firms.

It quickly became apparent that, to be a successful real-estate enterprise, the building must be distinctive and have an "address." We could not, in other words, just put four or five anonymous floors of rental space on top of the selling floors and guarantee success. So the Simpson Tower project on the corner of Queen and Bay streets was conceived. It would adjoin the store and be connected to it in certain key areas. At first designed as a twenty-storey concept, it was later replanned as a thirty-two-floor tower. I approached John B. Parkin Associates, architects, to produce the design, in association with Bregman and Hamann. The whole project was to be completed by 1967 in time for the Centennial celebrations.

The building of the tower also triggered a great deal of reconstruction within the main store itself. New escalators on the north side replaced old elevators from the basement to the eighth floor and the Arcadian Court. New elevators were installed on the south side, and a million-dollar facelift of the Court itself was done by Parkin. A series of construction strikes during the local building boom in the mid-sixties added months to the completion dates of several major projects in town, including the Simpson Tower, which was not completed until 1968.

During this period, Edgar suffered increasing discomfort from angina. He was hospitalized at the Toronto General but got out of bed and was driven down to see the completed but not-yet-opened Simpson Tower. He died shortly afterwards. His death changed many things. Much of the responsibility of the relationship with Sears, Roebuck had been Edgar's responsibility. Now it became mine, but with a difference. I became chairman and president of Simpsons Limited, following Edgar's death in 1968, and while I had a fine working relationship with the operating men of Simpsons-Sears, many of whom, like Jack C. Barrow, were Simpsons men by training. Others, like Major-General Douglas Peacher, who became president of Sears, were Sears, Roebuck-trained, and some, like Doug Peacher, became fiercely proud of Canada and things Canadian.

Jack Barrow had become chairman of Simpsons-Sears in 1966, as I had become chairman and CEO of Simpsons Limited. An old Simpsons man, Barrow had my complete trust, and, thinking to bridge the gap to Sears, I suggested he be invited to join the Simpsons board. This was probably a mistake as it placed him in an embarrassing position. On several occasions, he had a conflict of interest between his operating position and his Simpsons board responsibilities. There was never the slightest suggestion that Jack did other than fill his double role well. But his final loyalty had to be to his company, and ultimately to Sears when they decided to cut us adrift years later. Jack's rise in Simpsons-Sears had been rapid, from buyer, Girls' Wear, in 1952 to chairman and CEO in 1966. The tradition that had evolved over the years was that Sears, Roebuck produced and supplied the president and chief operating officer, but the chairman and CEO was a Canadian – Simpsons-trained.

I had adopted the practice years before, when Jim Button, merchant and amateur artist of some ability, came to us from Sears as the new president, of inviting the new man to accompany me for a week's shooting or fishing, as deep in Canada as circumstances permitted. My theory was that, after being isolated for a week, we would end up either life-time friends or wary enemies. I am happy to report that in every case we became good friends.

Jim Button's successor was Major-General Douglas Peacher, U.S. Marines (Ret.). When Doug was appointed, I gave him the option of shooting or fishing. Doug chose shooting. He was still very much involved with the Marines. In fact, he was the senior ranking reserve officer in the Marines and a member of the officer selection committee of the Marine General Command in Washington. This was at a time when the Vietnam War was at its height and in Canada we were plagued with U.S. draft dodgers. I jokingly asked Doug if they knew he was in Canada with the rest of them!

Each year I went to Saskatchewan for duck shooting. Several times I went with John Howard, grain farmer and veteran, as was I, of the Italian campaign. John had been a war correspondent. When John heard a U.S. Marine general was our guest, he laid on a goose shoot near Cumberland House, about forty miles west of The Pas, Manitoba, in an area of four hundred square miles of silt basin, lakes, marsh, and muck. This area is roughly where the North and South Saskatchewan rivers meet and divide into hundreds of rivulets, as confused and numerous as the veins on the back of an old man's hand.

I had dreamed of a spectacular and relatively comfortable "stubble" shoot with Doug and my son Jamie. We flew to Prince Albert by jet and there transferred to a single-engine float plane, a Beaver. Doug, a World War II Marine pilot in the South Pacific, shook his head when he saw the huge load of cases of shotgun shells, baggage, guns, and one-too-few seats for passengers. Our flying time to the Carrière Camp was about three hours, and the only identification from the air in this vast wilderness was one white-roofed and one red-roofed cabin.

Jamie and I jumped into the two seats behind the pilot and buckled up. The other "seat" between us was a couple of blankets on top of several cases of ammunition. I shouted down to the new Simpsons-Sears president, "Jump up, General, you can sit between us. There is no seat belt, but Jamie and I will link arms with you and hold on till the last possible moment!"

The General looked grim. We relented, having had our joke, and he sat on the right of the bush pilot. After about two hours of flying over mile after mile of sloughs, silt, and scrub – we flew at about a thousand feet – I noticed a couple of moose and pointed down, saying,

"General, down below, a couple of your customers. All this part of Canada belongs to you."

Doug saw the doubtful humour and then spoke up for the first time to the pilot, "Have you been to the Carrière Camp before?"

"Nope."

"What compass bearing are you flying on?"

"Well, General, see that hole in the instrument panel there? If the compass was in there, we'd be flying on about 45 degrees N.E., but compasses aren't very reliable up here!"

The General kept his composure, went a shade paler, and came back bravely, as one flyer to another, "Of course, you are in radio contact with Cumberland House."

"Well, sir, normally we would be, but you see that other hole in the instrument panel? That's where the radio should be, but I had to send it in for repair yesterday. It wasn't operating worth a damn!"

Major-General Douglas Peacher, U.S. Marines (Ret.), and brand-new president of Simpsons-Sears, went distinctly white and turned to me and said, "Allan, I think we are in trouble."

"Not yet," I replied.

"Are we in trouble?" I asked the bush pilot.

"A bit lost, but motor is still running, lots of gas, not in real trouble yet."

Just then our spirits rose as a red roof and a white roof suddenly appeared below, and we began a long glide down to a narrow, muddy, swiftly flowing river for our landing. As we approached the shoreline, against which a couple of shabby canoes were tethered, some three or four of the roughest-looking villains you could imagine came out of a cabin to stare at our approach in a most unfriendly manner. I thought to myself, if this is the Carrière Camp, I'll shoot John Howard just before doing away with myself.

We landed and the conversation went like this:

"Is this Jim Carrière's Camp?"

"No."

"We were told it had a red-roofed cabin and a white-roofed cabin."

"Well, this ain't it."

"Do you know of another camp with a red and a white roof nearby?"

"Nope, but I heard tell of one about forty miles away in that direction."

Glad to leave, we floated downstream about two miles before the pilot could turn the plane upstream against the muddy current.

We took off and soon found the Carrière Camp "away in that direction," where we were warmly greeted by Jim Carrière and reservedly accepted by the rest of the guides, who were all Cree Indians.

The camp was bare basic. The food was edible, if unusual, and ranged from ground moose to ground skunk, laced with plenty of onions and beans. It was below freezing at night but pleasantly warm during the day. We were in the middle of the vast breeding ground of hundreds of thousands of Canada geese, five thousand wild, white swans, countless mallards, teal, and other ducks. Northern pike swam in the muddy rivers and moose and bear roamed nearby. And at night, we heard a chorus of wolves whose serenade to the northern lights blended into a blood-stirring, wild-swelling volume of music like an organ played by a madman.

In camp we all felt warm and small and friendly in this vastness, as we listened to our Cree hosts tell of their winter trap lines, and why they liked the Canada jay, the whiskey jack, and why they hated bears most of all. We learned that the greater Canada geese in this area run to fourteen pounds in weight and more, and are slightly less clearly defined in their white, black, and goose-grey colourings than the regular Canadas. They were so naïve it was not necessary to put out decoys. The Indians would call them in a vocabulary of sounds extending to about twenty words or phrases, and the lovely birds would respond and fly low over us.

Jim Carrière, the camp operator, had been a sniper in Italy with the South Saskatchewan Regiment. When he discovered I was also a "spaghetti-eater," he took me as his "sport." We were in hip-waders all the time as, whenever you were not in a boat, you were slowly sinking into the muck, which I found less than pleasant. I was told, if you go down too fast, the thing to do is sink to your knees to spread the weight. If you are still sinking, lie flat out and roll to sounder ground! Jim called a flight of about three hundred huge geese from two miles away, which obediently came right over our heads about twenty feet up. I did not shoot.

"You didn't shoot," said Jim.

"No. They were too close," I lied.

Jim shook his dark head and said, "Well, I'll call them around again."

Around they came, obedient to his urgent calls, this time about forty feet in the air. They were so beautiful, I gawked at them, mouth open, and let them fly by without firing.

"You didn't shoot," said Jim, by this time visibly annoyed.

"No," I replied. "I have never seen such a beautiful sight so close. I just wanted to see them go by once more."

I know from experience that guides compete fiercely among themselves, and I was not co-operating. Jim Carrière glowered at me and said, "I'll bring them around one more time, and you shoot them or I'll shoot you!"

I figured he meant it. No one else was within miles, and not wishing to become a "hunting-accident" statistic, I got ready. The flock, now quite agitated, came in high and I aimed and fired at the lead goose, bringing down the one on its extreme right, which landed nearby with a tremendous thump. Jim gave me hell for not bringing down the leader. I did not have the nerve to tell him that the leader bore a charmed life. The most disconcerting thing was that the huge flock did not break up, but merely closed the gap left by their fallen comrade and flew off, filling the air with their excited chatter. I did not really want to shoot another goose. By the end of our stay, Doug and I had become good friends, and over the years we became best friends. We went salmon fishing together for many years on the Restigouche River as members of the Ristigouche Salmon Club.

Some years after Doug became president of Simpsons-Sears, he was honoured by the Marine Corps at his retirement parade at their headquarters in Washington, the one building in Washington not burned by the British when they set fire to the White House. Some say the building was saved because it was defended by the U.S. Marines. Pete Scott and I, with our wives, attended the ceremony as invited guests. Major-General Douglas Peacher headed a large uniformed parade with full band, and was awarded the fourth highest decoration the United States can bestow for meritorious service, after which there was a reception and a small private dinner given in his honour by the Commanding General and his wife.

It was significant that the two friends and wives invited to attend this prestigious ceremony were Canadians and Simpsons people, not Sears or Simpson-Sears people. We felt we had had a hand in the Canadianization of a Tennessee-born U.S. Marine. Trained by Sears originally, Doug Peacher did a lot for Simpsons-Sears, and was a good supporter of Simpsons and Canada, without betraying his native loyalties in any way.

• • •

My father had set an example as a public-spirited businessman and as a civic leader for all of us to see and admire. He was active with the YMCA, Big Brothers, the Toronto Board of Trade, church groups, and served as the founding chairman of the Toronto Industrial Commission in 1929. My brother Edgar was equally busy as first president of the Community Chest, as the United Way was then known, and of the Toronto Board of Trade, the Toronto Symphony, and the board of the Toronto General Hospital. So it was quite natural that I would serve on public bodies in my turn.

In the 1960s, public service grew at a fast pace across North America. Appeals and causes were legion, and much executive time was wasted in overlapping and competition for charitable dollars. Money was flowing. The country was once more growing with a large influx of immigrants. One could almost feel the exciting, pulsing heartbeat of building and progress. I cut my social, fund-raising teeth as campaign chairman of the Toronto Red Cross, then the YWCA Building Fund – yes, the YWCA, not the YMCA, which my father had presided over – followed by Cedar Glen, the United Church Conference camp project. This last-named project, on or adjacent to the Cold Creek Conservation Area, caught my interest largely because I felt that young people would learn more about God's wonders in the great outdoors than in a hundred damp church basements. I have never liked the false *bonhomie* of church basements.

All of these positions prepared me for the biggest task of all – being chairman of the United Appeal of Metropolitan Toronto in 1961. That year was the toughest and, in many ways, my most rewarding year. I felt obliged to take on this task because in my Red Cross days I had been part of a group that had convinced the hospitals of the fact that blood could be supplied on a "free" basis by the Red Cross more efficiently than it could be purchased on a hit-and-miss basis from interns and transients. I was also on the committee that recommended that the Toronto chapter of the Red Cross join the United Appeal as an associate member.

So, when I was invited to be vice-chairman to Harvey Cruickshank's chairmanship of the United Appeal, I agreed. Harvey was a vice-president of Bell Telephone and had a medical degree in psychiatry. It was an interesting experience throughout to be psychoanalysed by Harvey, morning, noon, and night whenever we met. He did an excellent job as chairman and brought great credit to his company. Bell Canada has always been most generous in supplying their men to aid in local charitable causes, as has Simpsons. Not all firms had this far-seeing attitude at the time. The very wealthy preferred private charities or a highly directed use of their benefactions, as was the case with the Eaton family. We had been brought up to believe that while the munificent charitable outpouring of the Eatons was awe-inspiring, it was also well known that no Eaton manager in the old days was allowed to spend the firm's time working for charitable organizations. He was expected to work full time for Eaton's. Eaton's, in turn, prided themselves on giving twice as much money as a company than any of their competitors, particularly Simpsons.

Simpsons did not have as much money to give but, because of my father's liberal instincts, provided many workers to a host of worthy causes with much benefit, publicity, and public recognition to our company and the men themselves. After all, we were serving our customer in yet another way, a customer we knew as a person. Service to the customer was ingrained in us, so public service came easily and naturally as part of the total job.

One of my early assignments was serving as a member of the National Industrial Design Council (NIDC) formed in 1947. The original group was under the chairmanship of R.C. Berkinshaw, chairman of the Goodyear Tire and Rubber Company. "Berk" was a marvellous example of the public-spirited businessman. He was tall, thin, almost ascetic-looking, a gently spoken Christian gentleman of great organizing ability and clarity of mind. I learned much from him on the art of chairmanship. He reconciled our somewhat divergent views and ruled us in a kindly fashion. He wrote the terms of reference himself for the fledgling NIDC. Mitchell Sharp, then Deputy Minister of Public Works, was our government "watchdog," because the NIDC, like the National Gallery of Canada, drew its budget money from public works. Culture was not high on the government's list of priorities.

Mitchell Sharp did a good job for us, as did Donald Buchanan, of the National Gallery, who was our secretary. Don himself was quite an interesting man, the antithesis of Berkinshaw in appearance. Short, compact, nervously active, his square, plain looks belied the fact that he was extremely knowledgeable about art and artists. In fact, he was editor of the magazine *Artscanada*. Don was quite deaf. A huge wad of cotton was lodged in the cavity of one ear, where some surgeon had removed the entire hearing apparatus. The other ear sprouted a healthy growth of hair to filter the sound. His face flashed into huge, wide-mouthed grins of good humour, as he grasped the gist of the conversation. He was intelligent and witty. Most importantly, he knew how to manoeuvre between the political shoals and rocky places of government bureaucracy. He was of great help to us in Ottawa.

I was given the task of writing the Awards to Industry program to recognize designers and industrial products of good design produced in Canada. It was our first important program. A number of industrial designers and manufacturers tried to insist that only "pure" Canadian designs by Canadian designers be given awards, while I, and most others, insisted that good design produced in Canada was the most important thing. We argued further that if "outsiders" of international calibre were excluded from consideration, Canadian designers would never know if they could compete with the best in the world. Our view was accepted.

The selection jury of prominent designers and architects, including some well-known Americans, chose among the first year's winners a small, cast-iron Quebec stove, designed in the late nineteenth century and made for many years by Charles Fawcett of Sackville, N.B. It bore a name like "Twilight Delight" cast in its footplate, but in spite of its cast-iron, acanthus-leaf decoration in bas-relief and its mica window, its practical efficiency was hard to beat. No one was more surprised at being given an award than the "Twilight Delight" owner, Charles Fawcett, who immediately saw the merit in international competition rather than in being classed as "quaint Canadian." The other winners were contemporary designs by young industrial designers or architects. The National Housing Design Council was formed a few years later and, as chairman of NIDC, I was asked to serve on that as well.

The 1960 civic handbook of the City of Toronto included the following statement: "A special committee will take a close look at the waterfront, earmarking areas for industry and play. . . . Another committee, made up of the community's top business leaders, will study redevelopment of the downtown area, with a view to making it a better place in which to work and shop. . . ." And in another section it said: "Change will come, partly to conform with Toronto's role as the cultural heart of Metropolitan Toronto, partly to meet the new cosmopolitan flavour of Toronto. . . . A Civic Square and a new City Hall will be created. The University Avenue Armouries will be razed to make way for a new Metropolitan Court House. The block on the south side of Queen, between Bay and York, will be redeveloped. Work on an East-West subway line will commence. The long-awaited O'Keefe Centre will be opened, giving Toronto one of the finest auditoria on the continent."

The city celebrated its 125th anniversary in 1959, with Her Majesty Queen Elizabeth II and Prince Philip in attendance, to the delight of all, but especially Mayor Nathan Phillips. Nate, "the mayor of all the people," as he liked to call himself, was first elected to city council in 1924 as an alderman, in which capacity he served for decades before being elected as mayor in 1955 and re-elected several consecutive times through 1961. Nate was the first Jewish mayor of Toronto, which in itself indicated the changing city structure and the growing importance of the Jewish community. For most of his years as alderman, Nate gave every appearance of being a nice but uninspired wardheeler type, but when he became "the mayor of all the people," he grew with the job – not an easy one, with controllers like William R. Allen (a future Metro chairman), Donald D. Summerville and William Dennison (both future mayors), and a radical young alderman, Philip G. Givens (also a future mayor), to keep in line. One could argue that it was because Nate had such outstanding men and women on his council that he was successful. But much credit has to go to the mayor's leadership in starting things like the Redevelopment Advisory Council, and then letting people do the work allotted while giving them full support.

Nate recognized the important role business could play in building his city. He asked me to bring together the top businessmen to advise him and work with the planning director on the redevelopment of the core area of the city. I agreed to select the group and write the terms of reference for council's approval. I was advised before proceeding any further with planning the Redevelopment Advisory Council that I would be wise to consult the Metro chairman, known in the press as "Big Daddy."

Frederick G. Gardiner was an extraordinary man, in appearance and in action. A former reeve of the Village of Forest Hill, he was appointed the chairman of the potpourri of mayors and reeves who represented the City of Toronto and the boroughs that made up the new and forward-looking amalgam called Metropolitan Toronto. Fred Gardiner and Metro took over the departments of Finance, Roads,

Sewage, and Police, and began developing a plan for the 248 square miles of Metro and a large area beyond. Fred was equal to the monumental task handed him by the premier of Ontario, and in the real meaning of leadership, "letting the other fellow do what you want him to do," he coerced, cajoled, and ceaselessly manoeuvred so "his" Metro would get the money and political support needed to embark on massive capital expenditures required for the veins and arteries of a metropolis.

Fred was respected by all and feared by some, a non-elected politician whose power exceeded that of the elected representatives. He was physically a large man. His bulky figure was surmounted by a large head and a rugged, friendly face of mastiff quality, whose intelligent eyes warned one not to play games with him. So, with some trepidation, I called him before Christmas 1959 to invite him to have lunch with me to talk about the proposed Redevelopment Advisory Council. A date was quickly set for the two of us to meet at the York Club at twelve noon. I reserved the breakfast room and used the dining-room table as a bar and work space for our papers, while a small luncheon table set for two was placed in the middle of the sizeable room.

"Would you like a drink, sir?" I greeted him as he strode into the room.

"Dry martini on the rocks – double – and keep them coming until I tell you to stop!" was Big Daddy's reply.

Thus began one of the longest and most interesting luncheons I have ever experienced. It was over four hours long. The martinis never ceased flowing, keeping pace with the fast-flowing conversation, mostly one-sided, while Fred disclosed to me the pitfalls and sheer excitement of creating a metropolis. We had not even started on food by 3:30 p.m. We had been interrupted three or four times by frantic callers from Gardiner's office trying to reach him by phone. To each message he responded, "Tell them I am on holidays, celebrating Christmas." He was obviously getting the worse for wear, so I pressed him to eat. At 4:00 he ate quickly, and then I helped him into his official car. As he drove off, I thought, "What a waste of time. He won't remember a thing."

To my astonishment, the next morning, when I arrived at my office at 9:00 a.m., I found on my desk a letter from that amazing man – four typewritten pages, with explicit instructions and suggestions, fully recounting our discussions, supported by no less than a dozen exhibits, all in order in a fat, brown envelope. I could not have been more impressed with this virtuoso performance, or more relieved, because Big Daddy assured me of his complete support and approval of the council as I had outlined it to him.

We are lucky we had a development-minded mayor like Phillips at this vital point in our city's history, and not a mayor like David Crombie or John Sewell who, after our development – the envy of the continent – had taken place, ran on anti-development tickets. Sewell, I always felt, was an embittered anti-business, anti-establishment person. The city council marked Simpsons' one hundredth year of business in Toronto in 1972 and presented us with an illuminated scroll. Alderman Sewell rudely interrupted the proceedings when the mayor began to introduce me. In his leather jacket and turtleneck sweater, Sewell made a demonstration of protest. He got up and stalked out, saying that he was not going to waste his time on such nonsense, or words to that effect. He did so to get publicity. It was a cheap stunt, and it pleased me that the photographers and TV cameramen refused even to follow him out. Later one of the cameramen said, "Allan, I hope you noticed that we didn't fall for Sewell's dramatics. We let the S.O.B. leave without coverage." Up to this point I had never met Alderman Sewell, and after this demonstration had little wish to do so. He was a product of the times and an astute enough politician to get himself elected as mayor. But I cannot think of anything memorable he accomplished.

David Crombie was known as "the Tiny Perfect Mayor." He was not so anti-business as he was pro-neighbourhood. He was more notorious for installing annoying "speed bumps" on some neighbourhood streets than he was renowned for the large, low-cost government-financed housing development near the St. Lawrence Market that bears his name. I believe Mayor Crombie was right in promoting this development because it helped to rehabilitate and revitalize many of the old buildings in and around the historic St. Lawrence Hall. But major commercial developments found little support from him.

The planning director of the City of Toronto was Matthew Lawson. He and I from the first saw eye-to-eye. Together we wrote the terms of reference of the Redevelopment Advisory Council. I drew up the list of twenty-five top business leaders who were also owners of core properties and got their acceptance to act. Matt, as he was known to us, saw a marvellous opportunity to educate the businessmen in town-planning principles, while selling them the plans that he and his staff had drawn up, so that we could, when we approved them, sell them to council. We had no staff. My secretary did most of the work, and sometimes the secretaries at the Planning Board. We decided we would accept no money from the city, but that the businessmen would subscribe to a budget the council would set for itself. Also, we decided that we would only have the presidents or the CEOs of business on the council, no alternates, and agreed that the council members were serving as individuals and not as representatives of their organizations, companies, or industries as such. The council alone would select and appoint its members. Further, we asked for the right to study and comment on city core plans before they were presented to city council so that projects would be presented with comments or approval appended. This was a unique arrangement and it worked extremely well for all concerned, city council and Planning Board.

I remember vividly the day I attended the city council meeting in the old City Hall, to stand before council to secure their agreement to our terms of reference. His Worship, Mayor Nathan Phillips, was presiding. I was ushered into the council chamber and stood in front of him, facing the controllers and aldermen, while he introduced me. I stressed the high quality of the men whom I had selected for the first council, who had agreed to act at their own expense, and read the terms of reference. I had been tipped off to expect strong opposition from Controller Don Summerville and Alderman Philip Givens over the fact that our meetings would be held in private. There was opposition. Controller Summerville was currently raising hob with the Canadian National Exhibition over just that point, and Phil Givens wanted to see labour representation on the council. Nate was agitated and whispered to me, "Colonel, you don't have to put up with this. Let me handle them for you."

To which I replied, in a low voice, "Nate, if I can't handle these guys, I have no right to try to run Simpsons!" To Controller Summerville, I said, "No, our meetings will be private. You may have to wash your dirty linen in public, but as long as we pay our own way, we don't." To Alderman Givens, who also claimed that we would be representing "vested" interests, my answer was, "Of course, we will. As owners of the properties to be developed, who have a better right to declare their vested interest in what happens to them? Why should we abdicate our responsibilities to someone from North Toronto or Etobicoke?"

The council voted unanimously to accept the terms of reference. No doubt the fact that it cost them no money made the pill easier to swallow. We got along well with them all, in an atmosphere of mutual respect, for several years after this. Naturally Matt was delighted and immediately set about putting us to work on a short but very intense course in town-planning principles. A three-day seminar was held at the Guild of All Arts at which we decided to see first-hand what other eastern-seaboard cities of the United States were doing.

Preston Gilbride and Matt planned a multi-city tour over several days, which included Newark, Philadelphia, Washington, and Baltimore. This was the first of two trips, the second taking us to Chicago, Pittsburgh, and Detroit. We learned much on these trips, most of which made us even prouder of our own local accomplishments. For instance, the cost of land assembly for redevelopment in the United States was 80 per cent paid for by the federal government. Our development was done by private owners without government funds. At that time we did not have real slums or racial problems like the older American cities. Since World War II, Toronto had developed 3.5 million square feet of office space and was planning on at least 10 million more in the next five years, while Charles Centre, Baltimore's showpiece of redevelopment, was planning to build one million square feet of office space over the following three years. Subsequently, largely due to the council's efforts, Toronto built some 15 million square feet, worth more than one billion dollars, in the ten years between 1960 and 1970, and became the envy of every other city in North America. Among the developments were the Toronto-Dominion Centre, the Sheraton Centre, the Thomson Building, and the Simpson Tower. The list could be extended. There was a pause when the anti-development mayors were in office. Since then have come the Eaton Centre, the Commerce Court, the Royal Bank Plaza, and the Harbourfront Complex. In the future are the development projects of the Bank of Nova Scotia, the Bell Canada Place, and the Railway Lands' Domed Stadium. Eric Arthur was right when he called Toronto "no mean city."

The Redevelopment Advisory Council served a purpose. Under a different name it continues to define the needs of the city more than a quarter-century later.

# DISCUSSIONS
# WITH THE BAY

# 15

The Hudson Bay Company's managing director, Richard Murray, and I met several times casually at retail organization meetings in the mid-sixties. It became increasingly apparent that Hudson Bay stores were not doing particularly well because the company's policy precluded expansion into shopping centres. The fact that control rested in the committee in London, U.K., made quick decisions impossible. Dick told me that plans were afoot to bring the ancient charter from England to Canada, so that for the first time in three hundred years the Hudson Bay Company would be a Canadian company. With management control in Canada, a vigorous new attitude to expansion and modernization would ensue. It was obvious to the analysts and others in the retail business who were caught up in the dizzy pace of expansion in the suburbs that the Bay was being left behind.

They were falling behind in the West, their main stronghold, where the fierce competition came from Woodward's, Eaton's, and Simpsons-Sears. In the East, as competitive retailers, they were hardly a factor to be reckoned with, except for their large but antiquated downtown store in Montreal, formerly Morgan's. Their few small, plaza-type shopping centres, with inadequately sized suburban stores, were quickly overshadowed by such huge regional centres as Yorkdale in Toronto that had large, modern Eaton's and Simpsons stores as the drawing power. However, the Bay was "stirring," and once the charter "emigrated" to Canada, a new phase would begin.

Simpsons, in the meantime, as one of the planned options to becoming "national" in scope, considered that the western store strength of the Bay, fast-becoming overshadowed as it was, made a good fit with Simpsons' stores, along with their other assets, and our expansion plans in the East. A marriage between Simpsons and the

Bay, and then a merger with Simpsons-Sears, would result in a company with sales of over $3 billion annually, the largest retailers in Canada, with everything from fur trading in the North to the most modern shopping centres in the urban areas; huge mail-order facilities and a stake in Hudson Bay Oil and Gas, not to mention the benefits of a continuing association with Sears, Roebuck.

Simpsons could not even begin to take that particular dream any further without the approval of our partner, Sears, Roebuck. So I flew to Chicago and had a series of meetings with Gordon Metcalfe, then chairman of Sears, and other senior Sears officers, including Crowdus Baker and Art Wood, two of the negotiators with Simpsons when the original deal was signed. I had gone to considerable work to prepare for such an exploratory meeting, making appreciations from the points of view of Simpsons, Sears, and the Bay as I saw them, listing the factors, the courses open, the advantages and disadvantages, and finally recommending a plan. Sears were intrigued at the possibility of getting a piece of Hudson Bay Oil and Gas, but realized that their resulting interest in Simpsons-Sears, after the three-way merger, would drop from 50 per cent to approximately 33 per cent. Gordon Metcalfe said, "Well, Allan, I compliment you on the ideas presented. We are willing to give you a 'hunting licence' to explore the next stage."

This was really all I was asking. The next stage had many problems and difficulties to overcome and questions that needed answering, such as, "What would the Anti-Combines Committee in Ottawa think of a situation where one owner controlled three-quarters of the department-store business in one city?" I was bothered by how meetings between Simpsons and the Bay would be kept secret so that wild rumours would not flood the market and cause speculation and even anguish.

Dick Murray and I met clandestinely in New York to discuss the range of topics we wished to cover at the first meeting. We planned as we walked in the moonlight of a crisp fall night around Central Park Lake, an impossible journey today without getting mugged or worse! Dick had briefed his London committee on my proposal and reported that they were ready to discuss the intriguing proposition of a three-way union in greater detail. I had received both permission from the Simpsons board to take things the next step and a "hunting licence" from Sears. Edgar abstained from taking an active role because of his conflicts of interest as a director of Sears in Chicago, the chairman of Simpsons-Sears, and the chairman of Simpsons! So I turned more and more to Pete Scott, our senior vice-president and chairman of Wood Gundy, who was like an old fire horse that, having heard the siren and felt the harness descend on his back, was champing at the bit to be off and running. His fertile and greatly experienced brain was reliving and enjoying hundreds of major corporate deals he had overseen over the years in his long career with Wood Gundy, and mentally adding up the problems of finance and government that pertained to this complex suggestion of a three-way merger. C.L. Gundy, slower to excite, was nevertheless equally intrigued. After all, he and the Wood Gundy officers owned about 10 per cent of Simpsons directly, and both he and Pete had a sentimental attachment to the company. Pete Scott often said that the forming of Simpsons Limited in 1929 by my father, C.L. Gundy's father, J.H. Gundy, and Simpsons' employees to buy out the interests of Sir Joseph Flavelle, put Wood Gundy into the big time. So Simpsons was as dear to their hearts as it was to mine.

Simpsons, being the initiators, acted as hosts for the first meeting, held in a large, mirrored private dining-room of the Waldorf-Astoria. Representing Simpsons were myself, Pete Scott, C.L. Gundy, Jim Tory, our legal representative, and Ken Kernaghan, Simpsons' secretary, on whose shoulders fell the administrative details. The Hudson Bay Company's delegation was led by the Governor, Viscount Amory, several directors, who included Graham Towers, a former governor of the Bank of Canada, Donald Gordon, as well as a former governor of the Bank of England, and, of course, Dick Murray. We assumed that such a formidable group would not have assembled had the Bay not been keen to bargain.

We met in Pete Scott's suite to plan strategy before going down to the formal meeting. We had asked the Bay to review the timing, circumstances, and implications in the move of the charter to Canada, and we had to review the practicality of the merger, what assets each had to offer to balance a "troika," and what sort of organization would control it. First and foremost, we wished to hear directly from the governor of the Bay what they would include in the sale of the new company. As the moment of truth neared, I felt the sudden weight of the events that had grown from Dick Murray's and my early talks and rather clandestine meetings, but drew comfort from the expertise represented by Pete Scott, who so obviously relished the whole exercise. Bowing to Pete's years of experience in this corporate poker game, I said, "Of course, Pete, you'll take over once we get downstairs."

To which he replied, "Like hell, I will. It's your show, you carry on and we'll support you. But let's hear what the Bay has to say first. Let them play a few cards. You can always call them later."

We descended to the private dining-room, now fitted out with a long table covered in green baize cloth, a long row of golden chairs down each side. A picture that I had once seen in a history book of the signing of the Armistice in the Hall of Mirrors at Versailles flashed through my mind as we solemnly took our seats on opposite sides of the long table, myself and Viscount Amory facing each other. My opposite number, Derek Amory, was a warm, approachable human being, and I could not help liking him on first sight. He had, as a fifty-year-old brigadier, elected to parachute into Arnhem, Holland, with the paratroopers, in spite of the fact that he had never jumped before. He shattered both hips on landing, proving in this case that he was more brave than wise. He had a painful, limping gait for the rest of his life. He was a Cabinet minister in Churchill's short-lived, postwar government. Finally seated, Viscount Amory said, "Well, Allan, seeing you are the host, we feel that you should make the first statement."

"Gladly," I replied, thinking, "let him play his cards first." I welcomed the Hudson Bay governor and directors to the meeting with the hope that our deliberations would be fruitful. I outlined briefly my clearance from Sears, my mandate from Simpsons, and the generalities that Murray and I had discussed. "Now we wish to hear from you, your views and what you bring to the party."

"Okay," said Derek Amory, a broad grin on his face. "We'll commence."

The meeting went smoothly and well all morning. We had separate lunches and reassembled for another session. To our delight they seemed very keen to make a deal. But they hedged somewhat on Hudson Bay Oil and Gas, saying that it would have to be considered further. We set the date for our second meeting for a couple of weeks later, also in New York.

I went back to Chicago to report. Gordon Metcalfe, Sears' chairman, listened intently and extended my "hunting licence" to another meeting. Before I left he said, "Allan, if they exclude Hudson Bay Oil and Gas from the deal, they won't have enough to make it worthwhile. In my opinion we can go farther and faster together without them." He had a point about faster, and unless we broke our agreement with Sears, Roebuck, or he agreed to the new merger proposal, there would be no deal anyway. At the next meeting it was obvious that Hudson Bay did not want to include its oil and gas interest. So, sadly I returned home and killed the deal, agreeing with Sears that we would go farther and faster together without the problems and drag of the Hudson Bay retail stores.


His Grace The Duke of Northumberland, and his lovely duchess, Elizabeth, were guests of the Royal Agricultural Winter Fair in 1958. The Duke, who served as Hunter Judge at the Royal Horse Show, was during World War II an Officer in the Blues, the Royal Horse Guards, and he was master and huntsman of the family pack of hounds, "the Percy." He hunted the country around Alnwick Castle, as generations of Percys have done for centuries.

We invited the Duke and Duchess to have a day with the Eglinton Hunt, of which Major Charles Kindersley and I were joint masters. We met at Brigadier Eric Wallace's Rolling Hills Farm, then at Leslie and Steeles Avenue, and I was assigned, as Joint Master, to see to the well-being of our distinguished visitors from England. Major Kindersley was hunting hounds, as usual. After drawing one or two covers blank, the hounds raced away on a hot scent. As we galloped along in close pursuit, the Duke exclaimed happily, "This is marvellous. It reminds me so much of my country. You must come and hunt with me one day." All of this was said at full gallop, side by side.

"Sir," I replied, "you should never say that to a Canadian unless you mean it!"

"Sir," the Duke replied, "a Northumbrian never says anything unless he means it."

To which I lightheartedly replied, "Okay, when?"

We finished a great run, the fox as usual saving his brush by dodging into one of the many groundhog holes. Jogging home together, flushed and happy, Hugh – we were by now on a first-name basis – said that he would arrange a week for us at Alnwick Castle as his guests so we could hunt with him in his country. Sporting dates like this are often bandied about in the heat of the moment, but true to his word we soon received an invitation for the Brigadier and myself to hunt next March with the Percy hunt, and to bring our wives, Vera and Audrey, to stay in Alnwick Castle as the guests of the Duke and Duchess of Northumberland.

The four of us flew on to London and put up at the old Berkley Hotel on Piccadilly, now, sad to say, demolished and replaced with a modern hostelry of no grace or comeliness. We arrived on a Saturday morning, thinking to rest up on Sunday to recover from jet-lag and proceed to Northumberland on Monday. We made the mistake of phoning Alnwick to inform the Duke that we had, in fact, arrived. He insisted on us getting on the day-train on Sunday so that the hunting week would not be interfered with!

It was obvious that the Duke of Northumberland had not been on a Sunday day-train from London in recent years. But as we had received a near-Royal command, and as we did not know any better, we boarded and had seven hours of the coldest, dampest, most dismal, jolting train trip one could imagine. Sunday is the day when all heavy maintenance work is done on the tracks, so we jounced and jolted our way through diversions and detours covering most of the English Midlands on the journey, until we came to Newcastle-upon-Tyne in the dark, and a few minutes later, Alnwick Station, where we descended, four cold and weary travellers, surrounded by mounds of our own baggage, not sure what would happen next. As we were the only people who descended from the train, we were not difficult to identify, and the Duke's chauffeur cum valet quickly loaded us into the Landrover, packed as tight as sardines. Except for the smartly turned-out driver, we looked like refugees from a gypsy encampment. Off we went to the castle.

We did not know what to expect. After passing the Percy monument in Alnwick, and almost without leaving the main street of the town, we turned sharp right into the first of five keeps, each with a portcullis, the first of the walled areas that turned out to be the size of three or four football fields. Eventually we passed through the last gateway into a relatively small, cobble-stoned courtyard, and pulled up under a large stone *porte-cochère*, to find our hunting host, Hugh Percy, the Duke himself, waiting in the huge doorway, silhouetted by the light of the "wardroom" behind him. That is what the entrance hall of a medieval castle was, a place where the ward-guard slept and lived. The Duke greeted us warmly and led up several flights of stairs, past acres of the great castle rooms, to the warm, cosy, and relatively small living-quarters that the Percy family inhabited.

We were intrigued when we first entered the "wardroom" to see a huge billiard table occupying most of the room, the walls of which were completely covered with enough eighteenth-century horse pistols and heavy sabres to outfit a company of mounted men.

The billiard table, we found out, was used solely as a large area on which to lay out the caps, gloves, whips, spurs, sandwiches, and other supplies needed for each day's hunt!

We were quickly made at home in the drawing-room, given a drink, and told to dress in black tie for dinner, which formality surprised me, it being Sunday evening. I was somewhat taken aback by all the obvious trappings of antiquity, and thought I must have been very presumptuous in calling the Duke by his first name, so I reverted once again to calling him "Your Grace," at which he turned sharply on me and in reprimand said, "Allan, don't call me that. Only the servants do that. Please call me Hugh." Dressed, we reassembled in the drawing room, having been joined by the Duke's younger brother and the dowager duchess, his mother, when my friend Hugh made his entrance in a black velvet smoking jacket, with a white silk scarf carelessly knotted at his throat. Hugh's brother jumped to his feet and very formally said, "Good evening, sir," as one would do when his commanding officer entered the mess.

Audrey was assigned to a huge bedroom with an immense four-poster bed, which one occupied by climbing up four steps, the bed and canopy all heavily and gorgeously hung with green silk damask. I was shown down the hallway to a small, elegant room with a single, late-eighteenth-century mahogany officer's travelling bed, a miniature four-poster in Regency style, complete with three horse-hair pads in lieu of a mattress. The valet had already unpacked me and I found out that he decided from my meagre wardrobe what I should wear for each occasion. The hair mattress was as comfortable as anything I had ever experienced. I quickly fell asleep.

As dawn broke next morning, I awoke to a raspy, grating chorus of sounds that could only come from the ancient hinges of a dozen heavy doors swinging in the wind. Looking out my window, anxious to get a glimpse of this mysterious castle by first light, I discovered the sound came from families of rooks in a distant fringe of trees, shrouded in morning mist, which also blurred and softened the outlines of the dozen or so full-sized leaden figures of soldiers of another era on the battlements, constantly "on watch" for yet another invasion of the Scots from the north of the border. Alnwick Castle had been built in the fourteenth century and completed in the fifteenth by Henry Percy, the Earl of Northumberland, known as Hotspur in Shakespeare's *Henry IV*. Local and old wives' tales maintained that it would fall if ever the local rooks disappeared, for their constant raspy complaints were the castle's early warning system!

Immersed in history but shuddering from the damp chill, I realized that nature's call could no longer be denied. So I made my way to the "loo" down the hall. The loo, so named after King Louis XIV of France who had the first water-closet facility in the Western world, turned out to be a tiny room with an unglazed arrow slit for a window, cold as a grave, so I did not linger. Invigorated, chilled, and missing Audrey, I decided to share her huge, warm four-poster for a few minutes. But after climbing the steps and finding my wife hidden amid mounds of down comforters on the truly king-size bed, I kissed her and departed to my Spartan and chilly room to climb into my heaviest tweeds. Eric and I and our wives would be "hill-top" watching the hunt, because the Duke had warned us he could mount us for three days but not for four.

The Percys hunted four days a week. There were no subscribers, the small field of forty or fifty being mostly the Duke's tenant farmers or retired military personnel. I quickly found out that some of the "tenant" farmers farmed as much as six thousand acres apiece, and their ancestors had rented the land from the dukes of Northumberland for three hundred years or more. We were trying to catch glimpses of the hunt from a roadside, high on a hill, when two horsemen, mounted on magnificent but substantial horses, came trotting toward us. "What are you doing here?" brusquely demanded one of them.

"Watching the hunt," I replied.

"Why aren't you hunting then?"

"Because the Duke said he could mount us for three days but not for four. We are staying at Alnwick Castle," I replied.

"Oh you are, are you," they said in unison, jumping off their horses. "Here, take our horses, and go see the hunt properly," they said, introducing themselves as Harry Sordy and Danny Morallee. "We'll do something for you a duke can't do!"

The sound of the hounds in full cry in the distance was more than Eric and I could stand, so forgetting we were only in casual tweeds, we both mounted and left our wives to the tender mercies of the two Northumbrians. After twenty minutes or so, and a few fences later, Eric and I realized we would never find the hunt and large patches of skin had been rubbed off my knees by my rough tweeds. So we found our way back to our car to find our wives and Danny and Harry, all now on a first-name basis, having a grand picnic. We dismounted and tried to return their horses to them, but they denied ever having met us before. Having demolished my flask of whisky, they wondered aloud where those fine-looking horses had come from! This marked the first of nearly fifteen years of happy hunting experiences in the Percy country.

Curiously, all my ancestors had come from within fifty miles either side of the border between Scotland and England. Some say that the result of breeding between Cupar in Fifeshire and Yorkshire will give you the meanest "cross" in the world. Curiously, while I had no knowledge of any living relatives in these areas, I understood the dialects and accents of most of the locals I met without undue difficulty, and we got along as if I had come home. This intrigued the Duke greatly, because many of his visitors did not fit in with his people at all. This further cemented our friendship over the years. The week vanished quickly, as we hunted Monday, Thursday, and Saturday with the Percy in beautiful, rolling grass country, among friends of high and low estate, all keen sportsmen and women, glowing with health and the gentle, rugged humour of country people. Northumberland is no place for weaklings!

Before this memorable visit was over, I had an unusual offer from the Duke, who offered me a Joint Mastership with himself at the Percy. I was flattered because never before in the history of the pack, since its founding in the early eighteenth century, had the dukes of Northumberland ever had a Joint Master, the Duke traditionally filling the roles of Huntsman and Master himself. I thanked him, saying that I realized what an honour it was to be even considered for the task, but added that I must refuse.

"Why?" he asked me.

"Well," I replied, "possibly because you have met an honest man. I must refuse because, at my stage in my business career, I couldn't hunt with you enough to justify the title."

Hugh asked me to withhold my final answer until he showed me a house and farm he could let me have. The next morning, early, Hugh and I drove out from Alnwick Castle to a nearby farm, on which stood a lovely stone, Georgian manor house with suitable stables and farm buildings. "I will see that the farm is managed for you, and it will be available whenever you can be with us. The house and one hundred acres for one hundred pounds per acre."

The house in question was the spitting image of Limestone Hall, which was built in 1853 near Milton, Ontario, where I live. Limestone Hall is typical of the fine Georgian manor houses in the northern border areas between England and Scotland. "I am very tempted, Hugh, but I can't," I said.

Annoyed, he spoke sharply to me, saying, "Possibly you don't realize what I am offering you. I am offering you this land *freehold* and we never do that!"

I replied, "Then it is even more important that you are dealing with an honest man. Attractive as it is, I would rather be your friend than your serf!"

The Duke smiled broadly and said, "How very perceptive of you, Allan. Okay, we'll be friends. Whenever you come this way, we'll see that you are put up and have a good horse."

I subscribed to the Percy for many years, and had many excellent days, one of which to this day is talked about locally as the greatest hunt in the past seventy-five years.

A couple of years after this first meeting, several of the hunting farmers, all tenants of the Duke of Northumberland, each farming more than one thousand acres, came to attend an agricultural seminar at the University of Guelph. They came to visit me at my home, Limestone Hall, Walker's Line, which is surrounded by our four hundred acres of mixed farming. In their envy, they expressed wonder at being able to *own* – or, as they would express it, own "freehold" – such a beautiful and productive property. My mind flashed back to the Duke's offer, and I had the feeling then and there that if I had gone into their midst, having accepted the Duke's offer, *owning* my farm, we would no longer have been able to be the close friends that we became.

In a further curious turn of events, our oldest daughter Gail, then a nurse in the emergency ward of the Toronto General Hospital, met, fell in love with, and then married a young, Northumbrian chief intern, Dr. John Kendall. His father, Dr. Ernie Kendall, lived in Newcastle-upon-Tyne and delivered most of the offspring of my hunting friends at the Percy, as *his* father, also a doctor, had done before him! Now I had yet another reason to visit that great country, hunted by the Percy and our ever-widening circle of friends.

We continued our fox-hunting odyssey and were invited to have a day with the fastest and most fashionable hunt in the world, the Quorn, as guests of Robert Hanson, M.F.H. Bob Hanson was a bluff, north-country Englishman, a great judge of horse flesh, having purchased remounts for the British cavalry in Ireland in World War I.

He was also a canny horse-trader, whose family business had been as drovers. In western Canada he would have been known as a "horse hawler." Bob had had wealth forced on him when the British socialist government nationalized all transport companies, including Hanson's Haulage. He became Master of Fox Hounds of a good Midlands pack, near Huddersfield, his home base.

In 1948, when the postwar Olympics were held in Helsinki, Bob provided the British show-jumping team's leader, Col. Lewellyn, a big brave bay horse named Fox Hunter. Col. Lewellyn and Fox Hunter became famous throughout the Continent and North America, after winning the gold medal in Helsinki for Great Britain. They won internationally at White City, London, Rome, Paris, New York, and Toronto against the finest in the world. I suspect that Bob hoped for at least a peerage as a reward for his largesse, but he did get a C.B.E. eventually. The honour had to wait until his son James was elevated to the peerage as Sir James, and more recently to the Lords as Lord Hanson. This latter recognition was due to James's highly successful international business accomplishments in Hanson Trust, which now is a hugely profitable conglomerate of everything from banks in Jersey Island to hot-dog companies in New Jersey, U.S.A.

But on this famous Quorn day, we met at Widmerpool. There were three hundred mounted followers in the field, all beautifully turned-out in their scarlet coats, ladies in black, and about one hundred car followers jamming the roads. The Quorn country is hedge-and-ditch and mile after mile of fast-galloping grass meadows. The elegant field, most mounted on well-bred, beautifully groomed horses, had a reputation of its own. The "Quorn bitches" did not refer to the female hounds, known as the "bitch pack," but to the elegant women who rode over everything in their path and cursed the laggards like the old campaigners they were.

Bob warned me about the "Quorn bitches." They gave no quarter and expected none, so ride over them if you can, he advised. Bob, in his experience and wisdom, said the best thing to do is pick a "pilot," one who can outride the field, and stick with him. The "pilot" he picked out for me to follow was a female, a girl-woman, huge with pregnancy, mounted on a fire-eating thoroughbred, which stood about seventeen hands high. Being six months pregnant, she could not get into her regular hunting clothes, so she was turned out in a brown velvet corduroy jacket and breeches, but still looked very business-like.

After two hours of pushing and shoving through gaps and narrow gates and cursing under my breath at the rest of the three hundred in the field, we found a fox. Suddenly, all hell broke loose! The
hounds went off in full cry, the huntsman, blowing his horn in the
exciting "Ta-ta, ta-ta" of a fox gone away, was very red in the face as
he galloped by. To my amazement, each of the three hundred mounted
followers seemed to be starting off at a dead gallop for every point of
the compass! I followed my pilot, and soon found out why the less
brave went the other ways. We sailed over a huge hedge and ditch
that only a handful of us took, so the hunt suddenly came down to a
dozen of us with hounds, the rest left half a mile or more behind. We
flew hedge after hedge till I lost count, eyes glued on my pregnant
"pilot," who rode fearlessly and magnificently. We ran for fifty-six
minutes without "drawing rein." Eric, who was parallel with me,
and I, were in the first dozen when the hounds finally checked, the
fox having gone to ground near Willoughby-on-the-Wold.

I bought the horse I rode at the Quorn from Bob Hanson, a magnificent bay, sixteen hands three inches and very strong. He was called
Joker. I hoped the name was not symbolic because I paid a high price
for him.


Simpsons was ninety years old in 1962. To mark the anniversary, we
published a booklet called *Simpsons 90th Anniversary News*. I contributed an article to the publication called "The Quality of Simpson
People." A few passages may seem like self-evident truths to someone in the retail business, but what they say is often overlooked today.

In my opinion the most important single factor in the steady and
vast growth of our companies over the past ninety years has been
the very special qualities that have distinguished Simpson people.
These qualities have been based on principles of courtesy, service and value, and a genuine human interest in people that started
with Robert Simpson himself, as he served tea each afternoon to
customers on his main floor . . . sound merchandising principles
laid down by Mr. H.H. Fudger . . . by the very human qualities
of C.L. Burton and the practical steps he took in Profit Sharing, so
that every one of us has a real sense of owning as well as belonging to a Simpson family.

It is said that a merchant is a man whose whole business is to recognize "customer wants," quickly and accurately, and fill them as efficiently as possible. We have always prided ourselves on being "good merchants" and cleanliness has been our passion. Many of our good merchants in bygone days were "characters" in their own right – they imbued sales staff, servicemen, and customers with enthusiasm about the things they bought and so we have become known as a quality store.

Let us always reserve the right to be brilliant merchants and eager shopkeepers and, above all, human beings.

Edgar, who was chairman and president of Simpsons at this time, wrote:

Simpsons in its ninetieth year is in the midst of the most important expansion program in its history. . . . The Cedarbrae Store, which opened recently in Scarborough, is typical of the kind of suburban stores we are planning for the Toronto and Montreal areas.

Important progress is being made in the construction of our large Yorkdale Store at the corner of 401 and Dufferin. . . . It will undoubtedly attract customers from many miles beyond the limits of the Metropolitan area.

In Montreal we have just completed negotiations for the purchase of property west on the Metropolitan Boulevard, on which a major department store will be erected within the next year. In Halifax there are new escalators, air conditioning, and in London and Regina, major additions and improvements to our facilities. Extensions to our Lawrence Avenue Service Building in Toronto and a large new Service Building will be built in Montreal within the next few months.

In all Simpson stores we will continue to feature quality merchandise, give complete service and credit facilities. While we must operate our stores as economically as possible in today's highly competitive market, we should never do anything to change the superior character of our stores. We look forward to the future with renewed vigour and confidence.

Everyone was excited about Canada's Centennial year, 1967, and planning began long in advance for celebrations and events to mark the occasion. Important landmarks, monuments to corporate virility and pride, such as the Simpson Tower, were planned and built. Unfortunately, prolonged industrial strife and strikes delayed many of these noble projects and prevented them from opening until 1968. The lowly labourers suddenly discovered, through their "organized" bosses, that no work could be done without them, so they were instructed – many of them recent, uneducated immigrants – that they should demand equal wages with educated and trained mechanics like electricians and plumbers! The idea was so far-fetched that, while they were successful in closing down many important jobs for months, they finally had to reduce their demands to start working again. Several investigations by police and others followed, trying to prove that local Mafia members were in charge, rather than the union bosses.

In 1965 I became honorary lieutenant-colonel of the Governor General's Horse Guards, and in 1967 I had the pleasure of seeing my son James riding as officer in charge of the mounted escort we put on for the visit of our new honorary colonel, His Excellency the Governor General of Canada, Roland Michener, Q.C. My pride in seeing him an officer in my regiment and officer of the mounted guard was understandable when His Excellency inspected his regiment on the occasion of the Centennial.

The Horse Guards go back to 1812, when Capt. John Button raised a cavalry troop to fight with Sir Isaac Brock at Niagara against the American invaders. They were present at the capitulation of Detroit. In 1837, Button's troop and Denison's formed the Queen's Light Dragoon Guards, having survived the breakup of the militia which followed in the 1850s. At the time of the Fenian raids of 1866, we were designated the Governor General's Body Guard of Upper Canada. The motto *Nulli Secundus* ("Second to None") was adopted in 1876. The regiment served in the North West Rebellion of 1885, our first "battle honour." A painful and hazardous march across Jackfish Bay in Lake Superior enabled the Body Guard to arrive in the West in time to cut off Louis Riel's forces before they could seek refuge in the United States.

The regiment had a most profound effect on me during my youthful years and certainly prepared me and my family to accept the trials and tribulations, the loneliness, the homesickness, and the yearning for loved ones forced on us by World War II. It helped us after the war to attack the peace with hard work, joy, and gratitude, as each day dawned one upon the other.

Being a member of the board of directors of a company has some obvious benefits and some potentially serious hazards, should the director not show "due diligence" in his approach to the job. The outside director is the representative of the minority shareholders. Yet as an "insider" with access to privileged information, he must be careful when dealing with the company's stock.

Bell Canada Enterprises is, without doubt, one of the best-managed companies on the North American continent, and one that makes full use of those who serve on its board of directors, and whose directors, in turn, give the company dedication and loyalty.

The Royal Bank of Canada's board is among the most prestigious in Canada because of the bank's pre-eminent position among Canadian banks and its international position in the top seven of world banks. My twenty-two years on the Royal board have been a constant learning experience, and the fellowship and friendship of the top business leaders and executive of the bank assume an importance in my life, exceeded only by the importance of my family and my regiment. This is not to downgrade or denigrate the other fine companies and their managements.

The importance of the outside or independent director is never more obvious than when your company is in a merger or takeover position. Then the full responsibility of the role of the director as the minority shareholders' representative is brought home, as you fulfil the legal requirements of putting out director's circulars to inform the shareholders of your independent view of the offer in hand. Many intense meetings, unscheduled and called as changing circumstances dictate, become the order of the day, and the company under attack, in a friendly or unfriendly takeover, becomes the most important company with which you have an outside association, regardless of its size or relative importance.

The whole system is so complicated now that corporate takeovers are virtual bonanzas for lawyers, accountants, and financial advisers. There is little evidence that the upset caused by the takeover or merger does much, if anything, to improve the fortunes of the "taken-over" company. Bell Canada Enterprises is one of the few large organizations that can take over companies with benefit to both, or so it seems.

When Edgar died in 1968 and I was appointed chairman and president of Simpsons Limited, we were still, as a nation, on the high created by Expo '67 and the Centennial. Simpsons was busy planning for its own upcoming centennial in 1972 and coping with the never-ceasing plans for expansion in both Simpsons and Simpsons-Sears.

Edgar's death put our relationship with Sears in Chicago in a new light. Instinctively I knew that as long as we held 50 per cent of the voting stock of Simpsons-Sears, we could manage without using our ultimate right of veto, but the cast of characters was changing fast. Now Edgar and General Wood, the originators of the scheme, were gone. My father and Norman Urquhart were also gone, and the day was fast approaching when there would be no one left on either side who was an originator of the scheme. Crowdus Baker and Art Wood, senior officers of Sears, were near retirement, and they were the only ones left in Sears, Roebuck who understood the unwritten customs and nuances of our inter-company relationships that made our continued expansion in so many fields possible.

We were now gradually considering allowing the entrée of Simpsons-Sears into some of our eastern trading areas, without changing the written agreement, because they were better equipped to deal with "secondary" locations than we were, and in our view "half a loaf" was better than seeing a direct competitor occupy these places. So a great deal of thought and discussion went into a new and rejuvenated Simpsons board of directors and our marketing strategy for the seventies. By all predictions, the seventies would be the "Soaring Seventies," establishing new records for business, and in particular for Simpsons.

Our continuing relationship with Sears, Roebuck was of prime importance. Fortunately, General Douglas Peacher, Simpsons-Sears' president, appointed by Sears, remained a close personal friend of mine. We saw eye-to-eye on most things, and he was direct enough and outspoken enough to indicate to his American mentors that he intended to run Simpsons-Sears entirely from a Canadian point of view. Doug, a genuine admirer of Canada and Canadians, understood better than the average of his colleagues that many things in Canada are distinctly different from their American counterparts and that not everyone shared a belief in "the American way," as the only desirable way of life.

We had a small board of directors at Simpsons Limited, an average of fourteen members, with a majority of outside or independent directors. Fourteen to sixteen people is an ideal workable size for a board, according to business-school thought. Independently we found this to be so. I deliberately set out to recruit prominent men and women, leaders in their fields of endeavour, to balance the officers, the directors, and the traditional representation of Wood Gundy, as benign as financial advisers can be! I believe that at one time we had the finest "small" board of any company in Canada. Members included Ian Sinclair, chairman of the CPR, now a senator; Brig. F.C. Wallace, D.S.O., M.C., chairman of Duplate of Canada and a member of the Atomic Energy Commission; Betty Kennedy, O.C., CFRB's public affairs editor, whose daily radio show had a loyal audience of over 100,000 (Simpsons' customers we hoped); Tom Bell, M.C., the head of Abitibi, the world's largest producer of newsprint, and an astute businessman with a fine war record; Alfred Powis, chairman of Noranda, the huge mining company with world-wide interests, who was only in his thirties when made president of that organization; Raymond LaVoie, a distinguished Québécois who headed up the French-owned Crédit Foncier; William Wilder, head of Canadian Arctic Gas; W.P. (Pete) Scott, chairman of Wood Gundy; and C.L. Gundy, president of Wood Gundy, our financial advisers. I was complimented on having the confidence to surround myself with such strong personalities. I was amazed that the leader of an enterprise would not want the brightest and most highly respected people on his side.

When one is asked to join the board of a company, there are many questions one must ask himself or herself. First, is it the type of enterprise that I wish to be associated with? Second, does it conflict with my own business interests or unduly restrict my scope in my chosen field? Third, are the members of the board, as it exists, mainly top company officers or is the board balanced with respected business and professional people with whom I would be honoured to associate myself? Fourth, can I devote sufficient time to the new company's affairs to represent its shareholders as a director, while continuing to manage my own company's affairs to the satisfaction of my own directors, the approval of my own shareholders, without becoming an absentee manager as far as my own co-workers are concerned? The continuing growth and health of one's own organization must come first.

In searching for a suitable member of the board, one looks at the candidate's over-all position, his standing in the business community, possible conflicts in his present business interests, and the strengths and weaknesses in his personal character. Will the candidate be a strong, useful member of the board and yet congenial? What special advice or expertise may we expect from the candidate? Finally, will there be mutual respect? In our case at Simpsons, we had to include, in our view, the new candidate's attitude to our American partners, Sears, Roebuck, and our offspring, Simpsons-Sears.

In some instances, directors represent special-interest groups, such as women, labour, francophones, etc. Each new director was chosen because the individual was the person we wanted, not because Betty Kennedy was a woman, Ian Sinclair a former labour lawyer, or Ray LaVoie a Québécois. Yet all these facets became bonuses when we faced our competition and our business associates.

On June 6, 1970, I experienced a real-life crisis, the sort of thing that always happens to "the other guy." I found myself in the intensive care unit of Joseph Brant Hospital, after a heart attack, sweating from pain and apprehension. An intravenous needle was taped to the back of my left hand and cardiograph terminals to my chest and side, hooked to a monitor that showed my pulse, pittering and pattering up and down on a TV monitor by my bed, the duplicate of one in the nurses' station.

"Oh God!" I thought in near panic. "What am I going to do?" It was not so much the fear of the possibility of dying that distressed me as the sheer frustration of being a prisoner in solitary. I could not communicate. I was immobilized, and Audrey and I had some four hundred people of the Twenty-Five Year Club from all parts of the country arriving for our annual garden party. A huge marquee had been installed on one of the lawns at Limestone Hall, our home. One year a mini-tornado blew the tent down – a minor crisis, not to be compared to this one!

I spent the first hot and humid night restlessly floating in and out of consciousness. It was as long a night as any I can remember. "Our Father, which art in Heaven . . . ." Think, think! What do I have to do? How will the market react when word gets out I am ill? "Forgive me my sins . . . as . . . ." Concentrate, concentrate! Calm down. "Thank you, nurse." She completely remade my sodden bed with clean, dry sheets for the third time in as many hours.

Finally I slept, weighed down by the monitor cables and by not knowing what tomorrow would bring. The next morning I was bathed. Then, much more relaxed, I was wheeled into a room closer to the nurses' station. When I first opened my eyes that morning, to sunshine and the buzz of calm efficiency of the duty nurses completing their tasks and waiting for the new shift to relieve them, I watched a good-looking nurse – I later dubbed her "Lady Dracula" – draw her daily quota of blood from her captives. I could once more begin to think, but I had no answers.

Dr. John Kendall, who was in charge of the intensive care unit and a renowned cardiologist as well as being my son-in-law, slipped in to tell me that Pete Scott had to see me urgently with papers to sign. Audrey would be in later. Strange, I thought. It was almost as perplexing as the fate of the patient who had occupied the bed I was now in. Did he die or was he well enough to move upstairs to the normal ward? Strange that W.P. Scott, vice-president of Simpsons Limited and chairman of Wood Gundy & Co., should be my first visitor, coming even before family. Yet Pete was like a second father to me.

Pete, hale and bluff and hearty, was a welcome sight as he approached my bed. After the usual "How are you feeling?" he cheerfully said, "Allan, I have come to tell you you are fired!"

The wind knocked out of me, I replied, "Thanks a lot, you sure know how to cheer up a man!"

Pete continued quickly, seeing the stunned disbelief on my face. "We had a board meeting, which I chaired as senior vice-president, and we decided that the only way you will recover is to relieve you of all responsibility. We have named Jack Porter as chairman and chief executive officer, pro tem. As soon as you can resume your work, the situation will reverse itself, and automatically you will become chairman and CEO and president once more."

Immensely relieved, I said, "I understand, but will there be an announcement in the papers of the change? No? Well, okay, but please tell Jack Porter I would like to see him as soon as it is convenient."

Jack Porter, a most loyal Simpsons man and friend, would keep the team together. And he did the job magnificently with no public recognition.

For the first time I became aware of the patient in the next bed. His name was Jim Anderson and he listened to all the foregoing with considerable interest because he was also *hors de combat*. He was the head of his own construction company, as I was head of Simpsons, until a few minutes ago at least. Jim said, "That was the damnedest thing I ever witnessed. Imagine firing a guy like that when he's down! But you're lucky, I have no one to fire me, and that's why I am in here with my second heart attack, I guess."

Jim was the spitting image of Dick Martin, the comedian of Rowan and Martin TV fame. He had a great sense of humour, a lopsided grin, and an ability to say outrageous things to nurses that would set us all, including the nurses, laughing – things that, if he had not been tied down, would have had him charged with sexual harassment in today's militant, feminist work world.

Almost before Pete Scott left the hospital, a message was smuggled in to me from the York Club, Toronto. I was chairman of their wine committee. The York Club has a well-rounded and extensive cellar, one of the best in any club in North America. The message said, in effect, that a crisis had developed. The club had less than five years' worth of vintage port left! This "intelligence" seemed so ludicrous – arriving at a time when I was not too sure whether I had one month or ten years left to live – that I started to laugh. Recovering, I wrote out an order for forty cases of vintage port – twenty of Adams, 1963, and twenty of Cockburn, 1963. I wrote at the bottom, "Not fit to open until 1975, and I will open the first bottle!" The wine was ordered and binned, and at a ceremony at the York Club in 1975, I *did* open the first bottle of this fine vintage port.

All in all, the intensive-care experience was one of the most interesting in my life. Jim and I quickly got the ward organized. John Kendall had slipped me a bottle of my Glen Grant, twenty-seven-year-old, single-malt whisky, which I hid in my night table. Each evening, at five, it was sampled by whichever doctors happened to be on duty, checking charts, pressures, and pulses. Later I added a Dry Sack sherry from another well-wisher. As each new patient was wheeled into our ward, and after the nurses had left, Jim and I would size up the newcomer. We recognized in the new patient the signs of the pale misery of inner terror that the intravenous and monitor-terminals stuck on him created in his mind as he tried to sort out his life. After finding out his name and where he came from, I would ask him what he would like to drink, Scotch or sherry? Horrified, the newcomer would whisper, "You can't drink in here!"

Laughing, we would reply, "Don't be silly. We wouldn't be here if we couldn't have a drink!"

With that, Jim would roll over and turn off his monitor, which would ring a bell in the nurses' station. The absence of a signal on the monitor would bring a nurse running, while I got out the appropriate bottle. "Would you please get us three clean glasses, nurse?" Jim would solemnly ask, while the long-suffering nurse would once more lecture us and scold us on the extreme danger of fooling with the monitors, before going off to fetch some glasses. Over a small drink we would then settle back while the new man told us his life story, more or less. The nurses finally had to separate Jim and me to save us from each other. But we laughed, the nurses laughed, the patients laughed, and most of the patients got better sooner than expected! Our medicine, laughter, was fine medicine!

Being in the hospital was like being in the war. Having survived the ordeal, I found it most interesting to see all conditions of people, stripped of social grace or importance, able to laugh at some of life's more ridiculous situations. What is more, the survivors, while we might never meet again, became friends who shared in common experience – the danger of losing life made survival all the sweeter. As well, the doctors and nurses were wonderful, caring human beings.

Dear Audrey carried on as hostess of the garden party in my absence, read my laboured little greeting, and was, as usual, a rallying point for the family during my weeks of recovery.

# CRISES OF
# THE SEVENTIES

## 16

The year 1973 marked a turning-point in the postwar era. The Mid-East oil embargo, which followed the formation of the Organization of Petroleum Exporting Countries (OPEC), had serious repercussions, deep and shattering, in Great Britain and in those European nations that looked to the Middle-Eastern countries for up to 70 per cent of their energy fuel needs. England was forced to shut down its factories for two days a week. Gasoline was rationed throughout the United States, and Canadians began to economize when hit by high prices and rumours of cutbacks in production. The labour situation worsened. Wage demands increased by leaps and bounds in an effort to nullify the effects of ever-increasing inflation and rising costs. In July there was a national rail strike.

We started out the year with high hopes that our great success of 1972, Simpsons' centennial year, would be repeated in our 101st, but the euphoria of our centennial, the hundredth birthday of ''One of the Great Stores of the World,'' the catch phrase that our president, Charles Stewart, had coined, began to dissipate slowly but surely as the year wore on. But the deepening world panic was not well out in the open until fall.

John David Eaton, after a lengthy decline in health, died. At Simpsons we expressed our sympathy by running a full-page advertisement in *The Globe and Mail* in memorial, a tribute we usually reserved for the death of the monarch. Eaton's had run a full-page ad to mark our centennial, congratulating Simpsons on being ''a great store of the world.'' Eaton's and Simpsons were engaged in a hard-fought, daily battle from coast to coast. We had each learned over the century to respect and even admire the men and women on both sides who dedicated their lives to serve their customers. I received a warm, emotional letter of thanks from John Craig Eaton, the oldest son of John David, who suddenly was faced with the awesome task of running that huge and very private company. Our personal friendship grew from that moment on.

Ian Sinclair, then chairman of Canadian Pacific Railway, now a senator, agreed to join the Simpsons board of directors. It was a coup for us as it would be for any company. Then my close friend and adviser, Pete Scott, told me he had to go to the hospital for tests. It turned out he was suffering from a brain tumour. My jubilation at having a great businessman like Sinclair join the Simpsons board was dampened by the news that Scott would be out of action for some time to come. Our relationship with Sears, Roebuck, while on the surface courteous and friendly for nearly twenty-two years, was showing certain strains and stresses. The deaths of my brother Edgar and of Norman Urquhart meant that Pete Scott's counsel and advice were much sought after. Now that was in jeopardy.

The expansion of Simpsons-Sears was increasingly costly. The capital could be raised from the money markets or generated from profits withheld from dividend payouts and ploughed back into more stores and facilities. We had already raised millions of dollars to honour Simpsons' end of the agreement, and we needed a consistent payout of dividends to help meet our interest costs. The only concern of Simpsons-Sears was to increase its own business, and at this point Sears, Roebuck could not care less if it received a few million Canadian dollars in dividends from our joint venture. Simpsons itself was in a most vigorous expansion phase, with four joint shopping-centre ventures coming up over the next four years, each requiring from ten to twenty million dollars for Simpsons' own purposes.

The atmosphere was friendly but increasingly tense at Simpsons-Sears meetings. All projects were bedevilled with high costs, much higher than the original projections. The bank's prime lending rate had reached 9 per cent, and construction costs were forecast to increase 20 per cent annually for the next five years. The stock market was as jittery as a young girl with acne at her first formal ball, and money was becoming scarcer and more expensive. After the Hudson Bay negotiations had fallen through in 1965, we looked westward to our counterpart in Vancouver, Woodward's. Chunky Woodward and I had become close friends, and the similarities in our respective businesses, and the lack of overlap of existing facilities, East and West, made us consider the pros and cons of a merger between Simpsons and Woodward's. Each of us suffered or rejoiced as the East or the West in turn prospered or suffered. We were both too regional and would benefit by becoming national in scope. Under our Sears agreement, for Simpsons to do anything of this nature would need Sears' sanction. Chunky, while he controlled much of the family stock, would have to win others in his family over to such a national move. After all, it was Chunky's father who angrily told Edgar, when Simpsons-Sears opened its first store in Vancouver, that Woodward's would run us out of town! But that was in May 1954, and times had changed.

Charlie Stewart and I flew to Chicago and met with Art Wood, Sears' chairman, and Gordon Metcalfe, ex-chairman and director, both of whom I knew well. After several hours, I once more got a "hunting licence." In other words, Sears granted me permission to discuss the situation with Woodward's in more detail. On returning to Toronto, I was horrified to discover that there was a major crisis in Simpsons Credit Department. We had been well in the forefront of automating our Credit Department, and were in the process of increasing our capabilities manyfold by switching from a 360 IBM computer to the more advanced 370 IBM, when the electronic authorizer shorted the electronic head, wiping out the entire disc record of hundreds of thousands of accounts in Toronto and Montreal! A minor disaster! It took three days and nights to re-record the records, and an estimated 2 per cent of accounts could not be re-established, a serious profit loss.

I flew to Vancouver with Charlie Stewart and spent two or three days with Chunky Woodward, viewing his stores and warehouse facilities. I arranged that he would, in turn, visit us, bringing his comptroller with him to see if our accounting systems were compatible, to see if we could bring off this marriage of two great retailers!

The international situation was not the best. In addition to inflation and spiralling costs, there were the Watergate scandals, with revelations of wrong-doing and cover-up. We watched our television sets, fascinated as this American soap opera unfolded day by day. But I had far more immediate things on my mind. Just a few days apart I got the depressing news that Chunky Woodward had been stricken with a virus and was in hospital, paralysed from the waist down, and the tragic news that Pete Scott's brain tumour was malignant and the prognosis was for three weeks or so. It was especially hard on Miss Ross, Pete's secretary of forty years, who had to sit and write while Pete dictated his complete funeral arrangements before his operation. It was horrible to think of the man already dead, but he had to make his arrangements, as we had to envision what being without Pete's wisdom and friendship would mean to us as well. He had a love of Simpsons and a wealth of wisdom in certain areas that no one else available to me then had.

I spoke to Bill Wilder about succeeding Pete Scott on the Simpsons board. Neil McKinnon, newly retired as chairman of the Canadian Bank of Commerce, came through loud and clear as being available to be a Simpsons director. Although Neil and I had been good friends for twenty years, it was evident that he was under much mental and emotion strain because of his retirement from the bank. I was cool to his approach.

Charlie Gundy's nephew sold a large block of Simpsons' stock, some 40,000 shares I was told, when it became clear I was not going to make him a director. Maybe it was shrewd of him because the stock market in early December 1973 took its greatest drop since 1956 when the Toronto Stock Exchange started keeping records. Stockbrokers were close to panic, consumers were nervous, and the professional managers were jittery. I was ashamed that I "blew my stack" at my senior men in a meeting, when they began to complain about Simpsons-Sears encroaching on our areas, about the state of business, about the performance of the stock market, and about the world in general as they saw it. I told them, in a burst of unusual anger, "If you don't like the game, retire and get out!" None of them did. Good friends and associates, they understood the pressures of the moment. The next day we set an all-time record for one day's business, an achievement that always restores good humour!

In addition, as the year came to its close, I received more and more letters complimenting us on Simpsons' excellent service. One satisfied customer enclosed a copy of a letter she had written to Eaton's, cancelling her account at that store and telling them how good Simpsons was! The Christmas surge in sales came but it was too late to set any sales records. The company about matched the previous year's profit, in spite of strong sales increases of up to 20 per cent. On Christmas Eve I went to the hospital to see Pete Scott, who clasped my hand to his breast and would not let me go until his lovely wife, Joan, slipped her hand in place of mine. Pete could no longer talk. On Christmas Day it poured rain. The countryside was flooded, as if with the world's tears.

• • •

In January 1974, there was hope that the effect of the oil embargo on the world economy would be less severe than it had been in 1973, as the various countries adjusted to rationing and conservation of energy. The need for self-sufficiency in oil, gas, and uranium was matched by the further development of Canada's nuclear and hydro alternatives. The country has vast, untapped potentials of raw energy, so the future still looked bright for us, despite drawbacks.

Jules Léger was sworn in as the twenty-first governor general, the fourth Canadian to hold that office. He succeeded our old friend, Roland Michener. To our consternation and in an ominous forecast of French-Canadian sentiment, Léger refused to be associated with anything royal – the Royal Canadian Military Institute, the Royal Ontario Museum, and so on. He balked at becoming the honorary colonel of our beloved Governor General's Horse Guards! I wondered why or how he pretended to represent Her Majesty the Queen in Canada.

My diary recorded the following:

"January 20th, 59th Birthday.

"Severe ice storms, party cancelled.

"Power off for 4 1/2 hours – high winds, drifting snow.

"My birthday parties have never been very successful. George V died on my twenty-first birthday and everything closed down in mid-evening. Another party cancelled. The only reason to celebrate your birthday, anyway, is to supply evidence that you are still alive. However, I will try for another next year!

"It gets increasingly difficult to justify higher salaries for those not pulling their weight, or justification for keeping them on. Inflation now 9.3 per cent." These words came from an entry in my diary a few days later. I noted further, "In the past ten years the federal government has destroyed many of our important employee benefits, i.e., profit-sharing (which we have had since 1916), stock options, and even the right to be wrong as an investor in capital gains. I start a full study of our benefits. Money isn't enough. Security isn't enough. Generous retirement provisions aren't enough. What is today's answer to get from employees the extra loyalty, extra effort, the hidden extra 10 per cent in hard work, as 'Big Daddy' Gardiner, Metro Chairman, used to say?"

Pete Scott died on January 31. My dear friend, sage, financier, businesman, fishing companion, and wise and loyal Simpsons director was dead. A few days earlier I phoned Betty Kennedy in Bermuda to formally ask her to join the board as a director. She was thrilled and accepted, and would be elected at the next meeting in March.

We were very pleased to have Betty join the board. In her hour-long, daily radio show on CFRB, Toronto, she interviewed some two thousand people a year from all walks of life and many diverse disciplines. She has been acknowledged to be one of the best radio interviewers anywhere. With a daily listening audience of one hundred thousand, she has the largest anywhere. Naturally many people thought we were just bowing to the increasingly popular trend to have a woman on the board, and lucky to have an intelligent, strikingly beautiful one at that! From our point of view, Betty, possibly more than any other outside director, knew and understood our customers, many of whom she interviewed or listened to on her show. In addition, she had coast-to-coast recognition, having been on CBC television weekly on *Front Page Challenge* for over twenty years. She had served on the Complaints Board of the Ontario College of Physicians and Surgeons and on a special Ontario government committee to review spending. To cap all this, she was a charming lady in the best sense of the word, one who was not afraid to speak her mind. We, on the board, were elated and proud when she accepted.

We left the "news" of the announcement to her old friend and long-time associate Gordon Sinclair, on his regular CFRB broadcast. Sinclair, as unpredictable as the weather, left it to the end of his newscast, and reported, grumpily, "Today Betty Kennedy became a director of Simpsons Limited – bully for Betty." Fortunately, Jack Dennett, in his newscast over the same station later in the day, reported, "She is a great Canadian, who will do a great job for one of Canada's greatest merchants."

Public-service strikes of all kinds beset the country in the first four months of 1974, wreaking havoc with commerce and business. There were postal strikes and air traffic controllers' strikes. The ship pilots on the St. Lawrence went on strike, and there were transportation workers' strikes in Laval and Montreal. Canada got a well-deserved reputation internationally for poor labour relations. The mood of the country was one of selfishness, not service.

I was invited by Robert Scrivener, then chairman of Bell Canada, to join the Bell board, one of the most prestigious in Canada. I was very pleased to accept. Bob Scrivener had, years ago, when he was Bell's general manager in Toronto, helped me raise money for the Red Cross when I was chairman of the Red Cross annual appeal for funds. We also had a hand in starting the Toronto-area, free-blood program of the Red Cross and led the Red Cross in becoming an associate of the United Appeal.

It was my lot, as chairman of Simpsons, to entertain and be entertained by a constant stream of business events. A memorable luncheon was one I gave for Joy Adamson, the author of *Born Free*. She had won the confidence of wild lions in Africa. After raising a lioness called Elsa, she had returned Elsa to her wild state, teaching her to survive and hunt and find a mate. Joy, tanned as old shoe leather, had only half a hand, the result of a clawing by one of her lions. She was a spunky lady.

A not-so-pleasant dinner was an official reception at the Royal York for Governor General Jules Léger. Normally decorations and medal miniatures would be worn at such an affair, but two major-generals who worked for the Ontario government, William Anderson and George Kitching, had been told not to wear their well-earned battle medals and that only the Order of Canada would be recognized. My old friends, Harry (Red) Foster and Ruth Frankel, had been instructed to wear their Order of Canada medals. I was furious at the inference that my wartime D.S.O. and campaign medals were "foreign" medals, so I wore my miniatures. Not to be outdone, both Anderson and Kitching put up theirs, having had them in their pockets!

Léger arrived with no aide-de-camp. There was no royal salute. Four people invited failed to show at our table, so Audrey and I sat in conspicuous prominence. It was becoming more and more obvious that Léger was uncomfortable as Her Majesty's representative, and there were widespread rumblings of discontent, even among Liberals. As my late father used to say, "There are only two classes of people in Canada, Liberals and disgruntled Liberals."

After a holiday spent trout fishing on the Rolling Rock Club stream, Audrey detected a lump in her left breast. She had a full medical examination, and a few days later, almost before we were aware of the seriousness of the situation, her breast was removed in an operation that was described as a modified radical mastectomy. Nowadays only the small growth area is removed and the survival rate seems to be the same. This avoids the horrible trauma of disfigurement and shock caused by the radical operation that Audrey endured. Weeks went by and the wound did not heal properly. Our lives changed drastically. Without the wonderful services of the Victorian Order of Nurses, one of whose nurses came daily to change the dressings, I do not know how we would have managed, living as we did in the country. Audrey was so upset that, from the moment of disfigurement to her dying day, I was never permitted to see the terrible wound. I had to be very gentle when I held her in my arms.

Fatigue became a constant companion. Night after night our sleep was interrupted several times by her terrible pain. Our children drew closer and, surrounded by their love, Audrey slowly grew stronger. It was almost a respite to bury myself in the constant stream of business meetings. New stores were built, and new shopping-centre partnerships were undertaken. There were meetings of the Industrial Commission, the Hospital for Sick Children, on whose board I had served for the past eleven years, and those of the York Club, of which I was then chairman.

Audrey's wound healed, but her back and rib cage gave her constant pain. It was suggested that the cause was a pinched nerve. Hurting as she was, she insisted on attending the annual dinner of the Twenty-Five Year Club, given in the Arcadian Court. We even danced a number. The next day we greeted four hundred Simpsons people and their spouses at a luncheon at our farm near Milton. Audrey stood beside me for an hour to greet our guests before she excused herself to fight her continual battle with pain alone in her room, without complaint. Most of those attending knew her problem and admired her for the wonderful, warm, caring person she had always been.

A few days later she once more summoned up her courage and insisted on accompanying me to a dinner at the Rosedale Golf Club. It was given by my Joint Masters and members of the Eglinton and Caledon Hunt to honour me for my twenty-three years as Joint Master and sometime amateur huntsman. They presented me with a beautiful, sterling-silver hunting horn, suitably inscribed. To Audrey they presented a huge, gold fox-mask pin as a memento of the many hours she had waited for me to return from yet another fox-hunting day, tired, dirty, and happy. We even enjoyed a dance to Peter Appleyard's orchestra. Peter was himself a fox-hunter with the Eglinton Hunt.

The next day, as Audrey rested, I attended the annual meeting of Standard Broadcasting Limited as a director of the company. Bud McDougald was chairman. Eric Warren also attended. Eric, an heir to the Gutta Percha rubber money, was a well-known eccentric who spent much of his time attending shareholders' meetings, often asking penetrating questions. He delighted in doing something to upset the composure of the chairman. He cared little for the opinions of his behaviour held by others. Seeing me in the front row of the meeting with the directors, and always having been courteous and friendly to me at Simpsons meetings, he shouted, "Allan Burton, what's a fine gentleman like you doing with a crowd like this?" The cry startled Bud McDougald who, as chairman of Standard Broadcasting as well as of the Argus Corporation and the Toronto Club, considered himself pretty well on top of the social flagpole. The meeting got started and suddenly Eric moved to the centre of the aisle and placed the Standard annual report on the carpet. He then stood on his head and said, "Mr. Chairman, you may be wondering why I am standing on my head. Well, it's the only way I can make head or tail of the upside-down figures in your financial report!" Eric was never malicious and often quite amusing in making his point of view known.

Bud McDougald, who was known to have done some corporate juggling in the past, retained his composure and passed off the incident. Eric, before leaving the meeting, sprayed some cheap, sickly perfume from a spray can and threw the can to me, saying, "Allan, if you are going to stay with this bunch, you'll need this more than me." The printed label on the can read "Bullshit Remover."

As the year wore on, the prime rate reached a dizzy 11.5 per cent. Sales and consumer demand remained strong, but salaries and expenses of all sorts climbed more rapidly than inflation and ate into profits at an alarming rate. With huge sales increases, profits were marking time. I purchased Pete Scott's Rolls-Royce, which had only five thousand miles on it, from his son Mike, but could not use it because I had just started an all-out economy drive to control expenses. Instead I drove a modest Mercury for the next year.

Near the end of July, Bill 22, the French-language bill, was made law in Quebec. It set up tribunals to police the hiring of francophones and the use of French in the workplace. This was the forerunner of the infamous Bill 101, which forbade the use of English and all other languages except French on signs and advertisements. Many of its other restrictions shocked the business world and started an exodus of executives and businesses from Quebec. For a nation-wide business, it meant one arm had a tourniquet on it that stopped the natural flow of talent between units.

Audrey was in almost continual pain and discomfort, and sud-

denly, without the slightest warning, there was another medical crisis. After working in the greenhouse one hot afternoon, both my
kidneys ceased functioning entirely. Hospitalized, I was forbidden
food or water for thirty hours, while I was probed and prodded internally by Dr. Kinsey Smith. He and his colleagues were mystified but
relieved when, within forty-five minutes of going on a dialysis, or
artificial kidney machine, slowly, painfully, my kidneys began to operate once more. I wrote in my diary on July 31, "Now I start a mad
course of guarding and recording each drop as more precious than
gold! My entire concentration is on this waterway! 2500 ccs in and a
miraculous 2450 ccs out – voided! The doctors profess themselves to
be very relieved, and I have been doing all the relieving!" The doctors said I could not get out of hospital for the holiday weekend, at
which poor Audrey, whose hurts had been momentarily eclipsed by
this new crisis, blew her top and said, "You are getting better on
your own. They are not doing anything for you here. They might as
well do nothing for you at home!" Her logic prevailed and I was
released.

The cause of my malaise was still a mystery, but eventually we
determined that I had nearly killed myself spraying a lethal mixture
in our greenhouse while clad only in shorts. Apparently the "bug
spray" was absorbed through my skin and immobilized my kidney
function, a painful lesson learned.

Toronto Transit Commission employees went on strike in July.
Downtown business slumped by 50 per cent, and David Crombie,
our "Tiny Perfect Mayor," was on vacation, apparently unconcerned.
His Honour was maliciously called "Mayor Zombie" in business circles. In August there was a subway strike in Montreal as well. The
TTC strike alone cost Simpsons some $750,000 in lost profit before
any level of government acted to stop the bleeding. Ontario Premier
William Davis threatened to call back the members of the legislature
from their vacations to pass a "back-to-work" bill, but the union said it
would defy any government "back-to-work" order!

On September 7 there was good news. Limestone Hall Farms
won first prize for corn in Halton County at the Milton Fall Fair. We
were fully regarded as a professional farm operation by our dairy-
men neighbours.

At the mid-September board meeting, I asked Bill Wilder, Charles
Gundy, Alf Powis, and Betty Kennedy to each give his or her view of
the present economic situation and their predictions for spring 1975.

Wilder and Powis were particularly pessimistic, even talking depression. We all agreed that the next few months would be very difficult and dangerous for firms or individuals who were over-extended during this period of recession.

Our planning staff, headed by Elmer Rounding and myself, reviewed no fewer than nineteen different projects we had on our platter at Simpsons. We unanimously decided to cancel or postpone all but six on account of deteriorating business conditions and the difficult money market.

On September 23 we sent Ted Burton on the advanced executive management course at Harvard for thirteen weeks, hoping that this would round out his business experience. We had to pull some strings to get him admitted. Ted was hard-working and had wide and varied experience in merchandising and business generally, but he had allowed himself several emotional outbursts. He was uneven in his handling of subordinates, to the extent that Charles Stewart had to correct him sharply. At this stage in his otherwise promising career, it could hardly be put down to immaturity. He would not be the first person in my experience to suffer "battle fatigue."

The advance executive management course at the Harvard Business School was specially designed to expose government servants, diplomats, and business leaders to a final "baptism of fire and learning" from their peers before advancing to their top positions. The course was limited to presidents of corporations, major-generals or above in the military, senior diplomats in the foreign service, and so on, and was an intensive three-and-a-half month, live-in experience, where enrollees worked in syndicates to solve their problems. This was the most advanced and expensive course on which we had ever sent anyone.

For twenty years we had run a management trainee course, a year-long, in-house exposure to every facet of the business. The Business School at the University of Western Ontario trained for six weeks each year several of our best, up-and-coming senior management prospects. But this was the first time any Simpsons person had been selected to attend the Harvard course. Dean Swift, president of Sears, Roebuck, a graduate of the course, had recommended it.

On October 3, 1974, Simpsons stock traded a large block of 121,000 shares at a new low price of $5.25. Earlier in the year it had traded at $7.50. We had maintained an unusually high price on our stock, and a high multiple of up to nineteen-times earnings. At $5.25, we now were about ten-times earnings, a much more normal multiple for most listed companies. On October 23, Simpsons' stock was traded once more in the $7.00 range.

I announced a new pension plan to freeze and replace profit-sharing, now dead and gone due to the tax department's rulings, the funds of which would form the basis of the new pension scheme. The retirement benefits in the new plan were greater, but the immense pride and loyalty generated by profit-sharing, in which I firmly believe, were gone.

At a December economic briefing at the Royal Bank, we were told that things had worsened dramatically in the United States, and to a lesser degree in Canada, in the past month. The prediction was that 1975 would be the slowest growth year in Canada since World War II. This did not stop the Members of Parliament in Ottawa from voting themselves salary increases of 50 per cent. Our salary and bonus increases, which amounted to 11 per cent, seemed small in comparison. Then an outraged cry from across the country forced Parliament to withdraw the increase for MPs.

We enjoyed a full Christmas at home with all the family. Audrey insisted on doing all the usual things for everybody. But on Boxing Day, our world came crashing down. Dr. John Kendall brought the news that Audrey's cancer had, in fact, spread to various areas, shoulder and hips. He was upset because he had lied to us on Christmas Eve about her condition, thinking it was better that way. Audrey now needed deep therapy at Princess Margaret Hospital to ease the intense pain. There was little we could do but pray.

We had planned for the next day a cocktail party at Limestone Hall for thirty-three of our friends, and Audrey refused to cancel it. She arranged to be driven into town to have her hair done, and with coolness and courage she played the part of the charming hostess. For the next two days she could hardly move. On December 30, it took me fifteen minutes to get her upright and out of bed, she was so stiff.

She had a full morning of X-rays at Princess Margaret Hospital. The head of the cancer clinic phoned and asked to see me that afternoon. He and another doctor told me they were putting her on pills and that she should come back in a month. I was thunder-struck when I heard this because there was no way she could cope at home as she was. The doctors asked me to describe her problems, which I did, upon which they said she should be admitted immediately to start treatment. They had asked to see me privately because they both felt that Audrey was not describing her problems fully. As usual, when they questioned her, she had made light of her pain. Audrey took the news calmly that she would have to remain in the hospital.

On New Year's Eve, Audrey was admitted to Princess Margaret Hospital. Our daughter, Lynn, delayed indefinitely her return to Sotheby's in London. We took Audrey a bottle of champagne to have a New Year's drink with her. Audrey had a small drink of Seagram's V.O., her usual "moose milk," as she called it. Lynn and I toasted her in champagne as we said silent prayers. Our New Year's wish was for a miracle for Audrey.

The miracle was not to be granted. Audrey was confined in the Princess Margaret for the next two months, while her body was bombarded with thirty-seven cobalt radiation treatments and massive injections of many different poisons in the vain hope that one of them would kill the disease without killing the patient. The doctors and staff were caring and concerned. The facilities were grossly overloaded, and there was little or no privacy for the poor patients. They had to sit in wheelchairs in the public aisles, their pride making them cover their faces to hide their anguish and apprehension, sometimes for hours, as the pitiful traffic of wheelchairs inched forward to the treatment room.

At the end of the first month we were told by the doctors that Audrey's cancer was still spreading. We learned the further depressing news that Betsy Rutherford, the wife of Col. Bob Rutherford, a regimental friend, had died of cancer. We attempted to withhold the news from Audrey. They had worked together in the GGHG Ladies' Guild during World War II, when Audrey was its president.

Early in the second month, Audrey required blood transfusions before she could go on with a new series of treatments. The heavy doses of radiation were destroying the healthy bone marrow as fast as they destroyed the cancer cells. Yet without the radiation, the pain was unbearable. Her spirits were low and she was convinced she had little chance. Her stomach was so sore from her spinal bombardment that even a drink of water hurt. Then, after three months in hospital, she came home.

Early in May, Audrey had to go back into the Princess Margaret for neck and head x-rays. The doctor wanted a complete scan. She was getting increasingly severe headaches, which added to her woes, and the doctors thought it might be because of wide fluctuations in blood pressure. The X-rays might reveal a new lesion.

On June 17, Audrey had a complete barium X-ray. Good news – they showed no new outbreaks. The severe headaches were put down to high blood pressure. But Audrey was down to about eighty-five pounds. We seemed to be dogged by the evil forces of the year. Fred Agnew, our farm manager, had a stroke and was dead within minutes. John Kendall phoned me the news in Montreal, where I was attending a regular Bell Canada meeting. I had talked to Fred only that morning, on my way to the airport, and he had been in excellent spirits. I hurried home. Audrey, typically, sent Mike Thomas to get a large Arcadian Court chicken pie for the Agnews, so that the widow, Ruth, could serve the crowd of relatives who invariably appear at such times.

On October 6, the full force of Audrey's pain returned, and we were unable to control it with drugs. We were up all night, her stomach rebelling at the medicine. All her regular doctors were away so, in desperation, I phoned my brother, Dr. Carl Burton, to see if he could describe to me the symptoms of an overdose or prescribe the maximum that could be given in a short time.

On October 12, Dr. Kendall sent her to Joseph Brant Hospital because she had a temperature of 101 degrees as well as terrible pains. The decision was then made to send her directly to Princess Margaret by ambulance from Burlington. She was disoriented. A week passed and Audrey was sick of hospitals, and I was sick of running back and forth. But what could we do? Everything seemed uncertain and unstable, at least the grand life we had enjoyed, if not our love for each other or the strength of the family drawing together. Then Audrey was released to go to our city apartment, with nurses. There, we observed her sixtieth birthday. Three days of chemotherapy followed.

On November 18, I was shocked to hear that Betty Kennedy's husband, Gerhard, had severe internal bleeding and was not expected to last the night. I was so immersed in our problems, I did not at first recognize the seriousness of Gerhard's illness. I remembered that Gerhard and Betty were Audrey's first visitors a year ago in Princess Margaret Hospital, before Gerhard knew of his own illness.

Then Audrey was readmitted to the Princess Margaret. She was so emaciated and weak she felt that she would never leave. She could not bear the sight or smell of food, and slowly withered away before our eyes. She floated in and out of consciousness. The doctors felt she may have had a small stroke. She did suffer a small heart failure.

I was sick at seeing my love in pain and discomfort. I would certainly not have allowed an animal to suffer like that. A doctor came in and asked, automatically, "How are you?" Amazingly, Audrey fought back to consciousness, opened her eyes wide, and, with veiled sarcasm, whispered, "Oh, I am just fine, Doctor!" I believe that was the last thing she said, except to me, for she added, "Love you!" She turned her face away and drifted away again. The doctor said she would not have any more procedures and promised to make her as comfortable as possible.

On November 29, I was wakened at 2:00 a.m. by the resident doctor, who told me that Audrey had passed away. I agreed to an autopsy. For once the spirit has flown, the poor, wizened remains might help provide some clues for future help.

After the long ordeal at Miles Funeral Parlour, during which I was on my feet from noon to 9:00 p.m., there was a constant stream of visitors. I was touched when Betty Kennedy came in to pay her respects, in spite of her own problems. She is a lovely person.

On December 2, a family funeral was held in the small rural Church of St. George's Anglican, Lowville, which is only a couple of miles away from the farm Audrey loved so much. The Rev. Paul Moore conducted a simple service attended by our farming neighbours and the immediate members of our family – the Brock Harrises, the Craig Reids, Clayton Hadfield, Bill and Kay Shields – all descendants of original settlers of this district, and wonderful friends, who had accepted us as belonging here with them. The casket was covered with a large bouquet of yellow roses. I believe Audrey would have approved.

The next two days I spent much time at the farm looking for pictures of Audrey, but I think she had deliberately destroyed them all, except the one I had on my dresser. The nostalgia of the afternoon let my grief come out at last, in full force, alone. I hardly slept all night and woke to hear the sad news that Gerhard Kennedy had passed away during the night. I felt great empathy with Betty's grief, and my heart went out to her.

Audrey's memorial service in Rosedale United Church was packed with family and friends from all walks of life. Pauline McGibbon, lieutenant-governor, and Premier William Davis attended. The Rev. Doug Stewart delivered the eulogy and sermon. The only flowers were two huge bouquets of yellow roses and white carnations on either side of the steps leading to the chancel. Our oldest friend, Alec Boothe, had a marvellous way with the ushers, mostly old friends from our regiment, the Governor General's Horse Guards.

I was sorry once more when Lynn finally returned to her work in London. Sotheby's had been most understanding and generous with her time. Gail and Jamie and I did the carol-singing tradition at Simpsons. There was an even bigger turnout of employees and customers than usual, several hundred people in all.

Regular Simpsons meetings filled the days and nights. I set up an ad hoc committee to advise us on the senior appointment, the president's job when Charlie Stewart retired. An all-time record for sales was set in the Toronto area of $2.5 million. The downtown store alone contributed $1,257,000 of the total.

For Christmas there was plenty of snow. There was a knot in my stomach at dinner. We toasted Audrey, for whom Christmas, especially at Limestone Hall, had meant so much.

The mid-1970s were not good years for the country. Inflation continually worsened. Labour strikes, particularly in the public sector, mail and transport in particular, disrupted the economy. The policies of the Trudeau administration were widely disliked both at home and in the United States where Trudeau himself was derided as a "tea drinker." Scandal caused problems for both the federal Minister of Labour and the Ontario Minister of Justice. There was little good news in the outside world. Even airport runway cleaners and mail handlers were on strike again. Jamie, while in London on a buying trip, was in sight and sound of three bombings by Irish terrorists.

Simpsons' wage bill rose by the annual rate of six million dollars, as we strove to compete with the wages and demands of civil servants and labourers. Eaton's appointed its first non-Eaton to be president. Robert Butler was made chairman of Eaton's and another outsider, Earl Orser, was named president. Orser had a reputation as a hatchetman. He was a chartered accountant and former vice-president, Finance, for Air Canada, but had no retail experience.

At a dinner meeting of the Redevelopment Advisory Council, we had Mayor David Crombie as our guest. He tried to explain his idea of making a pedestrian mall on Yonge Street, Metro's main north-south traffic artery, in spite of the combined opposition of the Police

Department, the Fire Department, and all the Yonge Street merchants. I wrote in my diary, "The plain arrogance of the little man made me cross, and I am afraid I blasted him about some of his stupid statements." He could not – or would not – give us his reasons for wanting to close this important thoroughfare. Because it was a Metro road, over which he as mayor of the City of Toronto did not have jurisdiction, I got the feeling his motives were purely political to declare Toronto's sovereignty over this thoroughfare. The council chairman, Sam Patton of the Toronto-Dominion Bank, thinking I was too forceful with the mayor, neglected to tell His Worship that it was the unanimous decision of the Redevelopment Advisory Council to oppose the mall idea. I was saddened by the chairman's lack of backbone in this regard, and I decided to resign. Fifteen years on the council I had started was enough. It was time for me to resign in favour of my nephew Ted, whose new job it was to deal with governments!

I was warned that a very militant group of women from the Training Department was bent on causing trouble in the store. Intrigued, I asked their spokesman (I hate the modern euphemism "spokesperson") to come and see me. I saw most of her points, which had to do with career opportunities within the organization, and promised I would do what I could as fast as was practical and sensible. Women's lib. did not start or stop at Simpsons. The tempest in the teapot subsided, at least temporarily.

Ted Burton returned from the advanced management course at Harvard, having learned many things from his peers. I made our new director, Betty Kennedy, chairman of Simpsons' Donation Committee. Simpsons-Sears was pressuring us to allow them to expand in our areas. But their expansion held little advantage for us except possibly in Kingston, Ottawa, and Oshawa. Sears would not reveal their plans to us, so we decided not to play until they did.

On June 16, 1975, Ted Burton was installed as the 102nd new president of the Toronto Board of Trade. Ted was the fourth Burton in the immediate family to have been so chosen, beginning with C.L. Burton, my father, continuing with my brother Edgar (Ted's father), and following with myself, and then Ted. No other family in the 130-year history of the board ever had more than one member serve.

John Turner, the new Minister of Finance, brought down his first budget, increasing taxes on incomes over $25,000 and raising the tax on gasoline. He imposed no controls but vowed to cut one billion dollars from government spending "as an evidence of good faith." I added in my diary, "About time in the wake of the most wasteful Government ever!"

I had a long chat with Art Wood, chairman of Sears, Roebuck, trying to impress upon him the fact that we had several well-qualified men in the company who could serve as president of Simpsons-Sears when Doug Peacher retired at year-end. A Canadian president would be good for morale, I argued. Charlie Gundy agreed and added to the argument. Sears, Roebuck, through Art Wood, was adamant they wanted an American president to serve under a Canadian chairman and CEO. So we had to agree, having done all in our power to secure the presidency for our candidate, Richard Sharpe. Dick, a top graduate of the School of Business of the University of Western Ontario, was a former Simpsons man, a first-class merchant, and a person of broad vision. Dick became chairman and CEO as soon as Jack Barrow vacated the post. I was elected to be chairman of the business advisory group of the School of Business on the retirement of Jack Brent, IBM chairman, who had done an outstanding job as chairman of the council.

Our six-month results in Simpsons were much worse than predicted. Stringent measures had to be taken. On September 2, at a Simpsons-Sears finance committee, after strenuous discussions, we reluctantly agreed to increase Simpsons-Sears equity by means of a rights issue – $24 million each to Simpsons Limited and Sears, Roebuck & Company, on condition Simpsons-Sears increased their dividend by two cents a share to help carry the burden of the interest costs. Charlie Gundy objected to the fact that we would be raising $24 million at 11.5 per cent to give to Simpsons-Sears for a return of 2 per cent. I felt much the same, but we had to agree. The market was poor and would probably get worse. All this was necessitated by the need to restore Simpsons-Sears debt-to-equity ratio to 60/40 from 63/37.

We flew to Chicago on September 15 to attend Simpsons-Sears and Allstate Insurance board meetings, following which Art Wood, chairman of Sears, Roebuck, gave a dinner at the Chicago Club for us to meet the Sears regional vice-presidents who were meeting in Chicago. Without prior warning, after a sumptuous dinner of wild game and fine wines, Art Wood announced that my friend, Major-General Douglas Peacher, and popular president of Simpsons-Sears would retire on January 1, 1976. Doug was embarrassed and furious. I never learned the background to the Sears, Roebuck decision, but I had to spend several hours after dinner with Doug, while he poured out his hurt at this peculiar treatment after years of loyal service to Sears. This action did not seem typical of the Art Wood whom I thought I knew quite well by this time.

All our Simpsons directors expressed shock that there would be a new American president for Simpsons-Sears when Dick Sharpe was here, already experienced and an excellent choice. Charles Gundy made a personal call to Art Wood and they agreed to come to Toronto to meet with us to discuss their reasoning, Gordon Metcalfe with him.

The market was very weak. I got a call from Jack Kincannon, Sears, Roebuck's vice-president of Finance, to suggest that the rights issue be done at a 10 per cent discount. The day before we had agreed on a 17.5 per cent discount. This meant that Simpsons would have to raise $25.6 instead of the $24 million originally agreed to. I flatly refused. I distrusted Kincannon's every motive and disliked his type. He never came clean, unlike most of the Sears men we had dealt with in the past twenty-three years.

I phoned Plaxton of Wood Gundy, who was with Kincannon on this deal, and gave him a piece of my mind. Charlie Gundy, Plaxton's boss, seemed unaware of these proposed changes in terms. We proposed 15 per cent – $8.50, which restored the debt-ratio of Simpsons-Sears to the classic 60/40, which was the object of the exercise. Art Wood agreed.

I went to hear a speech on free enterprise at the Canadian Chamber of Commerce. It was as exciting as watching paint dry. Someone said the speaker was so shy "he wouldn't steal a kiss at an orgy."

Shortly after the turn of the year I faced up to the fact that Charles Stewart would reach the age of retirement in 1976 and that a successor for his position as president of Simpsons Limited would have to be identified and approved. Choosing a president at the best of times is not the easiest decision to make, especially if one of the candidates is your nephew. Some of our best buyers and managers have been second- and third-generation "Simpsonites." I believe that nepotism has its good and bad sides. It had been successful in my own family. I firmly believe that the Burtons learned the basics of good shopkeeping as soon as we could walk and talk. We had a strict rule that as a Burton you could be employed by Simpsons in a lowly capacity to start, but that then you must go away and prove yourself with another firm, giving the Simpson company a chance to hire you if you wished to come back. This house rule, unwritten as it was, seemed to have worked quite well to date. My brother Edgar made his way in Carson, Pirie, and Scott in Chicago as a young man. I worked in New York at Schumacher's and in London at Trollope & Sons. My nephew Ted had worked for the J.L. Hudson Company in Detroit. In each case these "foreign" assignments at best qualified each of us for a position the equivalent of a junior buyer. Whatever progress up the ladder we made from there on was in competition with other worthies.

As Simpsons-Sears grew bigger and bigger, the presidency of Simpsons Limited required all the skills needed to operate our company profitably and all the skills of diplomacy as well as a deep understanding of people. The "people skills" do not come easily. Organizational methods and business strategy and tactics can be taught at universities and in business schools, but the ability to lead and to be considered worthy of leadership cannot. Yet clear and logical thought can be taught. One can learn the ability to think clearly and acquire the ability to describe concisely and accurately the object of the exercise. These abilities can be acquired and sharpened by experience.

I had some serious personal doubts about Ted's "people skills." On January 12, therefore, after discussing the situation with Charles Gundy, who at this time was the largest single shareholder of Simpsons' stock, I formed an ad hoc committee of the Simpsons board of directors to identify and recommend the next president of the company. I chose Tom Bell, chairman of Abitibi, as chairman, and deliberately chose the youngest directors on the board to act with Tom. These were Bill Wilder, then president of Arctic Gas, Mike Scott of Wood Gundy, and Jim Tory, director of Tory and Tory and our legal counsel. They had several months to do the necessary reviews.

Two days later we heard the astounding news that our chief competitor, Eaton's, had decided, after ninety-two years, to go out of the mail-order business and close their catalogue plants. They did about $400 million annually across the country, and lost $18 million a year doing it, while Simpsons-Sears was doing the same volume and making $18 million a year doing it!

It had been rumoured for some months that Eaton's had been trying to negotiate with J.C. Penney in the United States for an arrangement with Penney to match ours with Sears, Roebuck but it fell through. One commentator said, "It's sad to see an aging fighter hang up his gloves." The company had opted for sudden youth by hiring a couple of dozen MBAs and giving early retirement to men of experience, so they found themselves with men of insufficient depth and experience and little loyalty.

The newspapers were full of the closing of the Eaton's catalogue plants and the laying off of nine thousand people across the country. While one does not rejoice at the woes of a friendly competitor, by a modest estimate we calculated we might be able to win half their customers. That meant $200 million extra sales volume. I set up several teams to try to assess the "ripple effect" of this development and to advise how we could capitalize on the windfall.

Simpsons' main downtown Toronto store, built in 1871 and rebuilt several times, had been declared an historic building by the Historical Board of the City of Toronto. Max Miller, our staff architect, presented a plan to retain and refurbish the red-brick and terracotta exterior with improvements to the doorways and entrance lobby at Queen and Yonge streets. We had planned to have the face of the building "modernized" for 1972, our centennial year, but the aluminum sheeting, which was all the old building would bear, was so ghastly that we took another good look at the architecture of the store. It is one of the finest examples on the continent of what has been called the Chicago School – the late nineteenth-century designs that were functional but leaned toward Byzantine arches and moulded detail. In our case the detail was in terracotta.

Eaton's was far from being dead or dying. North of our store the huge Eaton Centre was rising to completion. The so-called "Miracle of Queen Street," with two of the largest and most prosperous department stores in the world facing each other across the street, was no more. The pedestrian traffic flow across Queen Street between Eaton's and Simpsons had been for years the heaviest pedestrian traffic in Metro Toronto. Now we would present a "quaint" appearance joined to the huge new Centre by a pedestrian bridge, like an umbilical cord, at the second-floor level.

The ad hoc committee, after having considered available alternatives, decided in favour of recommending that Ted Burton be made president of Simpsons Limited. I agreed, and decided that Charlie Stewart should become deputy chairman until his actual retirement, stay on as a director, and remain the chief administrator of the government's Anti-Inflation Board requirements. The Anti-Inflation Board limited increases for $25,000-a-year employees to a maximum of $2,400, and then took most of that away through a special 10 per cent surcharge. There were few personal incentives left. There was no company incentive left to increase proficiency or efficiency, so we might achieve the mediocre socialist state some said the prime minister, Pierre Trudeau, admired. The disheartening thing was that the civil servants had been granted "tenure" plus indexing of salaries, so they were not touched by the board's rulings. They became a massive drag on the economy.

Business generally was weak and the Anti-Inflation Board's restrictions were hurting. I set a goal to reduce our total staff by five hundred to weed out incompetents or "deadwood," and thus save $6 million a year in expenses. People who left would not be replaced. Such pruning was characteristic of the retail business. At least once a decade, retailers need to strike the balance between the number of staff required to maintain service to the customer and the number needed to form the small empires that grow up in various areas during good times.

# TWO PROPOSALS

## 17

Charles and Kay Stewart arranged a dinner party at their home at Ardwold Gate in Toronto and invited Betty Kennedy and me as the only guests. They suggested that I pick Betty up. I had begun to recognize that my friends were actively interested in match-making. They were not too enthusiastic about some of the partners others had chosen for me as dinner companions. These were perfectly nice ladies, but plump! Betty Kennedy was quite a different matter. We had enjoyed a pleasant but strictly business relationship as the chairman and a director of the board. I picked Betty up in the Rolls, which I am afraid only enhanced the chairman image and did little for me as an individual. I was so pleased to be with her, I talked too much, while she told me that she was joining the board of directors of a large, multinational American company called Akzona. She was not overly pleased when I admitted I had never heard of the company! We had a relaxing time, but Betty seemed quiet. She had to go to Ottawa the next day to cover the Conservative Party convention for CFRB, and no doubt she was already running over in her skilled and agile mind the questions she wanted to ask those she would interview. This was the convention that chose the unknown young man from Alberta, Joe Clark, as leader.

Some weeks later I saw Betty in an audit committee at Simpsons. She had a nice tan and said she had just returned from a vacation in Nassau. She had written a book, *Gerhard: A Love Story*, about life with her late husband after they learned of his cancer.

About this time I was invited to a luncheon at the Toronto-Dominion Centre by Leo Kolber of Cemp Investments and Charles Bronfman of Seagram's. The guest of honour was Sir Markus Sieff, head of Marks and Spencer of England, who was urging increased purchases from Israel as a practical means of keeping that country democratic. I was honoured to be seated on his right, and we got on well. He invited me to dinner when next in London. Mischievously, in my mind, I dubbed this fine retailer "Sir *Markdown* Sieff!"

I was beginning to come alive and enjoy life again. An amusing incident occurred on a commercial flight. The "white-knuckled" passenger next to me was an extremely nervous woman, who began to increase her intake of rye and ginger and tell me her life story. She said she worked at Eaton's. I said I worked at Simpsons.

"What department?" she asked.

"Chairman," I said.

"Oh my God!" she replied.

I said, "No. Chairman will be quite sufficient!"

One day I invited Betty Kennedy to attend a formal dinner-dance at the York Club as my guest. When I picked her up in the Rolls, I gave her a small present in a jewel case. Her joy seemed, to say the least, restrained. Later she told me she thought, "My God, it will be a diamond necklace or something that I can't accept. How can I refuse it without hurting his feelings?" Inside, when she opened it, she was surprised to find a gold-plated dog whistle on a gold chain, with a note that read: "If you ever need me, just whistle!" Betty was so relieved and amused that she laughed and relaxed. She said she saw me for the first time through different eyes. I was always the chairman of the board, and she said the best one she had ever seen. But she found it hard to put that image out of her mind. We had a very pleasant evening, and I invited Betty and her thirteen-year-old daughter, Tracy, to Limestone Hall to lunch and to see the marvellous display of daffodils down the mile-long farm lane. She arrived wearing the gold dog whistle on the gold chain. It did not escape my notice, although I said nothing. Before we had a chance to admire the daffodils, a freak snowstorm came off the lake and buried most of the flowers under two inches of wet snow! But we walked down the lane for the first time together. The peace and beautiful quiet of the countryside made conversation unnecessary. I was sure at this moment that I wanted to spend the rest of my life with this lovely person, but I was well aware that Betty was sure she would never marry again. She was still recovering from the trauma of Gerhard's death. I was determined not to spend the rest of my life making small conversation with strangers!

The same day Betty's book was launched at the Arcadian Court at Simpsons. Jean Chrétien spoke to a large crowd at the Royal York Hotel at lunch, and Betty and I were head-table guests. I took her to dinner at the York Club that night. She was relaxed and charming, but I noted in my diary that night, "I admire her tremendously but she is so deep in her work and the business world, we would find it very difficult to work out a partnership." At month's end I again took Betty to dinner at the York Club and we engaged in lively conversation. It was our first opportunity to talk about many things. I realized that as we talked we were holding hands! This raised several eyebrows, as I was chairman of the club and chairmen of the club do not generally show that much enthusiasm for anything. For the first time, I hoped that she felt as I did.

I then flew to London to attend a quarterly meeting of the directors of the Royal Bank of Canada, held for the first time in England. I recall a superb luncheon in our honour at the Vintners' Hall. I also remember phoning Betty long distance. She said she missed me and would be at the airport to meet me on my return.

My daughter Lynn, who was working at Sotheby's as administrator of the French Impressionist department, flew with me to visit Louis Vilard, the proprietor and owner of Château Cissac. He was a descendant of one of the French families that had made wine for over three hundred years. Louis had been on a continent-wide tour with the English winemaster and author Harry Waugh in 1972, and they were my weekend guests at Limestone Hall. I had not known either of them before, but both became my good friends. On the occasion of their visit we feasted on our own farm lamb and a Cheval Blanc (1966) from my cellar. To taste with some delicate cheese, I also produced an ancient bottle of 1918 Mouton, bottled before that celebrated house became known as Mouton-Rothschild. I made the experts open the bottle. Ancient wine, according to most authorities, should not be opened in advance, as you would to let a younger wine "breathe." To our delight and my surprise, the wine, although faded, was perfectly drinkable and improved noticeably with each glass. It may have been breathing its last breath, but there was still plenty of life left in it that evening! The two wine experts called on me to describe the wine. It was so delicate in bouquet and yet still with character in taste that I said, "It has the haunting fragrance of an elderly beauty who has just recently left the room." The experts applauded loudly, saying they could not have described it better!

Before he left, Louis Vilard walked with me over the fields and through the woods and said, "Allan, I have never been so happy since I left home. You must come and stay with me at Château Cissac, but you will come as a member of the family, not as a guest." It was a very rare honour to be invited into a Frenchman's home on that basis.

So Lynn and I flew to Bordeaux. Louis met us at the airport. My luggage did not arrive as it had been put on a plane for Bilbao, Spain! All I had were slacks, a shirt, and sweater, which added to the informality and the pleasure of the visit. We visited every famous *chai* and *cave* with Louis over the next few days, meeting his friends who made the famous wines. Avoiding the tourist groups, we had wine-tasting sessions from 10:00 a.m. to noon followed by a huge luncheon with three wines and tasting from 2:00 to 4:00 p.m. We sampled Lafite, Mouton, Cheval Blanc, Ducru Beaucaillou, La Lagune, and the 1975 vintages not yet bottled. The meals were of the countryside, and I never ate or drank better. To my surprise I lost a pound before the week was out. I ordered a large quantity of the wines we tasted for future delivery when bottled about two years down the road.

Lynn and I flew back to Paris, she to return to London to work, while I changed planes and flew to West Berlin. There I was met by a young British Guards officer in uniform who had the British commandant's Daimler at his disposal. Major-Gen. Sir Roy Redgrave, M.C., the commander of the British sector, had invited me to visit him and his wife, Valerie. We were old friends. Roy had commanded the Blues – the Royal Horse Guards (now the Blues and Royals) – when I was honorary colonel of the Governor General's Horse Guards. Our two regiments were affiliated.

I had not been in Germany since the war, and never to Berlin. The poor city was sliced in half by the infamous Berlin Wall, and West Berlin was itself divided into British, American, and French zones. Roy had the difficult and unenviable task of commanding the British sector along with its troops. He had the additional task of being chief judge and jury of every incident and crisis – and each incident had to be treated as a crisis – that took place within his zone. The British commander was on call twenty-four hours of every day, seven days a week, and his normal tour of duty was two years. The city was alive with intrigue, espionage, and counter-espionage. There were foreign delegations of all sorts; troops and civilians and industry were everywhere. In the air was a constant tension that one could feel. Just two days before my arrival a bomb had exploded in a U.S. officers' mess, killing some of the young soldiers. Villa Lemm, the

British General's house and grounds, was a walled domain. It looked out on the lake. The gardens were beautiful and peaceful except that they were patrolled by guard dogs at night. It was considered dangerous for me to stroll outside the grounds without an escort.

After a warm welcome from Roy and Valerie, I was assigned the Daimler once more, with two red-hatted members of the military police, one to guard and drive me and a Sgt. Clark to act as my guide. The Daimler was flying a large Union Jack from the post on its fender, or wing, as the British call it. I was to tour the entire length of the Berlin Wall from one end in the city to the Brandenburg Gate, places where tourists were not permitted to go. At selected spots, Sgt. Clark and I dismounted and through our binoculars viewed the many and varied in-depth defences – electrified fences, mine-fields, machine-gun nests, and guard dogs able to run one hundred yards back and forth, all on the same cable wire separated only by snarling inches. While we were examining these forbidding objects across a deadly desert of wasteland, without a blade of grass or vegetation, the East German soldiers in the huge watch-towers, which were spaced regularly the length of their line, poked out cameras with 300 mm and greater lenses to photograph me and my escort in great detail. The soldiers, I was told, were locked into their towers for twenty-four hours before being relieved by a new detail.

It was an interesting and disturbing experience. When I returned, Roy said, "Allan, I am sorry to have made a pigeon out of you. Your photograph from all angles and your description will be on file in every Communist country in the world within thirty-six hours." He went on to say, "You will keep them guessing for the next three weeks. You made a detailed tour of the line in my car, and they will wonder whether you are my replacement or a special agent to be dropped among them. It will take at least three weeks for them to find out you are a nobody! But that's the name of the game we play – keep them guessing! Sorry you can't go to East Berlin. The Canadian delegation wouldn't provide a car and escort for you. I can't send you in mine because you carry a Canadian passport, not British."

That evening we went to two diplomatic cocktail parties, one given in honour of British MPs who were in Berlin, three of them British Communists, to see whether the expenditure to maintain a British presence in Berlin was worthwhile. I talked to Austrians, Americans, Japanese, French, Swiss, and several members of delegations from Iron Curtain countries, all of whom were probing and curious about my presence. But the most curious were the British Communist MPs, who asked, "Who are you? What are you doing here?"

I said, "Special commercial attaché, okay?"

"Okay!" they said as they backed off.

Later Roy said, "I think I'll keep you here permanently. You were pleasant and they are still mystified."

Back in London, I phoned James Hanson and, to my surprise, he advised me that he had been knighted last May. He invited Lynn and me to a big party at Annabelle's, Berkley Square, to celebrate. Sir James and Geraldine, now Lady Hanson, were, as usual, excellent hosts and more. Lynn showed up with her escort, David Bennett, whom I met for the first time. I noted, "He's rather young and bearded."

The next day, feeling very liverish and low, I became homesick for Betty and for the tranquility of the farm. I phoned her. She insisted on meeting my plane the following Friday, which arrived three hours late. I kept telling myself, to insulate myself from the disappointment of not seeing her, that she would be too sensible to wait three hours. But there she was, with my driver, Mike Thomas, at her side.

Mike, after nearly twenty years' service with me, was more like a member of the family than he was a chauffeur. He had taken it upon himself to phone all my children to say that Mrs. Kennedy was meeting me at the airport and that they might want to phone or visit me the next day. He had also done the grocery shopping and drove us happily to Limestone Hall, for we had much to talk about!

We spent much of the evening talking about the complexities that faced us – boards of directors, families (twelve children between us, four of mine, four of Betty's, and four stepchildren from Gerhard's previous marriage). How could we live together and do our separate jobs? We walked down the farm lane through the woods under a lovers' moon. We did not want to say goodnight. We wondered if two people could be so lucky again, after each of us had been so happily married before. We reasoned we were the most fortunate couple alive to have each other as well as families who wished us well and a host of friends we both shared.

We tentatively set the following April as the month for our wedding. Tracy, Betty's thirteen-year-old daughter, asked her if we intended to marry. Betty replied, "Yes, dear, but not till spring."

"Why not now?" Tracy persisted, "why not this fall?"

Driving Betty to Ottawa to pick up Tracy, who had been at riding camp, we talked of love and marriage, and finally decided neither of us wished to face the winter alone. So we set a new date for fall.

We took the position that we would have only our children and their spouses to our wedding, a simple ceremony at Limestone Hall. Then about a week later we would have a big reception for all the other in-laws and close friends, at which the children would act as the hosts and hostesses. We set October 15, 1976, as the wedding date, the reception to follow on the 23rd, after which we would go to the Rolling Rock Club at Ligonier, Pennsylvania.

I took Jamie into my office to tell him the news and he was congratulatory. Barbara, his wife, who worshipped Audrey, was very silent, and Betty construed this to mean that she was upset with memories. Betty was tearful and we all had a good cry for days gone by, and then felt better. In the meantime, we kept mum about the forthcoming wedding, and we asked the members of our family to do the same.

One thing that was bothering me was the fact that while Simpsons and Simpsons-Sears were aggressively taking market share, Simpsons was sometimes forgoing possibilities of profit and expansion to accommodate Sears' stores. Our rationale was that as we owned half, half a loaf was better than none, and Sears could build new stores while we had our hands full with current projects.

I was surprised after a Simpsons-Sears directors meeting when Charles Gundy said he thought Simpsons' morale at the counter-level was not as high as Sears' morale. Charlie Stewart was upset because Gundy had no evidence to support his statement, and it seemed like a self-serving remark to make in front of the Sears, Roebuck people. We pointed out that Don Tigert of the University of Toronto, who does continuous surveys of habits and preferences, in his 1976 survey showed Simpsons as a two-to-one favourite over Eaton's in Toronto and doing well in Montreal. Simpsons-Sears was not included in this survey because they did not have a big enough retail base to compare. Simpsons and Eaton's were far ahead of the Bay, whose credit-card holders claimed they shopped many times more often at Simpsons than they did at the store whose credit card they held!

Roy Thomson, Lord Thomson of Fleet, died in 1976 in London, England. I knew him well when he was a Royal Bank director. He always had a fund of stories to match mine, no doubt an art learned when he was "on the road" selling radios in the old days in the North.

The story was that he had acquired a radio licence in the 1950s that had belonged to the Abitibi paper company for use in their logging operations. He set up a radio station to broadcast, but there were so few receivers in the countryside that he had little or no audience. Although by no means a young man at the time, he sold hundreds of radios, travelling the back roads to do so, thus creating his own market! This kind of drive and ingenuity, plus an amazing head for figures, led him to newspaper publishing. He found small papers around the world all very lucrative. Finally he acquired the prestigious *Scotsman* and *The Times of London* and was elevated to the House of Lords. His son, Kenneth, became Lord Thomson in turn, the title being one of the last hereditary ones awarded. Ken lives in Canada, by preference. Here he is known as plain Mr. Ken Thomson.

At Roy Thomson's memorial service, I ran into Gordon Sinclair of CFRB. He asked me if there was any truth to the rumours he had heard in Bala, Muskoka, where he summers. Without stopping to ask him what the rumours were, I said, "Sure."

Gordon, who could be an old curmudgeon, said generously, "Congratulations, I think it's a damn fine match." The rumour, it turned out, was that Betty and I had secretly married. What imaginations some people have!

The next day I got a call from Zena Cherry, a friend from high-school days, the leading social columnist in *The Globe and Mail*, to ask if the rumours were true. This time I asked, "What rumours?" On finding that we in fact were not yet married, having just set the date, Zena agreed to hold her column until it happened.

Gordon Sinclair called back to say the rumours were becoming more persistent and he felt we should make a statement. I hastened down to see Charlie Gundy and told him what was happening. Betty was a director on the Simpsons board. He was delighted and saw no reason why Betty should leave the board, although it was admittedly unusual for a chairman to marry one of his directors! Betty agreed a statement should go out. On August 11, Gordon Sinclair made the announcement on his noon broadcast. I got a call from Bud McDougald, chairman of Standard Broadcasting, who was delighted. He expressed relief that Betty intended to keep her show on the air as "The Betty Kennedy Show."

Betty and her daughter Tracy had been at Meech Lake, near Ottawa, for the past three weeks, so I drove up to see them for the final weekend and to drive home with them. On the way home we passed the roadway leading to the small village where Gerhard Kennedy's grave is located and left the main road to visit the site. High on a hill, under a huge and ancient pine tree, rests a large boulder of natural granite. It marks his grave, a place and circumstance that Gerhard himself had selected and planned before he died. It's a beautiful spot in the Gatineau Hills, amid the outdoor beauty of pines, hills, rocks, and clear skies that he loved so much. What we experienced was not a sad moment of tears, but one highly charged with memories and emotions and peace. Betty made an interesting remark, as we turned to leave. She called it "a final visit," and said, "We must now look forward to the wonderful life we will share in the future," to which I said a quiet "Amen." We felt very complete in our love for each other and had no hesitation in discussing the wonderful lives and loves we each had before.

Not long after this, at a Bell Canada meeting at which the late John Robarts and I were complimented by the chairman, he on his new and young bride and me on my impending marriage, John Robarts said, "Will you blush first or will I, Allan?"

I said, quickly, "I haven't anything to blush about, John, so you go right ahead!" I worried that my flip remark may have been taken as a "shot" at my old friend and fishing companion. But he took it in good spirit.

I had a most difficult meeting at the Royal Bank. The Bank Act had never contemplated two bank directors marrying each other, and so this Bible of bankers had no commandment for the eventuality. Seated next to me at luncheon was my chairman, Earle McLaughlin, who up to this point could not bring himself to appoint a woman a bank director. He suddenly said, "What are you going to do about possible conflict of interest in that Betty and you are directors of competing banks?"

I said, "I see no conflict. There are rules of confidentiality, and nothing in the Bank Act forbids two bank directors to marry. Surely you are kidding? No? Well, then, you can have my resignation right after lunch!"

"That's not what I had in mind," replied Earle.

"What did you have in mind?"

"I thought Betty would automatically resign from the Bank of Montreal," said Earle.

"Earle," I exclaimed in astonishment, "you are my boss. If you want my resignation, you have it forthwith. But you can't tell a director of the Bank of Montreal what to do, and I am not going to! What really bothers you about this?"

"Well, there are certain confidences between man and wife. . . ."

I quickly said, "Earle, are you trying to tell me that after every board meeting you go home and blab everything to Ethel?"

"Of course not," he replied indignantly.

"Then why am I any different from you?" I asked.

"A good point," said Earle, and the matter was not referred to again. Meanwhile, Fred McNeil, the chairman of the Bank of Montreal, had his board pass an official resolution congratulating Betty and me on our good fortune.

Earle McLaughlin was cool to me for a while because he was taking quite a pasting in the press for injudicious remarks he had made at a press conference. He mentioned the near-impossibility of finding a suitable female director as the reason or excuse for the fact that up to that time there were no women on the Royal Bank board. Fortunately our friendship resumed when Earle discovered the "tempest" was mainly in his own "teapot."

When I told Betty, she was concerned and wanted to resign. But I said, "No way."

"Love beareth all things, believeth all things," was the appropriate passage from the Bible we chose for our wedding, and the minister, the Rev. Douglas Stewart, was pleased with our choice. On September 23, 1976, Betty and I went to the municipal offices in Milton, Ontario, for our marriage licence. The only other customer in the room was a sad-looking, overweight teenage girl – alone.

Pierre Berton called Betty to say how pleased he was, mainly because he had been getting "hate mail" from fans, saying, "How could you leave your wife and seven children?" He was glad to have the proper Burton out in the open!

The large clans of offspring, spouses, and children began arriving from England and Germany as well as from British Columbia, Winnipeg, Toronto, Kitchener, Ottawa, Burlington, and Uxbridge.

October 15, the Wedding Day, was a beautiful and very happy day. I marvelled that all these young people from distant places were enjoying themselves, getting to know each other, and that no noses were put out of joint! As Betty and I both had meetings the next day and for several days to come, our honeymoon was postponed until later in the month.

On October 23, we had a reception at Limestone Hall for friends and relatives not invited to our wedding. One hundred and thirty people signed the register; only ten invitees could not come. They consumed thirty bottles of Comte de Champagne Blanc de Blanc and three punch bowls full of Pimm's. So, in retrospect, I felt it must have been a good party! Then we had a short shooting holiday cum honeymoon at Rolling Rock. We even had some of our children with us!

We were very concerned about the November 15 elections in Quebec. We felt that there would be difficulties ahead if Robert Bourassa's Liberals were defeated by the separatist Parti Québécois under René Lévesque, and so did Rowland Frazee, chief general manager of the Royal Bank, who pointed out at a meeting that the bank was already having problems with the hi-tech staff. So was Bell Canada. No one wanted to work in Quebec, which had the worst record for hours lost due to strikes in the Western world. Ontario had the doubtful distinction of being the second worst. The strikes amounted to near-anarchy – millions of dollars in damages on construction sites, and in public-service disruptions. Such stoppages were dragging us down economically and dividing us politically.

Betty interviewed Ed Broadbent of the NDP. She asked him, "What would you do if you were in power?"

He waffled, but noted that the NDP would correct injustice, level pay to a maximum of $100,000, and pay miners the same as doctors, equating danger with schooling.

In early November, strikes kept 180,000 people out of work in Quebec alone. Unemployment and unease held the economy back to a near standstill. Charles Bronfman of Seagram's said publicly that he would move out of Quebec if Lévesque won. But when Lévesque did win a landslide victory, Bronfman toned down his rhetoric. He was quoted in the papers as saying, "Primarily we are merchants, and business as usual, until or if new rules are made we can't do otherwise."

In early December the government put a sudden, sweeping embargo on all imports of textiles from all countries. To qualify for your quota, you had to fill out lengthy forms, more than we could accomplish to clear our Christmas goods already in customs! The year closed on a low note. Simpsons stock was down to $5.00, Simpsons-Sears $8.25. Our Limestone Hall Farm market steers brought 36 to 41 cents per pound, not enough to justify feeding them. There must be another, cheaper way to keep the barn warm!

I went to Vancouver with Betty, who was there to do *Front Page Challenge*. We had a pleasant dinner with Chunky Woodward and his new bride, Judy. I believe Woodward's results showed a major drop in net from 87 cents to 19 cents per share, reflecting the cost of opening his two new Alberta stores.

Lévesque made a speech in Montreal, attended by Mike Scott, Pete Scott's son, in which the Quebec premier said he intended to make an anglo in Quebec feel as uncomfortable as a francophone in Calgary! He said he would order Quebec financial institutions to take a proportion of Quebec underwritings if he could not sell his bonds!

On Christmas Day at Limestone Hall, we had a thirty-three-pound monster of a turkey, a gift from Bill Kennedy. In a disastrous mishap, eight of my best Spode (1850) dinner plates were dropped and shattered – a complete loss. Having "lived" for one hundred and twenty years, they "died" on Christmas Day.

The first few weeks of January 1977 gave warning that the new year was not going to be an easy year. In fact, life from here on in began to be lived on a day-by-day basis. The way to best convey the hectic nature of change is to follow the sequence of events as I recorded them in my diary.

On January 10, twelve inches of snow brought the Golden Horseshoe around Toronto to a standstill, the worst storm in one hundred years of record-keeping. The one bright spot was that in spite of the many countryside problems last year, it looked as if Simpsons would match last year's after-tax, per-share earnings – a great comeback from the disastrous spring of 1976.

About forty members of the press attended a press conference to hear about Simpsons' multi-million-dollar restoration and renovation plans for the exterior and interior of our downtown Toronto store. The press were delighted to be able to fill the news gap with our story, while they awaited the big news of the opening of the huge Eaton Centre immediately north of our store.

We told the news conference that the Eaton Centre was a great addition to the heart of downtown Toronto, but we left no doubt that we were "the heart," that good quality and good service would guarantee our prosperity, and that the customer would continue to "enjoy shopping at Simpsons." We did not have to tear down to build because we had one of "the great stores of the world" to build on!

At the annual drivers' banquet, held each year to honour Simpsons drivers for courtesy and accident-free driving, Mike Thomas, my driver of twenty years, was honoured specially by the Ontario government. He was designated a "Master Driver" for thirty-six years of accident-free driving, the only driver to achieve that record in Ontario. He was given a special "Master Driver" pin to wear on his cap.

On February 10, the new Eaton Centre officially opened. Premier William Davis, Lieutenant-Governor Pauline McGibbon, and Mayor David Crombie were all there, and the $250 million development saturated the news media. Simpsons ran a full-page advertisement in all the papers on the theme "The Miracle of Queen Street," emphasizing the hundred-year association in downtown Toronto of Eaton's and Simpsons across the street from each other. It was very well received, and Simpsons did an all-time record day's business of $1,440,000 in the area, an increase of $630,000 for the day. Our downtown store had a 77.3 per cent increase for the single day!

René Lévesque spoke to the New York Economic Club and shocked the audience and most Canadians by spending much of his time on Quebec's independence and very little time reassuring the financial community that their money was safe in Quebec. He likened the separatists to the revolutionaries who sparked the American War of Independence! The market reacted badly for those companies that had a large portion of their business in Quebec. There was, of course, no way we could move or walk away from our stores, but other prominent businesses with no such problems were planning moves if the Quebec business climate became more poisonous to non-francophones. A current joke went the rounds that, in the event of separation, the Quebec currency would be known as the "franc-a-phony."

Incredibly, Toronto experienced the worst fire since 1914, when entire blocks of King Street burned to the ground. The old Eaton's Annex started to burn about 1:30 a.m., and was completely demolished by fire. The centre of Toronto just avoided a holocaust. One hundred and fifty firemen and thirteen trucks took all night to get it under control. Old Holy Trinity Church and the Eaton Centre suffered nearly one million dollars in damages. Sixty-mile-an-hour winds fanned the huge flames, creating a "fire storm" of serious proportions. We at Simpsons had men hosing down the store's roofs all night, as huge, flaming cinders lit on them. The Bank of Nova Scotia's tower, two blocks south of our store on Bay Street, had its air-conditioning, penthouse, and elevator workings completely destroyed, burned out following a fire started by flaming cinders. The Toronto Fire Department did a magnificent job, but the downtown area around Bay Street and the old City Hall was closed to traffic.

I engaged Professor Nicholas Fry of the School of Business of the University of Western Ontario to work with us on a long-range plan to cover the next twenty years. An engaging and intelligent fellow, he received excellent co-operation from all our people. He put together various scenarios of the dangers and possibilities for Simpsons that could result from changing business conditions – demographics, lifestyles, and the implications of major changes in the balance of share ownership as large estates would be dispersed to dozens of heirs and institutions. He paid particular attention to political concerns over Quebec's future.

On May 13, I visited Charles Gundy, who was in hospital recovering from a coronary. He was the only "original" left from when the Simpsons-Sears deal was worked out with Sears, Roebuck.

I got the horrific news that we were $22 million over budget in inventory, due to the area managers sidestepping Doug Steele, the vice-president, Merchandising. I gave them hell and froze further buying. The president, Ted Burton, had some explaining to do on this. The Simpsons board meeting was a heavy experience. There was very little to be happy about in the figures. The so-called recession seemed to be getting worse, and people were being laid off and let go from many companies across the land. I heard a good line, "A company is known by the men it keeps." It was not until August 30 that Statistics Canada finally admitted that we were in a recession.

On July 20 in Toronto, the temperature rose to 101 degrees, the highest since 1854, when temperatures were first recorded.

The air-traffic controllers were finally legislated back to work on August 10. The public's support for them had vanished.

I had two personal projects underway. Gustave Weisman, the stained-glass artist, was preparing the memorial windows, one large window and five side windows at St. George's, Lowville, in memory of Audrey. The late Napier Simpson, the architect, who specialized in working on historic houses, was adding a California room to the farm. When I groaned at his estimates, Napier said, "Don't worry, Allan, you can't take it with you!"

I replied, "But I never thought you would get it all!"

In early September I went to Chicago to a Simpsons-Sears meeting. One of its associated companies, Allstate Insurance, had a $17 million profit, which we sorely needed, but which they had to turn back to the government under the rulings of the Anti-Inflation Board. We had not had a dividend in four years! Fortunately, business in July and August was quite a bit better than it had been. We recovered $800,000 in after-tax profit. Our expense controls were working.

Back in Canada I was thrilled to see at least forty, twenty-to-thirty-pound salmon struggling up Limestone Creek, the first this century. Also, there were five deer in the woods, and one hundred and fifty Canada geese on our pond near the house. Somehow this resurgence of nature cheered me up and gave me hope that we would survive as well.

In October, Betty and I were invited by the Young Presidents Organization to attend their first Canadian conference as resource people. The conference was held in Banff, and the two hundred YPOs, all under forty, gave us a very warm reception. It was strictly sweaters and slacks for the working sessions. Irving Gerstein, president of Peoples Jewellers Ltd., was the president of the YPO. Bert, his father, was one of the men who served on the first Redevelopment Advisory Council in Toronto in 1960.

The opening session was most impressive. A band played "O Canada" followed by "The Maple Leaf For Ever," which raised lumps in our throats as the young presidents raised their voices in song.

Phillipe de Gaspé Beaubien and David Leighton, the director of the Banff School, were the moderators. They opened with a mock news report from NBC, datelined 2001, New York, commenting on the tenth anniversary of the ten new Northern States joining the Union! There was a loud aside, "I wonder where they blew it!" Gordie Howe was still playing hockey at seventy-three, with his grandchildren – all playing for Mexico! This opening was followed by speeches by Jean-Luc Pépin and Senator Maurice Lamontagne. Then we broke into working groups. As well as Betty and myself, resource people included Conrad Black, Donald Macdonald, and Bryce Mackasey. We visited each group in turn, joining in the debate and answering questions.

The main theme was "Unity." There was no question in their minds that Lévesque wanted Quebec out of Canada, but the Quebec delegation professed not to feel cut off. "All French have suffered slights and hardships at the hands of *les maudits anglais.*" They talked about "new relationships." I was surprised no one mentioned the role of the monarchy or the sovereignty of Canada. I was also surprised at how deeply cut off from the mainstream of Canadian life those from British Columbia and Alberta felt. Surprise – there was great willingness to compromise, if only someone would lead the country! All in all it was a most exhilarating experience; the sheer vitality and enthusiasm of the YPOs were refreshing and infectious. Their wives took a most active part, a welcome sign of the times! We came home to Toronto emotionally drained by the Unity Conference – a great experience.

The long-range planning committee, consisting of Charles Stewart, Ted Burton, Dick Davidson, vice-president, Planning, Jim Tory, and myself, met each Tuesday for a full day for the next six months to consider the options open to us. This would prove interesting and rewarding and of extreme importance to our future as a company. I spoke to Jim Tory about my impending retirement in 1980, and asked him to monitor the directors for opinions as to future management.

We began a new phase in our activities which entailed a complete review in detail of every lease and agreement we had in Simpsons, including Simpsons-Sears, then all the real-estate opportunities and commitments. Fortunately, by November our expenses and inventory seemed to be under better control.

I agreed to let the Bay open next to our store in Scarborough Centre, but for a price. We got 10 per cent of the Centre profits *ad infinitum* by giving up our 10 per cent equity interest. I understood that Eaton's gave up their majority interest for what it cost them, with no future profits. We visited a site in Pickering for a future centre to be developed by Cadillac-Fairview. These decisions had to be made six to eight years in advance of opening.

Our new organization at Simpsons was announced: Dick Davidson as vice-president, Personnel; Ian McSweeney, vice-president, Merchandising; Ron Crichton, vice-president, Stores; and Ernie Wilkes, vice-president, Finance. All were long-time Simpsons men and as good as or better than any in the trade.

Our Simpsons' third quarter results showed a 60 per cent increase in sales and a 50 per cent increase in profit before taxes, $6.4 million versus $4.7 million last year! The very next day, the Royal Bank's economist gave us a very pessimistic outlook, slow growth of the economy for the next five years. We were officially in a recession!

Late in November, to add to our retail woes in Montreal, the bus and subway workers went on strike. Then Bill 101, the infamous language bill, was discussed on an hour-long program. We learned what it would mean for those doing business in Quebec. The air-traffic controllers were still acting up, so to fly to Toronto from Montreal, we had to file a flight plan to Syracuse, N.Y., and approach Toronto from the south, there being no agreement between Toronto and the U.S. controllers to delay traffic.

Good news! The union, which had been certified in our Montreal warehouse, lost its appeal to the labour tribunal and was decertified in the process. So we won one! No other parts of Simpsons had been unionized, largely due to profit-sharing. The employees, as shareholders, had a stake in the business.

The Simpsons-Sears November board meeting was a much happier affair than most had been. November was a record in both the mail order and stores, $10 million profit versus $6 million last year. But underlying our momentary joy was the unease of reading that INCO in Sudbury had laid off two thousand workers and Falconbridge, eight hundred. Inflation was rising again; unemployment was increasing. The times were worrisome, and people were nervous.

On December 19, our traditional carol singing in the downtown Toronto store, now in its fifty-third year, was featured in *The Toronto Star* with photos on page two of Betty and me and my daughter Gail and granddaughter Kathy Kendall. Several hundred customers came down specially to the main floor each day to sing with our store choir before store opening. I had given a luncheon for Sir Edward Heath, former prime minister of Britain, who was in town promoting his new book. It was a collection of Christmas carols. We had a signing in our store. He was shown on the CBC's national news leading our choir and singing with us!

In the first long-range planning session in early 1978, we examined two proposals for Simpsons. The first proposition was that we submerge – that is, we become a division of Simpsons-Sears, the original notion that Sears, Roebuck had in 1951 when the deal was struck. Our calculations proved that we would all be worse off financially if we followed this option. The second proposition was that we merge with Simpsons-Sears, but that Simpsons maintain its management and, to a degree, its autonomy in the new company. We agreed to examine this proposal in more detail.

That evening Betty and I went to A.J. Casson's one-man show at

Roberts Galleries in Toronto. Jack and Jenny Wildridge, the gallery owners, are old friends of ours, as is "Cass," as the artist is known to his friends. The show was a fantastic success. Casson, the youngest and only surviving member of the Group of Seven, saw upwards of $200,000 worth of his oils, watercolours, and pencil drawings snapped up in fifteen minutes! Oils sold for $14,000. Pencil sketches fetched $900. I bought one watercolour for $2,800. I never dreamed I would pay so much for a watercolour that was not by Russell Flint, but my Casson was a beauty. Betty bought a pencil sketch to match one Cass had given us for a Christmas present.

I admired Casson so much. He was eighty that year and very chipper and bright. He did not wear or need glasses. I was taken back in my memory to his first one-man show in 1957, when I paid $475 for a beautiful large oil, which now commands about $40,000! Yet I went home that evening in 1957 feeling quite guilty that I had spent so much on a painting.

The next day, we spent another full day on long-range planning. We looked at demographic changes since our stores were built. We examined past merger and amalgamation problems others had experienced. Our next consideration was "raidability" and what steps could be taken to prevent it. We decided that the raid we should fear the most was the quickie, highly leveraged financial "rape," where the raider would have no intention of trying to run or improve the company, and would be only interested in a quick profit, in getting the cash or in selling off assets. The rape was characterized as a takeover to get at Simpsons-Sears and then spin off Simpsons. We did a lot of thinking in these sessions, but we were unable to develop clear defences for the problems as they were outlined.

Simpsons in Montreal planned a large reception and invited Mayor Jean Drapeau and all the mayors of adjacent suburban towns. Also invited were several Parti Québécois ministers. The mayors turned out, as did 350 other guests, but not one Quebec provincial minister attended. Instead, the government sent a couple of Francization program officials to represent the government of Quebec.

Simpsons' results were good and well covered on the financial pages – $28 million net profit, up from $22 million last year; sales, $638 million, up 5.5 per cent. At the Simpsons-Sears board meeting, I tried to get an increase in their dividend allowable by the Anti-Inflation Board. I was supported by Jim Tory and Charlie Stewart, but Edward Telling, Sears' chairman, and Kincannon, vice-president,

Finance, of Sears, Roebuck, were dead against it. I did not contest the issue further because it was basically a psychological boost to the shareholders, but it was expected.

We examined the lists of all shareholders holding 20,000 or more Simpsons shares. There was no serious change from the previous year. The Burton family had about 8 per cent of the outstanding shares. Profit-sharing and management held over 20 per cent, but this was down from 30 per cent four or five years earlier.

We held another long-range planning session on western pros and cons. Ernest Wilkes, vice-president, Finance, prepared a paper on the viability of a merger or acquisition between Simpsons and Woodward's. His findings were pretty negative. Simpsons was in a poor bargaining position vis-à-vis Woodward's, because of the situation in Quebec and its uncertainties.

At a party at the home of Ray McConnell, the CBC producer of *Front Page Challenge*, I had a chat with Knowlton Nash about a business profile Patrick Watson wanted to do on me in the *Canadian Establishment* series. He assured me that they wanted to do a sympathetic portrait, but he did warn me that I should establish the story-line from the first interview! The story-line I chose would emphasize the human side of business. I then talked to Rowland Frazee of the Royal Bank about the CBC's proposal to cover the Royal's quarterly meeting in Vancouver. Several of the men they intended to profile would be at the meeting.

I met for the first time the CBC producer Ron Graham who was assigned my profile. We had a three-hour chat in which I found out that Chunky Woodward and I had been allotted fifteen-minute sections each to represent respectively the western and eastern retailers. That at least was the plan before the situation changed.

Not all business has to be conducted in boardrooms. It is more relaxing to combine work and play in a congenial surrounding. I flew to Vancouver and Chunky Woodward and I, in his beautiful cruiser *Pepi-San*, sailed for six hours at twenty knots until we came to Stewart Island, 120 miles north of Vancouver, at the southern extremity of the inland sea which runs nearly up to Alaska. This wild country, with immense trees and primeval rocks, is the home of the bald eagle. One hundred or more of these majestic birds follow the salmon on their migration to spawn.

The action of the tide, as it ebbs and flows, hitting an outcropping from shore, has created huge, thirty- or forty-foot swirling whirlpools, which materialize out of nowhere, never twice in the same place. Each has a vortex from six to ten feet deep. Not only are the salmon brought together by the swirling tide-water that surrounds the vortex, but hake and weaker swimming fish are cast up to the surface, the prey of fifty or more eagles. These huge birds swoop down and, with a graceful movement, impale the fish with their long talons, struggling to gain altitude once more with this bountiful load.

The fishing method we used on this trip was entirely new to me. Our guide identified a forming whirlpool and positioned our small boat on the edge as the swirling vortex disappeared in its dangerous cone-shape, ten feet or more below the level of the boat. Anglers in several other boats had the same idea, so as many as twenty lines were lowered in the water. If one or more fishermen's lines were hit by salmon or a small, shark-like dogfish, the changes were that the line was instantly interwoven with several others. The bald eagles were oblivious to all this and concentrated on swooping down, talons extended, to impale the hake or other fish forced to the surface around the edges of the whirlpool. Forty or fifty of these magnificent birds fished with us each day, swooping within feet of our heads as they impaled their chosen prey.

Less than half a mile away, on the other side of the inlet, a pod of six or seven killer whales (orcas) swam majestically in a family group looking for salmon. One dorsal fin was higher than the others, extending out of the water four or five feet – obviously the patriarch. On his command, all orca whales surrounded an area and, on another signal, all turned into the middle, savaging the fish caught in the middle of the killer whales' circle of death. It was a spectacular, if awesome sight, especially when seen at water level. They fished undisturbed by us or the eagles for the best part of an hour, an unforgettable sight of nature in balance. It struck me that we were the only creatures who seemed out of place in our less-than-graceful aluminum boat. Stewart Island has one of the highest rainfalls in British Columbia, but for three glorious days the sun shone from daybreak to sunset. Our guides were all divinity students, earning extra money to go back to school. I am sure I did far more praying on the edge of the whirlpool than they did!

. . .

When I returned home to Toronto, I gave a black-tie dinner at the York Club to introduce Ed Telling, chairman of Sears, Roebuck, to the business community. I invited eighty top businessmen, plus Simpsons-Sears' and Simpsons' directors. I was proud of the fact that I could introduce 95 per cent of the guests on a first-name basis, rank and company.

The luncheon of our annual Twenty-Five Year Club held at Limestone Hall was attended by about four hundred guests. It was the usual happy affair. I was wired for sound by the CBC, whose camera crew was well out of sight, using telescopic lenses. Ted Remorowski was in charge of the shooting. Ron Graham set up two more shooting dates for their camera crews. One was the opening of the St. Bruno Shopping Centre on Montreal's south shore.

A few days later, I received a surprise call from Ed Telling. He and Art Wood and Jack Kincannon were flying up from Chicago for the day. They wanted to see me alone! "Just a friendly meeting among owners," is the way they put it. They had not told anyone at Simpsons-Sears they were coming. I tried to contact Jim Tory, but could not reach him, so I got Tom Bell to discuss possible motives. Maybe it had something to do with the fact that the Hudson Bay had offered to buy a large interest in Zellers. The offer was one Bay share, plus $16 cash ($24 Canadian), for four Zellers shares.

Telling, Wood, and Kincannon arrived on August 4. I told Simpsons' vice-president and secretary, Ken Kernaghan, they were coming, but that I did not know why. He hit the nail on the head when he said, "With that combination, I suggest they will propose to merge Simpsons and Simpsons-Sears, with you as chairman." When we went into the board room at Simpsons, that is exactly what they did propose! Kincannon had worked out a proposal that gave Simpsons' shareholders a 40 per cent premium and a share exchange of one-to-one, plus a promise of a dividend increased by 37 per cent! They said I could write my own ticket on how long I wanted the job as chairman and CEO. They explained it was a great vote of confidence in me. They visualized a Simpsons-Sears division and a Simpsons division, one class of voting shares – result, 70 per cent Canadian, 30 per cent American.

I said I would call an early meeting the following Tuesday to consider the matter. I met with Wilkes, Tory, and Kernaghan to discuss the steps necessary to consider the proposal. The next day we flew to Chicago to discuss in detail the requirements of the Foreign

Investment Review Agency (FIRA). Sears cleared everything to see us. We were feeling our way because we were limited in what we could discuss, even with our directors, without making public utterances long before we should. I phoned Ian Sinclair and as many directors as I could. I hoped that we were doing the right thing. We were, from the shareholders' point of view – but emotionally it was difficult. We went back to Chicago and had a full and frank meeting. With me as chairman, the Sears division would operate under Dick Sharpe, the Simpsons division under Ted Burton. The restrictions of the Simpsons-Sears and Sears, Roebuck arrangement would be lifted, and the central management would formulate our co-operative plan for the country. We would become a $3 billion company, with Sears, Roebuck the largest shareholder.

I told Ted Burton, Jack Barrow, and John Taylor. Then at a corporate management meeting I informed my senior people and later held a news conference to explain our talks. Jim Tory called the Securities Commission to ask them temporarily to stop trading our shares if there was any unusual activity. Ed Telling agreed I would serve as chairman for the next three to five years to weld the new organization together. All outside Simpsons directors could become Simpsons-Sears directors, if they wished.

Were we doing the right thing? Had we any real choice? Our stock opened at $6.50 with 46,000 shares. At noon, with 100,000 shares, it was $6.54. By closing, 120,000 shares had traded. What had triggered the flurry? We had been careful about security. Simpsons-Sears went to $8.50 a share. I flew to Montreal to advise Ian Sinclair and Raymond LaVoie, our Montreal directors, of the latest situation. Telling flew from Chicago to discuss plans with Barrow and Taylor. I was advised by phone that the Toronto and Montreal exchanges had stopped trading in Simpsons and Simpsons-Sears, pending an announcement from the company. Our stock reached $7.00. I had the feeling we were being swept along on a riptide of events. We were paddling furiously to keep afloat. Were we headed in the right direction?

On August 16, we held a special Simpsons board meeting. Mike Scott, Alf Powis, and Jim Tory interrupted their holidays to attend. I secured unanimous agreement and then went to the Simpsons-Sears board meeting, which approved the deal. We made minor modifications to the press release on our joint behalf. FIRA and the exchanges were advised. The press reported their wild conjectures on why trading had been halted. We had agreed that only joint statements would be issued, so I was embarrassed and furious to read all sorts of quotes from Ted Burton in *The Globe and Mail*, especially as he had been instructed to say nothing!

There were a few reactions to the "American takeover," largely incited by *The Toronto Star*, which ran three or four articles based on the assumption that Simpsons had "sold-out" to the Americans. I wrote in my diary, "This is particularly hard for me to take, because the future of a 100 per cent Canadian Simpsons was clearly a holding pattern, and the investors gave us little or no credit for earnings of $10 million operating profit on our own."

I thought the furore and anxiety of the staff would be short-lived. It is unfortunate when one is forced to make disclosures long before one has the opportunity to establish a *modus operandi*, with the result that public relations becomes a make-up or patch-up job. Betty's comment was perceptive. She bet the CBC was jumping for joy at the announcement, and she was completely correct. The segment of the program devoted to me was expanded from fifteen minutes to a full fifty-minute episode! The target date to commence joint operation was set for January 31 of the following year.

Then, on September 6, Jack Kincannon, a man I never trusted, dropped a bombshell. He had spent all morning with Blake Cassels, the lawyers recommended by Jim Tory, and he came to our meeting to tell us that Sears, Roebuck could only agree to a "takeover" rather than a merger, because they might attract a U.S. tax of some $50 million the other way. Jim Tory was furious and I was thunderstruck! Kincannon's manner was peremptory to the point of rudeness. Alf Powis, meeting Kincannon for the first time, almost had words with him early on. The news was bad enough, but the public-relations aspect was even worse. We had to get 90 per cent of the shares to "squeeze in" the remainder.

I was ill with a temperature and swollen glands for two days, and so I postponed the press conference for two weeks. We were not ready to talk yet. I flew to Chicago and, in a meeting with Telling, asked him to meet again with his tax advisers to come up with a better arrangement than "takeover" because of the difficulties we had with that scheme.

On September 12, the workers of Toronto Transit Commission went on strike once more. This was disheartening news as a transit strike meant a substantial loss of business for us.

On September 14, we had our first meeting with FIRA about

approval for the merger. They seemed anxious to be helpful. The next day we got the shocking news that C.L. Gundy, our largest individual shareholder, had died. Despite this we proceeded with the board meeting as planned, and passed resolutions of sorrow and sympathy to the Gundy family. Two days later Charlie Gundy was buried, and I acted as an honorary pallbearer.

On September 25, we were hit with a mail strike, on top of the transit strike.

FIRA was a week late with its decision. Simpsons-Sears had had a great number of suggestions from them. The FIRA people were worse than horse-traders, and we postponed the press conference from the 24th to the 29th. We were not ready yet. I got a call from Chicago, asking for two more directors to be added to the board, and Jack Barrow, who was due to retire, to be put on the management committee. I phoned Telling and arranged to go to Chicago with Tory and Taylor, determined to settle the right to manage without undue interference once and for all. In Chicago we got a courteous reception from Telling, but it was obvious that Kincannon and I disliked each other. I simply did not trust his motives. Telling assured me of his complete support. We agreed to make Barrow vice-chairman of the board, with no duties. Part of my problem was Sears' lack of confidence in Ted Burton.

The press conference to announce the merger was called for October 26. I had a 9:00 a.m. meeting that morning with Simpsons officers to explain the news release and to answer questions. At 10:00 a.m., I repeated the question-and-answer period with the general managers and equivalent groups. The session lasted two hours. I had lunch with Barrow, Taylor, Dick Sharpe, Ted Burton, Jim Tory, and Norman Cuthbert (Public Relations) to review the morning's questions. Simultaneous sessions were going on at Simpsons-Sears. Then, at 2:00 p.m., there was a dress rehearsal for the press. Questions were fired at me until 3:40 p.m. I then changed my suit and went to the eighth-floor press conference room. The CBC crew was waiting for me and shot me going into the conference and filmed the entire ninety-minute session. I had become so used to them by now that the CBC crew might well have been part of the woodwork! Barrow, Taylor, and I fielded all the questions, with me taking most of them. About twenty-five press and media people attended.

"BURTON BOSS AT NEW SEARS" was the headline in *The Toronto Star*, which ran nearly a full page of story – good straightforward reporting on the merger. This time *The Globe and Mail* ran a snide article suggesting that Sears was now in full control of Simpsons. *The Toronto Sun* was not sure where it stood. It ran a full page that was quite complimentary to the Burtons, but it also ran a boxed column, written by a member of the Committee for an Independent Canada, which argued, of all things, that the Canadian Development Corporation should buy both Simpsons and Simpsons-Sears!

The "Canada-Firsters" were on the warpath, maintaining that the merger should not happen. They were on CBC Radio, and I was furious with Walter Gordon, former Minister of Finance, when he appeared on CBC-TV and made statements with not the slightest basis in fact; statements that I thought were unfounded and did him or his cause no credit. He said, "Once merged, Simpsons will buy 80 per cent of their merchandise in the United States, whereas now they purchase 80 per cent in Canada." The truth is that Simpsons-Sears, as well as Simpsons, purchased 80 per cent of their merchandise in Canada. His remarks were harmful to us and prolonged the FIRA investigations by another couple of weeks, while we once more attempted to "show benefit to Canada" in the merger, as the law required. The two-week delay triggered other developments that made FIRA more difficult and set the stage for third-party complications.

On October 31, Simpsons' third quarter and nine months' results were good. Third quarter sales were up 9.2 per cent, and our nine months' profit was up 80 per cent over 1977, sales up 6.2 per cent. I took a call from Jack Kincannon, who apologized for appearing to be rude. (He did.) He said, "Let's be friends." I accepted, with mental reservations.

Our legal costs in the merger were already over $250,000. The technical aspects were fantastically intricate. Ted Burton, a very disturbed man, talked to me about his responsibility to the shareholders and said he felt he should speak out against the deal. I said that if he truly felt that way he should speak out now, on the basis of some facts, or be prepared to resign. He did not seem to appreciate that we were all bound by what was best for our shareholders. He was giving expression to his own insecurities, not those of our shareholders. I pointed out to him that the shareholders generally did not seem to share his apprehension. We had received only three letters against the merger out of a possible 17,000, and the market had kept our share price up.

We held "boilerplate" meetings on November 9 of both the Simpsons board and the Simpsons-Sears board to clear the decks so we could act quickly when and if the FIRA agreed to the merger. I asked and got Ted Burton to move one or two of the most important motions, which Betty later said was Machiavellian of me. Ed Telling and John Gallagher of Sears came up from Chicago to the Simpsons-Sears board meeting. Telling was very friendly and even jovial.

We put the merger question to the trustees of the Profit-Sharing Fund. We spent all morning going into each document. Then there was a four-day lull before the storm. Ed Telling phoned me November 15 and I brought him up to date. It was the silence that precedes the battle.

# STORE WARS
# DECLARED!

## 18

On Friday, November 17, "war" was declared! At 8:00 a.m., I was about to leave the farm for the airport to fly to Florida when the phone rang. It was Donald McGiverin, president of Hudson Bay Company, to advise me that Dow Jones would carry a story this morning of a Hudson Bay takeover bid for Simpsons. He stressed there was no maliciousness in this. The Bay was friendly and wanted 100 per cent ownership, but a minimum of 60 per cent would do. They were not interested in the Sears part. If successful, I would be offered a directorship on the Bay board along with anyone else I wanted to be there. He went on to say they had great confidence in Simpsons' management and would not interfere, and so on. Needless to say, I cancelled the trip to Florida. All I could think of to say in reply was, "Thank you for letting me know," which apparently Don McGiverin thought was very funny because he repeated it to the press several times. "And all he had to say was thank you!"

The takeover bid was almost identical to an option we had considered as part of our long-range planning. While it was upsetting and undoubtedly would make our merger plans and life generally most confusing, we did not panic. I called a meeting for 10:00 a.m. to plan strategy. We would not know the details of the offer until Monday morning. In attendance with me were Jim Tory, Ted Burton, John Taylor, J.C. Barrow, and John Evans, lawyer for Simpsons-Sears, with Ted Medland and Ross LeMesurier of Wood Gundy.

The "war cabinet," as I chose to call it, of myself, J.C. Barrow, Jim Tory, Mike Scott, Ian Sinclair, Tom Bell, Jack Kincannon of Sears, and Ken Kernaghan met first thing Monday morning at 9:00 a.m., while other working groups of Simpsons' met over the weekend to update figures and consider areas of action. Fortunately, most of the information we needed was contained in a report done for us some months ago by Larry Smith and Company.

Next, I phoned all Simpsons directors and set up a full board meeting for next Wednesday. Then I phoned Earle McLaughlin, chairman of the Royal Bank, and caught him just as he was boarding a plane to Bermuda. I asked him to be prepared to back us up to $500 million. Earle's answer was, "Canadian or American?" I said Canadian would do. He said, "Okay, but I'll have to lay some off to other banks." I breathed a sigh of relief. Now we had some flexibility.

I got a phone call from Ian Sinclair, who said he would attend the board meeting, adding, "Don't worry, they can't push us around. We have some muscle, too, you know!"

Whatever would happen, I knew that Simpsons' shareholders would win financially. My only concern, I told Ted Burton, was that he run the business well while we were doing the fighting. Betty marvelled at my calmness. She suggested that Ron Graham of the CBC must be ecstatic – the plot was thickening. True, but I wished I were reading about someone else rather than myself!

Events moved so fast that FIRA's foot-dragging, the excessive demands they made on Sears, and the merger proposal itself were momentarily pushed off centre stage. Exhausted, I slept for fifteen hours on Sunday, November 19, the day before the day the Bay would unveil its offer to Simpsons' shareholders.

On November 20, the "war cabinet" met. Of necessity it included Sears and Simpsons-Sears people as well as Simpsons people, with myself as chairman. The new Bay offer, on top of our merger proposition, made each response a product of lawyers and investment dealers. The intricate security regulations and formal legal procedures in a takeover all allow the attacker to retain the initiative, while the company under attack can usually only respond in a cumbersome way, if at all. I was advised that Simpsons could not respond to certain articles that appeared in the press because we could not say anything publicly while FIRA had the case under review. I was told that the Royal Trust had 15 per cent of Simpsons' shares under nominee names, with permission to vote them as they saw fit. I soon realized that all the "raider" had to do was contact the roughly seventeen organizations, funds, and so on that represented about 40 per cent of our shares, while I had to contact 17,000 shareholders by mail. Any letter I sent would be overtaken by events before the shareholder received the formal notice. I personally contacted all the main fund managers, and all of them assured me that they would support Simpsons' management to the last possible moment. But, in the final analysis, they would have to take the best deal on the board. If we could not match it, they were sorry.

The first formal meeting of the "war cabinet" included Jim Tory, Mike Scott, Ted Burton, Tom Bell, and Ian Sinclair (by phone), Ed Telling, chairman of Sears, Jack Kincannon, Jack Barrow, and John Taylor of Simpsons-Sears, a man from Goldman Sachs, and Ross LeMesurier. Telling had brought the Goldman Sachs man from New York because they were experts in fighting takeovers and finding "white knights." I was to learn many new terms before this exercise was over. A "white knight" is a company of size or a financial group able to buy some or all of your major assets to frustrate the "attacker."

The leveraged takeover so common today was practically unknown in Canada at this time. It was not so long ago that we felt quite safe because it would take several hundred million dollars to buy us. I think the banks have much to answer for making it possible for the entrepreneur to "buy" a large company without putting up any money himself and allowing him to repay the bank by stripping the victim of assets. This was not the case in the Bay's offer for Simpsons, but we were told of all the doubtful practices going on in the United States.

We spent a long and frustrating day trying to work out combinations of extra dividends and "white-knight" situations to meet the Hudson Bay offer. We decided we could raise our dividend to the 45 to 50 cent range, with Simpsons-Sears raising theirs to 40 cents, which would be very constructive. But talking to Ian Sinclair, who had just arrived from Vancouver – we hoped as one of our "white knights" – he seemed less positive than I had originally been led to believe, or wished to believe. I went home feeling very let down – time was running out. Jim Tory and Jack Barrow flew to Ottawa and saw FIRA in an effort to speed the merger process.

On November 21, Simpsons stock opened at $7.50 to $7.75; Hudson Bay dropped to $20.00. By day's end, Hudson Bay had risen to $23.00, $25.00 asked. Someone was now after the Bay! Rumours flew. Was it Canadian Pacific? Weston's? Kay of Dylex? Cemp? Even Sears figured in the rumours! We worked on a long press release which said, in effect, that until November 27, when Hudson Bay Co. released its detailed offer to Simpsons shareholders, shares should not be tendered.

The situation was growing more confused. Doug Gardiner of the Royal Bank phoned to tell me that Chunky Woodward had called him from England to offer support for Simpsons in a most friendly way up to a minority position of 25 per cent! A nice show of confidence, which was much appreciated. Doug was a Woodward's director.

There was a long board meeting on November 22. A total of 480,000 Simpsons shares traded at $7.75, the largest number I ever remember in one day. CFTO-TV's Sandie Rinaldo interviewed me about the Bay offer, as did Richard Conrad of *The Star*, Terence Corcoran of *The Financial Times*, and Raoul Engel of Global TV. FIRA met again with Simpsons-Sears and then with Simpsons. I set up a meeting in Chicago with Telling, to suggest things Sears, Roebuck might consider.

FIRA met with Simpsons in an intense but positive session. The bureaucrats were excellent throughout, polite, and anxious to help. They said our co-operation was superb! We got the feeling that we had scored well, and that the conditions they recommended, while many in number, were not difficult for us to agree to. But several could only be undertaken by Sears, Roebuck. I thought they would recommend the merger, but I disliked the "horse-trading" approach of FIRA to Sears, where every concession was met with another demand.

Ray LaVoie informed me that McGiverin had given interviews in Montreal to *La Presse* and *Le Devoir*, in which he said that if the Bay had to divest themselves of Simpsons-Sears, they would adopt a passive attitude, that is, they would place no directors on the Simpsons-Sears board, they would exert no management influence, and so on. I pointed out, in quickly arranged interviews, it was hardly likely that, with an investment of $240 million, a public company could, in all honesty, be passive. McGiverin was deliberately drawing a "red herring" across our merger, and I branded him at least mischievous!

On November 24, McGiverin answered our criticism that the Bay had no clear dividend policy by raising the Bay's dividend from 60 to 80 cents. He also arranged to visit Sun Life and Royal Trust, to sway their votes on the Simpsons shares they controlled. He was a busy and canny fighter!

We were frustrated for the moment because the only sweetening of our pot could come from improved terms from Sears, Roebuck. We had no power at Simpsons to buy our own shares until a

shareholders' meeting voted a "continuance" under the new Corporations Act, which could well be too late. I still had not found a legitimate way to use the $500 million loan I had arranged with Earle
McLaughlin. I arranged to have dinner with Gardiner and Chunky
Woodward to discuss Woodward's minority offer.

Kincannon of Sears phoned me on November 25 and assured me
that they did not want Hudson Bay as a partner and they would fight.
My earlier feeling of frustration changed to relief that help was in
the wings. I was on the phone all day. I wrote a long letter to be sent
to family members who were shareholders.

On November 26, *The Toronto Star* ran a large cartoon about the
takeover of a large eagle battering a beaver. Kincannon called me
from Chicago, where they had been working all day. They suggested
a cash payment of $2.50 to all shareholders, including themselves.
This was not enough of a sweetener for Simpsons' shareholders to
combat the Bay offer.

I flew to Montreal on November 27. A heavy snowstorm made it
a two-hour trip just to get to Malton. I gave interviews to *La Presse*,
*Le Devoir*, and Radio-Canada. I dashed to the audit committee meeting of the Royal Bank, of which I was a member, and then to Place
Victoria to meet with Marcel Cazavan, president of Caisse de Depôt
et Placement du Québec. They had one million of our shares and
were very supportive of Simpsons – again, of course, until the last
possible moment. Then I went to a meeting with the Wood Gundy
people who put forward their "numbers" and suggestions as to what
we needed from Sears, Roebuck to sweeten the deal. Later I had dinner with Chunky Woodward, who had just arrived from England. I
was tired after that day!

The next day, before their quarterly board meeting, the directors of the Royal Bank discussed my interviews in the papers. One
picture of me in the *Gazette* showed me with one index finger in the
air, making a point. It looked as if I was making a rude gesture to
McGiverin and the Bay!

On November 29, I felt very tired and woolly headed in a meeting which went on from 10:00 a.m. to 2:30 p.m. before breaking for
lunch. We wanted to send out a chairman's letter to all shareholders
on the advice of Wood Gundy, but we had little to say without Sears
coming forward with something tangible. In the meantime, Hudson
Bay raised their dividend from 69 to 88 cents. Barrow and Taylor
talked turkey to Kincannon in Chicago. All we could get him to say

was Sears was working on improving their offer. Kincannon said he recognized that they had to come up with something meaningful by December 6 at the latest.

On November 30, there was a Simpsons board meeting to consider the Hudson Bay offer. It was another long and frustrating day, without many answers, and many more phone calls to Kincannon to get him to approve a press release saying Sears would improve their offer. The resulting press release was a much watered-down version, which said that Simpsons, Simpsons-Sears, and Sears, Roebuck were considering improvements in their offer. It also advised Simpsons' shareholders at this time not to put their shares with the Hudson Bay Company. Jack Barrow was uncomfortable discussing what Sears should do. In fairness to Sears, Roebuck, they had conceded a great deal to FIRA. They may not have been able to go further. The company was not doing all that well in the United States at that time.

December 1 was a long, full day in the Simpsons boardroom, trying to piece together some story-line for the press conference set for four days hence. We were very conscious of the December 7 date, the date beyond which Simpsons' shareholders could not retrieve their shares from the Bay, if deposited. We reserved space in all the major papers across the country for a full-page advertisement. It would reproduce my letter advising them to hold their shares until they heard from us. Jim Tory and Ross LeMesurier flew to Chicago in filthy weather – O'Hare Airport was closed because of snow – to hear a new proposal from Kincannon.

We got reports via Ottawa that the Ontario Liberal Cabinet ministers, led by Alastair Gillespie, were against the merger. Sears and Simpsons made promises to FIRA and were in agreement with that agency, so it was becoming a political battle. We found out later that McGiverin had hired Donald Macdonald to try to influence the Cabinet against the merger. I got a call from Tory on his return saying that Sears proposed to back out of the merger and had a different proposition for us.

On December 2, Kincannon suggested that Simpsons distribute Simpsons-Sears' ''B'' shares (our voting shares) to Simpsons' shareholders and make up the difference in some way – for instance, through a rights issue – so that our offer equalled the Bay's offer. We would then be free to merge with some other company. I cancelled the ads and the press conference and cooled the public-relations people to a standby position. Instinctively, I knew we were wrong to denude ourselves of our veto power in Simpsons-Sears by dissipating our voting shares, yet I also knew that the independence factor would be hailed by Simpsons' managers and that it could stop the Bay in their tracks. But all the plus factors of the merger would be wiped out – larger opportunities, financial flexibility, market research and development, and so on. Meanwhile, Sears attained all their objectives. I felt as if I had been used. It might have worked, but the Bay succeeded in killing it. Even if stripping the Simpsons-Sears shares and distributing them to Simpsons' shareholders worked, thus saving us from the Bay, we would still have had a huge load of debt from money raised for our investment in Sears without any concomitant income, a real drain. We might have won the battle and lost the war that way.

On December 4, Telling and Kincannon arrived in Toronto. Sears had nothing new to add, and I wondered why they had set up the meeting. Telling assured me, after some prodding, that they really did want to go ahead with the merger, but they were terrified by the possibility that they would end up with the Hudson Bay as their partner. I felt there was still a chance they would make some concessions yet. We were hanging in firmly. The Sears people went home to Chicago, taking Mike Scott and LeMesurier with them to continue the struggle.

I had a meeting of Toronto directors – Wilder, Powis, Tom Bell, Stewart, but without Barrow this time, because he was clearly in a conflict-of-interest position. Alf Powis came up with a suggestion that could have helped solve our dilemma. If FIRA gave us the favourable decision we expected, the federal Cabinet would consider our case the following Thursday. If I set up a board meeting for 5:00 p.m. on Thursday, in anticipation of a favourable answer from the Cabinet, we could close the deal. We got the bad news from Ottawa that the FIRA decision could not be given until a week from Thursday, which scuttled our plans.

Sears in Chicago came up with another plan to dividend out of Simpsons-Sears our share to the extent of $8.51 per share, but only if we could separate. Then they would not merge or buy us out. In other words, it was worth this amount to get rid of us and the Bay threat, a not-very-complimentary offer after twenty-five years of association! We would be stripped, sitting ducks if we accepted this. I felt, at that moment, like retiring and letting the Hudson Bay into the act.

No less than four companies associated with Simpsons' directors were under "takeover" fire – Abitibi (Tom Bell), Crédit Foncier (Ray LaVoie), Noranda (Powis), and Simpsons. Rumours and counter-rumours filled the days. Our directors were great. Bell was there in spite of his own Abitibi problems. I felt most sorry for Ray LaVoie, whose Crédit Foncier was being taken over by Central and Eastern Trust. Ray had forty-seven years with Crédit Foncier, and his French owners did not even tell him they were in the process of selling. He was furious, of course, and greatly saddened. Once more, Chunky Woodward contacted us, saying they would consider a share exchange with Simpsons if we needed another alternative.

Once more Sears, Roebuck came to Toronto. The meeting on December 7 was less than satisfactory. Ed Telling started by saying, "We are solidly behind the merger as proposed." Yet they were adamant that they could not increase their contribution to match the Bay's offer unless we gave up our rights under the agreement and stripped ourselves naked by dividending out to Simpsons' shareholders our Simpsons-Sears shares. We countered by saying, "We are willing to strip only if Sears agrees to a back-to-back merger with the bonuses suggested." Ed Telling was obviously nervous and upset. I did not discover until later that he had had a phone call from Chicago minutes before he came into the meeting room. Someone had stolen Sears, Roebuck's five-year plan and had leaked it to the press! We agreed only to talk further.

The Simpsons directors met at 5:00 p.m. We appointed Scott, Tory, and LeMesurier to continue negotiations. We needed a guarantee from Sears that they would proceed with the merger before dividending out our shares. We all felt quite low, and we were all very tired. Jim Tory, in particular, was carrying a very heavy load and was hoarse from talking.

We had expected the FIRA announcement from Cabinet on December 8, but the Prime Minister was in England having lunch with the Queen who, on his recommendation, appointed an NDPer, Ed Schreyer, as Governor General. Scott and LeMesurier went down yet again to Chicago where they wrangled all weekend with Kincannon. Every time we reached an agreement, Sears found a new excuse to dash our hopes. Each side heard only what it wanted to hear and understood things only its way. Underlying all this was my gut feeling that Sears wished to be rid of Simpsons, FIRA, and the liability of the takeover by the Bay at any cost to Simpsons. A new negotiating point was thrown in by Sears, that I retire at sixty-five and continue for three years as CEO as planned. I readily agreed. The fun was fast going from dealing with them. I found out much later that Kincannon had included that condition out of personal pique and that it did not come from Telling or Wood.

Finally we heard some good news. Tory phoned, "We think we have a deal!" Then, hours later, Tory phoned again, "No deal!" Once more they did not understand, or so Sears said. The only good news at that moment was that business was excellent.

We spent some time trying to estimate the political situation at the Cabinet level. It appeared that a large number of Cabinet ministers were against the merger. They were an uneven lot, Martin O'Connell, Norman Kafik, Judd Buchanan, led by Alastair Gillespie. Federal ministers Marc Lalonde and Jean Chrétien were strongly in favour of us – a much stronger pair than all the others. It was very frustrating to wait with the feeling that your future and the future of 17,000 others was in the hands of politicians who apparently make decisions only on the basis of what is best to get re-elected.

I got a phone call. The deal may be on again! Next morning, Tory called to say, "It's all off again!" I got mad and phoned Telling in Chicago, certain now they were toying with us. I told Telling I wanted face-to-face explanations from him as partners of twenty-five years. I did not think we were receiving good enough treatment. He agreed to meet me before the Simpsons-Sears meeting. I went to bed and slept little, trying to imagine what life under Bay ownership would be like.

Tory and I met with Ed Telling before our respective board meetings on December 11. We were struck by the fact that Telling was either ill-informed or misinformed about the cost to Sears of our proposal to sweeten the pot. He quoted the figure of $100 million. We were shocked because the real cost to them was only $2 million a year in lost revenue. They withdrew and came back. No dice. Jim Tory, worn out, then blew and berated Sears for not giving us "a proper day in court." Art Wood, smooth as ever, tried to get us to pass a resolution amending Simpsons' and Sears' agreement in their favour. We said, "Oh no, that would destroy our bargaining power." Telling and Wood, faces down, showed their disappointment.

It was a humourless Sears board meeting. Then we Simpsons directors went over to our own board meeting. Tory stayed behind in Simpsons-Sears while we, very depressed, started to work out our

*During the "store war" over Simpsons in 1979, the* Toronto Sun *ran this cartoon by Andy Donato.*

alternate plan to deal with McGiverin and the Bay. About 6:00 p.m., the phone rang. Tory advised, "The deal is on!" We had an alternative for our shareholders, which now exceeded in value the offer from the Bay. We worked until 10:00 p.m. on a new press release to be released at 9:00 a.m. next morning.

On December 12, Jim Tory phoned from the airport. "Hold the release!" We had run into a difficult problem in Ottawa with the tax department – frustration, fatigue, and phone calls. Newspaper articles claimed we were deliberately not giving out information. An interminable morning dragged by. At 11:00 a.m., Tory phoned, "Okay!" We were in business again! The news of our now-sweetened merger hit all the newscasts, and I did TV interviews with CFTO and CITY-TV. You could almost hear the sigh of relieved tension from the business district. It seemed the phone never stopped ringing.

The next day we held another press conference at Simpsons-Sears because McGiverin decried our offer, claiming it was only worth $7.60 against his $8.30. Not so. Wood Gundy had produced an explanation sheet for us giving comparative values, which not only educated the press but cleared up a couple of points for me. Cabinet support seemed to be going our way, but Gillespie, who was a member of the Committee for an Independent Canada, was dead against us. We issued a statement advising our shareholders to deposit their stock with their brokers. In the event we got a negative response from Cabinet, the Bay deal was the only one in town. McGiverin issued a statement saying the Bay would withdraw their offer if we split off the Simpsons-Sears "B" shares.

We won! On December 14, the federal Cabinet decided in our favour. We had won, or had we? Almost on the heels of our joy and jubilation came another dash of cold water. In spite of the agreement we had signed, Sears did not realize there was a purchase fund on the preferred shares and they pleaded with us to find a way around it. My spirits sank to a new low. I was running a temperature just under a hundred degrees and had a hacking cough. Jim Tory was very despondent and very tired.

As promised, we held a board meeting at Simpsons at 5:00 p.m., and voted to dividend out the "B" shares of Simpsons-Sears to Simpsons' shareholders. While we were in technical default with the Exchange for not allowing seven days' notice of dividend, we presumed that the Hudson Bay Co. would then withdraw their offer as they had previously announced and our merger would proceed.

Our stock had been suspended indefinitely by the Exchange. However, another disaster! The Bay did not withdraw their offer but amended it to include the Simpsons-Sears shares and did not withdraw as anticipated. So we were still in trouble. The situation was getting worse rather than better.

The next day we held a shareholders' meeting, which was quickly terminated. There were no questions from the few shareholders who turned out. I made a short speech, then Santa Claus in his red suit came up front to wish us all a merry Christmas! *Maclean's* took photos of me in front of the store and, cleverly as it turned out, some of McGiverin at the same time, so they could feature on their cover whoever won.

I no longer felt in charge of affairs. There were too many legal manoeuvres going on from different directions at the same time. I wrote in my diary, "We must trust Tory, LeMesurier, and God." I was not sure that was the correct order.

Jim Tory met all day with the Securities Commission and phoned after the session to say that we were in trouble. Tory and Blake Cassels had failed to convince the Commission that an offer for two stocks and two companies in one circular was not in accordance with the rules and should not be allowed to proceed as planned. This issue was now to be settled at a first-ever joint session of the Ontario and Quebec commissions to be held in Montreal on the next Monday. That evening we had fifty-seven people to dinner at Limestone Hall for our traditional Christmas neighbours' party.

It is almost impossible to describe adequately the tension and drama of those days. The only other time I had experienced anything like them was in World War II, but I was in my twenties then, not my sixties. On December 18th, I was up at 5:30 a.m. and flew to Montreal with Jack Barrow and John Taylor. Tory was already there. We drove to Wood Gundy's offices in Place Ville Marie to meet Mike Scott and to face yet another serious problem. In our merger arrangement with Sears, we had agreed that they could withdraw from the merger if any third party acquired sufficient shares of Simpsons to be entitled to receive on the merger more than 10 per cent of the merged enterprise. We could not ask the Securities Commission to invalidate the Bay bid unless Sears was unconditionally committed to our merger. Otherwise our shareholders might find they had neither offer available. We had felt that this was a "detail" and were shocked to find that the waiver was not given as a matter of course.

Was Sears still committed or had they again changed their minds? We phoned Telling two or three times and pleaded. We postponed the Securities meeting one hour while we pleaded, but to no avail. Jim Tory finally made an appearance and a statement saying that we were forced to withdraw from the hearing, stating that a misunderstanding had arisen between ourselves and Sears, Roebuck. Dow Jones came out that we would recommend for the Bay, which was not the case. I heard this over the public-address system in Gundy's offices. I had not had time to consult or advise my directors except for those with me. We flew home feeling sad and defeated.

At a board meeting at 9:00 a.m. the next day, Ian Sinclair was furious with me because he had not been advised. It was a very hectic day. Kincannon was on hand, but we elected to put out a Simpsons release, pointing the finger at Sears, Roebuck's lack of flexibility as the reason the merger was not consummated. The papers were full of the Bay's victory. I was supposed to have lunch with McGiverin but cancelled because our board meeting dragged on. Most directors present were in favour of keeping their stock. We offered our stockholders a choice – sell them to the Bay or retain them.

I spoke to all our senior area managers by conference call when a Sears, Roebuck release was put out from Chicago. Their release maintained that they were aware of no misunderstanding and that we withdrew from the merger. I issued one more release noting that I had read theirs and stuck with our version – a nasty turn.

Chunky Woodward phoned at 6:00 p.m. and said he would try and put in an offer for Simpsons. I sent our assistant controller, Stanley Nicholson, out to Vancouver with our latest figures. I hoped they would help him, but two days later Chunky phoned to say that his men had looked at the proposition again but could not make a bid for Simpsons after all. We got the encouraging news that the trustees of Simpsons-Sears' Profit Sharing Fund had voted 100 per cent to keep their Simpsons shares.

On December 23, there was Christmas carol singing on the main floor of the store, our fifty-fourth year of the tradition. I spoke to the several hundred customers who came down to sing with us each year, as I had done for the past twenty years. I thanked Elwood Glover, the announcer, who performed this "labour of love" for thirty-seven years. I also thanked Ellis McClintock and the members of his quintet as well as Joe Lindsell, who was in the choir for fifty-two of the fifty-four years. There was loud applause when I said Simpsons would survive because we and our customers wanted it to. I toured the kitchens and the sub-basement boiler rooms, as I had each year, to wish the people behind the scenes a Merry Christmas.

On Christmas Day, two inches of snow fell on Limestone Hall and made everything pure and calm. Surrounded by what seemed to be hordes of family and excited children, we sat down to a monstrous, thirty-three-pound turkey. I was tired but still able to count our blessings. On Boxing Day, we held our regular open house. Alan and Ruth Collier brought out A.J. and Margaret Casson as usual. "Cass" brought us an exquisite 1925 watercolour of his as a Christmas gift.

It was back to reality on December 27. The Hudson Bay Co. bid closed and they claimed to have 60 per cent of the stock. McGiverin, in announcing their control, reiterated that Simpsons would keep its name and identity and that no Simpsons employee need fear for his or her job or pension! They kept the offer open to January 10, 1979.

Betty and I and Tracy, along with Jim and Marilyn Tory, flew to Bermuda for much-needed rest and reflection at the Coral Beach Club. June Callwood and Trent Frayne, old friends, were on the same plane. New Year's Eve was spent with the Torys reminiscing about the events of the last few weeks. We continued to ponder Sears, Roebuck's true motives. We had done all we could and had no regrets.

The CBC was anxious to resume photographing for the *Establishment* series. I understand that my program had definitely advanced from a half-hour to an hour-long episode of its own. The producers had been filming for eighteen months. A lot had happened since they had started!

New Year's Day 1979 dawned bright and sunny in Bermuda, but I spent most of the day on the phone to Toronto. We had to decide whether to place our Simpsons stock with the Bay or retain Simpsons-Sears stock and see what happened to Simpsons. The overhang of the stock options was of considerable concern. Ted reported that we were under severe pressure from Wood Gundy and some of our directors to call a meeting to declare once more our intentions on the disposition of our stock. I set up a board meeting for Monday, January 8, and a meeting with the pension fund trustees at 2:00 p.m. I told Ted I would try to arrange a meeting with Don McGiverin on Sunday, the day before.

I had several mysterious phone calls. They were mysterious only because they had to be concealed from Betty, no small task when you are in a small cottage. Lorraine Thompson of *Front Page Challenge* phoned to ask me to be a mystery guest on the program. Of course, Betty must know nothing about it. They really do go to great lengths to keep their guests unknown to the panelists. I was not sure whether it was a good idea or not to go ''on air'' so soon, but I gave Lorraine a tentative okay.

Ted called on January 4 and reported current stock prices. I told him it was now a matter of individual choice whether he turned in his stock to the Bay. Don McGiverin called and we arranged to meet at Limestone Hall on Sunday afternoon. He was anxious to put to rest some apprehensions on the part of our people. I congratulated him on a well-fought battle and he seemed pleased. The Bay now owned in excess of 60 per cent of Simpsons, and I saw little value in being odd man out.

Our main concern now was a smooth transition of service from Simpsons-Sears to the Bay, while we unwound the merchandise agreements with Simpsons-Sears and rebuilt similar co-operative arrangements with the Bay. Only much later in the year was the depth of the twenty-five-year partnership sounded. There was a precipitous and immediate separation of goods and services. Such Sears products as Coldspot and Craftsman could no longer be used. But we had millions of dollars worth of inventory of products bearing these labels. This was a much more debilitating and costly exercise for both Simpsons and Simpsons-Sears than anyone had foretold, if indeed anyone had thought about it at all! The separation alone cost each of us several million dollars in labels, stationery, and signs of all sorts. We did all Sears' parcel delivery, which represented about 40 per cent of our daily parcel load, and our depots and equipment were designed for these loads. The Hudson Bay Co. in Toronto and Montreal was in no way able to make up these volumes. They just did not have the business.

McGiverin told me the Bay now had over 70 per cent and expected 80 per cent of our stock and that their deadline of January 10 would not be extended. This meant that there would be little or no market for Simpsons' stock, and wisdom dictated that we turn our stock in and take the premium. We put out the appropriate press release on the January 6, explaining that all officers and some directors were placing their shares with the Bay. We took this action because the size of the Bay's holding meant that there would be little chance of a meaningful market for Simpsons' shares in the future. This proved to be the case. The Bay's final offer was $8.25 per share. Thereafter 810,000 Simpsons shares traded on the market at $2.20.

On Sunday, January 7, Don McGiverin came to Limestone Hall, as planned, and we talked over drinks for three hours. He invited me to join the Hudson Bay board, but he added that because of their undertaking with the Combines Commission, no one could serve on the boards of both Simpsons and Simpsons-Sears. He wanted to place three people on Simpsons' board – himself as vice-chairman and Peter Wood and Alex MacIntosh (when Charlie Stewart retired). He wanted to speak to all our senior people in Toronto and Montreal to assure them that Simpsons would remain Simpsons. He said that the Bay admired Simpsons and wanted the company to continue to grow and prosper. All pensions and benefits would be maintained. Don McGiverin seemed very sincere. You could not help liking him. He allayed many apprehensions.

I received a letter that touched me deeply. It came from Dick Sharpe, vice-president, Merchandise, Simpsons-Sears, who had been designated to run the merged company under my chairmanship. He regretted that our association could not continue. I spent a long time composing a thoughtful reply. I thought a lot of Dick Sharpe and I was glad he had been designated to take over at Simpsons-Sears.

Don McGiverin, at the next managers' meeting, enlarged on the theme that Simpsons was "one of the great stores of the world." He announced that I had consented to join the Bay board, which drew a round of applause. Similar meetings were held in Montreal. McGiverin was impressed after a tour of the store's facilities. Our Montreal downtown store did about $90 million volume in 1978, when the Bay's bigger store (formerly Morgan's) only did $65 million. On January 14, Betty and I flew to Montreal to attend the annual meeting of the Bank of Montreal. I went in my official role as spouse of a director. This was our last official trip in our De Havilland 125 Jet, for it really belonged to Simpsons-Sears.

I spent much of January 16 going over salary and bonus sheets with Ted. For some years we had considered total remuneration – that is, salary and bonus, if any. So we corrected the salary lists to include the 1978 bonuses. From now on, there would be no bonuses payable in Simpsons, unless a new scheme was developed. Tom Bell, chairman of the Compensation Committee, met with McGiverin and got his sanction on the new lists.

The next day I received a letter from a consultant firm, which had 300,000 Simpsons shares, which said I should not serve on the board of the Bay! I discovered that I must retire as chairman to remain on the Bay board by the end of the year.

There was disturbing news in the business section of *The Globe and Mail* on January 19. Ralph Huband, secretary of the Bay, made an announcement that three Bay directors would be joining the Simpsons board, and that our dividend would be lowered! I cooled my anger before phoning McGiverin, who professed to be as upset as I was and promised to "muzzle the fellow." Huband had also stated that the Bay was not rushing things to give the Simpsons directors a chance to resign! Betty had already decided to resign from Simpsons, and it is obvious that Jim Tory would have to as well, with Alex MacIntosh coming on. I could not conceive of Ken Kernaghan, Simpsons' secretary, making these kinds of statements on behalf of Simpsons. I guessed I would have many differences to get used to if I remained on their board.

When McGiverin was in Chicago seeing Ed Telling of Sears, Roebuck to sort out their position with Simpsons-Sears, Telling asked him if they, Simpsons-Sears, could ask Wilder, Powis, and LaVoie to join Simpsons-Sears. Ian Sinclair had already indicated he must resign from Simpsons, as well as Betty and Jim Tory. Tom Bell was furious at Sears, Roebuck and voted to remain on Simpsons' board. I resigned from Simpsons-Sears forthwith.


I celebrated my sixty-fourth birthday on January 20. With my record of birthdays, I wondered what surprise this one would bring. I received a present and a beautiful note from Betty, as follows:

> *My dearest Allan—*
>
> *Your birthday is a special day for a very special person. My birthday wishes for you are filled with a deep and abiding love and enormous admiration for you with all your sense of fun, your integrity, and your courage! You are a marvelous man, my darling – hope your birthday is happy and that we share many more.*
>
> *With all my love,*
> *Betty*

To this I said "Amen." I was so touched I could not read it aloud, but passed it around to our children at the family party. I noted in my diary, "We love each other deeply and are very happy together and restless when apart." She is beautiful in mind and person.

Later that day we put on cross-country skis to get some exercise.

Unfortunately something interfered with my breathing, and I had a racking cough like bronchial asthma. We slowly made it home. I lost four pounds that night on trips to and from the bathroom with what I used to call the "old Italian complaint." To mark my birthday, I had picked up a bug.

The big event of the winter season in Quebec City is the carnival. I went there with the *Front Page Challenge* group. Betty and I stayed in the Château Frontenac overlooking the St. Lawrence River. Gordon Sinclair had the room next to ours. I invited him to share a room-service supper in our room, breaking out a bottle of Scotch to give him a pre-dinner drink.

We had a great time swapping yarns and managed to consume about two-thirds of the bottle before Gordon went to his room to bed. I worried whether or not I had done the right thing in giving him a drink at all. He was frail and had been known on occasion to go on a bender. So early the next morning, I phoned to see if he was all right. There was no answer. Alarmed that he might be ill, I went to his room about 8:00 a.m. and knocked on his door. Then Gordon came down the corridor toward me, bundled in his heavy coat with a Davy Crockett coon hat on his head, glowing with health and rosy-hued of cheek from the thirty-degrees-below-zero weather. He was humming happily to himself when he saw me. "Allan," he cried, "I have had the most marvellous morning. I was on the street by 6:00 a.m., and have done four interviews already for future shows, including one with the Grey Nuns!"

The guests for *Front Page Challenge* are carefully concealed from the panelists, so when Betty went off to make-up, Lorraine Thompson asked me if I would have an early dinner with the guests before the program started. I had a lively meal with the three mystery guests – Dr. Hans Selye, the pioneer in the study of stress, Mordecai Richler, the novelist, and a Parti Québécois minister with whom we had a spirited argument about Bill 101, the French-language charter so hated by the English.

The Hudson Bay Company delivered to me all the new organization charts for the Bay, Simpsons, and Zellers and asked me to distribute them to all managers. I called our management committee together and examined them in detail, finding a fair number of details that needed explaining. Don McGiverin came down to discuss the problems with us. I discovered that McGiverin did not like committees of any kind. In fact, he was trying to do far too much himself. He suggested he deal directly on operating matters with Ted Burton so he could get to know him better, and with me on all corporate matters. The arrangement suited me. At Simpsons' regular board meeting, the Bay nominees were added, and the resignations of Wilder and Powis were accepted. *Executive Magazine* ran a snarky article on McGiverin and me, criticizing me for not being more open during the takeover. The editors did not bother to find out why. FIRA restrictions, and so on, had required circumspection. Jim Tory advised me that he would resign from Simpsons' board and go on the Simpsons-Sears board.

The February weather was extremely cold. For the first time in living memory the Great Lakes were mostly ice-covered. My bronchial asthma attacks were getting worse by the day. I finally went to Arthur Squires at the Wellesley Hospital for the most complete medical I have ever had. Ten years before I had arranged for him to do annual medicals on all Simpsons' senior executives, but I had never gone myself. Dr. Squires called me, saying that he was going to retire one day and that he would like to do me before retiring to complete his Simpsons picture. It seemed like a reasonable request, and as Squires's reputation was enormous, I agreed. He sent me to a young respirologist for pulmonary checks on my bronchial asthma, who said, "I can cure your bronchitis in twenty-four hours." The drug Inderal, which I had been taking for my heart for nine years, was causing my distress! I was taken off the Inderal and my coughs and wheezes stopped as well.

Douglas Gardiner of the Royal Bank gave a small reception on February 2 for the West German minister of economics. Otto, Count Lansdorff was a short, balding man with curly fair hair who walked with a cane, limping slightly. He spoke perfect English and was obviously very knowledgeable and intelligent. He answered any and all questions after giving us a rundown on the economic situation in his country – 1.5 per cent inflation, 2 per cent unemployment. He spoke about the three-tiered boards of companies on which, by law, labour, management, and shareholders are represented. He said it would not be workable in North America because it was based on German constitutional law. He privately said that a management committee, an insider board, really ran each company and made decisions. The three-tiered boards were only window-dressing.

On February 22, I spent much of the morning going over my retirement estimates with Ian Gibson, treasurer. My service would be forty-four years and eleven months.

# THE HUNTER HUNTED

## 19

The Hudson Bay Company requested a cease-trading order on its stock. Rumour had it that either Brascan or Thomson Newspapers was buying in. The big news on March 2, 1979, was the Bay takeover bid by Thomson Newspapers. Thomson was buying 51 per cent of the shares at $31.00 a share. The Bay had closed at $23.00 the day before. Don McGiverin called me and said that at my first directors' meeting at the Bay we would be discussing the Thomson takeover bid. I replied, "Well you will have at least one experienced director then!"

At the regular Royal Bank meeting on March 7, there was much speculation about the Thomson takeover bid and its effect on Simpsons. I had a long chat with John Tory, Jim's brother – the power behind Ken Thomson's throne. I felt the takeover would be a constructive thing but decided to reserve my judgement until I had heard the Bay's side. The price was a nice further appreciation for Simpsons' shareholders!

At a budget meeting on March 12 with Ted Burton, Ronald Crichton, Ken Clarke, and Ernie Wilkes, we cut a proposed $20 million capital expenditure proposal to about $12.5 million. I reasoned that while the whole program should and probably would be implemented, $20 million represented more than could realistically be done in one year in any event. So we staged it over two years.

Three days later, Jack Barrow, John Taylor, and the officers of Simpsons-Sears gave a black-tie dinner at the York Club in honour of me, Tom Bell, and Ted, retiring as directors of Simpsons-Sears. We all made little speeches of regret that the merger had not succeeded. John Taylor told me that my letter to him was among his most treasured possessions.

In view of the Thomson bid, I chose not to join the Hudson Bay board until the annual meeting in May in Winnipeg. It seemed needlessly complicated to make out all the declarations needed for directors' circulars, and so forth, in respect to the Thomson bid for the Bay. I could not tell, for instance, what my position would be with respect to the "indirect" control of shares in the various trusts. The legalities of corporate life could be very complicated! I spent the whole of March 16 clearing out and shredding whole sections of files.

There was a regular meeting of the Royal Bank on March 21. It appeared as if money was getting tighter. The Bank of Canada was keeping the lid on money supply, but nothing was too serious yet. I then went to 10 Toronto Street to a board of directors meeting of Standard Broadcasting. Montegu Black, the new chairman, and Conrad Black were in attendance. It was quite a lively meeting, compared with the meetings Bud McDougald used to conduct. McDougald was very superstitious. I remembered one Standard meeting during which he, as chairman, would put his head in the door, ask a question, and disappear. All afternoon McDougald acted like a jack-in-the-box. The person next to me asked me if I knew what was going on. I said no. "Well," he continued, "if McDougald sits down, there will be thirteen at the table. So unless someone leaves, he won't come in!" Monty Black had no such hangups, but he no doubt had problems of his own.

I had a meeting with the Simpsons pension trustees who controlled 300,000 shares. We suggested that they accept the Thomson offer, if no better offer was forthcoming, but not to put their shares in until the Bay's circular and any other offer that may be better were considered. Don McGiverin called me and I assured him that the Bay's circular of the next day would be carefully considered before anything was done. The Pension Fund, with assets over $30 million, got a big injection after accepting the Bay offer of common, preferred, and cash. The preferred were sold. The Bay circular advised against selling out for those who were interested in the long term. It sounded very similar to our releases! We decided to defer any decision until April 4, the next scheduled trustees' meeting. We had until April 6 to turn in the stock. I was very glad I had decided not to go on the Bay board until May.

On April 6, there were sixty-miles-an-hour winds. The phones went out, but just before they did, Ruth Carlisle, my secretary, informed me that trading in Hudson Bay stock was halted, pending an announcement. Three days later the Bay directors advised their shareholders to accept the latest Thomson offer of $37 per share for 75 per cent of the stock and stated they would tender all their stock.

I flew to Quebec City on April 22 with John Robarts, Jim Kerr, and Douglas Gibson for the Bell Canada annual meeting. It was held in the Quebec capital for the first time. The Bell meeting was all in French with simultaneous translation. But to hear the flat, unemotional voice of a female translator when the chairman is speaking is undesirable. I could read his report with better understanding. The public-relations aspect of having the Bell annual meeting in Quebec City was good and the year's results were excellent. We flew home, tired but happy.

The next day I attended a luncheon in the Royal York, given by INCO for their directors and guests. I was seated next to George Richardson, governor of the Hudson Bay Company, and it was the first time I had had the opportunity to have a lengthy chat with him. He said, "I'll see you in May in Winnipeg," meaning I would join the Bay board then. I said I wasn't sure because my name had been omitted from the Bay information circular. Possibly since Thomson's had acquired 89 per cent of the Bay, things had changed. Not so, said he. Later, Ralph Huband, vice-president and secretary of the Bay, phoned to say the absence of my name was an oversight. His explanation did not impress me at all!

I phoned John Tory, who said that Thomson had no problem with my being on the board. He said he would support it personally, but that Thomson was very sensitive to the public suggestion of a Tory connection – Jim and John – and therefore they did not want me to appear to be their nomination. I felt somewhat less than welcome and probably should have told them to forget it, but I was still head of Simpsons, as chairman and CEO, and thought I could be of use on the Bay board while Simpsons and the Bay were working out their co-operative arrangements. An instance of how this could be of advantage involved Douglas Steele, a senior Simpsons merchant, who was seconded to the Bay. This occurred while the new Beaumark lines of heavy goods were designed and marketed to replace our Coldspot stoves, refrigerators, and other appliances. I think the Beaumark lines were very well designed, but the establishment of a completely new national line is very costly. Simpsons was allotted half the promotional expense, the Bay the other half. I thought this was disproportionate but there was nothing I could do about it at the time.

I wondered how Don McGiverin, long used to being his own boss, would get along under the new regime. I could hear a repetition of what he had told me, "We don't want to change anything, just be yourselves, but . . . ."

On April 20, the Simpsons board meeting passed all the "boilerplate," as routine legal resolutions are called in the trade, in connection with the new Corporations Act which required specified changes to ensure what is called "continuance." Don McGiverin, Peter Wood, and Alex MacIntosh attended for the first time. Don tried to explain the director bit to me, the confusion about the information circular and the lack of time to do it all properly. John Tory, Ken Thomson, and I would be put on the board at the directors' organizational meeting which followed the annual meeting. If we all survived the coming year, the shareholders would be able to vote on us in the normal fashion next year at the annual meeting.

Garth Turner of *The Toronto Sun* had a full-page article on April 22 titled "Take that, Mr. McGiverin." It strongly suggested that the "Tory connection," with my connivance, bought the Bay. I wrote in my diary, "What rot! And not helpful with any suspicion I was working against the Bay's owners." I was pleased that Thomson bought the Bay, but it was neither of my doing nor because of the "Tory connection," as far as I knew. I phoned Don to see if he was upset by it. His comment was, "Sure, I saw it, but I don't pay any attention to that crap!" All the same, from hunter to hunted is a big change, and it takes some adjusting! I wrote a letter of congratulations to Ken Thomson.

I came to the office on May 3 expecting to meet Jim Tory to go over a proper statement for the annual meeting about the dividending out of the Simpsons-Sears "B" stock. But Jim had left for Bermuda! Almost single-handedly, Jim Tory was making legal decisions, undertaking alone or with LeMesurier negotiations with Sears, Roebuck, the Securities Commission, or whatever government department we had to deal with. No one could have done more and no one worked himself nearer to exhaustion in our cause than he did. But only he can recount what went on, and in some cases why, in the complex legal and securities manoeuvres of those few days and weeks.

The Governor General's Horse Guards' reunion was held every five years to celebrate our first day in action in World War II, which took place at Cassino in the Liri Valley in Italy. It had been my first action, as well, where I commanded "C" Squadron. The reunion was held on May 12 in Denison Armouries in Toronto. Over four hundred veterans sat down to the memorial dinner. They had come from all parts of the continent. Five years ago we wondered how many veterans of the 1944 campaign would be around to celebrate in 1979, but the attendance was greater than ever. I met and drank with many of my "C" Squadron tank crews, old friends, like W.R. (Wally) Stitt, my wireless operator, whose skill more than once saved our network and ourselves from destruction. Wally professed to be a Fabian socialist, and when we were bedded down alongside our tank under a tarp, we would have long discussions on the subject of capitalism versus socialism. After the war he ran a successful business and, as far as I know, became a happy capitalist.

At the church parade and memorial service the next morning, I paraded with my veteran buddies. Along with the "spaghetti-eaters" of the Italian campaign and the regiment and regimental cadets, we filled the parade ground with a couple of hundred wives and sweethearts in the stands. "Men of Harlech," our regimental march, stirred our blood once more as our standard was paraded stiff with the gold embroidery of our battle honours.

I found it interesting that of the four hundred veterans, all but about three looked well and had good jobs and fine families. I was proud of my fellow Horse Guards.


My last Simpsons annual meeting was held on May 15. The usual 150 turned out, mostly employees. My speech was well applauded and no questions were asked. Don McGiverin was complimentary, and Tom Bell said it was one of the best speeches he had heard and asked for a copy. Tom's hearing was not too good, the result of having served in the artillery, and I did not remember what I said, but knowing my old friend and fellow Simpsons director, who was noted for directness of speech, he would not have praised the speech if it had not been up to standard! Ted Burton and I held a press conference, and as I had announced in my speech that I would be retiring on December 31, and that this was my last annual meeting as chairman, the press, of course, wanted to know my future plans. Betty and Ian Sinclair retired from the board by not standing for re-election, and special resolutions were passed thanking each of them for unique and special contributions. The next day Garth Turner of *The Toronto Sun* gave me a full-page spread, which was very complimentary, headlined "The Colonel Calls a Truce." I have it framed in my studio opposite me as I write. *The Toronto Star* and *The Globe and Mail* each had a good story on the annual meeting and Simpsons in general. My one regret was that I would miss forty-five years' service with Simpsons at the end of the year by only six months!

I flew out to Winnipeg, the Air Canada plane full of Bay people, for the Bay board meeting. The dinner of welcome was pleasant and everyone very friendly. I met Joe Segal, chairman of Zellers, for the first time. He was small but well turned out, quiet, and quite sensitive. Joe was complimentary about me and Simpsons. Of course, this helped me to admire his opinions and judgement! We sat up talking over nightcaps until 3:45 a.m., Toronto time!

I made a report on Simpsons to the Bay board meeting. The governor, George Richardson, was friendly and apparently quite pleased with his new allies. At noon on May 18, we assembled for the Hudson Bay Company's annual meeting. The governor seemed quite nervous and went into a long explanation about his January purchases of Bay stock being strictly "according to Hoyle." At the following directors' meeting, Ken Thomson, John Tory, and I were appointed directors of the Hudson Bay Company. I toured the main Bay store later with Wallace Evans, the Bay president, and though it was quite good, it was not up to Simpsons' standards.

A Horse Guards regimental dinner was held on May 25, and I attended, dressed in white tie, tails, and miniatures. The CBC crew and Ron Graham were on hand at the Denison Armouries, hoping to shoot more footage for my series, which we did before I had to go into the mess. I gave the toast to the regiment, the principal toast of the evening other than the one to the Queen. I said, "Tradition is a fine fabric woven of the souls of all who have served, embroidered by their deeds." The dinner was in honour of Dr. Magnus Spence; Col. Spence, to give him his military rank. "Mag" Spence had been the regimental medical officer as long as anyone could remember. He was beloved by all and was an extraordinarily good doctor. He had commanded the equivalent of a MASH unit in Italy and had served with great distinction.

I continued my tours of our various stores and facilities with Don McGiverin. In each location he addressed the assembled managers and assured them that it was the Bay's intention to be non-interfering.

We covered London and Windsor in one day, flying to Halifax the next day and then Montreal that night. McGiverin was complimentary about his impressions on seeing our stores and the people.

Halifax was the only place I knew where the store manager complained about a sunny day. They happened so infrequently that everyone stayed outside and no one shopped! In Montreal we toured our main downtown store, then those in St. Bruno, Anjou, Laval, Pointe Claire, and the St. James and St. Laurent warehouses. It was a gruelling day, but we were the better for the feeling of exhilaration that comes from being on the ground talking to our people, absorbing their enthusiasm, and seeing that the stores were in fine condition. Our stores did from 50 per cent to 100 per cent more sales per square foot than the Bay stores, and Don expressed some doubts about Bay décor and layout once he had seen ours. He mentioned several times how obvious it was that people across the country were pleased to see me. He was also impressed with my depth of knowledge about all details. Why not? I had built most of the stores.

There was yet another Twenty-Five Year Club dinner. It came and went on June 13. This one was for me a little sadder than the others because it would be my last as chairman. As usual the next day, some four hundred came to lunch at Limestone Hall. This time Don McGiverin, Ken and Marilyn Thomson, Ralph Huband, and Peter and Jane Wood came from the Bay.

At the Hudson Bay board meeting on June 22, it was suggested that I should not go into the meeting while the Simpsons-Bay merger was being discussed. This was a move designed to give minority shareholders another chance at a tax-free, roll-over exchange of Simpsons shares for Bay shares, or a cash equivalent for U.S. holders. Simpsons Limited would then disappear from the stock listings in the same way as we would have under the Simpsons, Simpsons-Sears merger proposal. There would be no change in our name or business as far as the public was concerned, or so the outside Simpsons directors were assured by Don McGiverin at our subsequent Simpsons board meeting. I found our outside directors were nervous and upset at the legal implications of agreeing to the Bay proposal. McGiverin denied that if it was successful they would be out of a job.

Mike Scott, Tom Bell, Ray LaVoie, Charles Stewart, Ted, Wilkes, and I decided to hire special counsel to monitor Tory's advice, and another investment company, Ames, to monitor Gundy's advice on the fairness of the offer. We could not fulfil our obligations to the minority Simpsons shareholders by "rubber-stamping" the Bay's proposal. We agreed to meet early the next week on the subject.

Ian McSweeney, Simpsons' vice-president, Merchandise, was due to take early retirement. Ted Burton suggested he could take on this job in addition to being president. Everyone was aghast at the thought, not because Ted was not a good merchant, he was, but the simple truth was that the one job was demanding enough.

We were steadily losing our good people from Simpsons. Some were leaving to join our competitors; others were taking early retirement, feeling that their positions were not secure. We had thousands of dollars invested in them and our investment was being lost. I was not in a good position to correct the situation because I was a "lame duck" with only a few months to go before retirement.

My daughter Lynn arrived home from Europe with the exciting news that she and David Bennett, her English boy-friend, intended to marry. I thought him young and bearded when I had met him at Sir James Hanson's party in 1976.

On July 29, Ken and Marilyn Thomson, their daughter Lynne, twenty, and sons David, twenty-six, and Peter, fourteen, came for swimming and lunch. Ken arrived in a not-very-new Pontiac Bonneville, with a few dents in the side, hardly one of his several hundred millions showing. The Thomsons, except for Marilyn, are all over six feet. Ken was very enthusiastic about Simpsons and his role as principal owner of the Hudson Bay Company. David was in McLeod, Young and Weir, Corporate Finance; Lynne, a teller at the Toronto Dominion Bank; and Peter, at Upper Canada College. It was a very pleasant day all round. I thought that Ken and Marilyn had a fine-looking family, as they should, she being a former model and a Miss Toronto to boot!

There were about 150 at the shareholders meeting on July 31, which turned out to be quite routine. I had rehearsed answers to the questions we had anticipated would be asked. In spite of all our preparations, there were no questions at all! So now Simpsons was wholly owned by and a subsidiary of the Hudson Bay Company. Our stock was delisted from the Toronto Stock Exchange after thirty-two years. Another milestone.

The Eaton Centre officially opened at 9:15 a.m. on August 8, 1979, and John Craig Eaton and I cut a ribbon on the pedestrian walkway over Queen Street between Simpsons and the new Centre. Then we followed pipers to the official platform where we joined Premier William Davis, Allan Lawrence, Minister of Consumer and Commercial Affairs, and Mayor John Sewell, who made a speech saying he had fought the Centre every foot of the way but felt it had turned out better than anticipated! Fifty ethnic school-children in national costumes, carrying various banners, formed an honour guard. The Governor General's Horse Guards' Band provided the music. The crowds were enormous. The skywalk joining Simpsons to this Centre would be most important for traffic. Simpsons had its best day in the Toronto area since the previous December, with sales of $1.7 million.

On August 16, I spent all morning going over Simpsons' six-month results, which overall were poor. High interest rates and the change-over were causing some trouble.

I worked all day on August 23 on my report for the Bay board meeting. The figures were confusing because the Bay accounting methods and ours were different. Stan Nicholson, Simpsons' comptroller, redid a great many of the figures and confirmed with Ian Ronald, Bay vice-president, that they had, in fact, included some things twice, worsening our result!

I gave my report to the Hudson Bay board meeting on August 24. Simpsons recorded $317 million in sales with $5.3 million profit before finance charges and taxes, while the Bay's sixty-eight stores (to our twenty) did $369 million for a loss of $4 million before finance charges and taxes.

Some of the directors were beginning to ask pointed questions. One, in particular, asked the chairman to have me explain why Simpsons was doing so much better than the Bay stores, which rather set me back. I answered that I really did not know that much about the Bay stores, but that Simpsons was well established in the strongest retail market in Canada, and if we had not been much more productive in these areas, we would have been very concerned. Also, if we were breaking ground in the West, the customer acceptance would no doubt be reversed.

When I took my seat next to the director who asked that question, I said to him in an undertone, "Thanks, pal, you have just killed me. In six months you'll see the figures being reversed. We have no control over what charges the Bay headquarters wants to lay on us!" Later, in private, I told him some of the reasons that I thought contributed to our better results. Our sales per square foot were more than double the Bay's. We turned our inventory more often and offered better services.

While I was in Halifax at the Royal Bank quarterly meeting, Don McGiverin had a meeting with Ted Burton and other Simpsons executives. He impressed on them that unless they could plan for a 15 per cent return on assets, heads would roll. That was on September 10, the same day the bank rate went up to 13 per cent, an all-time high. So the heat would be on more and more. I was glad I would be out of the rat race as of December 31.

On September 22, Ted Remorowski and the CBC crew came to the farm, and we drove up to Caledon to see the Eglinton Hunt's hounds move off. Charles Kindersley, M.F.H., was still hunting hounds, as he has for the past thirty or more years. Back at Limestone Hall, they set the camera up in the Orchid Room, looking through the doorway into the studio, and said, "Paint a picture." So I did a watercolour for them, not one of my best, but one that is of some curious significance due to the circumstances. They then shot footage of me leading horses, driving a tractor and discs, and in other poses.

It was not the happiest of times for me. I had little to do except clean out files. I had no purpose except as CEO. But I still had to take the rap if all went wrong. I attended a Hudson Bay board meeting in Vancouver on September 28. I was up at 6:00 a.m. and on the phone to Toronto for more figures for my report. The meeting went well, and at the luncheon afterward I was impressed with the calibre of the good-looking young Bay men in the room. Many of them knew their counterparts in Simpsons and expressed great pleasure at Simpsons being part of the organization.

Our sales were very disappointing. We were measuring our performance against last year's figures before the sales taxes were reintroduced in Ontario and Nova Scotia. We did a lousy job of budgeting. The recession was upon us. Finally, the competition was intense. I had lunch with Jamie. We had a good talk about his work and discussed some concerns in trying to remain with Simpsons.

On October 3, there was a sixtieth anniversary luncheon of Dominion Stores. I was seated with Conrad Black, Earle McLaughlin, Paul Higgins, and Charles (Chuck) Rathgeb. Conservative Cabinet Minister Sinclair Stevens hinted he might like my help on a group to advise the government on "privatizing" some Crown corporations.

"Privatizing" is a horrible word. The next day I had lunch with Don McGiverin. I briefed him to date and told him that the chain of command was being eroded faster than he could imagine. I was loath to come down hard on people, because with only two months to go and not being entirely sure what the Bay's intentions were for the end of the year, I felt I might do more harm than good.

More and more Bay people were dealing directly with their opposite numbers in Simpsons, and Ted himself was part of the problem. The vice-presidents seldom knew what he was doing, and apparently some no longer trusted his judgement in any major respect. They said it was hard to keep him on the point under discussion. He seemed to have lost his spark.

I was very annoyed at the picayune attitude of the Bay to directors' travel expenses and wrote and told Huband, the secretary, as much. I was reminded that, in 1937, Simpsons did the overseas or European buying for the Bay on a co-operative arrangement. The Bay would not give their buyers, who accompanied ours, enough to live on, so they cadged on our buyers. My father cancelled the co-operative arrangements forthwith when he could not see Ashley Cooper, the governor, on the subject when he was in London!

Betty's book, *Hurricane Hazel*, was launched on October 16 in the Arcadian Court. The launching was well-attended and successful. Previously that day I had attended funerals of Bill Finlayson and Norman Agar, Sr., Simpsons' long-time comptroller. A sad day with a happy ending!

Malcolm MacKenzie, the Bay's vice-president of Personnel, asked to see me in my office. We had one and three-quarter hours of the frankest talk yet. He came essentially to mollify me and to reassure me that the Bay would not renege on its employee benefit commitments. I told him I was concerned that Simpsons would succumb because our chain of command was "broken" by the Bay's whispered instructions. It was a good meeting, and it did make me feel that someone understood. In the future we would not pay attention to anything unless confirmed in writing.

An unexpected thing happened on October 29. I was summoned for jury duty in Milton. I made up my mind to serve if I was chosen, in spite of the fact that it was not very convenient to do so. But is it ever convenient? Some people said, "Oh, you can get out of that easily," which made me more determined to serve. The jury selection process was long and dull. Sixty names were put in a box and twenty at a time were drawn, while each potential juror faced the accused and counsel and crown attorney. I was selected number eleven on the panel. The accused were two youths, one white and one black, who were charged in a robbery case involving the sale of hashish and the theft of a car.

On day one, the potential jurors were a cross-section of society – an engineer, a plant superintendent, housewives, and sales clerks. Curiously, none of the long-haired youths, labourers, or coloured people were selected. All were challenged. The selection took all day.

Days two and three were long and arduous work, continuous except for a dinner break, and continued until 11:00 p.m. I was drained emotionally, physically, and mentally. We were sequestered incommunicado in the jury room. The only means of communication was a written message to the sheriff's deputy. Betty was waiting in her office in Toronto, already dressed in a new gown, purchased for the occasion – the King Tutankhamen Ball at the Art Gallery, the event of the season at $200 per ticket. My message to her via the sheriff's deputy was to go home. He was not too happy at having to phone long distance from Milton to Toronto!

I was impressed with the seriousness and conscientious manner all the jurors adopted in tackling a most difficult task. My two months sitting on courts-martial during the war were helpful. The real trouble was to convince some of the jurors, without exerting undue pressure, to stop trying to be judge and jury. Their only task was to find guilty or not guilty on the facts. Both defendants were found guilty. On discharge I said that if I ever needed a jury, I hoped I had as fine a panel as we were!

Worried about the breakdown in communications between the Bay and Simpsons, I wrote out my "communications" points and read them to McGiverin and MacKenzie over lunch. Don asked me to read them to the meeting to follow, just as I had to them. We had an excellent meeting at the Bay, which lasted three hours. My paper was well received, and I expected a lot of good would come of it. I made the point that the lateral communication between the Bay and Simpsons was destroying our organization faster than they ever could directly. It must be stopped immediately or the Bay would lose the Simpsons mystique and expertise. I went on to say that the delay in announcing the organization and succession after January 1, 1980, when I retired, had a disastrous effect on morale right down to the counter level!

I drove to London on November 8 and spent most of the day with Nick Fry and his fellow professors in the School of Business at the University of Western Ontario. The session went on all day through lunch until 3:30 p.m. I traced the early beginnings of Simpsons-Sears and read directly from my 1978 diary about the proposed merger, first with Sears, Roebuck and later with the Bay. They asked questions continuously. They said it was fabulous to hear first-hand all the details about FIRA, and other complications. I also spoke on the retailing challenge ahead – the need to use technology to the fullest as soon as possible but without losing the personal tone of the operation as customers and employees would remain much the same. It was a productive day for them, I hoped.

A Simpsons board meeting was followed by a Hudson Bay board meeting on November 15. My blast of the previous week was having a salutary effect on Simpsons-Bay relationships and communications. On November 24, I lunched with Don McGiverin and, in a very friendly exchange, he gave me a typewritten letter confirming my retirement at the end of the year, but with important and generous additions to the normal pension provisions.

The company undertook to provide me with a suitable office in the Simpson Tower for the next two years. It agreed to retain Ruth Carlisle, my secretary, on a full-time basis with benefits as my secretary. In addition, it agreed to give me the Simpsons Rolls-Royce as a parting gift in appreciation of my forty-four years and six months of service.

Don would assume the chairmanship and I would leave the Simpsons board; that is, I would not stand for re-election. My new office would not be on the executive floor, the thirty-second. Don said, further, he would give Ted Burton a chance as president. I could stay on the Hudson Bay board until I reached seventy, or 1985, all being well. I felt much relieved and appreciated the soul-searching that Don went through to arrive at this solution.

On November 29, as arranged with McGiverin, I called Alex MacIntosh, deputy governor of Hudson Bay, to co-ordinate with him advising inside and outside directors of the situation. At lunch he reaffirmed his complete belief in Simpsons and his support to see that Simpsons retained its own integrity. He told me of the days during which he accompanied the governor, George Richardson, on his tour of all the Bay stores except for a few of the northern ones, and how shocked he was at the state of them, which led them to hire Don McGiverin in 1969. Alex's assessment was that they had no choice but to improve their stores and then "invade the East," which they did. I, in turn, told him of the early days, as I knew them, at Simpsons, what I thought Simpsons stood for, and why it would be wrong to allow Simpsons to change radically. I warned him that the Bay people would not change Simpsons. Change would come from our own ranks through trying to please the Bay at all costs! I went on. Simpsons always put the customer first, the employees second, and the investor last. Today the order seemed to be the reverse – first the investor, second the employees, and last the customer. I pleaded with Alex to put the customer first and let the merchants run the business.

I spoke to Ted on November 30 and confirmed that I would retire as chairman on December 13, that Don McGiverin would fill that position as CEO, and that he, Ted, would be kept on as president, which I am sure was a relief to him. Crichton and Davidson, vice-presidents, would have to reconcile their differing views with Ted.

Indeed, December 13 was an historic day for me. I retired as chairman and CEO of Simpsons Limited after eleven years in that post, and after twenty-five years on the board of directors. Don McGiverin was duly elected chairman. I asked Tom Bell to propose and Mike Scott to second the resolution.

I was amazed and delighted, upon entering the Directors' Lounge, to see about forty prize-winning orchids in full bloom on display, plus a beautiful limited edition print of a Cattleya. Stuart Collins, my orchid man at Limestone Hall, was in attendance. He had begged, stolen, and searched for these rare specimens. This was my retirement gift from the directors. Thus ended a quarter century on the board of directors of Simpsons Limited.

Ted drove me on December 17 to the Toronto Club where he and the vice-presidents of Simpsons had arranged a black-tie dinner party in my honour. Ted Burton, Dick Davidson, Ron Crichton, Ken Kernaghan, Charles MacRae, Stan Nicholson, Ian Gibson – all close associates and old friends of many years – were present. They presented me with a most beautiful Stirrup Cup, in reality an *art-nouveau*, sterling-silver punch bowl, crafted in about 1900, an extremely rare piece. I thought it would be a brilliant idea to fill it with three bottles of Bollinger champagne, which we did and drank! I was greatly touched. Having given so many retirement parties and now being the recipient, I was a little saddened. The next day I wrote a personal note to each hung-over vice-president and, of course, to Ted. Then I went to the Royal Military Institute to have a Christmas drink with the GGHG officers with whom I had served in Italy and Europe in World War II.

On December 20, I gave a tea party for the secretaries and ladies of the thirty-second floor and their bosses. It was really a wine-and-cheese party held in the Directors' Lounge. It was probably a first and certainly a last, so I had everyone sign the guest book for the record. Betty and I then drove to Gail and John Kendall's for a surprise birthday party for Gail.

For the first time in years, I was able to attend the Members' Christmas party at the York Club with Jamie. It was ''old-home'' week. I had lunch with Jamie, Tom Bell, and Dave Weldon, who was president-elect of the Royal Winter Fair. Dave asked if I would consider being his vice-president immediately and president of the Royal three years down the road. I said, yes, I would be honoured.

Christmas at Limestone Hall saw no snow, but we did have a thirty-four-pound turkey and seventeen family members for dinner. And on Boxing Day we played host to dozens of good friends and relatives. It was a happy day on which to end a hectic year!

# AFTERWORD

Shortly after my official retirement from Simpsons at age sixty-five, Betty asked, "Why don't you start another business?"

I patiently explained it is a younger man's game. I would consider it if I were twenty years younger, but the hours of work and money invested might drain me dry before my allotted time, physically and financially, if not mentally.

The very thought repelled me because by mid-1980 we were heading for the worst economic recession in the past twenty-eight years, and interest rates were on their way up to twenty per cent or more. Every instinct I had told me to keep my head down, my financial powder dry, and enjoy our fine life together with our family.

In fact, I have had an enjoyable, busy, and full life since retirement, fulfilling my remaining business responsibilities, devoting more time to public works of my choice, rather than being expected to make an appearance at every dinner or reception as being head of Simpsons used to demand. Now I can be more discriminating in the use of my public time, such as fund-raising for the Halton Region Conservation Foundation, of which I am chairman. Our main project is the nature and conservation area on the Niagara Escarpment called Crawford Lake.

In addition to long-time involvement in hospital funds and health research projects, my connections with the Royal Bank and Bell Canada keep me current about world business. Also, I hoped I would be useful on the board of the Hudson Bay Company. With the best will in the world, Don McGiverin, Ken Thomson, and others of the Bay watched as Simpsons, the company they protested loudly they wanted to preserve and enhance, daily diminished even before their computer readouts gave them the bad news.

Many regular customers of department stores have switched to specialty shops, which give them the personal attention, quality, and design in merchandise that the modern large store seems unable or unwilling to provide any longer. More than any new owner's philosophy, the whole "takeover" trauma was largely to blame for the breakdown in customer satisfaction and the decline in sales. In our case, the abrupt severance of such services as delivery, shared by Simpsons and Simpsons-Sears for a quarter of a century, gave rise to immediate operating problems. In no way could the Bay stores come close to replacing the lost parcel volume, which resulted in cut services and closed excess plants. These very real operating problems were coupled with the highest prime interest rates anyone in business in Canada had ever known, spreading despair and despondency as published results worsened, lowering the morale of all concerned. The customer at the counter felt indifferent. There was a moan from the clerk that "things sure aren't what they used to be."

I watched this happening to Simpsons while I was a director of the Hudson Bay Company. I quickly found out that my opinion was not sought and, worse, I could officially get no information about what was happening to Simpsons at the operating level. As the Bay's results worsened, more and more the press releases "fingered" Simpsons as the major culprit, which made me not even want to enter one of our stores.

Ted Burton was relieved of the presidency of Simpsons nine months after I retired. Ron Crichton, vice-president, Stores, one of the best operators in the business, took early retirement because he felt a lack of support. Dick Davidson, vice-president, Personnel, was fired for suspecting the Bay was loading expenses on his organization to benefit the Bay stores. Dick was the only knowledgeable operator left in the top ranks, and his dismissal made it quite clear that by fighting too hard for things you believed in, you courted dismissal. It was Dick's opinion that the Bay accounting was allowing a Simpsons facility to be used by the Bay stores at 25 per cent less than we charged ourselves – in other words, here was a large subsidy at our expense, with both managements supposedly on similar bonus schemes. Within a month Dick Davidson found a higher-paying position in another service firm and is now its president. Charlie MacRae, a long-time Simpsons man and an excellent merchant in the heavy-goods group, was made president of Simpsons in due course, but, throughout the organization, lessons had been learned and individual initiatives had been moulded to the facts of survival.

My son Jamie had, meanwhile, on his own, decided to leave Simpsons because he felt he would like to go into business for himself. He was approaching forty and the "approaching forty" syndrome says "now or never." Jamie and his wife, Barbara, who was a top-marks graduate of a Boston retailing school, started a clothing business featuring classic country clothes. They called their new company Green River Clothiers, after the community where my grandfather had his general store and where my father was born. The name intrigued them. It was a difficult time to start a new business, but now they have three stores and a thriving business. They are building a loyal clientele by superior service, fine quality, and hard work.

The wheel has now gone full circle at Simpsons and the Bay. MacRae, who was president of Simpsons, has been replaced by a Bay man trained by Don McGiverin. While still bearing the title of governor, McGiverin has no longer any operating responsibility. Millions have been spent on refurbishing Simpsons' downtown store, and there is now hardly anyone in the organization, as far as I know, encumbered with "the old Simpsons tradition," which holds that the customer always comes first. Now all the focus is on the "bottom line." If it is not immediately profitable, get rid of it by franchise or curtail the service.

I find myself very busy. In addition to several public fund-raisings, from conservation and heritage to medical-research projects for hospitals, I paint in watercolours (although, latterly, writing these memoirs has consumed much of my studio time). Betty continues to amaze me, as she is mother and friend to all our children and their spouses, and yet she continues her own busy schedule of radio, television, and business. She has added membership on the executive committee of the board of directors of the Bank of Montreal to her work, membership in which would be a prized honour for any top executive in Canadian business.

And yet, our early morning walks down the farm lane and through the woods – reading animal signs and identifying bird-calls, even surprising a grazing doe and fawn in our fields or the coyotes who stalk them, while overhead gaggles of Canada geese settle in to our ponds, honking and chattering excitedly to each other – draws us ever closer together and somehow renews the excitement of life before once more the other realities of daily life must be faced in the city or on airplanes speeding to distant meetings. She is a great life companion and I am lucky.

Betty's children – four of her own and four step-children – are doing exciting, worthwhile things with their lives. Mark Kennedy has a Master's degree in Library Sciences as well as an M.A. in Philosophy from University of Toronto. He is working with Canada Consultants, an advisory group, and is married to an attractive woman from Marseilles, Anne Mirgalet, and they have a girl child, Allison, on whom Mark dotes outrageously.

Shawn Kennedy operates a gold prospecting company at Gold Bridge, B.C., and has staked 42,000 acres of claims around the Bralorne and Pilot mines. He is married to Beverley Stoughton, a slip of a girl, who loves to ride the mountain trails on horseback camping trips. They have two small but determined children, Haley and Dayton. Haley, a blonde girl child, has grown up in the B.C. wilds, as has Dayton, her brother. They live in "grizzly country" and are at one with nature. X-Cal Resources, Shawn's company, is the only mining company of the province that was listed on the Toronto Stock Exchange before being listed on the Vancouver Exchange.

D'Arcy Kennedy, a skilled mechanic, is currently on the Formula 2000 circuit, driving his own car and raising money for the project on an innovative scheme called Signature Racing. For a modest donation, your signature rides on his car, perhaps to victory.

Tracy Kennedy, Betty's daughter, is completing a film course at York University. She is a rider and a horse lover, carrying on my traditional fascination with horses. Her mare Cameo had a filly we call Capability, which won first foal at the Sutton Horse Show and first champion foal at the 1985 Canadian National Exhibition Horse Show.

My children are doing interesting things as well. Gail, the oldest daughter, a former R.N. and athlete, is married to Dr. John Kendall, a brilliant internist and world-class, long-distance runner. They have three children, all fine students. Hugh, graduated in first-class honours at Queen's University, has been accepted in the McGill Medical School. Kathy, when she completed Grade XIII at Branksome Hall, worked her way around the world for a year. Before leaving Canada, Kathy took part in the Junior Achievement program, becoming the successful president of her small clock-making and distributing company, earning praise and the offer of a job when she returned. She is back now and studying at Queen's University. Jamie, the youngest, is a student at Appleby College. He is the proud colour-bearer of the school Cadet Corps and majors in hockey and other sports.

My daughter Lynn married David Bennett (now no longer bearded as he was when I first met him in London). They have two children, Nicholas and Audrey Claire. Lynn worked for Sotheby's, the London auctioneers, for nine years, rising to be chief of administration. David, an aspiring author of suspense fiction, has now written three novels and takes trips to places like Colombia and Nepal for background information and colour.

My son Jamie is married to Barbara Winfree, whose father was a career diplomat in the U.S. Service. Barbara was born in Belgium and educated in Switzerland and India. She attended the Chamberlain School of Retailing in Boston, Mass., of which she became Head Girl. She was working at Eaton's when they first met. They have a daughter, Jennifer, who will be a beauty in her own right and whose passion is figure skating, and a son, Sean, a young man who is busy growing up and loves driving the garden tractor or chasing suckers in Limestone Creek. Barbara is a *cordon-bleu* cook as well as chief bookkeeper and personnel trainer for Green River Clothiers, Toronto.

My daughter Janice married Ronald Baker when they were both working in Simpsons' Display Department. They own and operate a business called Pegasus Designs. Janice is a good rider and used to hunt regularly with the Eglinton and Caledon Hunt while I was Master. They live in Kitchener, Ontario, and have two fine boys, Paul and Eric.

Then there are Betty's step-children, Gerhard's by his first marriage. Glen, a respected naturalist, is married to filmmaker Christopher Chapman and they have a son, Julian. Nancy Kennedy is merchandise manager of Sungsports Division of the Monaco Group. Gerhard is a major in the RCAF, stationed at Cold Lake, Alberta, site of the cruise missile testing and the F18s. Tony is an architect with UNICEF on assignment in Bangladesh.

So with all these healthy and happy people, our lives are full and never dull. Time is of the essence as, blessed with family and friends, we go busily on our chosen paths, yet with it all, horses still fascinate me almost as much as people!

# INDEX